Integrated Inferences

MW01098318

There is a growing consensus in the social sciences on the virtues of research strategies that combine quantitative with qualitative tools of inference. *Integrated Inferences* develops a framework for using causal models and Bayesian updating for qualitative and mixed-methods research. By *making*, *updating*, and *querying* causal models, researchers are able to integrate information from different data sources while connecting theory and empirics in a far more systematic and transparent manner than standard qualitative and quantitative approaches allow. This book provides an introduction to fundamental principles of causal inference and Bayesian updating and shows how these tools can be used to implement and justify inferences using within-case (process-tracing) evidence, correlational patterns across many cases, or a mix of the two. The authors also demonstrate how causal models can guide research design, informing choices about which cases, observations, and mixes of methods will be most useful for addressing any given question.

Macartan Humphreys is Director of the Institutions and Political Inequality group at the WZB Berlin, conducting research on postconflict development, ethnic politics, and democratic decision-making. He has been President of the American Political Science Association (APSA) Experimental Political Science section and Executive Director of the Evidence on Governance and Politics network. He holds honorary professorships at Trinity College Dublin and Humboldt University, Berlin.

Alan M. Jacobs is Professor of Political Science at the University of British Columbia, conducting research on comparative political economy in democratic settings. He has been President of the APSA's Qualitative and Multi-Method Research section, winner of the section's Mid-Career Achievement Award, and a regular instructor at the Institute for Qualitative and Multi-Method Research.

Strategies for Social Inquiry

Integrated Inferences: Causal Models for Qualitative and Mixed-Method Research

Editors

Colin Elman, Maxwell School of Syracuse University
John Gerring, University of Texas, Austin
James Mahoney, Northwestern University

Editorial Board

Bear Braumoeller[†], David Collier, Francesco Guala, Peter Hedström, Theodore Hopf, Uskali Maki, Rose McDermott, Charles Ragin, Theda Skocpol, Peter Spiegler, David Waldner, Lisa Wedeen, Christopher Winship

This book series presents texts on a wide range of issues bearing upon the practice of social inquiry. Strategies are construed broadly to embrace the full spectrum of approaches to analysis, as well as relevant issues in philosophy of social science.

Published Titles

Integrated Inferences

Causal Models for Qualitative and Mixed-Method Research

Macartan Humphreys
WZB Berlin

Alan M. Jacobs
University of British Columbia

CAMBRIDGE
UNIVERSITY PRESS

Shaftesbury Road, Cambridge CB2 8EA, United Kingdom

One Liberty Plaza, 20th Floor, New York, NY 10006, USA

477 Williamstown Road, Port Melbourne, VIC 3207, Australia

314–321, 3rd Floor, Plot 3, Splendor Forum, Jasola District Centre,
New Delhi – 110025, India

103 Penang Road, #05–06/07, Visioncrest Commercial, Singapore 238467

Cambridge University Press is part of Cambridge University Press & Assessment,
a department of the University of Cambridge.

We share the University's mission to contribute to society through the pursuit of
education, learning and research at the highest international levels of excellence.

www.cambridge.org
Information on this title: www.cambridge.org/9781107169623

DOI: 10.1017/9781316718636

First published 2023

A catalogue record for this publication is available from the British Library

A Cataloging-in-Publication data record for this book is available from the Library of Congress

ISBN 978-1-107-16962-3 Hardback
ISBN 978-1-316-62066-3 Paperback

Contents

Preface   *page* ix
    Quick Guide   ix
Acknowledgments   x

1   Introduction   1
   1.1 The Case for Causal Models   2
   1.2 Key Contributions   9
   1.3 The Road Ahead   14

Part I   Foundations

2   Causal Models   19
   2.1 The Counterfactual Model   19
   2.2 Causal Models and Directed Acyclic Graphs   27
   2.3 Graphing Models and Using Graphs   44
   2.4 Conclusion   55
   2.5 Appendix   55

3   Illustrating Causal Models   59
   3.1 Welfare State Reform   60
   3.2 Military Interventions   65
   3.3 Development and Democratization   69

4   Causal Queries   74
   4.1 Case-Level Causal Effects   75
   4.2 Case-Level Causal Attribution   78
   4.3 Average Causal Effects   80
   4.4 Causal Paths   82
   4.5 Conclusion   87
   4.6 Appendix   88

5   Bayesian Answers   100
    5.1   Bayes Basics   100
    5.2   Bayes Applied   116
    5.3   Features of Bayesian Updating   125

6   Theories as Causal Models   131
    6.1   Models as *Theories Of*   133
    6.2   Gains from Theory   138
    6.3   Formal Theories and Causal Models   147

Part II   Model-Based Causal Inference

7   Process Tracing with Causal Models   155
    7.1   The Intuition   157
    7.2   A Formalization of the General Approach   159
    7.3   Mapping from Models to Classic Qualitative Tests   169
    7.4   Assessing Probative Value from a Graph   170
    7.5   Principles of Learning   181
    7.6   Appendix: Process Tracing with `CausalQueries`   185

8   Process-Tracing Applications   189
    8.1   Inequality and Democratization   190
    8.2   Institutions and Growth   207
    8.3   Appendix: Forming Models in `CausalQueries`   215

9   Integrated Inferences   217
    9.1   From One Unit to Many   218
    9.2   General Procedure   221
    9.3   Payoffs   237
    9.4   Extensions   246
    9.5   Appendix: Mixing Methods with `CausalQueries`   253

10   Integrated Inferences Applications   259
    10.1 Inequality and Democratization   260
    10.2 Institutions and Growth   267
    10.3 Conclusion   278

11   Mixing Models   281

      11.1 A Jigsaw Puzzle: Integrating across a Model   283
      11.2 Combining Observational and Experimental Data   286
      11.3 Transportation of Findings across Contexts   291
      11.4 Multilevel Models, Meta-analysis   293

Part III   Design Choices

12   Clue Selection as a Decision Problem   301

      12.1 A Model-Informed Approach to Clue Selection   301
      12.2 Dynamic Strategies   314
      12.3 Conclusion   318

13   Case Selection   320

      13.1 Common Case-Selection Strategies   320
      13.2 No General Rules   323
      13.3 General Strategy   331
      13.4 Conclusion   345

14   Going Wide, Going Deep   347

      14.1 Walk-Through of a Simple Comparison   348
      14.2 Simulation Analysis   351
      14.3 Factoring in the Cost of Data   356
      14.4 Conclusion   357

Part IV   Models in Question

15   Justifying Models   361

      15.1 Justifying Probative Value   362
      15.2 Empirical Discovery of Causal Structure   368

16   Evaluating Models   372

      16.1 Four Strategies   372
      16.2 Evaluating the Democracy—Inequality Model   384
      16.3 Evaluating the Institutions—Growth Model   390
      16.4 Appendix   394

17   Final Words   396
      17.1 The Benefits   397
      17.2 The Worries   400
      17.3 The Future   403

Part V   Appendices

18   Glossary   409

      Bibliography   413
      Index   420

Preface

Quick Guide

This book has four main parts:

- Part I introduces causal models and a Bayesian approach to learning about them and drawing inferences from them.
- Part II applies these tools to strategies that use process tracing, mixed methods, and "model aggregation."
- Part III turns to design decisions, exploring strategies for assessing what kinds of data are most useful for addressing different kinds of research questions given knowledge to date about a population or a case.
- Part IV puts models into question and outlines a range of strategies one can use to justify and evaluate causal models.

We have developed an R package – CausalQueries – to accompany this book, hosted on CRAN. Supplementary Materials, including a guide to the package, can be found at https://integrated-inferences.github.io/.

Acknowledgments

We have very many people to thank for their intellectual companionship as we wrote and rewrote this book.

We finished a first draft of the manuscript during a year together in Berlin and held a book conference in May 2017, at a time when we reckoned that we had the book more or less written. Huge thanks to Stefanie Roth, Marion Obermaier, and Ina Thies-Hoelzmann for organizing this workshop and to Dorothea Kübler for so generously hosting us that year. We are grateful to participants at the workshop Jeyhun Alizade, Andrew Bennett (joining at impossible hours), Sebastian Bödeker, Kevin Clarke, Ruth Ditlmann, Tulia Falleti, Adam Glynn, Alexandra Hartman, Jan Paul Heisig, Michael C. Herron, Nahomi Ichino, Mark Kayser, Johannes Leutgeb, Anselm Rink, Ingo Rohlfing, Nicholas Weller, and Sherry Zaks for stimulating conversations that made us reconsider many aspects of the project. Collectively you set us back about five years.

As we rethought and rewrote the book, we continued to benefit from generous engagements from these and other friends and colleagues. We received very helpful feedback at a 2019 authors' workshop at the Institute for Qualitative and Multi-Method Research (IQMR) at Syracuse University, especially from Michael Findley, John Gerring, and Jason Seawright. At the WZB Berlin Social Science Center, colleagues in the causality project joined us in grappling with many of the core ideas; thanks especially to Michael Zürn, Steffen Huck, Johannes Leutgeb, and Julio Solis Arce for their insights. Other colleagues, often coming from quite different intellectual traditions, engaged us on many aspects of the approach as we refined the manuscript. We benefited greatly from one-on-one exchanges with P. M. Aronow, Tim Frye, Donald Green, John Huber, Thomas Leavitt, Winston Lin, Richard Nielsen, and Fredrik Sävje. Multiple in-depth discussions with Tasha Fairfield and Andrew Charman over the years helped us understand key points of difference between their approach and ours and sharpened our thinking. Conversations with Laura Garcia-Montoya and James Mahoney challenged us on ways of thinking about causal relations. Collaboration with members of the Process Outcome Integration with Theory (POInT) team – Elizabeth Allen, Calum Davey, Matt Juden, Tichaona Mapuwe Lily Medina, Henry Mwambi, Audrey Prost, and Rachel Sarguta – on applications of the `CausalQueries` package to a set of development studies advanced our thinking about practical uses of the approach. Seminar audiences at the Technical University of Munich, the University of Rochester, Northwestern, and Yale pointed us to conceptual ambiguities in the framework that needed work. We are especially grateful to David Collier for his early support of our work on Bayesian mixed-method inference and for his warm encouragement along the way.

Nothing helps clarify ideas more than having to teach them, and the book has been taught now at multiple summer schools. Macartan thanks participants at Empirical Implications of Theoretical Models (EITM) 2017 in Milan, who bravely worked with the earliest version of `CausalQueries`. Alan is grateful for the sharp and tough questions and the insightful suggestions from numerous cohorts of graduate students and junior faculty in the causal models module that he and Lily Medina taught at IQMR and that he taught at EITM in Ann Arbor.

Many others provided wonderful technical support and fresh reactions to the ideas developed in the book. Daniel Markovits prepped the data for the institutions and growth analysis and also ran and wrote up all the initial analyses using that data; big thanks to you for taking that so far. Yonel Admasu prepped the data for the democratization model analysis in Chapter 16; thanks for the careful scouting of multiple literatures.

Huge thanks to Manu Singh, one of the few to have read the whole book as it neared completion. Thanks for the careful read, the many improvements to the writing, and your insights into where weaknesses remained. Warm thanks to Beatrice Montano and Vartika Savarna too, for your careful reading and wonderful feedback. And our deepest gratitude to Sampada KC for your meticulous work constructing the book's index and reviewing the copyedits and proofs.

Our thinking about the book grew alongside the development of the accompanying R package, `CausalQueries`. Many talented people contributed to developing the package, and we owe them a lot. Jasper Cooper and Georgiy Syunyaev cracked some of the earliest challenges, Lily Mcdina developed the guts of the package, and she and Till Tietz saw it safely to CRAN. Clara Bicalho, Jonah Foong, Merlin Heidemanns, and Julio Solis Arce contributed innumerable improvements. Julian Cantor got deep into the weeds on figuring out probabilities of new data patterns after case selection. Till

Tietz dug deep to add elegance and speed. Sisi Huang developed a whole shiny application for the package and, as an early user, pointed to innumerable areas for improvement. Ben Goodrich gave us guidance on handling stan that was of huge consequence.

John Haslam at Cambridge has been a paragon of patience and a constant support at a distance. We are grateful to the *Strategies for Social Inquiry* series editors, Colin Elman, John Gerring, and James Mahoney, for letting us know early on that they thought this would be a book worth writing; the prospect of having this work appear in their great series has been a big motivation for us throughout. Our reviewer at Cambridge, Andrew Bennett, sent in 20 single-spaced pages of detailed, thoughtful, and incredibly constructive comments. You couldn't wish it on anyone.

Thanks to the Alexander von Humboldt Foundation and the Social Sciences and Humanities Research Council of Canada for financial support for many aspects of the project.

Thank you, last but not least, to our families for your support throughout this project, especially through a string of trans-Atlantic trips to "finish the book." Now we've really done it.

1 Introduction

We describe the book's general approach, preview our argument for the utility of causal models as a framework for choosing research strategies and for drawing causal inferences, and provide a roadmap for the rest of the book. We highlight the approach's payoffs for qualitative analysis, for combining intensive and extensive empirical strategies, and for making research design choices.

Here is the key idea of this book.

Quantitative social scientists spend a lot of time trying to understand causal relations between variables by looking across large numbers of cases to see how outcomes differ when postulated causes differ. This strategy relies on variation in causal conditions across units of analysis, and the quality of the resulting inferences depends in large part on what forces give rise to that variation.

Qualitative social scientists, like historians, spend a lot of time looking at a smaller set of cases and seek to learn about causal relations by examining evidence of causal processes in operation within these cases. Qualitative scholars rely on theories of how things work – theories that specify what should be observable within a case if indeed an outcome were generated by a particular cause.

These two approaches seem to differ in what they seek to explain – individual- or population-level outcomes, in the forms of evidence they require – cross-case variation or within-case detail, and in what they need to assume in order to draw inferences – knowledge of assignment processes or knowledge of causal processes.

The central theme of this book is that this distinction, though culturally real (Goertz and Mahoney, 2012), is neither epistemologically deep nor analytically helpful. Social scientists can work with causal models that simultaneously exploit cross-case variation and within-case detail, that address both case- and population-level questions, and that both depend on, and contribute to, developing theories of how things work.[1] In other words, with well-specified causal models, researchers can make integrated inferences.

In this book, we describe an approach to integrating inferences in which researchers *form* causal models, *update* those models using data, and then *query* the models to get answers to particular causal questions. This framework is very different from standard statistical approaches in which researchers focus on selecting the best estimator to estimate a particular estimand of interest. In a causal models framework, the model itself gets updated: We begin by learning about processes and only then draw inferences about particular causal relations of interest, either at the case level or at the population level.

We do not claim that a causal-model-based approach is the best or only strategy suited to addressing causal questions. There are plenty of settings in which other approaches would likely work better. For instance, it is hard to beat a difference in means if you have easy access to large amounts of experimental data and are interested in sample average treatment effects. But we do think that the approach holds great promise – allowing researchers to combine disparate data in a principled way to ask a vast range of sample- and population-level causal questions, helping integrate theory and empirics, and providing coherent guidance on research design. It should, we think, sit prominently in the applied researcher's toolkit.

Our goals in this book are to motivate this approach; provide an introduction to the theory of (structural) causal models; provide practical guidance for setting up, updating, and querying causal models; and show how the approach can inform key research-design choices, especially case-selection and data-collection strategies.

1.1 The Case for Causal Models

There are three closely related motivations for embracing a causal models approach. First is a concern with the limits of design-based inference. Second is an interest in integrating qualitative knowledge with quantitative

---

[1] We will sometimes follow convention and refer to "within-case" and "cross-case" observations. However, in the framework we present in this book, all data are data on cases and enter into analysis in the same fundamental way: We are always asking how consistent a given data pattern is with alternative sets of beliefs.

approaches. Third is an interest in better connecting empirical strategies to theory.

1.1.1 The Limits to Design-Based Inference

To caricature positions a bit, consider the difference between an engineer and a skeptic. The engineer tackles problems of causal inference using models: theories of how the world works, generated from past experiences and applied to the situation at hand. They come with prior beliefs about a set of mechanisms operating in the world and, in a given situation, will ask whether the conditions are in place for a known mechanism to operate effectively. The skeptic, on the other hand, maintains a critical position, resisting basing conclusions on beliefs that are not supported by evidence in the context at hand.

The engineer's approach echoes what was until recently a dominant orientation among social scientists. At the turn of the current century, much analysis – both empirical and theoretical – took the form of modeling processes (data-generating processes) and then interrogating those models (King, 1998).

Over the last two decades, however, skeptics have raised a set of compelling concerns about the assumption-laden nature of this kind of analysis, while also clarifying how valid inferences can be made with limited resort to models. The result has been a growth in the use of design-based inference techniques that, in principle, allow for model-free estimation of causal effects (see Dunning (2012), Gerber et al. (2004), Druckman et al. (2011), and Palfrey (2009) among others). These include lab, survey, and field experiments and natural-experimental methods exploiting either true or "as-if" randomization by nature. With the turn to experimental and natural-experimental methods has come a broader conceptual shift, with a growing reliance on the "potential outcomes" framework, which provides a clear language for articulating causal relations (see Rubin (1974), Splawa-Neyman et al. (1990) among others) without having to invoke fully specified models of data-generating processes. See Aronow and Miller (2019) for a thorough treatment of "agnostic statistics," which shows how much can be done without recourse to commitments to models of data-generating processes.

The ability to estimate average effects and to characterize uncertainty – for instance, calculating p-values and standard errors – without resorting to models is an extraordinary development. In Fisher's (2017) term, with these tools, randomization processes provide a "reasoned basis for inference," placing empirical claims on a powerful footing.

At the same time, excitement about the strengths of these approaches has been mixed with concerns about how the approach shapes inquiry. We highlight two.

The first concern – raised by many in recent years (e.g., Thelen and Mahoney, 2015) – is about design-based inference's scope of application. While experimentation and natural experiments represent powerful tools, the range of research situations in which model-free inference is possible is limited. For a wide range of questions of interest, both to social scientists and to society, controlled experimentation is impossible, whether for practical or ethical reasons, and claims of "as-if" randomization are not plausible (Humphreys and Weinstein, 2009).[2] Thus, limiting our focus to those questions for which, or situations in which, the credibility of causal claims can be established "by design" would represent a dramatic narrowing of social science's ken.

To be clear, this is not an argument against experimentation or design-based inference when these can be used; rather, it is an argument that social science needs a broader set of tools.

The second concern is more subtle. The great advantage of design-based inference is that it liberates researchers from the need to rely on models to make claims about causal effects. The risk is that, in operating model free, researchers end up learning about effect sizes but not about models. Yet often, the model is the thing we want to learn about. Our goal as social scientists is to come to grips with how the world works, not simply to collect propositions about the effects that different causes have had on different outcomes in different times and places. It is through models that we derive an understanding of how things might work in contexts and for processes and variables that we have not yet studied. Thus, our interest in models is intrinsic, not instrumental. By taking models out of the equation, as it were, we lose the baby with the bathwater.

We note, however, that although we return to models, lessons from the "credibility revolution" permeate this book. Though the approach we use relies on models, we also highlight the importance of being skeptical toward models, checking their performance, and – to the extent possible – basing them on weaker, more defensible models. In practice, we sometimes find that progress, even for qualitative methods, relies on the kind of background knowledge that requires randomization. (See our discussions in Sections 11.2 and especially 15.1.1.)

---

[2] Of course, even when randomization is possible, the conditions needed for clean inference from an experiment can sometimes be difficult to meet (Cook, 2018).

1.1.2 Qualitative and Mixed-Method Inference

Recent years have seen the elucidation of the inferential logic behind "process-tracing" procedures used in qualitative political science and other disciplines. On our read of this literature, the logic of process tracing depends on a particular form of model-based inference.[3] While process tracing as a method has been around for more than three decades (e.g., George and McKeown, 1985), its logic has been most fully laid out by qualitative methodologists in political science and sociology over the last 20 years (e.g., Bennett and Checkel, 2015b; Brady and Collier, 2010; George and Bennett, 2005; Hall, 2003; Mahoney, 2010). Whereas King, Keohane, and Verba (KKV) (1994) sought to derive qualitative principles of causal inference within a correlational framework, qualitative methodologists writing in the wake of KKV have emphasized and clarified process tracing's "within-case" inferential logic: In process tracing, explanatory hypotheses are tested principally based on the observations of what happened within a case rather than on the observation of covariation of causes and effects across cases.

The process-tracing literature has also advanced increasingly elaborate conceptualizations of the different kinds of "probative value" that within-case evidence can yield. For instance, qualitative methodologists have explicated the logic of different test types ("hoop tests," "smoking gun tests," etc.) involving varying degrees of specificity and sensitivity (Collier, 2011; Mahoney, 2012; Van Evera, 1997).[4] Other scholars have described the leverage provided by process-tracing evidence in Bayesian terms, moving from a set of discrete

---

[3] As we describe in Humphreys and Jacobs (2015), the term "qualitative research" means many different things to different scholars, and there are multiple approaches to mixing qualitative and quantitative methods. There we distinguish between approaches that suggest that qualitative and quantitative approaches address distinct, if complementary, questions; those that suggest that they involve distinct measurement strategies; and those that suggest that they employ distinct inferential logics. The approach that we employ in Humphreys and Jacobs (2015) connects most with the third family of approaches. Most closely related to political science is work of Glynn and Quinn (2011), in which researchers use knowledge about the empirical joint distribution of the treatment variable, the outcome variable, and a posttreatment variable, alongside assumptions about how causal processes operate, to tighten estimated bounds on causal effects. In the present book, however, we move toward a position in which fundamental differences between qualitative and quantitative inferences tend to dissolve, with all inference drawing on what might be considered a "qualitative" logic in which the researcher's task is to confront a pattern of evidence with a theoretical logic.

[4] A smoking-gun test seeks information that is only plausibly present if a hypothesis is true (thus generating strong evidence for the hypothesis if passed), a hoop test seeks data that should certainly be present if a proposition is true (thus generating strong evidence against the hypothesis if failed), and a doubly decisive test is both smoking-gun and hoop (for an expanded typology, see also Rohlfing (2013)).

test types to a more continuous notion of probative value (Bennett, 2015; Fairfield and Charman, 2017; Humphreys and Jacobs, 2015).[5]

Yet, conceptualizing the different ways in which probative value might operate leaves a fundamental question unanswered: What gives within-case evidence its probative value with respect to causal relations? We do not see a clear answer to this question in the current process-tracing literature. Implicitly – but worth rendering explicit – *the probative value of a given piece of process-tracing evidence always depends on researcher beliefs that come from outside the case in question.* We enter a research situation with a model of how the world works, and we use this model to make inferences given observed patterns in the data – while at the same time updating those models based on the data.

A key aim of this book is to demonstrate the role that models can – and, in our view, must – play in drawing case-level causal inferences and to clarify conditions under which these models can be defended. To do so, we draw on an approach to specifying causal models developed originally in computer science and that predates most of the process-tracing literature. The broad approach, described in Cowell et al. (1999) and Pearl (2009), is consistent with the potential outcomes framework, and provides rules for updating population- and case-level causal queries from different types of data.

In addition to clarifying the logic of qualitative inference, we will argue that such causal models can also enable the systematic integration of qualitative and quantitative forms of evidence. Social scientists are increasingly developing mixed-method research designs and research strategies that combine quantitative with qualitative forms of evidence (Small, 2011). A typical mixed-methods study includes the estimation of causal effects using data from many cases as well as a detailed examination of the processes taking place in a few cases. Classic examples of this approach include Lieberman's study of racial and regional dynamics in tax policy (Lieberman, 2003), Swank's analysis of globalization and the welfare state (Swank, 2002), and Stokes' study of neoliberal reform in Latin America (Stokes, 2001). Major recent methodological texts provide the intellectual justification of this trend toward mixing, characterizing small-n and large-n analyses as drawing on a single logic of inference (King et al., 1994) and/or as serving complementary functions (Collier et al., 2010; Seawright, 2016). The American Political

---

[5] In Humphreys and Jacobs (2015), we use a fully Bayesian structure to generalize Van Evera's four test types in two ways: first, by allowing the probative values of clues to be continuous; and, second, by allowing for researcher uncertainty (and, in turn, updating) over these values.

Science Association now has an organized section devoted in part to the promotion of multimethod investigations, and the emphasis on multiple strategies of inference research is now embedded in guidelines from many research funding agencies (Creswell and Garrett, 2008).

However, while scholars frequently point to the benefits of mixing correlational and process-based inquiry (e.g., Collier et al., 2010, p. 181), and have sometimes mapped out broad strategies of multimethod research design (Lieberman, 2005; Seawright, 2016; Seawright and Gerring, 2008), they have rarely provided specific guidance on how the integration of inferential leverage should unfold. In particular, the literature has not supplied specific, formal procedures for aggregating findings – whether mutually reinforcing or contradictory – across different modes of analysis.[6] As we aim to demonstrate in this book, however, grounding inference in causal models provides a very natural way of combining information of the X, Y variety with information about the causal processes connecting X and Y. The approach that we develop here can be readily addressed both to the case-oriented questions that tend to be of interest to qualitative scholars and to the population-oriented questions that tend to motivate quantitative inquiry.

As will become clear, when we structure our inquiry in terms of causal models, the conceptual distinction between qualitative and quantitative inference becomes hard to sustain. Notably, this is not because all causal inferences depend fundamentally on covariation but because in a causal-model-based inference, what matters for the informativeness of a piece of evidence is how that evidence alters beliefs about a model and, in turn, a query. While the apparatus that we present is formal, the approach – in asking how pieces of evidence drawn from different parts of a process map onto a base of theoretical knowledge – is arguably most closely connected to process tracing in its core logic.

---

[6] A small number of exceptions stand out. In the approach suggested by Gordon and Smith (2004), for instance, available expert (possibly imperfect) knowledge regarding the operative causal mechanisms for a small number of cases can be used to anchor the statistical estimation procedure in a large-N study. Western and Jackman (1994) propose a Bayesian approach in which qualitative information shapes subjective priors that in turn affect inferences from quantitative data. Relatedly, in Glynn and Quinn (2011), researchers use knowledge about the empirical joint distribution of the treatment variable, the outcome variable, and a posttreatment variable, alongside assumptions about how causal processes operate, to tighten estimated bounds on causal effects. Coppock and Kaur (2022) show how bounds can be placed on causal quantities following qualitative imputation of missing potential outcomes for some or all cases. Seawright (2016) and Dunning (2012) describe approaches in which case studies are used to test the assumptions underlying statistical inferences, such as the assumption of no-confounding or the stable-unit treatment value assumption.

1.1.3 Connecting Theory and Empirics

The relationship between theory and empirics has been a surprisingly uncomfortable one in political science. In a prominent intervention, for instance, Clarke and Primo (2012) draw attention to – and critique – political scientists' widespread reliance on the "hypothetico-deductive" (H-D) framework, in which a theory or model is elaborated, empirical predictions derived, and data sought to test these predictions and the model from which they derive. Clarke and Primo draw on decades of scholarship in the philosophy of science pointing to deep problems with the H-D framework, including the idea that the truth of a model logically derived from first principles can be *tested* against evidence.

In fact, the relationship between theory and evidence in social inquiry is often surprisingly unclear, both in qualitative and quantitative work. We can perhaps illustrate it best, however, by reference to qualitative work, where the centrality of theory to inference has been most emphasized. In process tracing, theory is what justifies inferences. In their classic text on case-study approaches, George and Bennett (2005) describe process tracing as the search for evidence of "the causal process that a theory hypothesizes or implies" (6). Similarly, Hall (2003) conceptualizes the approach as testing for the causal-process-related observable implications of a theory; Mahoney (2010) indicates that the events for which process tracers go looking are those posited by theory (128); and Gerring (2006) describes theory as a source of predictions that the case-study analyst tests (116). Theory, in these accounts, is supposed to help us figure out where to look for discriminating evidence.

What is not clear, however, is how deriving within-case empirical predictions from theory provide leverage on a causal question. From which elements of a theory can scholars derive informative observable implications? How do the evidentiary requisites for drawing a causal inference, given a theory, depend on the particular causal question of interest – on whether, for instance, we are interested in identifying the cause of an outcome in a case or estimating an average causal effect in a population? Perhaps most confusingly, when a theory tells us what to look for to draw an inference, are we to make inferences about the theory or are we making theory-*dependent* inferences?[7] In short, how exactly can we ground causal inferences from

---

[7] More precisely, it is not always clear whether the strategy is of the form: (1) "if theory T is correct we should observe K," with evidence on K used to update beliefs about the theory; or (2) "According to theory T, if A caused B then we should observe K," in which case K is informative about whether A caused B *under* T.

within-case evidence in background knowledge about how the world works?

Much quantitative work in political science features a similarly weak integration between theory and research design. The modal inferential approach in quantitative work, both observational and experimental, involves looking for correlations between causes and outcomes, with less regard for intervening or surrounding causal relationships.[8] If a theory suggests a *set* of relations, it is common to examine these separately – does *A* cause *B*?; does *B* cause *C*?; are relations stronger or weaker here or there? – without standard procedures for bringing the disparate pieces of evidence together to form theoretical conclusions. More attention has been paid to empirical implications of theoretical models than to theoretical implications of empirical models.

In this book, we seek to show how scholars can simultaneously make fuller and more explicit use of theoretical knowledge in designing their research projects and analyzing data, and make use of data to update theoretical models. Like Clarke and Primo, we treat models not as veridical accounts of the world but as maps – maps, based on prior theoretical knowledge, about causal relations in a domain of interest. Also, as in Clarke and Primo's approach, we do not write down a model in order to test its veracity (though, in later chapters, we do discuss ways of justifying and evaluating models). Rather, our focus is on how we can systematically *use* causal models – in the sense of *mobilizing background knowledge of the world* – to guide our empirical strategies and inform our inferences. Grounding our empirical strategy in a model allows us, in turn, to update our model as we encounter the data, thus letting our theory evolve in the face of evidence.

1.2 Key Contributions

This book draws on methods developed in the study of Bayesian networks, a field pioneered by scholars in computer science, statistics, and philosophy to represent structures of causal relations between multiple variables. Judea Pearl's *Causality* provides an indispensable guide to this body of work (Pearl, 2009). Although work in this tradition has had limited traction in political science to date, the literature on Bayesian networks and their graphical counterparts, directed acyclic graphs (DAGs), addresses very directly the

---

[8] There are of course many exceptions, including work that uses structural equation modeling, and research that focuses specifically on understanding heterogeneity and mediation processes.

kinds of problems with which qualitative and quantitative scholars routinely grapple.[9]

Drawing on this work, we show in the chapters that follow how a theory can be formalized as a causal model represented by a causal graph and a set of structural equations. Engaging in this modest degree of formalization yields enormous benefits. It allows us, for a wide range of causal questions, to specify causal questions clearly and to draw inferences about those questions from new data.

For scholars engaging in process tracing, the benefits of this approach are multiple. In particular, the framework that we describe in this book provides:

- A clear language for *defining* causal questions of interest, consistent with advances using the potential outcomes framework and those using graphical causal models.
- A strategy for assessing the "probative value" of evidence drawn from different parts of any causal network. The approach yields a principled and transparent approach to answering the question: How should the observation of a given piece of data affect my causal beliefs about a case?
- A transparent, replicable method for aggregating inferences from observations drawn from different locations in a causal network. Having collected multiple pieces of evidence from different parts of a causal process or case context, what should I end up believing about the causal question of interest?
- A common approach for assessing a wide variety of queries (estimands). We can use the same apparatus to learn *simultaneously* about different case-level and population-level causal questions, such as "What caused the outcome in this case?" and "Through what pathway does this cause most commonly exert its effect?"
- Guidance for research design. Given finite resources, researchers must make choices about where to look for evidence. A causal model framework

---

[9] For application to quantitative analysis strategies in political science, Rohrer (2018) and Glynn and Quinn (2007) give clear introductions to how these methods can be used to motivate strategies for conditioning and adjusting for causal inference. García and Wantchekon (2015) demonstrate how these methods can be used to assess claims of external validity. With a focus on qualitative methods, Waldner (2015) uses causal diagrams to lay out a "completeness standard" for good process tracing. Weller and Barnes (2014) employ graphs to conceptualize the different possible pathways between causal and outcome variables among which qualitative researchers may want to distinguish. Generally, in discussions of qualitative methodology, graphs are used to capture core features of theoretical accounts, but are not developed specifically to ensure a representation of the kind of independence relations implied by structural causal models (notably, what is called the "Markov condition" in the literature). Moreover, efforts to tie these causal graphs to probative observations, as in Waldner (2015), are generally limited to identifying steps in a causal chain that the researcher should seek to observe.

can help researchers assess, *a priori*, the relative expected informativeness of different evidentiary and case-selection strategies, conditional on how they think the world works and the question they want to answer.

The approach also offers a range of distinctive benefits to researchers seeking to engage in mixed-method inference and to learn about general causal relations, as well as about individual cases. The framework's central payoff for multi-method research is the systematic integration of qualitative and quantitative information to answer any given causal query. We note that the form of integration that we pursue here differs from that offered in other accounts of multi-method research. In Seawright (2016)'s approach, for instance, one form of data – quantitative *or* qualitative – is used to draw causal inferences, while the other form of data is used to test assumptions or improve measures employed in that primary inferential strategy. In the approach that we develop in this book, in contrast, we are always using *all* information available to update causal quantities of interest.

In fact, within the causal models framework, there is no fundamental difference between quantitative and qualitative data, as both enter as values of nodes in a causal graph. This formalization – this reductive move – may well discomfit some readers. We acknowledge that our approach undeniably involves a loss of some of what makes qualitative research distinct and valuable. Yet, this translation of qualitative and quantitative observations into a common, causal-model framework offers major advantages. For scholars seeking to mix methods, these advantages include the following:

- Transparency. The framework makes manifest precisely how each form of evidence enters into the analysis and shapes conclusions.
- A procedure for justifying inferences. We use case-level information to learn about populations and general theory. But at the same time, we can then also use what we have learned about populations to justify inferences about causal relations within individual cases.
- Cumulation of knowledge. A causal model framework provides a straightforward, principled mechanism for building on what we have already learned. As we see data, we update our model, and then our updated model can inform the inferences we draw from the next set of observations and give guidance to what sort of future data will be most beneficial. Models can, likewise, provide an explicit framework for positing and learning about the generalizability and portability of findings across research contexts.

- Guidance for research design. With a causal model in hand, we can formally assess key multi-method design choices, including the balance we should strike between breadth (the number of cases) and depth (intensiveness of analysis in individual cases) and the choice of cases for intensive analysis.

Using causal models also has substantial implications for common methodological intuitions, advice, and practice. To touch on just a few of these implications:

- Our elaboration and application of model-based process tracing shows that, given plausible causal models, process tracing's common focus on intervening causal chains may be much less productive than other empirical strategies, such as examining moderating conditions.
- Our examination of model-based case selection indicates that, for many common purposes, there is nothing particularly special about "on the regression line" cases or those in which the outcome occurred, and there is nothing necessarily damning about selecting on the dependent variable. Rather, optimal case selection depends on factors that have to date received little attention, such as the population distribution of cases and the probative value of the available evidence.
- Our analysis of clue selection as a decision problem shows that the probative value of a given piece of evidence cannot be assessed in isolation, but hinges critically on what we have already observed.

The basic analytical apparatus that we employ here is not new. Rather, we see the book's goals as being of three kinds. First, we aim to import insights: to introduce social scientists to an approach that has received little attention in their fields but that can be useful for addressing the sorts of causal questions with which they are commonly preoccupied. As a model-based approach, it is a framework especially well suited to fields of inquiry in which exogeneity frequently cannot be assumed by design – that is, in which we often have no choice but to be engineers.

Second, we draw connections between the Bayesian networks approach and key concerns and challenges with which the social sciences routinely grapple. Working with causal models and DAGs most naturally connects to concerns about confounding and identification that have been central to much quantitative methodological development. Yet we also show how causal models can address issues central to process tracing, such as how to select cases for examination, how to think about the probative value of causal process observations, and how to structure our search for evidence, given finite resources.

Third, we provide a set of usable tools for implementing the approach. We provide software, the `CausalQueries` package, that researchers can use to make research design choices and draw inferences from the data.

There are also important limits to this book's contributions and aims. First, while we make use of Bayesian inference throughout, we do not engage here with fundamental debates over or critiques of Bayesianism itself. (For excellent treatments of some of the deeper issues and debates, see, for instance, Earman (1992) and Fairfield and Charman (2017).)

Second, this book does not address matters of data collection (e.g., conducting interviews, searching for archival documents) or the construction of measures. For the most part, we assume that reliable data can be gathered (even if it is costly to do so), and we bracket the challenges that surround the measurement process itself.[10] That said, a core concern of the book is using causal models to identify the *kinds* of evidence that qualitative researchers will want to collect. In Chapter 7, we show how causal models can tell us whether observing an element of a causal process is potentially informative about a causal question; and in Chapter 12 we demonstrate how we can use models to assess the likely learning that will arise from different clue-selection strategies. We also address the problem of measurement error in Chapter 9, showing how we can use causal models to learn about error from the data.

Finally, while we will often refer to the use of causal models for "qualitative" analysis, we do not seek to assimilate all forms of qualitative inquiry into a causal models framework. Our focus is on work that is squarely addressed to matters of causation; in particular, the logic that we elaborate is most closely connected to the method of process tracing. More generally, the formalization that we make use of here – the graphical representation of beliefs and the application of mathematical operations to numerically coded observations – will surely strike some readers as reductive and not particularly "qualitative." It is almost certainly the case that, as we formalize, we leave behind many forms of information that qualitative researchers gather and make use of. Our aim in this book is not to discount the importance of those aspects of qualitative inquiry that resist formalization, but to show some of the things we *can* do if we are willing to formalize in a particular way.

---

[10] See Mosley (2013) for a treatment of complexities around interview research in political science and Lieberman (2010) on strategies for historically oriented research.

1.3 The Road Ahead

This book has four parts.

In the first part, we present the framework's foundational concepts. In Chapter 2, following a review of the potential outcomes approach to causality, we introduce the concept and key components of a causal model. Chapter 3 illustrates how we can represent causal beliefs in the form of causal models by translating the arguments of several prominent works of political science into causal models. In Chapter 4, we set out a range of causal questions that researchers might want to address – including questions about case-level causal effects, population-level effects, and mechanisms – and define these queries within a causal model framework. Chapter 5 offers a primer on the key ideas in Bayesian inference that we will mobilize in later sections of the book. In Chapter 6, we map between causal models and theories, showing how we can think of any causal model as situated within a hierarchy of complexity: Within this hierarchy, any causal model can be justified by references to a "lower level," more detailed model that offers a theory of why things work the way they do at the higher level. This conceptualization is crucial insofar as we use more detailed (lower level) models to generate empirical leverage on relationships represented in simpler, higher level models.

Though some of the material in this first part is technical, we try throughout to keep the discussion jargon free. We couldn't eliminate jargon entirely though and so we provide a glossary in Chapter 18 which you can refer to in times of need.

In the second part, we show how we can use causal models to undertake process-tracing and mixed-method inference. Chapter 7 lays out the logic of case-level inference from causal models: The central idea here is that what we learn from evidence is always conditional on the prior beliefs embedded in our model. In Chapter 8, we illustrate model-based process tracing with two substantive applications: one on the issue of economic inequality's effects on democratization and a second on the relationship between political institutions and economic development. Chapter 9 moves to mixed-data problems: situations in which a researcher wants to use "quantitative" (broadly, X, Y) data on a large set of cases and more detailed ("qualitative") data on some subset of these cases. We show how we can use any arbitrary mix of observations across a sample of any size (greater than 1) to update on all causal parameters in a model, and then use the updated model to address the full range of general and case-level queries of interest. In Chapter 10, we illustrate this integrative approach by revisiting the substantive applications introduced in Chapter 8. Finally, in Chapter 11, we take the project of integration a step further by showing how we can use models to integrate findings across *studies* and across *settings*. We show, for instance, how we can learn jointly from the data generated by an observational study and an experimental study of the same causal domain and how models can help us reason in principled ways about the transportability of findings across contexts.

In the third part, we unpack what causal models can contribute to research design. In terms of the Model-Inquiry-Data strategy-Answer strategy framework from Blair et al. (2023), we can think of Chapters 2, 4, and 5 as corresponding to models, inquiries, and answer strategies, while Data strategies are dealt with in this third part. Across Chapters 12, 13, and 14 we demonstrate how researchers can mobilize their models, as well as prior observations, to determine what kind of new evidence is likely to be most informative about the query of interest, how to strike a balance between extensiveness and intensiveness of analysis, and which cases to select for in-depth process tracing. Consistent with the principle in Blair et al. (2023) to design holistically, we find that questions around data-selection strategies cannot be answered in isolation from model and query specification.

The fourth and final part of the book steps back to put the model-based approach into question. Until this point, we will have been advocating an embrace of models to aid inference. But the dangers of doing this are demonstrably large. The key problem is that with model-based inference, our inferences are only as good as the model we start with. In the end, while we advocate a focus on models, we know that skeptics are right to distrust them. The final part of the book approaches this problem from two perspectives. In Chapter 15, we demonstrate the *possibility* of justifying models from external evidence, though we do not pretend that the conditions for doing so will arise commonly. In Chapter 16, drawing on common practice in Bayesian statistics, we present a set of strategies that researchers can use to evaluate and compare the validity of models, and to investigate the degree to which findings hinge on model assumptions. The key point here is that using a model does not require a commitment to it. Indeed, the model itself can provide indications that it is doing a poor job.

In the concluding chapter, we summarize what we see as the main advantages of a causal-model-based approach to inference, draw out a set of key concerns and limitations of the framework, and identify what we see as the key avenues for future progress in model-based inference.

Here we go.

Part I

Foundations

2 Causal Models

We provide a lay-language primer on the counterfactual model of causality and the logic of causal models. Topics include the representation of causal models with causal graphs and using causal graphs to read off relations of conditional independence among variables in a causal domain.

Causal claims are everywhere. Causal knowledge is often not just the goal of empirical social science, it is also an *input* into causal inference.[1] Causal assumptions are hidden in seemingly descriptive statements: Claims that someone is guilty, or exploited, or powerful, or weak involve beliefs about how things would be if conditions were different. Even when scholars carefully try to avoid causal claim-making, causal verbs – depends, drives, produces, influences – are hard to avoid.

But while causal claims are commonplace, it is not always clear what exactly is meant by a causal relation and how causal knowledge about one thing can be marshaled to justify causal claims about another. For our purposes, the counterfactual view of causality addresses the first question. Causal models address the second. In this chapter, we discuss each in turn. The present chapter is largely conceptual, with ideas worked through with a couple of "toy" running examples. In Chapter 3, we then apply and illustrate many of the key concepts from this chapter by translating a few prominent arguments from the field of political science into the language of structural causal models.

2.1 The Counterfactual Model

We begin with what we might think of as a meta-model, the counterfactual model of causation. At its core, a counterfactual understanding of causation

---

[1] As nicely put by Nancy Cartwright: no causes in, no causes out (Cartwright 1989). We return to the point more formally later.

captures a simple notion of causation as "difference-making."[2] In the coun-terfactual view, to say that X caused Y is to say: *had X been different, Y would have been* different.

A causal effect, in this view, is the difference between two things (two values of Y) that might have happened. This means that *by definition, causal effects are not measurable quantities.* They are not differences between two observable outcomes in the world, but, at best, differences between one observable outcome and a second counterfactual outcome. For this reason, causal effects need to be inferred, not measured.

In this view, the antecedent, "had X been different," imagines a *controlled* change in X – an intervention that alter X's value – rather than a naturally arising difference in X. The usual counterfactual claim, then, is not that Y is different from how it might have been had circumstances been such that X were different; it is, rather, that if one could somehow have *made X* different in a case, then Y would have been different in that case.[3]

Consider a simple example. Teacher A is extraordinary. Students with teacher A do not study and would perform well whether or not they studied. Students with teacher B perform well if and only if they study. Moreover, students with teacher B do in fact study. And all perform well.

When we say that one of teacher B's students did well *because* they studied, we are comparing the outcome that they experienced to the outcome that they would have experienced if (1) they had had teacher B, as they did but (2) counterfactually, had *not* studied.

Notably, when we define the effect of studying, we are *not* comparing the realized outcome of the studiers to the outcome of the students who *in fact* did not study. That is because the students who in fact did not study had teacher A, not B. Moreover, we are not comparing the realized outcome of a student of teacher B to what that same student would have achieved if they had had teacher A (and for that reason, had not studied). The reason again is that this comparison includes the effect of having teacher A and not the effect of studying *given* they had teacher B.

---

[2] The approach is sometimes attributed to David Hume, whose writing contains ideas both about causality as regularity and causality as counterfactual. On the latter, Hume's key formulation is, "if the first object had not been, the second never had existed" (Hume and Beauchamp, 2000, Section VIII). More recently, the counterfactual view has been set forth by Splawa-Neyman et al. (1990) and Lewis (1973). See also Lewis (1986).

[3] In the terminology of Pearl (2009), we can represent this quantity using a "do" operator: $Y(\text{do}(X = x))$ is the value of Y when the variable X is *set* to the value x.

Here is a second example, drawn from a substantive domain that we will return to many times in this book. In his seminal book on democracy and distribution, Carles Boix argues that low economic inequality is a cause of democratization (Boix, 2003). At high levels of inequality, Boix argues, the elite would rather repress the poor than submit to democracy and its redistributive consequences; at low levels of inequality, in contrast, redistribution under democracy will be less costly for the elite than would continued repression. Now, in light of this theory, consider the claim that Switzerland democratized $(D = 1)$ because it had a relatively low level of economic inequality $(I = 0)$. In the counterfactual view, this claim is equivalent to saying that, if Switzerland had had a *high* level of inequality, the country would not have democratized. Low economic inequality made a difference. The comparison for the causal statement is with the outcome Switzerland would have experienced under an intervention that boosted its historic level of economic inequality (but made no other change) – *not* with how Switzerland would have performed if it had been like one of the countries that *in fact* had higher levels of inequality, cases that likely differ from Switzerland in other causally relevant ways.

2.1.1 Potential Outcomes

Researchers often employ what is called the "potential-outcomes" framework when they need precise formal language for describing counterfactual quantities (Rubin, 1974). In this framework, we characterize how a given unit responds to a causal variable by positing the outcomes that the unit *would* take on at different values of the causal variable. Most commonly, $Y_i(0)$ and $Y_i(1)$ are used to denote the values that Y *would* take for unit i if X were 0 and 1, respectively.[4]

One setting in which it is quite easy to think about potential outcomes is medical treatment. Imagine that some individuals in a diseased population have received a drug $(X = 1)$ while others have not received the drug $(X = 0)$. Assume that, subsequently, a researcher observes which individuals become healthy $(Y = 1)$ and which do not $(Y = 0)$. Given the assignments of all other individuals,[5] we can treat each individual as belonging to one of four

---

[4] To avoid ambiguity, we prefer $Y_i(X = 0)$ and $Y_i(X = 1)$. Alternative notation, used in Holland (1986) for instance, places the treatment condition in the subscript: $Y_t(u)$, $Y_c(u)$, with u used to capture individual level features. Sometimes the pairs are written Y_{u0}, Y_{u1}.

[5] We note that we are conditioning on the assignments of others. If we wanted to describe outcomes as a function of the *profile* of treatments received by others, we would have a more complex type space. For

Table 2.1 Potential outcomes: What would happen to each of four possible types of case if they were or were not treated.

	Type a	Type b	Type c	Type d
	adverse	beneficial	chronic	destined
Outcome if not treated	Healthy	Sick	Sick	Healthy
Outcome if treated	Sick	Healthy	Sick	Healthy

unobserved response "types," defined by the outcomes that the individual *would have* if they received or did not receive treatment:[6]

- **a**dverse: Those individuals who would get better if and only if they do not receive the treatment
- **b**eneficial: Those who would get better if and only if they do receive the treatment
- **c**hronic: Those who will remain sick whether or not they receive the treatment
- **d**estined: Those who will get better whether or not they receive the treatment.

Table 2.1 maps the four types (a, b, c, d) onto their respective potential outcomes. In each column, we have simply written down the outcome that a patient of a given type would experience if they are not treated, and the outcome they would experience if they are treated. We are here always imagining *controlled* changes in treatment: the responses if treatments are changed without changes to other background (or pre-treatment) conditions in the case.

We highlight that, in this framework, case-level causal relations are treated as deterministic. A given case has a set of potential outcomes. Any uncertainty about outcomes enters as incomplete knowledge of a case's "type," not from underlying randomness in causal relations. This understanding of causality – as ontologically deterministic, but empirically imperfectly understood – is compatible with views of causation commonly employed by qualitative

instance, in an $X \rightarrow Y$ model with 2 individuals, we would report how (Y_1, Y_2) respond to (X_1, X_0); each vector can take on four values producing a type space with 4^4 types rather than 2^2. The complex type space could be reduced back down to four types again, however, if we invoked the assumption that the treatment or non-treatment of one patient has no effect on the outcomes of other patients – an assumption known as the stable unit treatment value assumption.

[6] See Copas (1973) for an early classification of this form. The literature on probabilistic models also refers to such strata as "principal strata," "canonical partitions," or "equivalence classes."

Table 2.2 Mapping types to potential outcomes: the values Y takes on if X were set at 0 or 1

	$a: \theta^Y = \theta^Y_{10}$	$b: \theta^Y = \theta^Y_{01}$	$c: \theta^Y = \theta^Y_{00}$	$d: \theta^Y = \theta^Y_{11}$
Set $X = 0$	$Y(0) = 1$	$Y(0) = 0$	$Y(0) = 0$	$Y(0) = 1$
Set $X = 1$	$Y(1) = 0$	$Y(1) = 1$	$Y(1) = 0$	$Y(1) = 1$

researchers (see, e.g., Mahoney, 2008), and with understandings of causal determinism going back at least to Laplace (1901).

As we will also see, we can readily express this kind of incompleteness of knowledge within a causal model framework: Indeed, the way in which causal models manage uncertainty is central to how they allow us to pose questions of interest and to learn from evidence. Certainly, there are situations we could imagine in which one might want to conceptualize potential outcomes themselves as random (for instance, if individuals in different conditions play different lotteries). But for the vast majority of the settings we consider, not much of importance is lost if we treat potential outcomes as deterministic but possibly unknown: Every case *is* of a particular type; we just do not know which type that is.

2.1.2 A Generalization

Throughout the book, we generalize from this simple setup. Whenever we have one causal variable and one outcome, and both variables are binary (i.e., each can take on two possible values, 0 or 1), there are only four sets of possible potential outcomes, or "types." More generally, for variable Y, we will use θ^Y to capture the unit's "type": the way that Y responds to its potential causes.[7] We, further, add subscripts to denote particular types. Where there are four possible types, for instance, we use the notation θ^Y_{ij}, where the first subscript, i, represents the case's potential outcome when $X = 0$; and the second subscript, j, is the case's potential outcome when $X = 1$.

Adopting this notation, for a causal structure with one binary causal variable and a binary outcome, the four types can be represented as $\{\theta^Y_{10}, \theta^Y_{01}, \theta^Y_{00}, \theta^Y_{11}\}$, as shown in Table 2.2

Returning to the matter of inequality and democratization to illustrate, let $I = 1$ represent a high level of economic inequality and $I = 0$ its absence; let $D = 1$ represent democratization and $D = 0$ its absence. A θ^D_{10} (or a) type is a

---

[7] Later, we will refer to these as "nodal types."

case in which a high level of inequality, if it occurs, *prevents* democratization in a country that would otherwise have democratized. So the causal effect of high inequality in a case, i, of θ_{10}^D type is $\tau_i = -1$. A θ_{01}^D type (or b type) is a case in which high inequality, if it occurs, generates democratization in a country that would otherwise have remained non-democratic (effect of $\tau_i = 1$). A θ_{00}^D type (c type) is a case that will not democratize regardless of the level of inequality (effect of $\tau_i = 0$); and a θ_{11}^D type (d type) is one that will democratize regardless of the level of inequality (again, effect of $\tau_i = 0$).

In this setting, a causal *explanation* of a given case outcome amounts to a statement about its type. The claim that Switzerland's low level of inequality was a cause of its democratization is equivalent to saying that Switzerland democratized and is a θ_{10}^D type. To claim that Benin democratized because of high inequality is equivalent to saying that Benin democratized and is a θ_{01}^D type. To claim, on the other hand, that Malawi democratized for reasons having nothing to do with its level of economic inequality is to characterize Malawi as a θ_{11}^D type (which implies that Malawi would have been democratic no matter what its level of inequality).

Now let us consider more complex causal relations. Suppose there are two binary causal variables X_1 and X_2. We can specify any given case's potential outcomes for each of the different possible combinations of their causal conditions. There are now four such conditions since each causal variable may take on 0 or 1 when the other is at 0 or 1.

As for notation, we now need to expand θ's subscript since we need to represent the value that Y takes on under each of the four possible combinations of X_1 and X_2 values. This requires four, rather than two, subscript digits. We map the subscripting for θ_{hijk} to potential outcome notation as shown in Equation (2.1).

$$\theta_{hijk}^Y \begin{cases} Y(0,0) = h \\ Y(1,0) = i \\ Y(0,1) = j \\ Y(1,1) = k \end{cases} \tag{2.1}$$

where the first argument of $Y(.,.)$ is the value to which X_1 is set and the second is the value to which X_2 is set.

Thus, for instance, θ_{0100}^Y means that Y is 1 if X_1 is set to 1 and X_2 to 0 and is 0 otherwise; θ_{0011}^Y is a type in which $Y = 1$ if and only if $X_2 = 1$; θ_{0001}^Y is a type for which $Y = 0$ unless both X_1 and X_2 are 1.

Table 2.3 Two binary causes yield 16 causal types

θ^Y	if $X_1 = 0, X_2 = 0$	if $X_1 = 1, X_2 = 0$	if $X_1 = 0, X_2 = 1$	if $X_1 = 1, X_2 = 1$
θ^Y_{0000}	0	0	0	0
θ^Y_{1000}	1	0	0	0
θ^Y_{0100}	0	1	0	0
θ^Y_{1100}	1	1	0	0
θ^Y_{0010}	0	0	1	0
θ^Y_{1010}	1	0	1	0
θ^Y_{0110}	0	1	1	0
θ^Y_{1110}	1	1	1	0
θ^Y_{0001}	0	0	0	1
θ^Y_{1001}	1	0	0	1
θ^Y_{0101}	0	1	0	1
θ^Y_{1101}	1	1	0	1
θ^Y_{0011}	0	0	1	1
θ^Y_{1011}	1	0	1	1
θ^Y_{0111}	0	1	1	1
θ^Y_{1111}	1	1	1	1

We now have 16 causal types for this node: 16 different patterns that Y might display in response to changes in X_1 and X_2. The full set is represented in Table 2.3, which also illustrates how we read types off of four-digit subscripts. For instance, the table shows us that for nodal type θ^Y_{0101}, X_1 has a positive causal effect on Y but X_2 has no effect. On the other hand, for type θ^Y_{0011}, X_2 has a positive effect while X_1 has none.

The 16 types also capture interactions. For instance, for a θ^Y_{0001} type, X_2 has a positive causal effect if and only if X_1 is 1. For that type, X_1 and X_2 serve as "complements." For θ^Y_{0111}, X_2 has a positive causal effect if and only if X_1 is 0. For that type, X_1 and X_2 are "substitutes."

This is a rich framework in that it allows for all the possible ways in which a set of multiple causes can interact with each other. Often, when seeking to explain the outcome in a case, researchers proceed as though causes are necessarily *rival*, where X_1 being a cause of Y implies that X_2 was not. Did Malawi democratize because it was a relatively economically equal society *or* because of international pressure to do so? In the counterfactual model, however, causal relations can be nonrival. If two out of three people vote for an outcome under majority rule, for example, then both of the two supporters caused the outcome: The outcome would not have occurred if *either* supporter's vote were different. A typological, potential-outcomes conceptualization provides a straightforward way of representing this kind of complex causation.

Because of this complexity, when we say that X caused Y in a given case, we will generally mean that X was *a* cause, not *the* (only) cause. Malawi might not have democratized if *either* a relatively high level of economic equality *or* international pressure had been absent. For most social phenomena that we study, there will be multiple, and sometimes a great many, difference-makers for any given case outcome.

We will mostly use θ^Y_{ij}-style notation in this book to refer to types. We will, however, occasionally revert to the simpler a, b, c, d designations when that eases exposition. As types play a central role in the causal-model framework, we recommend getting comfortable with both forms of notation before going further.

Using the same framework, we can generalize to structures in which a unit has any number of causes and also to cases in which causes and outcomes are nonbinary. As one might imagine, the number of types increases rapidly (very rapidly) as the number of considered causal variables increases; it also increases rapidly if we allow X or Y to take on more than two possible values. For example, if there are n binary causes of an outcome, then there can be $2^{(2^n)}$ types of this form: that is, $k = 2^n$ combinations of values of causes to consider, and 2^k distinct response patterns across the possible combinations. If causes and outcomes are ternary instead of binary, we have $3^{(3^n)}$ causal types.

Nevertheless, the basic principle of representing possible causal relations as patterns of potential outcomes remains unchanged, at least as long as variables are discrete.

2.1.3 Summaries of Potential Outcomes

So far, we have focused on causal relations at the level of an individual case. Causal relations at the level of a population are, however, simply a summary of causal relations for cases, and the same basic ideas can be used. We could, for instance, summarize our beliefs about the relationship between economic inequality and democratization by saying that we think that the world is comprised of a mixture of a, b, c, and d types, as defined above. We could get more specific and express a belief about what proportions of cases in the world are of each of the four types. For instance, we might believe that a types and d types are quite rare while b and c types are quite common.

Moreover, our belief about the proportions of b (positive effect) and a (negative effect) cases imply a belief about inequality's *average* effect on democratization as, in a binary setup, this quantity is simply the proportion of b types minus the proportion of a types. Such summaries allow us to move from the discussion of the cause of a single outcome to discussions of average effects, a distinction that we take up again in Chapter 4.

2.2 Causal Models and Directed Acyclic Graphs

So far we have discussed how a single outcome is affected by one or more possible causes. However, these same ideas can be used to describe more complex relations between collections of variables – for example, with one variable affecting another directly as well as indirectly via its impact on a third variable. For instance, X might affect Y directly. But X might also affect Y by affecting M, which in turn affects Y. In the latter scenario, M is a mediator of X's effect on Y.

Potential-outcomes tables can be used to describe such relations. However, as causal structures become more complex – especially, as the number of variables in a domain increases – a causal model can be a powerful organizing tool. In this section, we show how causal models and their visual counterparts, directed acyclic graphs (DAGs), can represent substantive beliefs about counterfactual causal relationships in the world. The key ideas in this section can be found in many texts (see, e.g., Galles and Pearl, 1998; Halpern and Pearl, 2005), and we introduce here a set of basic principles that readers will need to keep in mind in order to follow the argumentation in this book.

As we shift to talking about networks of causal relations between variables, we will also shift our language. When talking about causal networks, or causal graphs, we will generally refer to variables as "nodes." And we will sometimes use familial terms to describe relations between nodes. For instance, if A is a cause of B, we will refer to A as a "parent" of B, and B as a "child" of A. Graphically, we have an arrow pointing from the parent to the child. If two variables have a child in common (both directly affecting the same variable), we refer to them as "spouses." We can also say that a variable is a "causal ancestor" of another variable (its "causal descendant") if there is a chain of parent–child relations from the "ancestor" to the "descendant."

Returning to our running democratization example, suppose now that we have more fully specified beliefs about how the level of economic inequality can have an effect on whether a country democratizes. We might believe

A model of inequality's effect on democratization

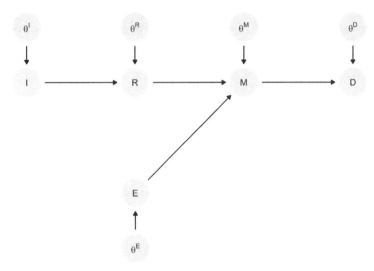

Figure 2.1   A simple causal model in which high inequality (*I*) affects democratization (*D*) via redistributive demands (*R*) and mass mobilization (*M*), which is also a function of ethnic homogeneity (*E*). Arrows show relations of causal dependence between variables

that inequality (I) affects the likelihood of democratization (D) by generating demands for redistribution (R), which in turn can cause the mobilization (M) of lower-income citizens, which in turn can cause democratization (D). We might also believe that mobilization itself is not just a function of redistributive preferences but also of the degree of ethnic homogeneity (E), which shapes the capacities of lower-income citizens for collective action. We visualize this model as a *directed acyclic graph* (DAG) in Figure 2.1. In this model, R is a parent of M. I is an ancestor of M but not its parent. R and E are spouses, and M is their child (i.e., mobilization depends on both redistributive preferences and ethnic demography).

Fundamentally, we treat causal models like this as formal representations of *beliefs* about how the world works – or, more specifically, about causal relations within a given domain. We might use a causal model to capture our own beliefs, a working simplification of our beliefs, or a set of potential beliefs that one might hold. The formalization of *prior* beliefs in the form of a causal model is the starting point for research design and inference in this book's analytic framework.

We now provide a formal definition of a causal model (Definition 2.1) as used in this book, and then unpack the definition.

Definition 2.1. Causal model

A "**causal model**" is:

1.1: An ordered list of n endogenous nodes, $\mathcal{V} = (V^1, V^2, \ldots, V^n)$, with a specification of a range for each of them

1.2: A list of n exogenous nodes, $\Theta = (\theta^1, \theta^2, \ldots, \theta^n)$

2: A list of n functions $\mathcal{F} = (f^1, f^2, \ldots, f^n)$, one for each element of $\mathcal{V}$ such that each f^i takes as arguments θ^i as well as elements of $\mathcal{V}$ that are *prior* to V^i in the ordering

and

3: A probability distribution over Θ

This definition corresponds to Pearl's definition of a "probabilistic causal model" (Pearl, 2009, Definition 7.1.6). Also following Pearl, we use the term "structural causal model" to refer to a model that specifies parts 1.1, 1.2, and 2 of this definition but without part 3 (see, e.g., Pearl, 2009, Definition 7.1.1).[8]

The three components of a causal model then are (1) the nodes – that is, the set of variables we are focused on and how they are defined, (2) the causal functions – which characterize which nodes are caused by which other nodes and how, and (3) probability distributions over unexplained elements of a model (in our framework, the θ nodes). We discuss each in turn.

2.2.1 The Nodes

The first component of a causal model is the set of variables (nodes) across which the model characterizes causal relations.

We have two sorts of variables: the named, "endogenous," nodes, $\mathcal{V}$, and the unnamed "exogenous" nodes, Θ.[9]

On the graph (DAG) in Figure 2.1, the five endogenous nodes are lettered. All these endogenous nodes have an arrow pointing into them indicating that

---

[8] We note however that this terminology is not always used consistently in the literature and the term "structural causal model" is sometimes used coextensively with what we have defined above as a causal model.

[9] In many treatments, $\mathcal{U}$ is used for the exogenous nodes. We use Θ to denote these unobserved, unspecified influences in order to emphasize their particular role, as direct objects of interest in causal inquiry.

the node at the end of the arrow is (possibly) caused in part by (or, "depends on") the node at the beginning of the arrow.

Nodes R, M, and D are all obviously endogenous because they depend on other named variables. I and E are not endogenous to other nodes in $\mathcal{V}$, but we still call them endogenous because they depend on other nodes in the model, specifically on nodes in Θ. We will use the term "root nodes" to indicate nodes like this that are in $\mathcal{V}$ but are not endogenous to other nodes in $\mathcal{V}$.

Our definition specified that the endogenous nodes should be *ordered*. We can in fact specify different orderings of nodes in this example. For instance we could have the ordering $<E, I, R, M, D>$, or the ordering $<I, R, E, M, D>$ or even $<I, E, R, M, D>$. The ordering *matters* only to the extent that it constrains the causal functions: f^j can take as arguments only θ^j and elements of $\mathcal{V}$ that come before j in the ordering. In practice, this prevents us from having a variable that is both a cause and a consequence of another variable.

In specifying these nodes, we also need to specify the ranges over which they can vary. We might specify, for instance, that all the endogenous nodes in the model are binary, taking on the values 0 or 1. We could, alternatively, define a set of categories across which a node ranges or allow a node to take on any real number value or any value between a set of bounds.

The exogenous nodes, Θ, require a little more explanation since they do not describe substantive nodes. Five such exogenous nodes are shown on the graph, one for each endogenous node (note though, very frequently we do not include the exogenous nodes explicitly when we draw a graph, but we should still imagine them there, pointing into each endogenous node).

In our discussion above, we introduced θ notation for representing types. Here, we simply build these types into a causal model. We imagine a θ term pointing into every node (whether explicitly represented on the graph or not). We can think of θ terms as unobservable and unspecified inputs into a causal system. These might include random processes (noise) or contextual features that we are unable to identify or do not understand, but that both affect outcomes and condition the effects of other, specified variables on outcomes.

As we will show, consistent with our discussion of potential outcomes and types, in discrete settings *we can think of* θ nodes as capturing the functional relations between variables and, as such, as being quantities of direct interest for causal inquiry. We more fully develop this point – returning to the notion of θ terms as receptacles for causal effects – below.

2.2.2 The Functions

Next, we need to specify our beliefs about the causal relations among the nodes in our model. How is the value of one node affected by, and how does it affect, the values of others? For each endogenous node – each node influenced by others in the model – we need to express beliefs about how its value is affected by its parents (its immediate causes). We do this using a function f^i for each node i. We will usually refer to these functions as "causal functions" to highlight the fact that they capture causal relations between nodes.[10] Critically, these functions contain all the information needed to construct potential outcomes (see Note 2.1 on these connections).

We can think in a qualitative and quantitative way about how one variable is affected by others. Qualitatively, if a variable i depends on the value of another variable j (given other variables prior to i in the ordering), then that variable j enters as an argument in f^i. In that case, j is a parent to i. Whether a variable is a parent or not depends on the nodes in the model: if we think A causes B and B causes C and A causes C only via B then A is not a parent of C in a model that includes B among the endogenous nodes; but A would be a parent of C in a model that does not include B.

Graphically, we can represent all such relations between variables and their parents with arrows, and when we represent the relations in a causal model in this way, we get a DAG – where the acyclicality and directedness are guaranteed by the ordering requirements we impose when we define a causal model.

Thus, the DAG already represents a critical part of our model: The arrows, or directed edges, tell us *which nodes we believe may be direct causal inputs into other nodes*. So, for instance, we believe that democratization (D) is determined jointly by mobilization (M) and some exogenous, unspecified factor (or set of factors), θ^D. As we have said, we can think of θ^D as all of the other influences on democratization, besides mobilization, that we either do not know of or have decided not to explicitly include in the model. We believe, likewise, that M is determined by I and an unspecified exogenous factor (or set of factors), θ^M. And we are conceptualizing inequality (I) and ethnic heterogeneity (E) as shaped solely by factors exogenous to the model, captured by θ^I and θ^E, respectively.

---

[10] These causal functions relate to "structural equations" in a simple way: structural equations place an endogenous variable on the left hand side and the causal function together with the parents on the right hand side. Thus for example $Y = f^Y(\mathrm{pa}(Y), \theta^Y)$ is a structural equation, as is $Y = X + \theta^Y$ where implicitly $f^Y(\mathrm{pa}(Y), \theta^Y) = X + \theta^Y$.

Beyond the qualitative beliefs captured by the arrows in a DAG, we can express more specific *quantitative* beliefs about causal relations in the form of a causal function. A function specifies how the value that one node takes is determined by the values that other nodes – its parents – take on. Specifying a function means writing down whatever general or theoretical knowledge we have about the direct causal relations between nodes.

We can specify this relationship in a vast variety of ways. It is useful, however, to distinguish broadly between parametric and nonparametric approaches. We take a nonparametric approach in this book – this is where our types come back in – but it is helpful to juxtapose that approach with a parametric approach to causal functions.

2.2.2.1 Parametric Approaches

A parametric approach specifies a functional form that relates parents to children. For instance, we might model one node as a linear function of another and write $D = \alpha + \beta M$. Here, β is a parameter that we may not know the value of at the outset of a study but about which we wish to learn. If we believe D to be linearly affected by M but also subject to forces that we do not yet understand and have not yet specified in our theory, then we might write: $D = f^D(M, \theta^D) = \alpha + \beta M + \theta^D$. (This functional form may be familiar from its use in linear regressions.) In this function, α and β might be the parameters of interest – features of the world that we seek to learn about – with θ^D treated as merely a random disturbance around the linear relationship.

We can also write down functions in which the relations between nodes are left wholly or partially unspecified, for instance, governed by parameters with unknown values. Consider, for instance, the function $D = \beta M^{\theta^D}$. Here, D and M are linearly related if $\theta^D = 1$. (If $\theta^D = 1$, then the function just reduces to the linear form, $D = \beta M$.) However, if θ^D is not equal to 1, then M's effect on D can be nonlinear. For instance, if θ^D lies between 0 and 1, then M will have a diminishing marginal effect on D. Here, θ^D itself would likely be a quantity of interest to the researcher since it conditions the causal relationship between the other two nodes.

The larger point is that functions can be written to be quite specific or extremely general, depending on the state of prior knowledge about the phenomenon under investigation. The use of a structural model does not require precise knowledge of specific causal relations, even of the functional forms through which two nodes are related.

2.2.2.2 The Non-parametric Approach

With discrete (non-continuous) data, causal functions can take fully *non-parametric* form. That is, nonparametric functions can allow for *any possible relation* between parents and children, not just those that can be expressed in an equation.

We use a nonparametric framework for most of this book and thus spend some time developing the approach here.

We begin by returning to the concept of types. Drawing on our original four types and the democratization example from earlier in this chapter, we know that we can fully specify causal relations between a binary M and a binary D using the concept of a type, represented by θ^D. We think of θ^D as akin to a variable that can take on different *values* in different cases, corresponding to the different possible types. Specifically, we allow θ^D to range across the four possible values (or types) $\{\theta^D_{10}, \theta^D_{01}, \theta^D_{00}, \theta^D_{11}\}$. For instance, θ^D_{10} represents a negative causal effect of M on D while θ^D_{00} represents D remaining at 0 regardless of M.

So the value that θ^D takes on in a case governs the causal relationship between M and D. Put differently, θ^D represents *the nonparametric function that relates M to D*. We can formally specify D's behavior as a function of M and θ^D in the following way:

$$f^D(M, \theta^D_{ij}) = \begin{cases} i & \text{if } M = 0 \\ j & \text{if } M = 1 \end{cases}$$

Here, we are saying that D's value in a case depends on two things: the value of M and the case's type, defining how D responds to M. We are then saying, more specifically, how D's value is given by the subscripts on θ once we know M's value: If $M = 0$, then D is equal to the subscript i; if $M = 1$, then D is equal to j. Note that θ^D's possible values range over *all possible* ways in which D's value can relate to M's.

How should we think about what kind of *thing* θ^D is, in a more substantive sense? It is helpful to think of θ^D as an unknown and possibly random factor that conditions the effect of mobilization on democratization, determining whether M has a negative effect, a positive effect, no effect with democratization never occurring, or no effect with democratization bound to occur regardless of mobilization. A little more generally it can be thought of as describing a "stratum" – a grouping together of units that may differ in innumerable ways but that, nevertheless, respond in the same way at the node in question given values of other nodes in the model (Frangakis and Rubin,

2002). Importantly, while we might think of θ^D as an unknown or random quantity, in this framework θ^D should not be thought of as a nuisance – as "noise" that we would like to get rid of. Rather, under this nonparametric approach, θ terms are *the very quantities that we want to learn about*: We want to know whether M likely had a positive, negative, or no effect on D. We elaborate on this point in Chapter 4.

More generally, we can use θ terms to capture causal functions involving any number of parent nodes. Every substantively defined node, J, in a graph can be thought of as having a θ^J term pointing into it, and the (unobservable) value of θ^J provides the mapping from J's parents (if it has any) to the value of J.

The ranges of each θ^J node depend on the number of parents J has, as well as the ranges of J and its parents. Thus, as described in Section 2.1.2, binary nodes with n parents can take on 2^{2^n} values. Each value corresponds to a unique combination of 0s and 1s for each of the 2^n combinations of values that the nodes' parents can have.

Applied to the binary nodes in Figure 2.1, θ^J ranges as follows:

- **Nodes with no parents**: For a parentless node, like I or E, θ^J represents an external "assignment" process that can take on one of two values. If $\theta^J = \theta^J_0$, we simply mean that J has been "assigned" to 0, while a value of θ^J_1 means that J has been assigned to 1. For instance, θ^I_0 describes a case in which exogenous forces have generated low inequality.
- **Binary nodes with one binary parent**: For endogenous node R, with only one parent (I), θ^R takes on one of the four values of the form θ^R_{ij} (our four original types, θ^R_{10}, θ^R_{01}, etc.).
- **Binary nodes with two binary parents**: M has two parent nodes. Thus, θ^M will take on a possible 16 values of the form θ^M_{hijk} (e.g., θ^M_{0000}, θ^M_{0001}, etc.), using the syntax detailed earlier in this chapter and unpacked in Table 2.3.

Nodal types and causal types. So far, we have been talking about types operating at specific nodes. For instance, we can think of the unit of Malawi as having a θ^D value – the type governing how D responds to M in this case. Let's call this Malawi's *nodal* causal type, or simply nodal type, for D. But we can also conceptualize the full collection of Malawi's nodal types: the nodal types governing causal effects in Malawi for all nodes in the model. This collection would include Malawi's nodal type values for θ^I, θ^E, θ^R, θ^M, and θ^D. We refer to the collection of nodal types across all nodes for a given unit (i.e., a case) as the case's *unit causal type*, or simply *causal type*. We denote a causal

Table 2.4 Nodal types, causal types

Term	Symbol	Meaning
Nodal type	θ^J	The way that node J responds to the values of its parents. Example: θ_{10}^Y: Y takes the value 1 if $X = 0$ and 0 if $X = 1$.
Causal type	θ	A causal type is a concatenation of nodal types, one for each node. Example: $(\theta_0^X, \theta_{00}^Y)$ is a causal type that has $X = 0$ and that has $Y = 0$ no matter what the value of X. Types like this are written in code in `CausalQueries` as X0.Y00.

type by the vector θ, the elements of which are all of the nodal types in a given model (θ^I, θ^E, etc.). For analytic applications later in the book, this distinction between nodal types and causal types will become important.

We will sometimes refer to a unit's causal type – the values of θ – as a unit's *context*. This is because θ captures all exogenous forces acting on a unit. This includes the assignment process driving the model's exogenous nodes (in our example, θ^I and θ^E) as well as all contextual factors and any idiosyncratic unit level features that shape causal relations between nodes (θ^R, θ^M, and θ^D). Put differently, θ captures both how a unit reacts to situations and which situations it is reacting to. Table 2.4 summarizes the difference between nodal types and causal types and their associated notation.

If we knew a unit's causal type – all nodal types operating in the unit, for all nodes – then we would know everything there is to know about that unit. We would know the value of all exogenous nodes as well as how those values cascade through the model to determine the values of all endogenous nodes. So a unit's causal type fully specifies all nodal values. More than that, because the causal type contains all causal information about a unit, it also tells us what values every endogenous node *would* take on under *counterfactual* values of other nodes. Of course, causal types, like nodal types, are fundamentally unobservable quantities. But (as we discuss later in the book) they are quantities that we will seek to draw inferences about from observable data.

A few important aspects of causal functions are worth highlighting.

1. These functions express *causal* beliefs. When we write $D = f^D(M, \theta^M) = \beta M$ as a function, we do not just mean that we believe the values of M and D in the world to be linearly related. We mean that we believe that the value of M *determines* the value of D through this linear function. Functions are, in this sense, *directional* statements, with causes on the right-hand side and an outcome on the left.

2. The collection of simple functions that map from the values of parents of a given node to the values of that node are sufficient to represent potentially complex webs of causal relations. For each node, we do not need to think through entire sequences of causation that might precede it. We need only specify how we believe it to be affected by its parents – that is to say, those nodes pointing *directly* into it. Our outcome of interest, D, may be shaped by multiple, long chains of causality. To theorize how D is generated, however, we write down how we believe D is shaped by its parent – its direct cause, M. We then, separately, express a belief about how M is shaped by *its* parents, R and E. A node's function must include as inputs all, and only, those nodes that point directly into that node.[11]

3. As in the general potential-outcomes framework, all relations in a causal model are conceptualized as deterministic at the case level. Yet, there is not as much at stake here as one might think at first; by this we simply mean that a node's value is *determined* by the values of its parents *along with* any stochastic or unknown components. We express uncertainty about causal relations, however, as unknown parameters, the nodal types.

Note 2.1. *Potential outcomes and causal functions*

We sometimes describe the values of outcomes using causal functions and sometimes we use potential-outcomes notation. These two representations relate to each other in a simple way.

Causal functions are part of the definition of causal models. A causal function (such as f^Y) takes as arguments *only the parents of a node* (along with the nodal type). It can only be evaluated if values for the parents of the node are provided. For instance, say Y depends directly on X and indirectly on X via M. We can then calculate the value that Y takes when $X = 1$ and $M = 1$ via $f^Y(X = 1, M = 1, \theta^Y)$. But we cannot use f^Y alone to assess the value of Y when $X = 1$ but the value of M is unspecified. The key point is that the number of arguments in a causal function is fixed and limited to the parents plus the nodal type.

When we use potential-outcomes notation (like $Y(X = 1)$), we describe outcomes given the values of other nodes *that may or may not be the parents*

---

[11] The set of a node's parents is required to be minimal in the sense that a node is not included among the parents if, given the other parents, the child does not depend on it in any state that arises with positive probability.

of the node of interest. Thus when we write $Y(X = 1)$, we are not specifying M, only X. The interpretation is that we are requesting the value of Y when X is set to 1 and M takes on whatever value it takes on in that condition. Similarly, $Y(M = 1)$ asks what value Y takes on when M is set to 1 but X takes on whatever value it takes on naturally. We can also ask about these values given other conditions that might obtain but were not controlled. Thus, $\Pr(Y(M = 1) = 1 | X = 1)$ is the probability that $Y = 1$ for cases in which M has been *set* to 1 and X just happens to be 1.

These two ways of describing outcomes are related since the potential-outcomes quantities can be derived from the causal functions. Thus, in the example above in which X has a direct and indirect effect on Y via M, we can calculate $Y(X = 1)$ – interpreted as the value Y takes when X is set to 1 and M takes whatever value it would take naturally (given X is set to 1) – using a causal function nested within a causal function: $f^Y(X = 1, M = f^M(X = 1, \theta^M), \theta^Y)$. Similarly, in a $X \to M \to Y$ chain model, we can write $Y(X = 1)$ *even though* X is not a parent of Y, and calculate its value via $Y(X = 1) = f^Y(M = f^M(X = 1, \theta^M), \theta^Y)$.

2.2.3 The Distributions

Putting collections of nodes and causal functions that relate these to each other together gives us what we call a *structural causal model*. A structural causal model expresses our beliefs about the skeletal structure of causal relations in a domain: It tells us which nodes are exogenous (entirely caused by things outside the model), which nodes are endogenous (caused by exogenous nodes or other endogenous nodes), and which nodes can have effects on which other nodes.

But this only takes us so far in inscribing our causal beliefs about the world. In particular, we have not said anything here about how *likely* different sets of conditions are, what values different nodes – whether endogenous or exogenous – are likely to take on, or the kinds of causal effects we expect most commonly to operate between linked nodes on the graph.

To incorporate these features we need two things. We need to include probability distributions over exogenous nodes. And we need to understand how distributions over exogenous nodes imply distributions of the values – actual or counterfactual – of endogenous nodes.

2.2.3.1 Probability Distributions over Exogenous Nodes

When we add information on the distribution of exogenous nodes, we move from having a structural causal model to having a *probabilistic* causal model, or simply a causal model, as we have defined it above. These probability distributions may represent our "priors" – our beliefs before seeing any data – or they may represent beliefs having seen data, our "posteriors."

Intuitively, it can be helpful to think of the structural model as providing a collection of rules or mechanisms that can produce different outcomes depending on the context, and to think of the collection of nodal types for a unit – that unit's causal type – as capturing the context itself. Indeed, a set of realized values on all exogenous nodes is sometimes referred to simply as the context. To understand anything about actual outcomes we first need to understand the context.

Thus, for instance, a structural causal model consistent with Figure 2.1 stipulates that democratization may be affected by mobilization, that mobilization may be affected by ethnic homogeneity and redistributive demands, and that redistributive demands may be affected by the level of inequality. But it says nothing about the context: the values that we think the exogenous nodes tend to take on in the world. And it says nothing about how likely (or how common) we think different contexts are. We have not said anything, that is, about how common high inequality is across the relevant domain of cases or how common ethnic homogeneity is. Put differently, we have said nothing about the *distribution* of θ^I or of θ^E. Similarly, we have said nothing yet about the nature of the causal effects in the model: for instance, about how commonly mobilization has positive, negative, or null effects of democratization; about how commonly redistributive demands (R) and ethnic homogeneity (E) have different possible joint causal effects on M; or about how commonly inequality (I) has different possible effects on redistributive demands (R). That is, we have said nothing about the distribution of θ^D, θ^M, or θ^R values in the world.

We make progress by specifying probability distributions over the model's nodal types – its θ^J terms, specifying $\Pr(\theta^J = \theta^J_k)$, for each node J and each nodal type potentially operating at J (i.e., each possible value of θ^J). At the case level, we can think of this probability distribution as a statement about our beliefs about the unit's type or about the context. If we think in terms of populations, we might think in terms of the *proportion* of units in the population of interest that have different values for θ^J – which we will call λ^J – and then think of the unit's type as a draw from this population. (We may also need to specify beliefs about how cases are drawn from the population.)

For instance, our structural causal model might tell us that E and R can jointly affect M. We might, then, add to this a belief about what kinds of effects among these variables are most common. For instance, we might believe that redistribution rarely has a positive effect on mobilization when ethnic homogeneity is low. Well, there are four specific nodal types in which R has a positive effect on M when $E = 0$: θ_{0010}^M, θ_{0110}^M, θ_{0111}^M, and θ_{0011}^M. (Look back at Table 2.3 to confirm this for yourself, substituting E for X_1 and R for X_2.) Thus, we can express our belief as a probability distribution over the possible nodal types for M, θ^M, in which we place a relatively low probability on θ_{0010}^M, θ_{0110}^M, θ_{0111}^M, and θ_{0011}^M, as compared to θ^M's other possible values. This is akin to saying that we think that these four nodal types occur in a relatively small *share* of units in the population of interest.

Of course, when we are thinking about populations, we will usually be uncertain about these kinds of beliefs. We can then build uncertainty into our beliefs about the "shares" of different nodal types in the population. We do this by thinking of the shares as nodes in their own right and specifying a probability distribution over these shares (see, e.g., (Chickering and Pearl, 1996)). For instance, rather than stipulating that λ_1^E (the share of cases that have θ_1^E) is exactly 0.1, we can specify a distribution over shares, centered on a low value but with our degree of uncertainty captured by that distribution's variance.[12] Similarly, we can specify a distribution over the shares of θ^M types, λ^M. In consequence, our uncertainty about a unit's type might reflect uncertainty about the features of the unit given the population, or uncertainty about the population itself.

In the default setup, we assume that each θ term (θ^I, θ^E, θ^R, etc.) is generated independently of the others. So, for instance, the probability that I has a positive effect on R in a case bears no relationship to the probability that M has a positive effect on D. Or, put differently, those cases with a positive $I \rightarrow R$ effect are no more or less likely to have a positive $M \rightarrow D$ effect than are those cases without a positive $I \rightarrow R$ effect. This independence feature is critical for allowing a causal graph to reveal relationships among nodes in a model (see, in particular, our discussion of conditional independence below). See Note 2.2 on the "Markov condition" that relates the structure of the graph to the types of independence statements implied by the graph (Spirtes et al., 2000).

One subtlety is that violations of independence can arise even if we are certain that θ^X and θ^Y are drawn independently from different distributions.

---

[12] We say more about these distributions when we turn to a discussion of Bayesianism in Chapter 5.

Specifically, it is possible for our *beliefs* about the distributions from which X and Y are drawn not to be independent even if we believe that the draws *are* independent. Consider an example. We might have every reason to believe that X is randomized and so think that θ^X is independent of θ^Y – so there is no confounding between the two. However, we might be uncertain about the assignment probability (a belief about λ^X). Moreover, we might believe that a world in which the probability of assignment to $X = 1$ is high is also a world in which treatment effects are strong (a belief about λ^Y), and that a world with low assignment probabilities is also likely a world of weak treatment effects. In this situation, even though we are sure there is randomization of the treatment – and, indeed, conditional on the true values of (λ^X, λ^Y) we know that θ^X and λ^Y are independent – the value of θ^X is related to the value of θ^Y *in our beliefs*. Specifically, when we learn $X = 1$ for a random case we think it is more likely we are in the high assignment-large effects world. Thus, independence is violated.[13]

If the assumption of independence cannot be maintained, then the model might have to be enriched to ensure independence between exogenous nodes. Otherwise, nonindependence has to be taken into account when doing analysis.[14] Graphically we represent such failures of independence by using curved two-headed arrows. More on this in Section 2.3.1.

2.2.3.2 Induced Distributions over Endogenous Nodes

When we provide a distribution over exogenous nodes, we have all we need to calculate a distribution over endogenous nodes since these nodes are all ultimately functions of exogenous nodes.

Figuring out the induced probability distribution of endogenous nodes is conceptually not so hard. We can imagine calculating these distributions by first looking at root nodes. For a root note V^1, say, the distribution of V^1, depends only on θ^1. If we figure out what values of θ^1 give rise to a particular value of V^1, say $V^1 = v^1$ when $\theta^1 = \theta_1^1$, then the probability that $V^1 = v^1$ is just the probability that $\theta^1 = \theta_1^1$. For non-root nodes, we proceed similarly except that we first calculate the probability of different possible values for their parents. For V^2, for instance, we assess what values of θ^2 and V^2's parent, V^1 say, give rise to particular values of V^2, and then deduce from the causal

---

[13] For more on violations of independence arising from correlations in beliefs about population quantities, see Section 9.5.3.

[14] In the `CausalQueries` software package, we can specify nodal types as having joint distributions.

function for what set of values of θ^1 and θ^2 we would observe $V^2 = v^2$, say. Then we have enough to figure out the probability that $V^2 = v^2$ from the joint probability of θ^1 and θ^2. And so on for subsequent nodes in the ordering.

Taking this one step further, it's not hard to see that from the distribution of the exogenous nodes, we have enough to determine not just what outcomes arise in a given context but also what would arise if we *intervened* in that context. In that case we proceed as before, but now the probability of a node on which we have intervened is *known*, not inferred from $\Pr(\theta)$.

2.2.4 Conditional Independence

Importantly, even if we assume that the exogenous nodes in a model are independently distributed, we are not likely to think that the endogenous ones are. In fact, insofar as one node depends on another, it is obvious that they are not. As a result, the induced probability distribution over endogenous variables might be quite complicated.

Fortunately, however, the structure provided by a causal model makes it possible to use statements about "conditional independence" (see Definition 2.2) to generate relatively simple statements about the joint probability of all nodes.

> **Definition 2.2.** Conditional independence
>
> Nodes A and B are "**conditionally independent**" given C if $P(a|b, c) = P(a|c)$ for all values of a, b, and c.

So let's unpack the idea of conditional independence. The key idea is that two variables are *independent* when knowing something about one is not helpful for making inferences about the other (we get to the "conditional" part in a moment). Conversely, when there is a *dependence* between two nodes, then knowing something about one of them is informative about the other.

These relations of dependence and independence between nodes can result from the structure of causal relations. Intuitively, we can usefully think of dependencies as arising from the ways information flows along causal pathways. For instance, in Figure 2.1, the arrow running from I to R means that R is causally dependent on I. This dependence, moreover, implies that if we know something about I, then we expect to know something about R.

Concretely, we might expect I's and R's values to be correlated with each other.[15]

The graph in Figure 2.1 thus implies that, if we measured redistributive preferences, we would also be in a better position to infer the level of inequality, and vice versa. Similarly, I and M are linked in a relationship of dependence, one that is mediated by R. Since inequality can affect mobilization (through R), knowing the level of inequality would allow us to improve our estimate of the level of mobilization – and vice versa.

In contrast, consider I and E, which in this model are *independent* of one another. In this model these two nodes have no common ancestor, which means that the forces that set a case's level of inequality are (assumed to be) independent of the forces that determine its level of ethnic homogeneity. So learning the level of inequality in a case, according to this model, would give us no information whatsoever about the case's degree of ethnic homogeneity and vice versa.

So dependencies between nodes can arise from those nodes lying along a causal chain. Yet they can also arise from nodes having common causes (or ancestors). Consider Figure 2.2. Here, we are indicating that war (W) can cause both excess deaths (D) and price inflation (P). Casualties and inflation may then be correlated with one another because of their shared cause. If we learn that there have been military casualties, this information will lead us to think it more likely that there is also war and, in turn, that there is price inflation (and vice versa). When two outcomes have a common (proximate or distant) cause, observing one outcome might lead us to believe it more likely that the other outcome has also occurred.

Now let's turn to the "conditional" part. The key idea here is that sometimes what we learn from an observation depends on *what we already know*. An everyday example can help us wrap our minds around this intuition. Suppose that, on a winter's day, I want to know whether the boiler in my basement, which provides steam to the heating system, is working properly. I usually figure out if the boiler is working by reading the temperature on the thermometer on my living room wall: This is because I believe that the boiler's operation *causes* the room temperature to rise (implying $B \rightarrow T$). Under this causal dependency, the temperature in the living room is generally

[15] Though we sometimes use "correlated" and "uncorrelated" to describe dependence and independence between variables, *independence* is in fact a stronger idea than *uncorrelated*. Two variables might be uncorrelated but still not be independent of each other. For instance, imagine X is evenly distributed over $\{0, 1, 2\}$ and $Y = 1$ if and only if $X = 1$. Then X and Y will be uncorrelated but you can nevertheless learn a lot (everything!) about Y from learning about X.

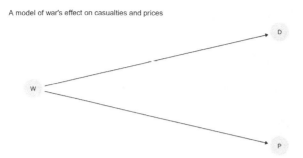

A model of war's effect on casualties and prices

Figure 2.2   A simple causal model in which war (*W*) affects both excess deaths (*D*) and price inflation (*P*)

informative about the boiler's operation. If the room is warm, this makes me
believe that the boiler is probably operating; if the room is cold, then I come
to think it's less likely that the boiler is running. (Similarly, if I go down to
the basement and can see whether the boiler is fired up, this will shape my
expectations about how warm the living room is.)

However, I also believe that the boiler affects the room's temperature
through a change in the temperature of the radiator ($B \rightarrow R \rightarrow T$), and
that this is the only way in which the boiler can affect the room temperature. So suppose that, before reading the thermometer on the wall, I touch
the radiator and feel that it is hot. The radiator's temperature has, of course,
given me information about the boiler's operation – since I believe that the
boiler's operation has an effect on the radiator's temperature ($B \rightarrow R$). If
the radiator is hot, I judge that the boiler is probably running. But now, having already observed the radiator's temperature, can I learn anything *further*
about whether the boiler is operating by taking a reading from the thermometer on the wall? No, I cannot. Everything I could possibly learn about the
boiler's status from gauging the room's temperature I have *already* learned
from touching the radiator – since the boiler's effect on the room's temperature runs entirely *through* the radiator. One way to think about this is that, by
observing the radiator's temperature, we have fully intercepted, or "blocked,"
the flow of information from the boiler to the wall thermometer.

In sum, the room's temperature *can* be informative about the boiler, but
whether it is informative hinges on whether we already know if the radiator
is hot. If we know *R*, then *B* and *T* are uninformative about one another.
Formally, we say that *B* and *T* are *conditionally independent given R*.

Turning back to Figure 2.1, imagine that we already knew the level of redistributive preferences. Would we then be in a position to learn about the level
of inequality by observing the level of mobilization? According to this DAG,

we would not. This is because R, which we already know, *blocks* the flow of information between I and M. Since the causal link – and, hence, the flow of information – between I and M runs through R, and we already know R, there is nothing left to be learned about I by also observing M. Anything we could have learned about inequality by observing mobilization is already captured by the level of redistributive preferences, which we have already seen. We can express this idea by saying that I and M are *conditionally independent given R*. That is, observing R makes I and M independent of one another.

Note 2.2. *The Markov Condition*

The assumptions that no node is its own descendant and that the θ terms are generated independently make the model *Markovian*, and the parents of a given node are Markovian parents.

Knowing the set of Markovian parents allows us to write relatively simple factorizations of a joint probability distribution, exploiting the fact ("the Markov condition") that all nodes are *conditionally independent* of their nondescendants, conditional on their parents.

Consider how this property allows for simple factorization of P for an $X \rightarrow M \rightarrow Y$ DAG. Note that $P(X, M, Y)$ can always be written as:

$$P(X, M, Y) = P(X)P(M|X)P(Y|M, X)$$

If we believe, as implied by this DAG, that Y is independent of X given M, then we have the simpler factorization:

$$P(X, M, Y) = P(X)P(M|X)P(Y|M)$$

More generally, using pa_i to denote the parents of i, we have:

$$P(v_1, v_2, \ldots, v_n) = \prod P(v_i|pa_i) \tag{2.2}$$

More generally, knowing if two nodes are or are not conditionally independent of each other tells us if we can learn about one from values of the other.

2.3 Graphing Models and Using Graphs

While we have already been speaking about causal graphs throughout this chapter, we want to take some time to unpack their core features and uses.

A key benefit of causal models is that they lend themselves to graphical representations. In turn, graphs constructed according to particular rules can aid causal analysis. In the next subsection, we discuss a set of rules for representing a model in graphical form. The following subsection, then demonstrates how access to a graph facilitates causal inference.

2.3.1 Rules for Graphing Causal Models

The diagram in Figure 2.1 is a causal DAG (Hernán and Robins, 2006). We endow it with the interpretation that an arrow from a parent to a child means that a change in the parent can, under some circumstances, induce a change in the child. Though we have already been using this causal graph to help us visualize elements of a causal model, we now explicitly point out a number of general features of causal graphs as we will be using them throughout this book. Causal graphs have their own distinctive "grammar," a set of rules that give them useful analytic features.

Directed, acyclic. A causal graph represents elements of a causal model as a set of nodes (or vertices), representing variables, connected by a collection of single-headed arrows (or directed edges). We draw an arrow from node A to node B if and only if we believe that A can have a direct effect on B. Thus, in Figure 2.1, the arrow from I to R means that inequality can directly affect redistributive demands.

The resulting diagram is a DAG if there are no paths along directed edges that lead from any node back to itself – that is, if the graph contains no causal cycles. The absence of cycles (or "feedback loops") is less constraining than it might appear at first. In particular, if one thinks that A today causes B tomorrow which in turn causes A the next day, we can represent this as $A_1 \rightarrow B \rightarrow A_2$ (rather than $A \leftrightarrow B$). We timestamp the nodes, turning what might informally appear as feedback into a noncyclical chain.

Meaning of missing arrows. The *absence* of an arrow between A and B means that A is not a direct cause of B.[16] Here lies an important asymmetry: drawing an $A \rightarrow B$ arrow does not mean that we know that A *does* directly cause B; but omitting such an arrow implies that we know that A does *not* directly cause B. We say more with the arrows that we omit than with the arrows that we include.

---

[16] By "direct" we mean that the A is a parent of B: that is, the effect of A on B is not fully mediated by one or more other nodes in the model.

Returning to Figure 2.1, we have here expressed the belief that redistributive preferences exert no direct effect on democratization; we have done so by *not* drawing an arrow directly from R to D. In the context of this model, saying that redistributive preferences have no direct effect on democratization is to say that any effect of redistributive preferences on democratization *must* run through mobilization; there is no other pathway through which such an effect can operate. As social scientists, we often have beliefs that take this form. For instance, the omission of an arrow from R to D might be a way of encoding the belief that mass preferences for redistribution cannot induce autocratic elites to liberalize the regime absent collective action in pursuit of those preferences.

The same goes for the effects of I on M, I on D, and E on D: The graph in Figure 2.1 implies that we believe that these effects also do not operate directly, but only along the indicated, mediated paths.

Moreover, when we say that A does not have a direct effect on B – justifying an excluded arrow – we do not mean merely that A doesn't affect B *on average*. We mean that there is no chance that A affects B.

Possible-causes. The existence of an arrow from A to B does not imply that A always has (or certainly has) a direct effect on B. Consider, for instance, the arrows running from E and from R to M. Since M has two parents, assuming all variables are binary, we define a range of 16 nodal types for θ^M, capturing all possible joint effects of E and R. However, for some of these nodal types, E or R or both will have no effect on M. For instance, in the nodal type θ^M_{0011},[17] E has no effect on M while R has a positive effect. Thus, in a case with this nodal type for M, E is not a cause of M; whereas in a case with, say, θ^M_{0101}, E has an effect on M, while R has none. In this sense, the existence of the arrows pointing into M reflects that E and R are "possible causes" of M.[18]

No excluded common causes. Any cause common to multiple nodes on a graph must itself be represented on the graph. If A and B on a graph are both affected by some third node, C, then we must represent this common cause. Thus, for instance, the graph in Figure 2.1 implies that I and E have no common cause. If we believed that a country's level of inequality and its

---

[17] We are applying the subscript scheme from Table 2.3, where E plays the role of X_1 and R plays the role of X_2.

[18] Put in more general terms, a node's causal function must include all nodes pointing directly into it. We can imagine this same idea in a parametric setting. Imagine that M's causal function was specified as: $M = RE$. This function would allow for the possibility that R affects M, as it will whenever $E = 1$. However, it would also allow that R will have no effect, as it will when $E = 0$.

ethnic composition were both shaped by, say, its colonial heritage, then this DAG would *not* be an accurate representation of our beliefs about the world. To make it accurate, we would need to add to the graph a node capturing that colonial heritage and include arrows running from colonial heritage to both I and E.

This rule of "no excluded common causes" ensures that the graph captures all potential relations among nodes that are implied by our beliefs. If I and E are in fact driven by some common cause, then this means not just that these two nodes may be correlated but also that each may be correlated with any consequences of the other. For instance, a common cause of I and E would also imply a dependence between R and E. R and E are implied to be independent in the current graph but would be implied to be dependent if a common node pointed into both I and E.

Of particular interest is the implied independence of θ terms from one another, noted earlier. In Figure 2.1, imagine, for instance, that the distribution of θ^D and θ^I was dependent: that is, if the distribution of θ^D were different when $I = 0$ than when $I = 1$. This could be because some other factor, perhaps a feature of a country's economy, affects both its level of inequality and the response of its elites to mobilization from below. Such a situation would represent a classic form of confounding: the assignment of cases to values on an explanatory node (I) would depend on the case's potential outcomes on D. The omission of any such common cause is equivalent to expressing the belief that I is exogenous, that is, (as if) randomly assigned. If we believe such a common cause to be operating, however, then we must include it as a node on the graph, pointing into both I and D.

Representing Unobserved Confounding

It may be, however, that there are common causes that we simply do not understand. We might believe, for instance, that some unknown factor (partially) determines both I and D. We refer to this situation as one of *unobserved confounding*. Even when we do not know what factor is generating the confounding, we still have a violation of the assumption of independence and need to be sure we are capturing this relationship in the graph. We can do so in a couple of ways. If we are representing all θ terms on a graph, then we can capture the relationship between θ^I and θ^D by including a single, joint term (θ^I, θ^D) that points into both I and D. Where the θ terms are not explicitly included in a graph (as is often the case), we can represent unobserved confounding by adding a two-headed arrow, or a dotted line, connecting nodes whose unknown causes are not independent. Either way, we are building in

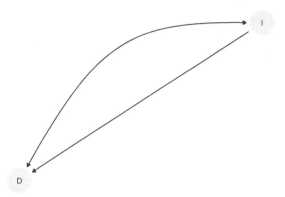

Figure 2.3   A DAG with unobserved confounding

the possibility of a joint distribution over the nodal types θ^I and θ^D. Figure 2.3 illustrates for the I and D relationship.

We address unobserved confounding in more detail later in the book and show how we can seek to learn about the joint distribution of nodal types – that is, how we can learn even about confounders that we cannot observe – in such situations.

License to exclude nodes. The flip side of the "no excluded common causes" rule is that a causal graph does not need to include everything that we know about a substantive domain of interest. We may know quite a lot about the causes of economic inequality, for example. But we can safely omit any factor from the graph as long *as it does not affect multiple nodes in the model.* Indeed, θ^I in Figure 2.1 already implicitly captures all factors that affect I. Similarly, θ^D captures all factors *other than* mobilization that affect democratization. We may be aware of a vast range of forces shaping whether countries democratize, but we can choose to bracket them for the purposes of an examination of the role of economic inequality. This bracketing is permissible as long as none of these unspecified factors also act on other nodes that *are* included in the model. For instance, we have chosen to exclude from the model the existence of international pressure on a state to democratize, even though this is another potential cause of democratization. This exclusion is permissible as long as we believe that international pressure does not have an effect on the level of inequality, a state's ethnic makeup, redistributive demands, or mobilization.

Similarly, we do not need to include all mediating steps that we believe might be operating between two causally linked variables. In Figure 2.1, we could choose to exclude R, for instance, and draw an arrow directly from I to M. We could also exclude M, if we wished to. (Since E points into M, removing M would mean that we would have E point directly into R – a point that we return to below.) And, of course, the model that we have drawn leaves out numerous other mediating steps that we might imagine – such as the role of elites' perceptions of the costs of repression as a mediator between mobilization and democratization. In other words, we generally have discretion about the degree of granularity to represent in our chains of causation. As we explain in Chapters 6 and 7, we will sometimes want to spell out more, rather than fewer, mediating steps in our models for reasons of research design – because of the empirical leverage that such mediating variables might provide. However, there is nothing about the rules of DAG-making that require a particular level of granularity.

We can't read causal functions from a graph. As should be clear, a DAG does not represent all features of a causal model. What it does record is which nodes enter into the causal function for every other node: what can directly cause what. But the DAG contains no other information about the form of those causal relations. Thus, for instance, the DAG in Figure 2.1 tells us that M is a function of both R and E, but it does not tell us whether that joint effect is additive (R and E separately increase mobilization) or interactive (the effect of each depends on the value of the other). Nor does it tell us whether either effect is linear, concave, or something else.

This lack of information about functional forms is puzzling at first: Surely, it would be convenient to visually differentiate, say, additive from interactive effects. As one thinks about the variety of possible causal functions; however, it quickly becomes clear that there would be no simple visual way of capturing all possible causal relations. Moreover, causal graphs do not require a specification of causal functions in order to perform their main analytic purpose – a purpose to which we now turn.

2.3.2 Conditional Independence from DAGs

If we encode our prior knowledge using the grammar of a causal graph, we can put that knowledge to work for us in powerful ways. In particular, the rules of DAG construction allow for an easy reading of whether and when variables in the model are likely to be independent of each other. More formally, we say that we can use a DAG to identify the *conditional independencies* that are implied by our causal beliefs. (For a more extended treatment of the ideas in this section, see Rohrer (2018).)

In Section 2.2.4, we introduced the idea of conditional independence. A major benefit of a DAG is that, if we have followed the rules for DAG construction correctly, we can read relationships of conditional independence directly from the graph.

Such relations of conditional independence are central to the strategy of statistical control, or covariate adjustment, in correlation-based forms of causal inference, such as regression. In a regression framework, identifying the causal effect of an explanatory node, X, on a dependent node, Y, requires the assumption that X's value is conditionally independent of Y's potential outcomes (over values of X) given the model's covariates. To draw a causal inference from a regression coefficient, in other words, we have to believe that including the covariates in the model "breaks" any biasing correlation between the value of the causal node and its unit-level effect.

As we will explore, however, relations of conditional independence are also of more general interest in that they tell us, given a model, *when information about one feature of the world may be informative about another feature of the world, given what we already know.* By identifying the possibilities for learning, relations of conditional independence can thus guide research design more broadly. We discuss these research-design implications in Chapter 7, but focus here on showing how relations of conditional independence operate on a DAG.

To see more systematically how a DAG can reveal conditional independencies, it is useful to spell out three elemental structures according to which information can flow across a causal graph.

For each of the three structures in Figure 2.4, we can read off whether nodes are independent both in situations when other nodes are not already observed and in situations in which they are. We discuss each of these structures in turn. For each, we first specify the unconditional relations among nodes in the structure and then the relations conditional on having already observed another node. When we talk about "unconditional" relations, we are asking: What does observing one node in the structure tell us about the other nodes? When we talk about "conditional" relations, we are asking: If we have already observed a node (so, conditional on that node), what does observing a second node tell us about a third node?

(1) A Path of Arrows in the Same Direction

Unconditional relations. Information can flow unconditionally along a path of arrows pointing in the same direction. In Panel 1 of Figure 2.4, information

(1) A path of arrows pointing in the same direction

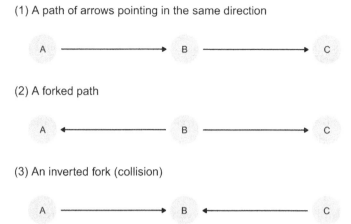

(2) A forked path

(3) An inverted fork (collision)

Figure 2.4   Three elemental relations of conditional independence

flows across all three nodes. If we have observed nothing yet, learning about any one node can tell us something about the other two.

Conditional relations. Learning the value of a node along a path of arrows pointing in the same direction *blocks* flows of information that passes through that node. Knowing the value of B in Panel 1 renders A no longer informative about C, and vice versa. This is because anything that A might tell us about C is already captured by the information contained in B.

(2) A Forked Path

Unconditional relations. Information can flow unconditionally across the branches of any forked path. In Panel 2, if we have observed nothing already, learning about any one node can provide information about the other two nodes. For instance, observing only A can provide information about C and vice versa.

Conditional relations. Learning the value of the node at the forking point *blocks* flows of information across the branches of a forked path. In Panel 2, learning A provides no information about C if we already know the value of B.[19]

(3) An Inverted Fork (Collision)

Unconditional relations. When two or more arrowheads collide, generating an inverted fork, there is no unconditional flow of information between

---

[19] Readers may recognize this statement as the logic of adjusting for a confound that is a cause of both an explanatory node and a dependent node in order to achieve conditional independence.

the incoming sequences of arrows. In Panel 3, learning only A provides no information about C, and vice versa, since each is independently determined.

Conditional relations. Collisions can be sites of *conditional* flows of information. In the jargon of causal graphs, B in Panel 3 is a "collider" for A and C.[20] Although information does not flow unconditionally across colliding sequences, it does flow across them *conditional* on knowing the value of the collider node or any of its downstream consequences. In Panel 3, learning A *does* provide new information about C, and vice versa, *if* we also know the value of B (or, in principle, the value of anything that B causes).

The last point is somewhat counterintuitive and warrants further discussion. It is easy enough to see that, for two nodes that are correlated unconditionally, that correlation can be "broken" by controlling for a third node. In the case of collision, two nodes that are *not* correlated (or more generally, independent) when taken by themselves can *become* correlated when we condition on (i.e., learn the value of) a third node into which they both point, the collider. The reason is in fact quite straightforward once one sees it: If an outcome is a joint function of two inputs, then if we know the outcome, information about one of the inputs can provide information about the other input. For example, if I know that you are short, then learning that your mother is tall makes me more confident that your father is short. Crucially, it is knowing the *outcome* – that you are short – that makes the information about your mother's height informative about your father's.

Looking back at our democratization DAG in Figure 2.1, M is a collider for R and E, its two inputs. Suppose that M is determined by the parametric causal function $M = RE$. Knowing about redistributive preferences alone provides no information whatsoever about ethnic homogeneity since the two are determined independently of one another. On the other hand, imagine that we already know that there was no mobilization. Now, if we observe that there *were* redistributive preferences, we can figure out the level of ethnic homogeneity: it must be 0. (And likewise in going from observing homogeneity to inferring redistributive preferences.)

Using these basic principles, conditional independencies can be read off of any DAG. If we want to know whether two nodes are conditionally independent, we do so by checking every path connecting them. And we ask whether, along those paths, the flow of information is open or blocked, given any other nodes whose values are already observed. Conditional independence is

---

[20] In the familial language of causal models, a collider is a child of two or more parents.

established when *all* paths are blocked given what we have already observed; otherwise, conditional independence is absent.

Following Pearl (2009), we will sometimes refer to relations of conditional independence using the term *d-separation*. We say that variable set C *d*-separates variable set A from variable set B if A and B are conditionally independent given C. For instance, in Panel 2 of Figure 2.4, B *d*-separates A and C. We say that A and B are *d*-connected given C if A and B are *not* conditionally independent given C. For instance, in Panel 3, A and C are *d*-connected given B.

Readers are invited to practice reading relations of conditional independence off of a DAG using the exercises in Appendix, Section 2.5.3. Analyzing a causal graph for relations of independence represents one payoff to formally encoding our beliefs about the world in a causal model. We are, in essence, drawing out implications of those beliefs: Given what we believe about a set of direct causal relations (the arrows on the graph), what must this logically imply about other dependencies and independencies on the graph, conditional on having observed some particular set of nodes? We show in a later chapter how these implications can be deployed to guide research design by indicating which parts of a causal system are potentially informative about other parts that may be of interest.

2.3.3 Simplifying Models

It is very easy to write down a model that is too complex to use effectively. In such cases we often seek simpler models that are consistent with models we have in mind but contain fewer nodes or more limited variation. As we have already suggested, we often have considerable discretion about how detailed to make our models. However, whenever we seek to simplify a more complex model, we must take care to ensure that the simplified model is logically consistent with the original model.

The main rule that we must follow when simplifying a model is to preserve dependencies implied by the original, more complex model. Consider a few examples drawing on our Inequality example. Suppose that we begin with a model that includes the following structure:

Mobilization ← Inequality → Mortality.

And suppose that we are not interested in inequality or its effects per se and so wish to eliminate it from the model. We can do so, but then we must retain the relationship between *Mobilization* and *Mortality* that is implied in the original model. We can do so by drawing a double-headed arrow between *Mobilization* and *Mortality*, implying unobserved confounding between the two. Another alternative could be to simplify the graph further and simply remove *Mortality* and its descendants from the graph, which we can safely do *if* none of these nodes point into other nodes that we are retaining (since, if they do, then another dependency would be lost by this simplification).

Another situation in which a dependency must be preserved is where the node we eliminate is a mediator, as when we remove *Mobilization* from

Inequality $\rightarrow$ Mobilization $\rightarrow$ Democratization

Since a dependency between *Inequality* and *Democratization* runs through *Mobilization* in the original model, we would preserve that dependency by linking the two, that is, with the structure:

Inequality $\dashrightarrow$ Democratization

Alternatively, suppose that, beginning with the model Inequality $\rightarrow$ Mobilization $\rightarrow$ Democratization, we wish to eliminate *Inequality*. Suppose further that *Inequality* is a root node (it has no substantive parents) with no children other than *Mobilization*. Then we can eliminate *Inequality* from the graph without taking further steps. This is because there are no dependencies among substantive nodes that operate via *Inequality*.

Similarly, if our model includes the structure Mobilization $\dashrightarrow$ Democratization $\leftarrow$ Growth, then we can safely and simply eliminate *Growth* from the model, as long as *Growth* is a root node with no other children besides *Democratization*.

As we discuss further in Chapter 6, eliminating nodes may change the meaning of the exogenous, θ terms in the graph. For instance, when we eliminate *Growth* from the model Mobilization $\dashrightarrow$ Democratization $\leftarrow$ Growth, leaving us with the simpler model Mobilization $\dashrightarrow$ Democratization, the term θ^D changes in its range and interpretation. With all variables binary, θ^D in the original model could take on any of 16 nodal types, representing all possible joint effects of *Mobilization* and *Growth*. In the simplified model, θ^D now ranges across only four possible nodal types. *Growth*'s effects, rather than being explicitly modeled through the nodal-type functions, become an unobserved source of variation in *Mobilization*'s effects – and are, thus, "absorbed" into the four remaining nodal types.

In sum, we can work with models that are simpler than our causal beliefs: we may believe a model to be true, but we can derive from it a sparser set of claims. There may be intervening causal steps or features of context that we believe matter but that are not of interest for a particular line of inquiry.

While these can be left out of our model, we nonetheless have to make sure that their *implications* for the relations remaining in the model are not lost. Understanding the rules of reduction allows us to undertake an important task: checking which simpler claims are and are not consistent with our full belief set.

2.4 Conclusion

In this chapter, we have shown how we can inscribe causal beliefs, rooted in the potential-outcomes framework, into a causal model. In doing so, we have now set out the foundations of the book's analytic framework. Causal models are both the starting point for analysis in this framework and the object about which we seek to learn. Before moving on to build on this foundation, we offer in the next chapter guidance by example on the construction of causal models, illustrating how a set of substantive social scientific arguments can be represented in causal model form.

2.5 Appendix

2.5.1 Steps for Constructing Causal Models

1. Identify a set of variables in a domain of interest. These become the nodes of the model.
   - Specify the range of each node: Is it continuous or discrete?
   - Each node should have an associated θ term pointing into it, representing unspecified other influences (not necessarily graphed)

2. Draw a causal graph (DAG) representing beliefs about causal dependencies among these nodes.
   - Include arrows for direct effects only
   - Arrows indicate *possible* causal effects
   - The absence of an arrow between two nodes indicates a belief of *no* direct causal relationship between them
   - Ensure that the graph captures all relationships between nodes. This means that either (a) any common cause of two or more nodes is included on the graph (with implications for Step 1) or (b) nodes that are not independent of each other are connected with a double-headed arrow or dashed, undirected edge.

3. Write down one causal function for each endogenous node.
   - Each node's function must include all nodes directly pointing into it on the graph as well as the θ terms
   - Functions may express arbitrary amounts of uncertainty about causal relations
   - In this book's non-parametric framework, the causal functions are captured entirely by the θ terms.

4. State probabilistic beliefs about the distributions of the θs.
   - How common or likely to do we think different nodal types are for each node?
   - Are the nodal types independently distributed? If in Step 2 we drew an undirected edge between nodes, then we believe that the connected nodes' types are not independently distributed.

2.5.2 Model Construction in Code

Our CausalQueries package provides a set of functions to implement all of these steps concisely for *binary* models – models in which all nodes are dichotomous.

```
# Steps 1 and 2
# We define a model with three binary nodes and
# specified edges between them:
model <- make_model("X -> M -> Y")


# Functional forms are unrestricted. Restrictions can
# be added. Here we impose monotonicity at each step
# by removing one type for M and one for Y
model <- set_restrictions(model, labels = list(M = "10", Y="10"))


# Step 4
# Set priors over the distribution of (remaining) causal types.
# Here we set "jeffreys priors"
model <- set_priors(model, distribution = "jeffreys")


# We now have a model defined as an R object.
# Later we will update  and query this model
```

Figure 2.5   An exercise: *A* and *D* are conditionally independent, given which other node(s)?

These steps are enough to fully describe a binary causal model. Later in this book, we will see how we can ask questions of a model like this but also how to use data to train it.

2.5.3 Exercise: Reading Conditional Independence from a Graph

We encourage readers to get some practice identifying the relations of conditional independence by analyzing the relationship between *A* and *D* in Figure 2.5. Try answering the following questions yourself, and then consult the answers provided below.

Are A and D independent:

1. unconditionally?

Answer

Yes. *B* is a collider, and information does not flow across a collider if the value of the collider node or its consequences is not known. Since no information can flow between *A* and *C*, no information can flow between *A* and *D* simply because any such flow would have to run through *C*.

2. if you condition on *B*?

Answer

No. Conditioning on a collider opens the flow of information across the incoming paths. Now information flows between *A* and *C*. And since information flows between *C* and *D*, *A* and *D* are now also connected by an unbroken path. While *A* and *D* were independent when we conditioned on nothing, they cease to be independent when we condition on *B*.

3. if you condition on *C*?

Answer

Yes. Conditioning on *C*, in fact, has no effect on the situation. Doing so cuts off *B* from *D*, but this is irrelevant to the *A*–*D* relationship since the flow between *A* and *D* was already blocked at *B*, an unobserved collider.

4. if you condition on B and C?

Answer

Yes. Now we are doing two countervailing things at once. While conditioning on B opens the path connecting A and D, conditioning on C closes it again, leaving A and D conditionally independent.

Illustrating Causal Models

We use three arguments from published political science research to illustrate how to represent theoretical ideas as structural causal models. We illustrate using Paul Pierson's (1994) work on welfare state retrenchment, Elizabeth Saunders' (2011) research on military intervention strategies, and Adam Przeworski and Fernando Limongi's (1997) study of the relationship between national wealth and democracy.

In this short chapter, we illustrate how we can encode prior knowledge in a causal model by asking how we might construct models in light of extant scholarly works. We do this drawing on three well-known publications in comparative politics and international relations: Paul Pierson's book on welfare state retrenchment (Pierson, 1994); Elizabeth Saunders' research on leaders' choice of military intervention strategies (Saunders, 2011); and Przeworski and Limongi's work on democratic survival (Przeworski and Limongi, 1997), an instructive counterpoint to Boix's argument about a related dependent variable (Boix, 2003). For each, we represent the causal knowledge that we might plausibly take away from the work in question in the form of a causal model.

Readers might represent these knowledge bases differently; our aim here is only to illustrate how causal models are constructed, rather than to defend a particular representation (or the works in question) as accurate.

Before we begin, we offer a caution about how the illustrations in this chapter should be understood. For simplicity, in each of the next sections we focus on a specific argument in the literature. We emphasize, however, that *in general* a causal model should be thought of as a representation of our state of knowledge or beliefs about causal relations within a domain. Suppose, for instance, that we are interested in testing a specific argument in which X affects Y through mediator M. In constructing a causal model to guide our empirical analysis, we cannot simply draw that argument in DAG form $(X \rightarrow M \rightarrow Y)$ and leave it at that. In line with the principles relating to conditional independence outlined in Chapter 2, we must consult our beliefs about this causal domain in a broader sense. For instance, given what we know about the domain from prior observations or studies, is it plausible that X could affect Y through a pathway that does not go through M? If we believe it is possible, then we must also draw a direct $X \rightarrow Y$ arrow, or our causal model will steer us wrong – even if our primary aim is to examine the pathway through M. Otherwise, our DAG will be enforcing a relation of conditional independence (X being conditionally independent of Y given M) that we do not believe holds. Thus, while we draw on specific works in the illustrations in this chapter, we urge readers to remember that in practice, when generating a causal model, one would want to characterize a broader prior knowledge base in relation to a causal domain.

With these exercises, we aim to illuminate a number of features of causal models and their construction. The examples demonstrate how graphs capture beliefs about relations of conditional independence and illustrate the potential complexity embedded in the causal structures implied by common social-scientific arguments. For each work, we also go beyond the graphs themselves to illustrate both a potential parametric rendering of the causal functions and a nonparametric formulation built on nodal types.

3.1 Welfare State Reform

The argument in Pierson's 1994 book *Dismantling the Welfare State?* challenged prior notions of post-1980 welfare state retrenchment in OECD countries as a process driven primarily by socioeconomic pressures (slowed growth, rising unemployment, rising deficits, aging populations) and the rise of market-conservative ideologies (embodied by the political ascendance of figures such as Margaret Thatcher and Ronald Reagan). Pierson argues that socioeconomic and ideological forces put retrenchment on the policy agenda, but do not ensure its enactment because retrenchment is a politically perilous process of imposing losses on large segments of the electorate. Governments will only impose such losses if they can do so in ways that allow them to avoid blame – by, for instance, making the losses hard to perceive or the responsibility for those losses difficult to trace. These kinds of blame-avoidance

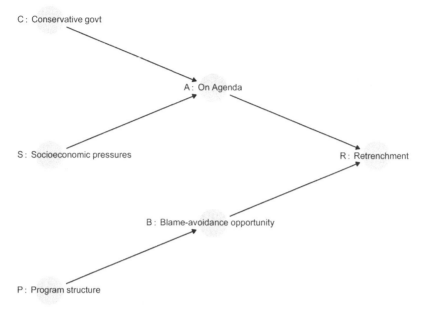

Figure 3.1   A graphical representation of Pierson's (1994) argument

opportunities are themselves conditioned by the particular social-program structures that governments inherit.

While the argument has many more specific features (e.g., different program-structural factors that matter, various potential strategies of blame-avoidance), its essential components can be captured with a relatively simple causal model. We propose such a model in a graphical form in Figure 3.1. Here, the outcome of retrenchment (R) hinges on whether retrenchment makes it onto the agenda (A) and on whether blame-avoidance strategies are available to governments (B). Retrenchment emerges on the policy agenda as a consequence of both socioeconomic developments (S) and the ascendance of ideologically conservative political actors (C). Inherited program structures (P), meanwhile, determine the availability of blame-avoidance strategies. To avoid cluttering the graph, we do not represent the θ terms, but implicitly every node on this graph has a θ node pointing into it.

A few features of this graph warrant attention. As we have discussed, it is the omitted arrows in any causal graph that imply the strongest statements. The graph implies that C, S, and P – which are neither connected along a directed path nor downstream from a common cause – are independent of one another. This implies, for instance, that whether conservatives govern is independent of whether inherited program structures will allow for blame-free retrenchment. Thus, as Pierson argues, a Reagan or Thatcher can come to power but nonetheless run up against an opportunity structure that would make retrenchment politically perilous. Given the absence of bidirectional arrows indicating confounding, the graph similarly implies that the nodal types for all nodes are independent of one another. So, for instance, conservatives are no more or less likely to come to power in places where the policy agenda is more likely to be responsive to conservative ideological demands (i.e., no confounding between C and A). These are all strong assumptions.

Further, this graph represents the belief that any effect of program structures on retrenchment *must* run through their effects on blame-avoidance opportunities. One could imagine relaxing this restriction by, for instance, drawing an arrow from P to A: Program structures might additionally affect retrenchment in other ways, such as through an impact on the fiscal costliness of the welfare state, thus helping to determine whether reform makes it onto the agenda. If the current state of knowledge suggested that program structures could affect retrenchment via a pathway other than blame-avoidance opportunities, then we would indeed want to include a direct $P \rightarrow A$ arrow.

Importantly, adding such an arrow would lend our prior beliefs *less* structure in the sense that we are ruling out fewer causal possibilities by assumption. Put differently, it is the model with *fewer* connections between nodes that represents the stronger claim about the world since an omitted arrow forbids particular direct effects. Moreover, as we discuss in later chapters, the choice about which nodes to connect or not to connect directly can have consequences for causal-model-based research, including for the inferences that we end up drawing. We also discuss, in Chapter 16, the possibility of empirically evaluating alternative model structures.

Where two variables *are* connected by an arrow, moreover, this does not imply that a causal effect will always operate. Consider, for instance, the arrow pointing from A to R. The fact that A sometimes affects R and sometimes does not is, in fact, central to Pierson's argument: Conservatives and socioeconomic pressures forcing retrenchment onto the agenda will *not* generate retrenchment if blame-avoidance opportunities are absent.

The graph also reflects a choice about where to begin. We could, of course, construct a causal account of how conservatives come to power in the first place, how socioeconomic pressures arise, or why programs were originally designed as they were. Yet it is perfectly permissible for us to bracket these antecedents and start the model with C, S, and P, as long as we do not believe that these variables have any antecedents in common. If they do have common causes, then this correlation should be captured in the DAG.[1]

The DAG itself tells us about the possible direct causal dependencies but is silent on the ranges of and functional relations among the variables. How might we express these? With three endogenous variables, we need three functions indicating how their values are determined. Moreover, every variable pointing directly into another variable must be part of that child's causal function.

One option would be to take a parametric approach and imagine specific functions connecting parents to children, with θ terms representing exogenous "noise." Let us assume that all variables (including the implied θ terms) are binary, with each condition either absent or present. Then, for instance, we can capture quite a lot of Pierson's theoretical logic with the following quite simple causal functions:

- $A = CS\theta^A$, capturing the idea that retrenchment makes it on the agenda only if conservatives are in power *and* socioeconomic pressures are high.
- $B = P\theta^B$, implying that blame-avoidance opportunities arise only when program structures take a particular form.
- $R = AB\theta^R$, implying that retrenchment will occur only if it is on the agenda and blame-avoidance opportunities are present.

In each equation, the θ term allows for random, exogenous forces that might block the outcome from occurring. In the last causal function, for instance, retrenchment will only occur if retrenchment is on the agenda and blame-avoidance opportunities are present – but even if both are present, the effect on retrenchment also hinges on the value of θ^R. When $\theta^R = 1$, the AB combination has a positive causal effect on retrenchment. When $\theta^R = 0$, AB has no causal effect: retrenchment will not occur regardless of the presence of AB. We can think of θ^R as capturing a collection of features of a case's context that might render the case susceptible or not susceptible to an AB causal effect. For instance, Pierson's analysis suggests that a polity's institutional structure might widely diffuse veto power such that stakeholders can block reform even when retrenchment is on the agenda and could be pursued without electoral losses. We could think of such a case as having a θ^R value of 0, implying that

---

[1] In DAG syntax, this correlation can be captured by placing the common cause(s) explicitly on the graph or by drawing a dashed line between the correlated nodes, leaving the source of the correlation unspecified.

AB has no causal effect. A $\theta^R = 1$ case, with a positive effect, would be one in which the government has the institutional capacity to enact reforms that it has the political will to pursue. Yet θ^R would also capture countless other forces, many of which we might not be able to theorize or observe, that might facilitate or block *AB*'s effect.

Alternatively, we could take a non-parametric approach, as we generally do in the remainder of this book. In a non-parametric setup, each node's θ term captures that node's nodal type. Each value of a θ term's range represents a possible way in which the node might respond to its parents. With all substantive variables being binary, we would define θ^A as taking on one of 16 values (16 types, given 2 parent nodes); θ^B as taking on one of four values; and θ^R as taking on one of 16 values; with θ^C and θ^S each taking on one of two values.

Thus, the central thrust of Pierson's argument about causal effects could then be represented in nodal-type form as:

- $\theta^A = \theta^A_{0001}$, meaning that $A = 1$ if and only if both of its parents (C and S) are 1, capturing the joint necessity of conservative leadership and socioeconomic pressures for putting welfare state reform on the agenda
- $\theta^B = \theta^B_{01}$, meaning that $B = 1$ if and only if its parent (P) is 1, capturing the role of favorable program structures in generating blame-avoidance opportunities.
- $\theta^R = \theta^R_{0001}$, meaning that $R = 1$ if and only if both of its parents (A and B) are 1, capturing the joint necessity of reform being on the agenda and blame-avoidance opportunities being available for retrenchment to occur.

In practice, we would not simply define each of these θ terms as taking on the indicated nodal types. Doing so would imply that we had complete certainty that causal relations in all cases behave according to Pierson's logic. Instead, we would normally allow for a probability *distribution* over each θ, representing our beliefs about what kinds of causal effects are most likely or most common. How we define the distributions over θ^A, θ^B, and θ^R depends on the degree of confidence that we want to express in Pierson's specific argument (given that we accept the DAG). To represent the belief that Pierson's argument is correct with certainty and operates in a uniform, deterministic fashion across units, we would simply have degenerate distributions for θ^A, θ^B, and θ^R, with a probability of 1.0 placed on the respective nodal types shown above. To capture uncertainty about the functional relations on any graph or if we believe that there is some heterogeneity of effects across units, we would disperse probability density across types for each θ. For instance, for θ^R we might want to put some weight on θ^R_{0011} (blame-avoidance opportunities alone are enough to generate retrenchment), θ^R_{0101} (conservative leaders alone are enough), θ^R_{0111} (either is enough), and θ^R_{0000} (retrenchment will not happen even when both conditions are present), while perhaps putting greatest weight on θ^R_{0001}.[2]

Our beliefs about the distribution of exogenous conditions – that is, how common conservative governments, socioeconomic pressures, and particular program structures are – would similarly be captured in distributions over the values of θ^C, θ^S, and θ^P, respectively.

3.2 Military Interventions

In her book *Leaders at War*, Saunders (2011) asks why, when intervening militarily abroad, leaders sometimes seek to transform the *domestic* political institutions of the states they target while sometimes seeking only to shape those states' *external* behaviors.

Saunders' central explanatory variable is the nature of leaders' causal beliefs about security threats. When leaders are "internally focused," they believe that threats in the international arena derive from the internal characteristics of other states. Leaders who are "externally focused," by contrast, understand threats as emerging strictly from other states' foreign and security policies.

These basic worldviews, in turn, affect the cost-benefit calculations leaders make about intervention strategies – in particular, about whether to try to transform the internal institutions of a target state – via two mechanisms. First, an internal focus (as opposed to an external focus) affects leaders' perceptions of the likely security gains from a transformative intervention strategy. Second, internal versus external focus affects the kinds of strategic capabilities in which leaders invest over time (Do they invest in the kinds of capabilities suited to internal transformation?); and those investments in turn affect the costliness and likelihood of success of alternative intervention strategies. Calculations about the relative costs and benefits of different strategies then shape the choice between a transformative and a non-transformative approach to intervention.

At the same time, leaders can only choose a transformative strategy if they decide to intervene in the first place. The decision about whether to intervene depends, in turn, on at least two kinds of considerations. The first is about

---

[2] In notation that we use later, these beliefs would be represented with a λ^R vector.

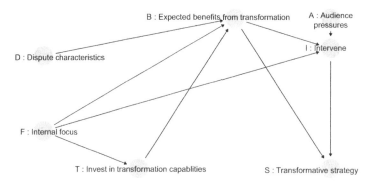

Figure 3.2   A graphical representation of Saunders' (2011) argument

fit: A leader is more likely to intervene against a target when the nature of the dispute makes the leader's preferred intervention strategy (transformative or non-transformative) appear feasible in a given situation. Second, Saunders allows that forces outside the logic of her main argument might also affect the likelihood of intervention: in particular, leaders may be pushed to intervene by international or domestic audiences.

Figure 3.2 depicts the causal dependencies in Saunders' argument in DAG form (again, with all θ terms left implicit). Working from left to right, we see that whether or not leaders are "internally focused" (F) affects the expected net relative benefits of transformation (B), both via a direct pathway and via an indirect pathway running through investments in transformative capacities (T). Characteristics of a given dispute or target state (D) likewise influence the benefits of transformation (B). The decision about whether to intervene (I) is then a function of three factors: the presence or absence of an internal focus (F), the expected relative net benefits of transformation (B), and audience pressures (A). Finally, the choice of whether to pursue a trans-formative strategy (S) is a function of whether or not intervention occurs at all (I), and of cost-benefit comparisons between the two strategies (B).

This DAG illustrates how readily causal graphs can depict the multiple pathways through which a given variable might affect another variable, as with the multiple pathways linking F to I and B (and, thus, all of its causes) to S. In fact, this graphical representation of the dependencies in some ways throws the multiplicity of pathways into even sharper relief than does a narrative exposition of the argument. For instance, Saunders draws explicit attention to the fact that causal beliefs (F) operate on expected net benefits via both a direct and indirect pathways: both shaping calculations of the net benefits of transformation and conditioning investments in capabilities. What is a bit easier to miss without formalization is that F also acts *directly* on the choice to intervene as part of the feasibility logic: When leaders assess whether their generally preferred strategy would be feasible if deployed against a particular target, the generally preferred strategy is itself a product of their internal or external focus. The DAG also makes helpfully explicit that the two main outcomes of interest – the choice about whether to intervene and the choice about how – are not just shaped by some of the same causes but are themselves causally linked: one can only decide how to intervene if one has intervened.

Omitted links are also notable. For instance, the lack of an arrow between D and A suggests that features of the dispute that affect feasibility have no effect on audience pressures. If we instead believed there could be other connections – for instance, that audiences take feasibility into account in demanding intervention – then we would want to include a $D \rightarrow A$ arrow.

Turning to variable ranges and causal functions, it is not hard to see how one might readily capture Saunders' logic in a fairly straightforward manner. All variables except S could be treated as binary with $F = 1$ representing internally focused causal beliefs, $T = 1$ representing investments in transformative capabilities, $B = 1$ representing expectations that transformation will be more net beneficial than non-transformation, $D = 1$ meaning that a dispute has characteristics that make transformation a feasible strategy, and so on. Although there are two strategies, we in fact need three values for S because it must be defined for all values of the other variables – that is, it must take on a distinct categorical value if there is no intervention at all. We could then define functions, such as:

- $B = FTD$, implying that transformation will be perceived to be net beneficial in a case if and only if the leader has internally focused causal beliefs, the military is prepared for a transformative strategy, and the dispute has characteristics that make transformation feasible.
- $I = (1 - |B - F|) + (|B - F|)A$, implying that intervention can occur under (and only under) either of two alternative sets of conditions: if the generally preferred strategy and the more net-beneficial strategy in a given case are the same (i.e., such that $B - F = 0$) or, when this alignment is absent (i.e., such that $|B - F| = 1$), where audiences pressure a leader to intervene.

As illustrated in the Pierson example, in a non-parametric framework, each parametric causal function represents one nodal type for the relevant θ. For instance, though we spare the reader the complexities of the corresponding subscript notation, there is a single value of θ^B under which the conditions $F = 1, P = 1$, and $T = 1$ generate $B = 1$, and we get $B = 0$ otherwise. Likewise, there exists a single value of θ^I under which $B = 1, F = 1$ and $B = 0, F = 0$ produce $I = 1$, for either value of A; and A has a positive effect on I whenever $B \neq F$. To work with this model, we would specify a probability distribution over all possible nodal types for each node on the graph.

This example also nicely illustrates how much potential causal complexity a moderately intricate argument and causal graph imply. The number of *possible* nodal types at each node depends on how many parents that node has. Looking at the endogenous nodes here, we have one binary node with one parent (T), implying 4 nodal types; two binary nodes with 3 parents (B and I), implying 256 nodal types each; and one ternary node (S) with two parents, implying 81 nodal types.[3] If we now conceptualize the set of possible "causal types" as containing all distinct combinations of nodal types – all ways in which a case might behave across all of its nodes (see Chapter 2) – then this graph implies over 21 million different ways in which the values of exogenous nodes (D, F, and A) might jointly produce patterns of outcomes across the graph. Saunders' argument effectively represents one of these 21 million possible sets of relations.

The framework that we outline in this book allows for updating our confidence in an argument like Saunders': We can ask how likely the specific causal type implied by this argument is relative to other causal types. Yet, as we will see, the approach lends itself to a much broader view of causal inquiry than simply asking whether an overall theory or argument is correct. In the approach that we develop here, we will use data to update our beliefs over *all* causal types allowed for in a model. We can then use these updated beliefs to answer any number of specific causal questions about relationships in the model. For instance, we can use a single set of data to update the model and then ask about the average effect of internal focus on the intervention; the likelihood of a positive effect of internal focus on the intervention; the relative importance of the expected-benefits pathway over the direct pathway in

---

[3] For S, we generalize the formula for calculating nodal types in a fully binary setting, given in Chapter 2 as $2^{(2^n)}$. More generally, for a node with m possible values, and n parents each of which has p possible values, the number of nodal types is $m^{(p^n)}$. For S, this becomes $3^{\left(2^2\right)}$.

generating a positive effect; or effects at individual steps in the causal chain, such as the effect of expected benefits on the choice of strategy.

3.3 Development and Democratization

Przeworski and Limongi (1997) argue that democratization occurs for reasons that are largely idiosyncratic (i.e., not driven by socioeconomic or macro-structural conditions); but once a country has democratized, a higher level of economic development makes democracy more likely to survive. Economic development thus affects whether or not a country is a democracy, but only after a democratic transition has occurred, not before. Thus, in their description – and contrary to Boix (2003) – democratization is not determined by other substantive variables in the model. The dynamic component of Przeworski and Limongi's argument – the fact that both the presence of democracy and the causal effect of development on democracy depend on whether a democratic transition occurred at a previous point in time – forces us to think about how to capture over-time processes in a causal model.

We represent Przeworski and Limongi's argument in the DAG in Figure 3.3. The first thing to note is that we can capture dynamics by considering democracy at different points in time as separate nodes. According to the graph, whether a country is a democracy in a given period (D_t) is a function, jointly, of whether it was a democracy in the previous period (D_{t-1}) and of the level of per capita GDP in the previous period, as well as of other unspecified forces θ^{D_t} (not pictured).

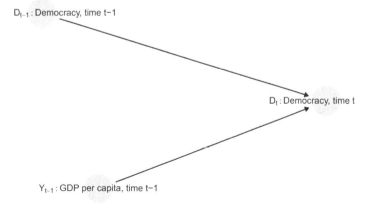

D_{t-1} : Democracy, time t−1

D_t : Democracy, time t

Y_{t-1} : GDP per capita, time t−1

Figure 3.3   A graphical representation of Przeworski and Limongi's (1997) argument

Second, the arrow running from Y_{t-1} to D_t means that Y *may* affect the presence of democracy, not that it always (or certainly) does. Indeed, Przeworski and Limongi's argument is that development's effect on democracy depends on a regime's prior state: GDP matters for whether democracies continue to be democracies, but not for whether autocracies go on to become democracies. The absence of an arrow between D_{t-1} and Y_{t-1}, however, implies a (possibly incorrect) belief that democracy and last period GDP are independent of one another.

This claim implies an asymmetric effect of national income on regime type: High GDP per capita can prevent a democratic state from reverting to autocracy, according to Przeworski and Limongi, but it cannot cause an autocracy to become a democracy. Interestingly, this argument means that even though high national income cannot cause a state to *transition to* democracy, it can still cause a state to be democratic. The posited causal effect is best understood in counterfactual terms: a democracy with high per capita GDP *would* have reverted to autocracy if it had had low per capita GDP. The argument might also be expressed as an interaction: If a state was an autocracy in the previous period, then GDP will have no effect on its regime type in the current period; national income has an effect only on states that were democracies in the previous period. The graph allows for this interaction – in making the current regime type dependent both on GDP and prior regime type – but the type of interaction would need to be specified in a causal function.

For a parametric representation of this asymmetric relationship, we can specify a function in which GDP can reduce the likelihood of a transition *away* from democracy but has no effect on the probability of a transition *to* democracy. One possible causal function that captures this argument is:

$$D_t = \mathbb{1}(\theta^{D_t} < (1 - D_{t-1})p + D_{t-1}Y_{t-1}q),$$

where

- D_t and D_{t-1} are binary nodes representing current and last-period democracy, respectively.
- Y_{t-1} represents national per capita GDP in the previous period, scaled to $0-1$.
- p is a parameter representing the probability that an autocracy democratizes.
- q is a parameter representing the probability that a democracy with $Y_{t-1} = 1$ remains democratic.

- θ^{D_t} represents a random, additional input into whether or not a state is democratic; we might think of this as distributed uniformly over $[0, 1]$.
- The indicator function, $\mathbb{1}$, evaluates the inequality and generates a value of 1 if and only if it is true.

Unpacking the equation, the likelihood that a country is a democracy in a given period rises and falls with the expression to the right of the inequality operator. This expression itself has two parts, reflecting the difference between the determinants of *transitions to* democracy (captured by the first part) and the determinants of democratic *survival* (captured by the second). The first part comes into play – that is, non-zero – only for non-democracies in the last period. For non-democracies, the expression evaluates simply to p, the exogenous probability of democratization. The second part is non-zero only for democracies, where it evaluates to q times Y_{t-1}: thus, remaining democratic is more likely as national income rises. The inequality is then evaluated by asking whether the expression on the left passes a threshold, θ^{D_t}. Thus, higher values for the expression on the left increase the likelihood of democracy while the randomness of the θ^{D_t} threshold captures the role of other, idiosyncratic inputs. The mean and variance of θ^{D_t} capture the overall likelihood of being a democracy as well as the importance of unspecified factors.[4] In a model like this, it would be natural to seek to estimate parameters p and q as well as try to understand the distribution of θ^{D_t}.

We can also, of course, represent the asymmetry in a binary setup with nodal types. Specifically, nodal type $\theta^{D_t}_{0001}$ represents a causal effect in which a democracy will remain democratic if it is wealthy, but will become authoritarian if it is not wealthy: $D_t = 1$ if both of its parents, Y_{t-1} and D_{t-1}, equal 1, and $D_t = 0$ if either of its parents are 0. We can see here the clear causal effect of Y_{t-1} for a country that was a democracy (i.e., $D_{t-1} = 1$): for such a unit, changing Y_{t-1} to 0 would change that country from a democracy to a non-democracy in the current period. We can also see, under this nodal type, that for a country that was *not* a democracy last period ($D_{t-1} = 0$), changing GDP will have no effect. Consider, in contrast, a $\theta^{D_t}_{0011}$ type: under this alternative nodal type, a non-democracy becomes a democracy if national income goes from low to high.

---

[4] Note how, while the causal function nails down certain features of the process, it leaves others up for grabs. In particular, the parameters p and q are assumed to be constant for all autocracies and for all democracies, respectively, but their values are left unspecified. And one could readily write down a function that left even more openness – by, for instance, including an unknown parameter that translates y into a change in the probability of reversion or allowing for nonlinearities.

Again, we can express our beliefs in the prevalence or likelihood of different causal effects on democracy by assigning a probability distribution over D_t's 16 possible nodal types.

Although we do not engage with dynamic models in this book, this model provides a useful opportunity for thinking through the implications of a given distribution of nodal types for a dynamic process. Imagine a setup in which, in each period, one half of units were of type $\theta_{0001}^{D_t}$, and one half of type $\theta_{1111}^{D_t}$, meaning that they will be democracies in the current period regardless of income level or prior regime status (with each unit's type assigned afresh in each period). Suppose, further, that all units' income level remains constant over time. Now, say that in an initial period, half the units were democracies, half the units had high income, and there was no correlation between these two features or between these features and nodal type. So, half the democracies were high income, half low income; half the non-democracies were high income, half low income; and the two nodal types are also distributed equally among all regime/income combinations.

How does this setup evolve over time? In particular, what happens over time to the association between income level and regime type? In the next period, half of the cases – the half that are of the $\theta_{1111}^{D_t}$ type – will be democracies *regardless* of their income level: half of these will be surviving democracies and the other half new democracies, simply because half of the cases of each type were initially democracies. Further, half of this set of democracies will be high income democracies, simply because half of the $\theta_{1111}^{D_t}$ cases were high income, and income is constant.

Of the other half of cases – the $\theta_{0001}^{D_t}$ types – one quarter will be surviving democracies that survived *because of* their income: These are the quarter of the $\theta_{0001}^{D_t}$ types that were both democracies and high income at the outset. The other three quarters will be autocracies: the quarter of the $\theta_{0001}^{D_t}$ types that were low-income democracies will be "backsliders," becoming autocracies because of their poverty; and half of the $\theta_{0001}^{D_t}$ types that were autocracies at the outset will *stay* autocracies regardless of income level, as all autocracies of this nodal type do.

So now a larger share of democracies are high income. Initially, half of the democracies were high income. Now half of the $\theta_{1111}^{D_t}$ democracies are high income (half of all cases), but *all* of the $\theta_{0001}^{D_t}$ democracies are high income (one-eighth of all cases). So now 0.6 of all democracies are high income. Similarly, the backsliding process boosts the share of autocracies that are low income, from one half to two-thirds.

With a fresh type draw for each unit after each round – randomly transitioning some countries into democracies – we get a similar sorting process in future periods. Each period, some autocracies become democracies, with the high income ones remaining democracies and the low-income ones remaining democracies only if they get assigned to the "always democratic" type $(\theta_{1111}^{D_i})$. Eventually, the system converges on a joint distribution in which wealthy states are all stable democracies and the poorer states transition back and forth between democracy and autocracy across periods – not a terrible approximation of the global state of affairs in the contemporary era.

4   Causal Queries

We describe major families of causal questions and illustrate how these can all be described as queries about the values of nodes in a causal model.

Although scholars share a broad common interest in causality, there is tremendous heterogeneity in the kinds of causal questions that scholars ask. Consider the relationship between inequality and democratization. We might seek to know inequality's average impact on democratization across some broad set of cases. Alternatively, we might be interested in a particular case – say, Mongolia in 1995 – and want to know whether inequality would have had an effect *in this case*. Or we might wonder whether the level of democracy in Mongolia in 1995 is *due* to the level of inequality in that case – yet another distinct question (in the same way that establishing that poison would make you sick does not imply that you are sick because of poison). In a different vein, we might be interested in *how* causal effects unfold, inquiring about the pathway or mechanism through which inequality affects democratization – a question we can also ask at two levels. We can ask whether inequality affected democratization in Mongolia through mobilization of the masses; or we can ask how commonly, across a broad set of cases, inequality affects democratization through mobilization of the masses. Pushing further, we might ask a counterfactual question of the form: Would inequality have produced democratization had mobilization been prevented from occurring?

Distinct methodological literatures have been devoted to the study of average causal effects, the analysis of case-level causal effects and explanations, and the identification of causal pathways. Fortunately, each of these questions can be readily captured as specific queries asked of (and answerable from) a causal model. As described by Pearl (2010), the goal is to deploy an "*algorithm* that receives a model M as an input and delivers the desired quantity $Q(M)$ as the output." More specifically, we demonstrate how, given a model as described in Chapter 2, a causal query can be represented as a question about the exogenous *nodes* on a causal graph (θ). When we assimilate our causal questions into a causal model, we are placing what we want to know in formal relation to both what we *already* know and what we can potentially *observe*. As we will see in later chapters, this move allows us then to deploy a model to generate strategies of inference: To determine which observations, if we made them, would be likely to yield the greatest leverage on our query, given our prior knowledge about the way the world works. And by the same logic, once we see the evidence, this integration allows us to "update" on our query – to figure out in a systematic fashion what we *have* learned – in a manner that takes background knowledge into account.

In the remainder of this chapter, we walk through the conceptualization and causal-model interpretation of four key causal queries:

- Case-level causal effects
- Case-level causal attribution
- Average causal effects
- Causal pathways

These queries are in no way exhaustive of the causal questions that can be captured in causal graphs, but they are among the more common foci of social scientific investigation. In Appendix, we describe a still richer set of queries, including "actual causes," and we show how the CausalQueries software package implements a general procedure for mapping queries onto causal types.

4.1 Case-Level Causal Effects

The simplest causal question is whether some causal effect operates in an individual case. Does X have an effect on Y in this case? For instance, is Yemen in 1995 a case in which a change in economic inequality would produce a change in whether or not the country democratizes? We could put the question more specifically as a query about a causal effect in a particular direction, for instance: Does inequality have a positive effect on democratization in the case of Yemen in 1995?

In counterfactual terms, a query about case-level causation is a question about what would happen if we could manipulate a variable in the case: If we could hypothetically intervene to change X's value in the case, (how) would Y's value change? To ask, more specifically, whether a positive or negative

A DAG capturing a case–level causal effect

Figure 4.1   A DAG that indicates how the effect of X on Y in a given case depends on the case's nodal type, represented by θ^Y

effect operates for a case is to ask whether a particular counterfactual relation holds in that case.

Consider the model in Figure 4.1. As introduced in Chapter 2, θ^Y here represents the nodal type characterizing Y's response to X and, if X and Y are binary, it can take on one of four values in this model: θ^Y_{10}, θ^Y_{01}, θ^Y_{00}, and θ^Y_{11} (which map onto our a, b, c, and d types, respectively).

In this model, then, the query, "What is X's causal effect in this case?" simply becomes a question about the value of the nodal type θ^Y. If $\theta^Y = \theta^Y_{10}$, for instance, this implies that X has a negative effect on Y in this case. If $\theta^Y = \theta^Y_{00}$, this implies that X has no effect on Y in this case and that Y will always be 0.

We can also pose probabilistic versions of a case-level causal effect query. For instance, we can ask, "What is the probability that X has a positive effect on Y in this case?" Answering this question requires assessing the probability that $\theta^Y = \theta^Y_{01}$.[1] We can also ask, "What is the probability that X *matters* for Y in this case?" Answering this question involves *adding* the probability that X has a positive effect to the probability that it has a negative effect. That is, it involves adding the probability that $\theta^Y = \theta^Y_{01}$ to the probability that $\theta^Y = \theta^Y_{10}$. And we can ask, "What is the *expected* effect of X on Y in this case?" To answer

---

[1] A little more carefully: Insofar, as we believe the effect is either positive or it is not, the true answer to the question – the estimand – is a yes or a no; the *probability* is an answer that captures our *beliefs* about the estimand. Alternatively, we could imagine asking about the *share* of a population for which a positive effect operates, a type of query that we use quite a bit later in the book.

this question, we need to estimate the probability that X has a positive effect *minus* the probability that it has a negative effect.

In sum, when posing probabilistic questions about case-level causal effects, we are still asking about the value of a θ term in our model – but we are asking about the *probability* of the θ term taking on some value or set of values. In practice, we will in this book most often be posing case-level causal-effect queries in probabilistic form.

We can conceptualize questions about case-level causal effects as questions about θ terms even if our model involves more complex relations between X and Y. The question itself does not depend on the model having any particular form. For instance, consider a mediation model of the form $X \rightarrow M \rightarrow Y$. In this model, a positive effect of X on Y can emerge in two ways. A positive $X \rightarrow Y$ effect can emerge from a positive effect of X on M followed by a positive effect of M on Y. Yet we will also get a positive $X \rightarrow Y$ effect from a sequence of negative intermediate effects: If an increase in X causes a *decrease* in M, while a decrease in M causes an *increase* in Y, then an increase in X will yield an increase in Y.

Thus, there are two chains of intermediate effects that will generate a positive effect of X on Y. Therefore, in this mediation model, the question, "What is the probability that X has a positive effect on Y in this case?" is asking whether either of those combinations of intermediate effects is operation. Specifically, we are asking about the following probability:

$$\Pr\left((\theta^M = \theta^M_{01} \& \theta^Y = \theta^Y_{01}) \text{ OR } (\theta^M = \theta^M_{10} \& \theta^Y = \theta^Y_{10})\right) \quad (4.1)$$

In a similar way, a negative effect of X on Y can emerge from a chain of opposite-signed effects: either positive $X \rightarrow M$ and then negative $M \rightarrow Y$, or negative $X \rightarrow M$ and then positive $M \rightarrow Y$. Thus, to ask, "What is the probability that X has a negative effect on Y in this case?" is to ask about the following probability:

$$\Pr\left((\theta^M = \theta^M_{01} \& \theta^Y = \theta^Y_{10}) \text{ OR } (\theta^M = \theta^M_{10} \& \theta^Y = \theta^Y_{01})\right) \quad (4.2)$$

Finally, to ask about the *expected* effect of X on Y in a case is to ask about the first probability (of a positive effect) minus the second (of a negative effect).

Notice that working with this more complex mediation model required us first to figure out which combinations of intermediate causal effects would generate the overall effect of X on Y that we were interested in. Mapping from sets of $X \rightarrow M$ and $M \rightarrow Y$ effects to the $X \rightarrow Y$ effects that they yield allowed us to figure out which θ^M and θ^Y values correspond to the overall effect that we are asking about. We will make use of these kinds of mappings at many points in this book. But for now the key point is that, regardless of the complexity of a model, we can always pose questions about case-level causal effects as questions about a case's nodal types or about the probability of it having a given set of nodal types.

4.2 Case-Level Causal Attribution

A query about causal attribution is closely related to, but different from, a query about a case-level causal effect. When asking about X's case-level effect, we are asking, "*Would* a change in X cause a change in Y in this case?" The question of causal attribution asks: "*Did* X cause Y to take on the value it did in this case?" More precisely, we are asking, "Given the values that X and Y *in fact* took on in this case, would Y's value have been different if X's value had been different?"

Consider an example. We know that inequality in Taiwan was relatively low and that Taiwan democratized in 1996, but was low inequality a *cause* of Taiwan's democratization in 1996? Equivalently: Given low economic inequality and democratization in Taiwan in 1996, would the outcome in this case have been different if inequality had been high? Notice that, when asking a causal attribution question, we are *conditioning* on the X and Y values that we in fact observe in the case.

Another way to put the point is that, when asking about causal attribution, we have already narrowed down the set of possible nodal types by observing the realized values of some nodes in the case of interest. For the simple $X \rightarrow Y$ model in Figure 4.1, if we observe $X = 1$ and $Y = 1$ in the case at hand, then we know that either X had a positive effect on Y in this case or this is a case in which $Y = 1$ regardless of X's value. So only two nodal types for Y are potentially in play: θ_{01}^Y and θ_{11}^Y. So the attribution question is: Given we know that $\theta^Y \in \{\theta_{01}^Y, \theta_{11}^Y\}$, does $\theta^Y = \theta_{01}^Y$? Or, probabilistically: What is $\Pr(\theta^Y = \theta_{01}^Y)$ given that $\theta^Y \in \{\theta_{01}^Y, \theta_{11}^Y\}$?

This query can be still defined as statements about nodal types when models are more complex. We may often think about matters of causal attribution in situations in which another potential cause of the outcome presents itself, and we want to know whether we can attribute the outcome to one condition or the other (or to both). Consider the slightly more complex setup in Figure 4.2. Here, Y is a function of two variables, X_1 and X_2. This means that θ^Y is somewhat more complicated than in a setup with one causal variable:

Did X=1 cause Y = 1?

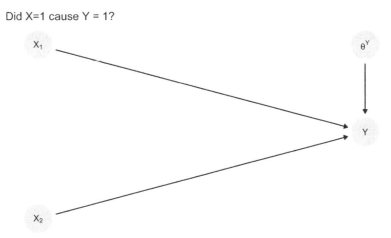

Figure 4.2   A causal model in which Y depends on two variables X_1 and X_2

θ^Y must here define Y's response to all possible combinations of X_1 and X_2, including interactions between them.

With this model, a query about causal attribution – whether $X_1 = 1$ caused $Y = 1$ – can take account of the value of X_2. Parallel to our Taiwan example, suppose that we have a case in which $Y = 1$ and in which X_1 was also 1, and we want to know whether X_1 caused Y to take on the value it did. Answering this question requires knowing whether the case's type is such that X_1 would have had a positive causal effect on Y, given what we know about X_2 – which we can think of as part of the context.

In this setup, we can answer the query by consulting the characterization of nodal types for a two-parent node that we provided in Table 2.3. From that table, we can figure out for which nodal types X_1 has a positive effect on Y given a particular value of X_2. Suppose that in the case at hand we observe $X_2 = 1$. In Table 2.3, we can then see that we have four rows – rows 9 to 12 – in which Y goes from 0 to 1 as X_1 goes from 0 to 1 while X_2 is fixed at 1. (The key columns here are the third and fourth, where for these rows we see that Y goes from 0 to 1 as we go from the third to the fourth column.) These four rows represent the four Y-nodal types: θ^Y_{0001}, θ^Y_{1001}, θ^Y_{0101}, and θ^Y_{1101}. In other words, we can attribute a $Y = 1$ outcome to $X_1 = 1$ if we are in the context $\theta^{X_2} = \theta^{X_2}_1$ and θ^Y is one of these four nodal types.

The *probability* that $X_1 = 1$ caused $Y = 1$ given $X_1 = 1$, $X_2 = 1$, and $Y = 1$ is the probability of these four types divided by the probability that

$Y = 1$ given $X_1 = 1$ and $X_2 = 1$. The latter probability is the probability of being in the last eight rows of Table 2.3, which are the eight Y-nodal types consistent with the observation of $X_1 = 1$, $X_2 = 1$, and $Y = 1$.

Thus, a question about causal attribution is a question not just about how a case would behave given an intervention, but a question that *conditions* on observed node values in the case – and then asks how the outcome would have been different *if* circumstances had been different from what we know them to have been in this case.

4.3 Average Causal Effects

While the queries we have considered so far operate at the case level, we can also pose causal queries at the level of populations. One of the most common population-level queries is a question about an average causal effect. In counterfactual terms, a question about average causal effects is: If we manipulated the value of X for all cases in the population – first setting X to one value for all cases, then changing it to another value for all cases – by how much would the average value of Y in the population change? Like other causal queries, a query about an average causal effect can be conceptualized as learning about a node in a causal model.

We can do this by conceiving of any given case as being a member of a population with each unit endowed with nodal types. When we seek to estimate an average causal effect, we seek information about the proportions or *shares* of these nodal types in the population.

More formally and adapted from Humphreys and Jacobs (2015), we can use λ_{ij}^Y to refer to the *share* of cases in a population that has nodal type θ_{ij}^Y. Thus, given our four nodal types in a two-variable binary setup, λ_{10}^Y is the proportion of cases in the population with negative effects; λ_{01} is the proportion of cases with positive effects; and so on. One nice feature of this setup, with both X and Y as binary, is that the average causal effect can be simply calculated as the share of positive-effect cases minus the share of negative-effect cases: $\lambda_{01}^Y - \lambda_{10}^Y$.

Graphically, we can represent this setup by including λ^Y in a more complex causal graph as in Figure 4.3. We might think of this graph as standing in for a still more complex graph in which we replicate the $X \rightarrow Y \leftarrow \theta^Y$ graph for as many units as we have and have λ^Y point into each θ^Y (see Figure 9.2 for an example).

Nodal types drawn from a common distribution

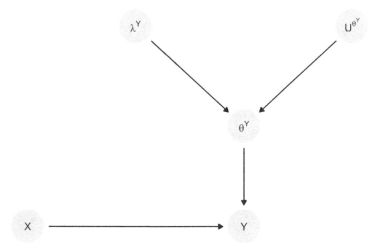

Figure 4.3   A causal model in which cases are drawn from a heterogeneous population. Here, λ parameterizes the multinomial distribution of nodal types in the population

As in our setup for case-level causal effects, X's effect on Y in a case depends on (and only on) the case's nodal type, θ^Y. The key difference is that we now model the case's type not as exogenously given, but as a function of two additional variables: the distribution of nodal types in a population and a random process through which the case's type is "drawn" from that distribution. We represent the type distribution as λ^Y: a vector of values for the proportions $\lambda^Y_{10}, \lambda^Y_{01}, \lambda^Y_{00},$ and λ^Y_{11}. We represent the random process for drawing a case's θ^Y value from that distribution as U^{θ^Y}.

In practice, it is the components of λ^Y – the shares of different nodal types in the population – that will be of substantive interest. In this model, our causal query – about X's average causal effect – is defined by the shares of negative- and positive-causal-effect cases, respectively, in the population. "What is X's average effect on Y?" amounts to asking: What are the values of λ^Y_{10} and λ^Y_{01}? As with θ^Y, λ^Y is not directly observable. And so the empirical challenge – to which we devote later parts of this book – is to figure out what we *can* observe that would allow us to learn about λ^Y's component values?[2]

We can, of course, likewise pose queries about other population-level causal quantities. For instance, we could ask for what proportion of cases in

---

[2] Note also that λ^Y can be thought of as itself drawn from a distribution, such as a Dirichlet. The hyperparameters of this underlying distribution of λ would then represent our uncertainty over λ and hence over average causal effects in the population.

the population X has a positive effect? This would be equivalent to asking the value of λ_{01}^Y, one element of the λ^Y vector. Or we could ask about the proportion of cases in which X has no effect, which would be asking about $\lambda_{00}^Y + \lambda_{11}^Y$, capturing the two ways in which there can be zero effect.

We can also ask conditional queries about average effects. For instance, for the DAG in Figure 4.2 with two causal variables, we can ask what is the average causal effect of X_1 on Y for units in which $X_2 = 1$. In this model, λ is a 16-element vector, with a share for each of Y's 16 nodal types, covering all possible joint effects of X_1 and X_2. So this query, conditioning on X_1, asks about the difference between the proportion of the population that is of a type in which X_1 has a positive effect when $X_2 = 1$ and the proportion in which X_1 has a negative effect when $X_2 = 1.$[3]

4.4 Causal Paths

To develop richer causal understandings, researchers often seek to describe the causal path or paths through which effects propagate. Consider the DAG in Figure 4.4, in which X can affect Y through two possible pathways: directly and via M. Assume again that all variables are binary, taking on values of 0 or 1. Here, we have nodal types defining M's response to X (θ^M) and nodal types defining Y's response to both X (directly) and M (θ^Y).

Suppose that we observe $X = 1$ and $Y = 1$ in a case. Suppose, further, that we have reasonable confidence that X has had a positive effect on Y in this case. We may nonetheless be interested in knowing whether that causal effect ran *through* M. We will refer to this as a query about a causal path. Importantly, a causal path query is not satisfied simply by asking whether some mediating event along the path occurred. We cannot, for instance, establish that the top path in Figure 4.4 was operative simply by determining the value of M in this case – though that will likely be useful information.

Rather, the question of whether the mediated (via M) causal path is operative is a composite question of two parts: First, does X have an effect on M in this case? Second, does that effect – the difference in M's value caused by

---

[3] As we discuss at greater length in Section 9.3.2 of Chapter 9, this conditional average effect query is subtly different from a case-level query about an observed case with a particular value on a variable. A case-level query might take the form: What would we believe the causal effect of X_1 on Y to be in a case randomly drawn from the population in which *we observed* $X_2 = 1$. In this latter query, the *observation* of a unit with particular features might provide information that would allow us to update on λ – that is, on what kind of world we are in. The conditional average effect query, in contrast, assumes a distribution over λ and simply queries that distribution.

A DAG with two causal paths

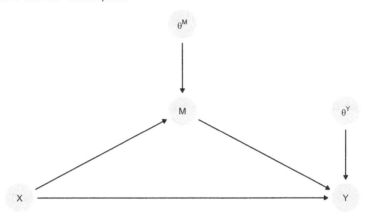

Figure 4.4 X affects Y both directly and indirectly through M

a change in X – in turn *cause* a change in Y's value? In other words, what we want to know is whether the effect of X on Y depends on – that is, *will not operate without* – the effect of X on M.

We take the question of whether a path is operative in producing an effect as the same as the question of whether there is an indirect effect as asked in mediation analysis. Indeed as emphasized in mediation analysis there are two types of "indirect effects" of X on Y via M (when X is fixed at $X = 0$ and at $X = 1$), and similarly two types of "direct" effects (when M is fixed at $M(X = 0)$ and at $M(X = 1)$).

Using potential outcomes notation, a positive indirect effect would be present (for $x \in \{0, 1\}$) if:

$$Y(X = x, M = M(X = 1)) > Y(X = x, M = M(X = 0)).$$

Written using causal functions this is:

$$f^Y(X = x, M = f^M(X = 1, \theta^M), \theta^Y)$$
$$> f^Y(X = x, M = f^M(X = 0, \theta^M), \theta^Y)).$$

Both expressions ask whether there would be an increase in the value of Y if M were to change in the way that it would change due to a change in X, but without an actual change in X (Imai et al., 2010; Pearl, 2009, p. 132). Note there are two versions of this query, one for $x = 0$ (holding X constant at 0) and one for $x = 1$ (holding X constant at 1).

Similarly, a positive direct effect would be present if:

$$f^Y(X = 1, M = f^M(X = x, \theta^M), \theta^Y)$$
$$> f^Y(X = 0, M = f^M(X = x, \theta^M), \theta^Y)).$$

Again there are two versions of the query, one for $x = 0$ and one for $x = 1$.

From these expressions we can see that asking whether a causal effect operated via a given path is in fact asking about a specific set of causal effects lying along that path, as captured by θ^M and θ^Y.

We now work through the logic that links queries to nodal types θ^M and θ^Y, focusing on positive effects of X on Y that work through M for a case with $X = 1$.

First, note that there are two sequences of effects that would allow X's positive effect on Y to operate via M: (1) X has a positive effect on M, which in turn has a positive effect on Y; or (2) X has a negative effect on M, which in turn has a negative effect on Y.

The first question then is whether X affects M in this case. This is a question about the value of θ^M. We know that θ^M can take on four possible values corresponding to the four possible responses to X: θ_{10}^M, θ_{01}^M, θ_{00}^M, and θ_{11}^M. For sequence (1) to operate, θ^M must take on the value θ_{01}^M, representing a positive effect of X on M. For sequence (2) to operate, θ^M must take on the value θ_{10}^M, representing a negative effect of X on M.

Next, note that θ^Y defines Y's response to different combinations of *both* X and M – since both of these variables point directly into Y. Given that Y has two binary parents, there are 16 possible values for θ^Y – again as shown earlier in Table 2.3, simply substituting X and M for X_1 and X_2. Note that these 16 nodal types capture the full range of causal possibilities. For instance, they allow for M to affect Y and, thus, to potentially pass on a mediated effect of X. They allow for X to have a *direct*, unmediated effect on Y. And there are nodal types in which X and M *interact* in affecting Y.

What values of θ^Y then are compatible with the operation of a positive effect of X on Y via M? Let us first consider this question with respect to sequence (1), in which X has a positive effect on M, and that positive effect is necessary for X's positive effect on Y to occur. For this sequence to operate, as we have said, θ^M must take on the value of θ_{01}^M. When it comes to θ^Y, then, what we need to look for are types in which X's effect on Y *depends on M's taking on the values it does as a result of X's positive effect on M*.

We are thus looking for nodal types for Y that capture two kinds of counterfactual causal relations operating on nodes. First, X must have a positive effect on Y when M undergoes the change that results from X's positive effect on M. This condition ensures simply that X *has* the required effect on Y in the presence of X's effect on M. Second, that change in M, generated by a change in X, must be *necessary* for X's positive effect on Y to operate. This condition specifies the *path*, ensuring that X's effect actually runs *through* (i.e., depends on) its effect on M.

1. Is $X = 1$ a counterfactual cause of $Y = 1$, given X's positive effect on M? Establishing this positive effect of X involves two queries:

   a) Where $X = 0$, does $Y = 0$? As we are assuming X has a positive effect on M, if $X = 0$ then $M = 0$ as well. So, we need that $Y = 0$ when $X = 0$, $M = 0$.
   b) Where $X = 1$, does $Y = 1$? Given X's assumed positive effect on M, $M = 1$ under this condition. So, we need $Y = 1$ when $X = 1$, $M = 1$.
2. Is X's effect on M necessary for X's positive effect on Y? That is, do we see $Y = 1$ *only* if M takes on the value that $X = 1$ generates (which is $M = 1$)? To determine this, we inspect the *counterfactual* condition in which $X = 1$ and $M = 0$, and we ask: Does $Y = 0$? Thus, we need $Y = 0$ when $X = 1$ but $M = 0$. In that case we know that M changing to 1 when X goes to 1 is *necessary* for X's effect on Y to operate (i.e., that the effect operates through the M path).

We now have enough to identify the types of θ^Y that answer the query. We again use notation of the form θ^Y_{wxyz} where:

- w is the potential outcome for Y when $(X = 0, M = 0)$
- x is the potential outcome for Y when $(X = 1, M = 0)$
- y is the potential outcome for Y when $(X = 0, M = 1)$
- z is the potential outcome for Y when $(X = 1, M = 1)$

The three conditions then imply that $w = 0$ (condition 1a), $z = 1$ (condition 1b), and $x = 0$ (condition 2). This leaves us with only two qualifying nodal types for Y: $\theta^Y = \theta_{0001}$ and θ_{0011}.

We can undertake the same exercise for when X has a negative effect on M, or $\theta^M = \theta^M_{10}$. Here, we adjust the three queries for θ^Y to take account of this negative effect. Thus, we adjust query 1a so that we are looking for $Y = 0$ when $X = 0$ and $M = 1$. In query 1b, we look for $Y = 1$ when $X = 1$ and $M = 0$. And for query 2, we want types in which Y fails to shift to 1 when X shifts to 1 but M stays at 1. Types θ^Y_{0100} and θ^Y_{1100} pass these three tests.

In sum, we can define this query about causal paths as a query about the value of θ terms on the causal graph. For the graph in Figure 4.4, asking

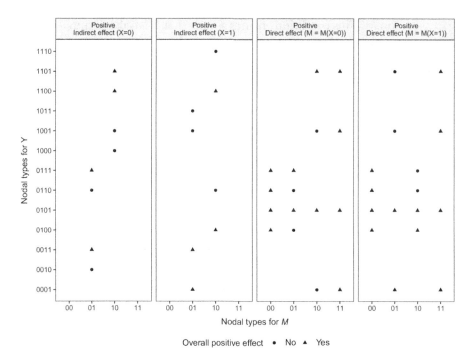

Figure 4.5   Combinations of nodal types for M and Y that generate direct, indirect, and overall positive effects together. The four digits in the nodal type labels for Y correspond to the potential outcomes for Y under four conditions: when $X = 0$ and $M = 0$, when $X = 1$ and $M = 0$, when $X = 0$ and $M = 1$, and when $X = 1$ and $M = 1$. The two digits in the nodal type labels for M correspond to the potential outcomes for M when $X = 0$ and when $X = 1$.

whether a positive effect of X on Y for an $X = 1$ case runs via the M-mediated path is asking whether one of four combinations of θ^M and θ^Y holds in the case:

- $\theta^M = \theta^M_{01}$ and $(\theta^Y = \theta_{0001}$ or $\theta_{0011})$
- $\theta^M = \theta^M_{10}$ and $(\theta^Y = \theta_{0100}$ or $\theta_{1100})$

The same kind of exercise can be conducted for other pathway inquiries. Thus, Figure 4.5 shows the combinations of θ^M and θ^Y that combine to make common pathway queries. Here, we distinguish between direct and indirect effects when there are and are not *overall* positive effects. The figure highlights the counterintuitive fact that it is possible to have different types of positive pathway effects without these producing an overall positive effect.[4]

---

[4] To choose one example, if $\theta^M = \theta^M_{01}$ and $\theta^Y = \theta^Y_{1001}$, then, Y would be 1 if either X and M were both 0 or if X and M were both 1. If X were 1, then we would have $M = 1$ and $Y = 1$, and $M = 1$ because

Finally, though stated here in terms of the case-level types that answer a pathway query, it is a conceptually small move to address population queries. As we did with average effects, these can now be constructed as statements about the shares of a population that answer different queries.

It is worth noting how different this formulation of the task of identifying causal pathways is from widespread understandings of process tracing. Scholars commonly characterize process tracing as a method in which we determine whether a mechanism was operating by establishing whether the events that are lying along that path occurred. As a causal-model framework makes clear, finding out that $M = 1$ (or $M = 0$, for that matter) does not establish what was going on causally. Observing this intervening step does not by itself tell us what value M *would* have taken on if X had taken on a different value, or whether this would have changed Y's value. We need instead to conceive of the problem of identifying pathways as one of figuring out the *counterfactual* response patterns of the variables along the causal chain.

4.5 Conclusion

For each of the causal queries we have described in this chapter, we have discussed several types of causal questions that social scientists often pose to their data and have shown how we can define these queries in terms of collections of nodal types on a causal graph.

In Appendix, we show how the mapping from causal questions to nodal types can be generalized to many different types of queries (as the CausalQueries software package does). These queries all involve summaries of the values of nodes given different types of interventions (or the absence of interventions) on other nodes. But we highlight that it is not hard to expand the set of queries still further to introduce broader, and more normative, considerations. Thus, for instance, one might ask whether an effect is large enough to merit some investment or whether the *distribution* of effects is justifiable given some normative considerations.

In connecting general queries to causal types, we prepare the ground for developing an empirical research design. Nodal types cannot themselves be directly observed. However, as we will demonstrate later in the book, defining

---

$X = 1$. And, given $X = 1$, $Y = 1$ only because $M = 1$ – which is due to X. Thus, there is an indirect effect. However, had X been 0 then M would have been 0 and Y would have been 1 – so no overall effect.

causal queries as summaries of causal types and links *observable* elements of a causal model to the *unobservable* objects of inquiry – allowing us to use the former to draw inferences about the latter.

4.6 Appendix

4.6.1 Actual Causes

In the main text, we dealt with causes in the standard counterfactual sense: antecedent conditions for which a change would have produced a different outcome. Sometimes, however, we are interested in identifying antecedent conditions that were not counterfactual difference-makers but that nonetheless *generated* or *produced* the outcome.

Though conceptually complex, queries of this form may be quite important for historical and legal applications and so we give an overview of them here though point to Halpern (2016) for an authoritative treatment of these ideas.

We will focus on situations in which an outcome was "overdetermined": Multiple conditions were present, each of which on their own, *could* have generated the outcome. Then, none of these conditions caused the outcome in the counterfactual sense; yet one or more of them may have been distinctively important in *producing* the outcome. The concept of an *actual cause* can be useful in putting a finer point on this kind of causal question.

A motivating example used in much of the literature on actual causes (e.g., Hall, 2004) imagines two characters, Suzy and Billy, simultaneously throwing stones at a bottle. Both are excellent shots and hit whatever they aim at. Suzy's stone hits first, knocks over the bottle, and the bottle breaks. However, Billy's stone *would* have hit had Suzy's not hit, and again the bottle would have broken. Did Suzy's throw cause the bottle to break? Did Billy's?

By the usual definition of causal effects, neither Suzy's nor Billy's action had a causal effect: Without either throw, the bottle would still have broken. We commonly encounter similar situations in the social world. We observe, for instance, the onset of an economic crisis and the breakout of war – either of which would be sufficient to cause the government's downfall – but with (say) the economic crisis occurring first and toppling the government before the war could do so. In this situation, neither economic crisis nor war in fact made a difference to the outcome: Take away either one and the outcome remains the same.

To return to the bottle example, while neither Suzy's nor Billy's throw is a counterfactual cause, it just seems obvious that Suzy broke the bottle, and Billy did not. We can formalize this intuition by defining Suzy's throw as the *actual cause* of the outcome. Using the definition provided by Halpern (2015), building on Halpern and Pearl (2005) and others, we say that a condition (X taking on some value x) was an actual cause of an outcome (of Y taking on some value y), where x and y may be collections of events, if:

1. $X = x$ and $Y = y$ both happened;
2. there is some set of variables, W, such that if they were fixed at the levels that they *actually took* on in the case, and if X were to be changed, then Y would change (where W can also be an empty set);
3. no strict subset of X satisfies 1 and 2 (there is no redundant part of the condition, $X = x$).

The definition thus describes a condition that *would* have been a counterfactual cause of the outcome if we were to imagine holding constant some set of events that in fact occurred (and that, in reality, might not have been constant if the actual cause had not in fact occurred).

Let us now apply these three conditions to the Suzy and Billy example. Conditions 1 and 3 are easily satisfied, since Suzy *did* throw and the bottle *did* break (Condition 1), and "Suzy threw" has no strict subsets (Condition 3).

Condition 2 is met if Suzy's throw made a difference, counterfactually speaking – with the important caveat that, in determining this, we are permitted to condition on (to fix in the counterfactual comparison) any event or set of events that actually happened (or on none at all). To see why Condition 2 is satisfied, we have to think of there being three steps in the process: (1) Suzy and Billy throw, (2) Suzy's or Billy's rock hits the bottle, and (3) the bottle breaks. In actuality, Billy's stone did not hit the bottle, so we are allowed to condition on that fact in determining whether Suzy's throw was a counterfactual cause (even though we know that Billy's stone *would* have hit if Suzy's hadn't). Conditional on Billy's stone not hitting, the bottle would *not* have broken had Suzy not thrown.

From the perspective of counterfactual causation, it may seem odd to condition on Billy's stone not hitting the bottle when thinking about Suzy not throwing the stone – since Suzy's throwing the stone was the very thing that prevented Billy's from hitting the bottle. It feels close to conditioning on the bottle not being broken. Yet Halpern argues that this is an acceptable thought experiment for establishing the importance of Suzy's throw since conditioning is constrained to the actual facts of the case. Moreover, the same logic shows why Billy is not an actual cause. The reason is that Billy's throw is only a cause in those conditions in which Suzy did not hit the bottle. But because Suzy *did* actually hit the bottle, we are not permitted to condition on Suzy not hitting the bottle in determining actual causation. We thus cannot – even through conditioning on actually occurring events – construct any counterfactual comparison in which Billy's throw is a counterfactual cause of the bottle's breaking.

The striking result here is that there can be grounds to claim that a condition was the actual cause of an outcome even though, under the counterfactual definition, the effect of that condition on the outcome is 0. (At the same time, all counterfactual causes are automatically actual causes; they meet Condition 2 by conditioning on nothing at all, an empty set $\mathcal{W}$.) One immediate methodological implication follows: Since actual causes need not be causes, there are risks in research designs that seek to understand causal effects by tracing back actual causes – that is, the way things actually happened. If we traced back from the breaking of the bottle, we might be tempted to identify Suzy's throw as the cause of the outcome. We would be right only in an actual-causal sense, but wrong in the standard, counterfactual causal sense. Chains of events that appear to "generate" an outcome are not always causes in the counterfactual sense.[5]

As with other causal queries, the question "Was $X = x$ the actual cause of $Y = y$?" can be redefined as a question about which combinations of nodal types produce conditions under which X could have made a difference. To see how, let us run through the Billy and Suzy example again, but formally in terms of a model. Consider Figure 4.6, where we represent Suzy's throw (S), Billy's throw (B), Suzy's rock hitting the bottle (H^S), Billy's rock hitting the bottle (H^B), and the bottle cracking (C). Each endogenous variable has a θ term associated with it, capturing its nodal type. We capture the possible "preemption" effect with the arrow pointing from H^S to H^B, allowing whether Suzy's rock hits to affect whether Billy's rock hits.[6]

---

[5] Perhaps more surprising, it is possible that the expected causal effect is negative, but that X is an actual cause in expectation. For instance, suppose that 10% of the time Suzy's shot intercepts Billy's shot but without hitting the bottle. In that case, the average causal effect of Suzy's throw on bottle breaking is -0.1, yet 90% of the time Suzy's throw is an actual cause of bottle breaking (and 10% of the time it is an actual cause of non-breaking). For related discussions, see Menzies (1989).

[6] We do not need an arrow in the other direction because Suzy throws first.

A DAG capturing an actual cause

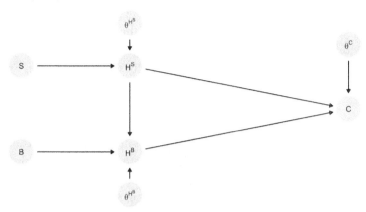

Figure 4.6   A causal model that allows preemption

For Suzy's throw to be an actual cause of the bottle's cracking, we need first to establish that Suzy threw ($\theta^S = \theta_1^S$) and that the bottle cracked ($C = 1$) (Condition 1). Condition 3 is automatically satisfied in that $\theta^S = \theta_1^S$ has no strict subsets. Turning now to Condition 2, we need Suzy's throw to be a counterfactual cause of the bottle cracking if we condition on the value of some set of nodes remaining fixed at the values they in fact took on. As discussed above, we know that we can meet this criterion if we condition on Billy's throw not hitting. To make this work, we need to ensure, first, that Suzy's throw hits if and only if she throws; so $\theta^{H^S} = \theta_{01}^{H^S}$. Next, we need to ensure that Billy's throw does not hit whenever Suzy's does: This corresponds to any of the four nodal types for H^B that take the form $\theta_{xx00}^{H^B}$. Those last two zeroes in the subscript mean simply that $H^B = 0$ whenever $H^S = 1$. Note that the effect of Billy throwing on Billy hitting when Suzy has *not* thrown – the first two terms in the nodal-type's subscript – does not matter since we have already assumed that Suzy does indeed throw.

Finally, we need θ^C to take on a value such that H^S has a positive effect on C when $H^B = 0$ (Billy doesn't hit) since this is the actual circumstance on which we will be conditioning. This is satisfied by any of the four nodal types of the form θ_{0x1x}^C. This includes, for instance, a θ^C value in which Billy's hitting has no effect on the bottle (perhaps Billy doesn't throw hard enough): for example, θ_{0011}^C. Here, Suzy's throw is a counterfactual cause of the bottle's cracking. And, as we have said, all counterfactual causes are actual causes.

They are, simply, counterfactual causes when we hold *nothing* fixed (W in Condition 2 is just the empty set).

Notably, we do not need to specify the nodal type for B: Given the other nodal types identified, Suzy's throw will be the actual cause regardless of whether or not Billy throws. If Billy does not throw, then Suzy's throw is a simple counterfactual cause (given the other nodal types).

The larger point is that actual cause queries can, like all other causal queries, be defined as questions about the values of nodes in a causal model. When we pose the query, "Was Suzy's throw an actual cause of the bottle cracking?," we are in effect asking whether the case's combination of nodal types (or its causal type) matches $\theta_1^S, \theta_x^B, \theta_{xx00}^{H^B}, \theta_{01}^{H^S}, \theta_{0x1x}^C$.

Likewise, if we want to ask *how often* Suzy's throw is an actual cause, in a population of throwing rounds, we can address this query as a question about the joint *distribution* of nodal types. We are then asking how common the qualifying combinations of nodal types are in the population given the distribution of types at each node.

Actual causes are conceptually useful whenever there are two sufficient causes for an outcome, but one preempts the operation of the other. For instance, we might posit that both the United States' development of the atomic bomb was a sufficient condition for US victory over Japan in World War II, and that US conventional military superiority was also a sufficient condition and would have operated via a land invasion of Japan. Neither condition was a counterfactual cause of the outcome because both were present. However, holding constant the *absence* of a land invasion, the atomic bomb was a difference-maker, rendering it an actual cause. The concept of actual cause thus helps capture the sense in which the atomic bomb distinctively contributed to the outcome, even if it was not a counterfactual cause.

An extended notion (Halpern, 2016, p. 81) of actual causes restricts the imagined counterfactual deviations to states that are more likely to arise (more "normal") than the factual state. We will call this notion a "notable cause." We can say that one cause, A, is "more notable" than another cause, B, if a deviation in A from its realized state is (believed to be) more likely than a deviation in B from its realized state.

For intuition, we might wonder why a Republican was elected to the presidency in a given election. In looking at some minimal winning coalition of states that voted Republican, we might distinguish between a set of states that *always* vote Republican and a set of states that usually go Democratic but voted Republican this time. If the coalition is minimal winning, then every state that voted Republican is a cause of the outcome in the standard (difference-making) sense. However, only the states that usually vote Democratic are notable causes since it is only for them that the counterfactual scenario (voting Democratic) was more likely to arise than the factual scenario. In a sense, we take the "red" states' votes for the Republican as given – placing them, as it were, in the causal background – and identify as "notable" those conditions that mattered and easily could have gone differently. By the same token, we can say that, among those states that voted Republican this time, those that more commonly vote Democratic are *more* notable causes than those that less commonly vote Democratic.

How notable a counterfactual cause is can be expressed as a claim about the distribution of a set of nodal types. For instance, if we observe $R_j = 1$ for state j (it voted Republican), then the notability of this vote directly increases with our belief about the probability that $\theta^{R_j} = \theta_0^{R_j}$ – that is, with the probability that the state's vote could have gone the other way. The higher the probability that a state could have voted Democratic, the more notable a cause we consider its voting Republican.

4.6.2 General Procedure for Mapping Queries to Causal Types

In the next parts of this appendix, we describe a *general* method for mapping from queries to causal types. In particular, we describe the algorithm used by the CausalQueries software package to define queries and a walk-through of how to use CausalQueries to identify the causal types associated with different queries.

The algorithm calculates the full set of outcomes on all nodes, given each possible causal type and a collection of controlled conditions ("do operations"). Then, each causal type is marked as satisfying the query or not. This in turn then tells us the *set* of types that satisfy a query. Quantitative queries, such as the probability of a query being satisfied, or the average treatment effect, can then be calculated by taking the measure of the set of causal types that satisfies the query.

First, some notation.

Let n denote the number of nodes. Label the nodes $V_1, \ldots, V_n$ subject to the requirement that each node's parents precede it in the ordering. Let pa_j denote the set of values of the parents of node j and let $V_j(pa_j, \theta_t)$ denote the value of node j given the values of its parents and the causal type θ_t.

The primitives of a query are questions about the values of outcomes, V, given some set of controlled operations x.

- Let $x = (x_1, \ldots, x_n)$ denote a set of do operations where each x_i takes on a value in $\{-1, 0, 1\}$. here -1 indicates "not controlled," 0 means set to 0 and 1 means set to 1 (this set can be expanded if V is not binary).
- Let $V(x, \theta_t)$ denote the values V (the full set of nodes) takes given θ_t.
- A "simple query" is a function $q(V(x, \theta_t))$ which returns TRUE if $V(x, \theta_t)$ satisfies some condition and FALSE otherwise.

Queries are summaries of simple queries. For instance, for nodes X and Y:

- Query Q_1: $\mathbb{1}(Y(X = 1) = 1))$ asks whether $Y = 1$ when X is set to 1. This requires evaluating one simple query.
- Query Q_2: $\mathbb{1}(Y(X = 1) = 1)\&\mathbb{1}(Y(X = 0) = 0))$ is composed of two simple queries: The first returns true if Y is 1 when X is set to 1, the second returns true if Y is 0 when X is set to 0; both conditions holding corresponds to a positive effect on a unit.
- Query Q_3: $E((\mathbb{1}(Y(X = 1) = 1)\&(Y(X = 0) = 0)) - (\mathbb{1}(Y(X = 1) = 0)\&\mathbb{1}(Y(X = 0) = 1))$ asks for the average treatment effect, represented here using four simple queries: the expected difference between positive and negative effects. This query involves weighting by the probability of the causal types.

Then, to calculate $V(x, \theta_t)$:

1. Calculate v_1, the realized value of the first node, V_1, given θ_t. This is given by $v_1 = x_1$ if $x_1 \neq -1$ and by $\theta_t^{V_1}$ otherwise.
2. For each $j \in 2 \ldots n$ calculate v_j using either $v_j = x_j$ if $x_j \neq -1$ and $V_j(pa_j, \theta_t)$ otherwise, where the values in pa_j are determined in the previous steps.

We now have the outcomes, V, for all nodes given the operations x and so can determine $q(V(x))$. From there, we can calculate summaries of simple queries across causal types.

A last note on conditional queries. Say, we are interested in an attribution query of the form: What is the probability that X causes Y in a case in which $X = 1$ and $Y = 1$? In this case, define simple query q_1 which assesses whether X causes Y for a given θ_t and simple query q_2 which assesses whether $X = 1$ and $Y = 1$ under θ_t. We then calculate the conditional query by conditioning on the set of θs for which q_2 is true and evaluating the share of these for which q_2 is true (weighting by the probability of the causal types).

4.6.3 Identifying Causal Types for Queries with `CausalQueries`

We first demonstrate how queries are calculated using the `CausalQueries` package for a chain model of the form $X \to M \to Y$ and then generalize.

Imagine first a chain model of this form in which we assume no negative effects of M on X or M on Y. We will also suppose that in fact $X = 1$, always. Doing this keeps the parameter space a little smaller for this demonstration but also serves to demonstrate that a causal model can make use of the counterfactual possibility that a node takes on a particular value even if it never does in fact.

We then ask two questions:

- Q1. What is the probability that X has a positive effect on Y? ("POS")
- Q2. What is the probability that $X = 1$ causes $Y = 1$ in cases in which $X = 1$ and $Y = 1$? ("POC")

To answer these two queries, we define a simple query q_1 which assesses whether X causes Y for each θ and a second simple query q_2 which assesses whether $X = 1$ and $Y = 1$ for each θ. In this example, the first simple query involves some do operations, the second does not.

Code to answering these two simple queries is shown below and the output is shown in Table 4.1 (one row for each causal type).

```
model <- make_model("X -> M -> Y") |>
         set_restrictions("X[]==0") |>
         set_restrictions("M[X=1] < M[X=0]") |>
         set_restrictions("Y[M=1] < Y[M=0]")


q1 <- "Y[X = 1] > Y[X = 0]"
q2 <- "X == 1 & Y == 1"


df <- data.frame(
  a1 = get_query_types(model, q1)$types,
  a2 = get_query_types(model, q2)$types,
  p  = get_type_prob(model))
```

The answer to the overall queries are then (1) the expected value of (the answers to) q_1 given weights p and (2) the expected value of (the answers to) q_1 given q_0 and weights p. See the next block of code for the implementation in `CausalQueries` and Table 4.2 for the results.

Table 4.1 Set of causal types in the model that satisfy q_1 and q_2 along with the probability of the type

Causal type	a1	a2	p
X1.M00.Y00	FALSE	FALSE	0.111
X1.M01.Y00	FALSE	FALSE	0.111
X1.M11.Y00	FALSE	FALSE	0.111
X1.M00.Y01	FALSE	FALSE	0.111
X1.M01.Y01	TRUE	TRUE	0.111
X1.M11.Y01	FALSE	TRUE	0.111
X1.M00.Y11	FALSE	TRUE	0.111
X1.M01.Y11	FALSE	TRUE	0.111
X1.M11.Y11	FALSE	TRUE	0.111

Table 4.2

Calculated answers to two queries

POS	POC
0.111	0.2

```
df |> summarize(
  POS = weighted.mean(a1, p),
  POC = weighted.mean(a1[a2], p[a2])
)
```

Given the equal weighting on causal types, these answers reflect the fact that for five of nine causal types, we expect to see $X = 1$ and $Y = 1$ but that the causal effect is present for only one of nine causal types and for one of the five causal types that exhibit $X = 1$ and $Y = 1$.

In practice, querying is done in one step. Like this for an unconditional query:

```
# POS
query_model(model, query = "Y[X = 1] > Y[X = 0]")
```

And like this for a conditional query:

```
# POC
query_model(model, query = "Y[X = 1] > Y[X = 0]",
            given = "X == 1 & Y == 1")
```

Table 4.3 Examples of queries and corresponding causal types. The probability of the query is the probability of the causal types that imply the theory

Model	Query	Given	Interpretation	Types
X -> Y	Y[X=1] > Y[X=0]		Probability that X has a positive effect on Y	X0.Y01, X1.Y01
X -> Y	Y[X=1] < Y[X=0]	X == 1	Probability that X has a negative effect on Y among those for whom X = 1	X1.Y10
X -> Y	Y[X=1] > Y[X=0]	X==1 & Y==1	Probability that Y = 1 is due to X = 1 (Attribution)	X1.Y01
X -> Y <- W	Y[X=1] > Y[X=0]	W == 1	Probability that X has a positive effect on Y for a case in which W = 1 (where W is possibly defined post treatment)	W1.X0.Y0001, W1.X1.Y0001, W1.X0.Y1001, W1.X1.Y1001, W1.X0.Y0011, W1.X1.Y0011, W1.X0.Y1011, W1.X1.Y1011
X -> Y <- W	Y[X=1, W=1] > Y[X=0, W=1]	W==0	Probability that X has a positive effect on Y if W were set to 1 for cases for which in fact W = 0	W0.X0.Y0001, W0.X1.Y0001, W0.X0.Y1001, W0.X1.Y1001, W0.X0.Y0011, W0.X1.Y0011, W0.X0.Y1011, W0.X1.Y1011
X -> Y <- W	Y[X=1] > Y[X=0]	Y[W=1] > Y[W=0]	Probability that X has a positive effect on Y for a case in which W has a positive effect on Y	W0.X0.Y0110, W1.X1.Y0001, W1.X1.Y1001, W0.X0.Y0111
X -> Y <- W	(Y[X=1, W=1] > Y[X=0, W=1]) > (Y[X=1, W=0] > Y[X=0, W=0])	W==1 & X==1	Probability of a positive interaction between W and X for Y; the probability that the effect of X on Y is stronger when W is larger	W1.X1.Y0001, W1.X1.Y1001, W1.X1.Y1011

Table 4.3 (cont.)

Model	Query	Given	Interpretation	Types
X -> M -> Y <- X	Y[X=1, M=M[X=1]] > Y[X=0, M=M[X=1]]	X==1 & M==1 & Y==1	The probability X would have a positive effect on Y if M were controlled to be at the level it would take if X were 1 for units for which in fact M==1	X1.M01.Y0001, X1.M11.Y0001, X1.M01.Y1001, X1.M11.Y1001, X1.M01.Y0101, X1.M11.Y0101, X1.M01.Y1101, X1.M11.Y1101
X -> M -> Y <- X	(Y[M=1] > Y[M=0]) & (M[X=1] > M[X=0])	Y[X=1] > Y[X=0] & M==1	The probability that X causes M and M causes Y among units for which M = 1 and X causes Y	X1.M01.Y0001, X1.M01.Y0011

Table 4.4 Coefficients on causal types for an interaction query

Coefficient	Causal types
−2	W1.X1.Y0110
−1	W1.X1.Y0100, W1.X1.Y0010, W1.X1.Y1110, W1.X1.Y0111
0	W1.X1.Y0000, W1.X1.Y1100, W1.X1.Y1010, W1.X1.Y0101,
	W1.X1.Y0011, W1.X1.Y1111
1	W1.X1.Y1000, W1.X1.Y0001, W1.X1.Y1101, W1.X1.Y1011
2	W1.X1.Y1001

The same procedure can be used to identify any set of types that correspond to a particular query. Table 4.3 illustrates the procedure, showing the syntax for model definition and queries along with the syntax for identifying implied types using get_query_types.

All of these queries correspond to the probability of some set of types. We might call these simple queries. Other complex queries (including the average treatment effect) can be thought of as operations on the simple queries.

For instance:

- the average treatment effect, Y[X=1] - Y[X=0] is the difference between the simple queries Y[X=1] > Y[X=0] and Y[X=1] < Y[X=0], or more simply the difference between the queries Y[X=1]==1 and Y[X=0]==1;
- the interaction query Q = (Y[X = 1, W = 1] - Y[X = 0, W = 1]) - (Y[X = 1, W = 0] -Y[X = 0, W = 0]) is similarly a combination of the simple queries (Y[X = 1, W = 1] ==1, Y[X = 0, W = 1]==1, Y[X = 1, W = 0]==1, and Y[X = 0, W = 0]==1).

For linear complex queries like this, we can proceed by identifying a set of positive or negative coefficients for each causal type that can be used to combine the probabilities of the types.

For instance, for the interaction query, Q, get_query_types(model, Q) would identify a set of positive or negative coefficients for each causal type that range from −2 to 2, with a 2, for instance corresponding to a type for which a change in W changes the effect of X from −1 to 1. See Table 4.4 for coefficients on types when $X = 1$ and $W = 1$.

5   Bayesian Answers

In this chapter, we outline the logic of Bayesian updating and show how it is used for answering causal queries. We illustrate with applications to correlational and process tracing analyses.

Bayesian methods are sets of procedures that allow us to figure out how to update beliefs in light of new information.

We begin with a prior belief about the probability that a hypothesis is true. New data then allow us to form a posterior belief about the probability of that hypothesis. Bayesian inference takes into account three considerations: the consistency of the evidence with a hypothesis, the uniqueness of the evidence to that hypothesis, and background knowledge that we have about the hypothesis.

In the next section, we review the basic logic of Bayesian updating. The following section applies that logic to the problem of updating on causal queries given a causal model and data. The last section discusses principles of learning that follow from the use of Bayesian updating.

5.1 Bayes Basics

For simple problems, Bayesian inference accords well with common intuitions about the interpretation of evidence. Once problems get slightly more complex, however, our intuitions often fail us.

5.1.1 Simple Instances

Suppose I draw a card from a deck. The chance that it is a Jack of Spades is just 1 in 52. However, suppose that I first tell you that the card is indeed a spade and then ask you what the chances are that it is a Jack of Spades. In this situation, you should guess 1 in 13. If I said it was a face card and a spade, on the other hand, you should say 1 in 3. But if I told you that the card was a heart, you should respond that there is no chance that it is a Jack of Spades.

All of these answers involve applications of Bayes' rule in a simple setup. In each case, the answer is derived by, first, assessing what is *possible*, given the available information, and then assessing how likely the outcome of interest is among those states of the world that are possible. We want to know the likelihood that a card is the Jack of Spades in light of the evidence provided. We calculate this thus:[1]

$$\text{Prob (Jack of Spades} \mid \text{Info)} = \frac{\text{Is Jack of Spades Consistent with Info? (0 or 1)}}{\text{How many cards are consistent with Info?}}$$

The probability that a card is the Jack of Spades given the available information can be calculated as a function of whether or not a Jack of Spades is at all *possible* given the information and, if so, of how many other types of cards would also be consistent with this evidence. The probability of a Jack of Spades increases as the number of other cards consistent with the available evidence falls.

Now consider two slightly trickier examples (neither original to us).

Interpreting Your Test Results. Say that you take a diagnostic test to see whether you suffer from a disease that affects 1 in 100 people. The test is strong in the sense that, if you have the disease, it will yield a positive result with a 99% probability; and if you do not have the disease, then with a 99% probability, it will deliver a negative result. Now consider that the test result comes out positive. What are the chances you have the disease? Intuitively, it might seem that the answer is 99% – but that would be to mix up two different probabilities: the probability of a positive result if you have the disease (that's the 99%) with the probability you have the disease given a positive result (the quantity we are interested in). In fact, the probability you have the disease, given your positive result, is only 50%. You can think of that as the share of people that have the disease among all those that test positive.

The logic is most easily seen if you think through it using frequencies (see Hoffrage and Gigerenzer (1998) for this problem and ways to address it). If 10,000 people took the test, then 100 of these would have the disease (1 in 100), and 99 of these would test positive. At the same time, 9,900 people tested

---

[1] The vertical bar, |, in this equation should be read as "given that." Thus, $Pr(A|B)$ should be read as the probability that A is true or occurs given that B is true or occurs.

would *not* have the disease, yet 99 of these would also test positive (the 1% error rate). So 198 people in total would test positive, but only half of them are from the group that has the disease. The simple fact that the vast majority of people do not have the disease means that, even if the false positive rate is low, a substantial share of those testing positive are going to be people who do not have the disease.

As an equation this might be written:

$$\text{Probability Sick} \mid \text{Test} = \frac{\text{How many are sick and test positive?}}{\text{How many test positive overall?}}$$
$$= \frac{99}{99 + 99}$$

Two-Child Problem. Consider, last, an old puzzle described in Gardner (1961). *Mr Smith has two children, A and B. At least one of them is a boy. What are the chances they are both boys?* To be explicit about the puzzle, we will assume that the information that one child is a boy is given as a truthful answer to the question, "Is at least one of the children a boy?"

Assuming that there is a 50% probability that a given child is a boy, people often assume the answer is 50%. But surprisingly, the answer is 1 in 3. The reason is that the information provided rules out only the possibility that both children are girls. So the right answer is found by readjusting the probability that two children are boys based on this information. As in the Jack of Spades example, we consider all possible states of the world, ask which ones are possible given the available information, and then assess the probability of the outcome we are interested in relative to the other still-possible states. Once we have learned that A and B are not both girls, that leaves three other possibilities: A is a girl, B is a boy; A is a boy, B is a girl; A and B are both boys. Since these are equally likely outcomes, the last of these has a probability of 1 in 3. As an equation, we have:

$$\text{Probability both boys} \mid \text{Not both girls} = \frac{\text{Probability both boys}}{\text{Probability not both girls}}$$
$$= \frac{1 \text{ in } 4}{3 \text{ in } 4}$$

5.1.2 Bayes' Rule for Discrete Hypotheses

All of these examples make use of Bayes' rule, a simple and powerful formula for deriving updated beliefs from new data.

A simple version of the formula – really the definition of a conditional probability – is:

$$\Pr(H|d) = \frac{\Pr(H, d)}{\Pr(d)} \qquad (5.1)$$

where H represents a hypothesis, and d represents a particular realization of new data (e.g., a particular piece of evidence that we might observe).

The elaborated version, which we call Bayes' rule, can be written:

$$\Pr(H|d) = \frac{\Pr(d|H)\Pr(H)}{\Pr(d)} = \frac{\Pr(d|H)\Pr(H)}{\sum_{H'}(\Pr(d|H')\Pr(H'))} \qquad (5.2)$$

where the summation runs over an exhaustive and exclusive set of hypotheses.

What this formula gives us is a way to calculate our *posterior* belief $(\Pr(H|d))$: the degree of confidence that we should have in the hypothesis *after* seeing the new data.

Inspecting the first line of the formula, we can see that our posterior belief derives from three considerations.

First is the strength of our prior level of confidence in the hypothesis, $\Pr(H)$. All else equal, a hypothesis with a higher prior likelihood is going to end up having a higher posterior probability as well. The reason is that, the more probable our hypothesis is at the outset, the greater the chance that new data consistent with the hypothesis has *in fact* been generated by a state of the world implied by the hypothesis. The more prevalent an illness, the more likely that a positive test result has *in fact* come from an individual who has the illness.

Second is the likelihood $\Pr(d|H)$: How likely are we to have observed this *particular* pattern in the data if the hypothesis were true? We can think of the likelihood as akin to the "true positive" rate of a test. If a test for an illness has a true positive rate of 99%, this is the same as saying that there is a 0.99 probability of observing a positive result if the hypothesis (the person has the illness) is true.

Third is the unconditional probability of the data $\Pr(d)$, which appears in the denominator. This quantity asks: How likely are we to have observed this pattern of the data *at all*, – regardless of whether the hypothesis is true or false? If this data pattern is something we might expect to see even if the hypothesis is not true, then seeing this data pattern will not weigh strongly in favor of the hypothesis. If positive test results are quite common regardless of whether someone has the illness, then a positive test result should not shift our beliefs much in favor of thinking that the patient is ill.

One helpful way to think about these last two quantities is that they capture, respectively, how *consistent* the data are with our hypothesis and how *specific* the data are to our hypothesis (with specificity higher for *lower* values of $\Pr(d)$). We update more strongly in favor of our hypothesis the more consistent the data that we observe are with the hypothesis; but that updating is dampened the more consistent the data pattern is with alternative hypotheses.

As shown in the second line of Equation (5.2), $\Pr(d)$ can be usefully written as a weighted average over different ways (alternative hypotheses, H') in which the data could have come about. If we have three alternative hypotheses, for instance, we ask what the probability of the data pattern is under each hypothesis and then average across those probabilities, weighting each by the prior probability of its associated hypothesis.

Assessing $\Pr(d)$ requires putting prior probabilities on an exclusive and exhaustive set of hypotheses. However, it does not require a listing of all possible hypotheses, just some *exhaustive* collection of hypotheses (i.e., a set whose probability adds up to 1). For example, in a murder trial, we might need to assess the unconditional probability that the accused's fingerprints would be on the door. We can conceive of two mutually exclusive hypotheses that are collectively exhaustive of the possibilities: The accused is guilty, or they are not guilty. We can average across the probability of the accused's fingerprints being on the door under each of these two hypotheses, weighting by their prior probabilities. What we do *not* have to do is decompose the "not guilty" hypothesis into a set of hypotheses about who *else* might be guilty. As a procedure for assessing the probability of the evidence under the not-guilty hypothesis, it might be helpful to think through who else might have done it, but there is no logical problem with working with just the two hypotheses (guilty and not guilty) since they together capture all possible states of the world. In Section 5.2.1.2, we work through an example in which we can calculate the probability of data conditional on some effect *not* being present.

Also, while the hypotheses that enter the formula have to be mutually exclusive, that does not prevent us from drawing downstream inferences about hypotheses that are not mutually exclusive. For instance, we might use Bayes' rule to form posteriors over which one of four people is guilty: an elderly man, John; a young man, Billy; an older woman, Maria; or a young woman, Kathy. These are mutually exclusive hypotheses. However, we can then use the posterior on each of these hypotheses to update our beliefs about the probability that a man is guilty and about the probability that an elderly person is guilty. Our beliefs about whether the four individuals did it will have knock-on effects on our beliefs about whether an individual with their characteristics did it. The fact that "man" and "elderly" are not mutually exclusive in no way means that we cannot learn about both of these hypotheses from an underlying Bayesian calculation, as long as the hypotheses to which we apply Bayes' rule are themselves mutually exclusive.

5.1.3 Continuous Parameters, Vector-Valued Parameters

The basic Bayesian formula extends in a simple way to continuous variables. For example, suppose we are interested in the value of some variable, β. Rather than discrete hypotheses, we are now considering a set of possible values that this continuous variable might take on. So now our beliefs will take the form of a probability *distribution* over possible values of β: essentially, beliefs about which values of β are more (and how much more) likely than which other values of β. We will generally refer to a variable that we are seeking to learn about from the data as a "parameter."

We start with a *prior* probability distribution over the parameter of interest, β. Then, once we encounter new data, d, we calculate a *posterior* distribution over β as:

$$p(\beta|d) = \frac{p(d|\beta)p(\beta)}{\int_{\beta'} p(d|\beta')p(\beta')d\beta}.$$

Here, the likelihood, $p(d|\beta)$, is not a single probability but a function that maps each possible value of β to the probability of the observed data arising if that were the true value. The likelihood will thus take on a higher value for those values of β with which the data pattern is more consistent. Note also that we are using integration rather than summation in the denominator here because we are averaging across a continuous set of possible values of β, rather than a discrete set of hypotheses.

We can then take a further step and consider learning about *combinations* of beliefs about the world. Consider a vector θ that contains multiple parameters that we are uncertain about the value of, say, the levels of popular support for five different candidates. We want to learn from the data which combinations of parameter values – what level of support for candidate 1, for candidate 2, and so on – are most likely the true values. Just as for a single parameter, we can have a prior probability distribution over θ, reflecting our beliefs before seeing the data about which combinations of values are more or less likely. When we observe data (say, survey data about the performance of the five candidates in an election), we can then update to a set of posteriors beliefs over θ using:

$$p(\theta|d) = \frac{p(d|\theta)p(\theta)}{\int_{\theta'} p(d|\theta')p(\theta')d\theta}.$$

This equation is identical to the prior one, except that we are now forming and updating beliefs about the vector-valued parameter, θ. The likelihood now has to tell us the probability of different possible distributions of support that we could observe in the survey under different possible true levels of support for these candidates. Suppose, for instance, that we observe levels of support in the survey of $d = (12\%, 8\%, 20\%, 40\%, 20\%)$. The likelihood function might tell us that this is a distribution that we are highly likely to observe if the true distribution is, for instance, $\theta = (10\%, 10\%, 10\%, 50\%, 20\%)$ but very unlikely to observe if the true distribution is, for instance, $\theta = (30\%, 30\%, 10\%, 5\%, 25\%)$. More generally, the likelihood function will generate a likelihood of the observed survey data for *all* possible combinations of values in the θ vector. Our posterior beliefs will then shift from our prior toward that combination of values in θ under which the data that we have observed have the highest likelihood.

5.1.4 The Dirichlet Family

Bayes' rule requires the ability to express a prior distribution over possible states of the world. It does not require that the prior have any particular properties other than being a probability distribution. In practice, however, when dealing with continuous parameters, it can be helpful to use "off the shelf" distributions.

For the framework developed in this book, we will often be interested in forming beliefs and learning about the *share* of units that are of a particular type, such as the shares of units for which the nodal type for Y is $\theta_{01}^Y, \theta_{10}^Y, \theta_{00}^Y,$ or θ_{11}^Y. Formally, this kind of problem is quite similar to the example that we just discussed in which public support is distributed across a set of candidates, with each candidate having some underlying share of support. A distinctive feature of beliefs about shares is that they are constrained in a specific way: Whatever our belief about the shares of support held by different candidates might be, those shares must always add up to 1.

For this type of problem, we will make heavy use of "Dirichlet" distributions. The Dirichlet is a family of distributions that capture beliefs about shares, taking into account the logical constraint that shares must always sum to 1. We can use a Dirichlet distribution to express our best guess about the proportions of each type in a population, or the "expected" shares. We can also use a Dirichlet to express our *uncertainty* about those proportions.

To think about how uncertainty and learning from data operate with Dirichlet distributions, it is helpful to conceptualize a very simple question about shares. Suppose that members of a population fall within one of two groups, so we are trying to estimate just a single proportion: for example, the share of people in a population that voted (which also, of course, implies the share that did not). Our beliefs about this proportion can differ (or change) in two basic ways. For one thing, two people's "best guesses" about this quantity (their expected value) could differ. One person might believe, for instance, that the turnout rate was most likely 0.3 while a second person might believe it was most likely 0.5.

At the same time, levels of uncertainty can also differ. Imagine that two people have the *same* "best guess" about the share who voted, both believing that the turnout rate was most likely around 0.5. However, they differ in how certain they are about this claim. One individual might have no information about the question and thus believe that any turnout rate between 0 and 1 is equally likely: This implies an expected turnout rate of 0.5. The other person, in contrast, might have a great deal of information and thus be very confident that the number is 0.5.

For questions about how a population is divided into two groups – say, one in which an outcome occurs, and another in which the outcome does not occur – we can capture both the expected value of beliefs and their uncertainty by using a special case of the Dirichlet distribution known as the Beta distribution. Any such question is in fact, a question about a single proportion – the proportion in one of the groups (since the proportion in which the outcome did not occur is just one minus the proportion in which it did). The Beta is a distribution over the [0, 1] interval, the interval over which a single proportion can range. A given Beta distribution can be described by two parameters, known as α and β. In the case where both α and β are equal to 1, the distribution is uniform: All values for the proportion are considered equally likely. As α rises, large values for the proportion are seen as more likely; as β rises, lower outcomes are considered more likely. If both parameters rise proportionately, then our "best guess" about the proportion does not change, but the distribution becomes tighter, reflecting lower uncertainty.

An attractive feature of the Beta distribution is that Bayesian learning from new data can be easily described. Suppose one starts with a prior distribution Beta(α, β) over the share of cases with some outcome (e.g., the proportion of people who votes), and then one observes a positive case – an individual

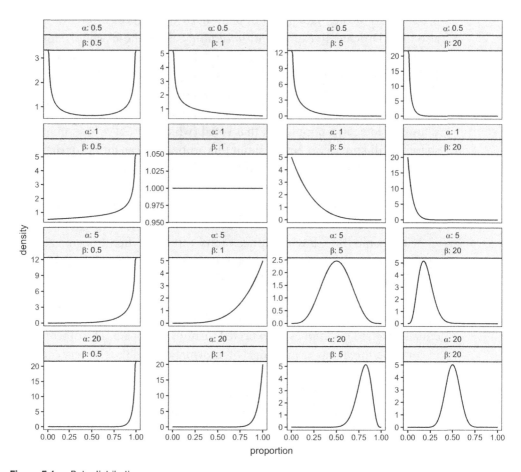

Figure 5.1   Beta distributions

who voted. The Bayesian posterior distribution is now a Beta with parameters $\alpha + 1, \beta$: the first parameter, relating to positive cases, literally just goes up by 1. More generally, if we observe n_1 new positive cases and n_0 new negative cases, our updated beliefs will have parameters $\alpha + n_1, \beta + n_0$. So if we start with uniform priors about population shares, and build up knowledge as we see outcomes, our posterior beliefs should be Beta distributions with updated parameters.

Figure 5.1 shows a set of Beta distributions described by different α and β values. In the top left, we start with a distribution that has even greater variance than the uniform, with alpha and beta both set to 0.5 (corresponding to the non-informative "Jeffrey's prior"). In each row, we keep α constant, reflecting observation of the same number of positive cases, but increase β

reflecting the kind of updating that would occur as we observe new negative cases. As we can see, the distribution tightens around 0 as β increases, reflecting both a reduction in our "best guess" of the proportion positive and mounting certainty about that low proportion. As we go down a column, we hold β constant but increase α, reflecting the observation of more positive cases; we see a rightward shift in the center of gravity of each distribution and increasing certainty about that higher proportion.

Note that we can think of proportions as probabilities, and we will often write somewhat interchangeably about the two concepts in this book. To say that the proportion of units in a population with a positive outcome is 0.3 is the same as saying that there is a 0.3 probability that a unit randomly drawn from the population will have a positive outcome. Likewise, to say that a coin lands on heads with 0.5 probability is the same as saying that we expect that 0.5 of all coin tosses will be heads.

The general form of the Dirichlet distribution covers situations in which there are beliefs not just over a single proportion or probability, but over collections of proportions or probabilities. For example, if four outcomes are possible and their shares in the population are $\theta_1, \theta_2, \theta_3$, and θ_4, then beliefs about these shares are distributions over all four-element vectors of numbers that add up to 1 (also known as a three-dimensional unit simplex).

The Dirichlet distribution always has as many parameters as there are outcomes, and these are traditionally recorded in a vector denoted α. Similar to the Beta distribution, an uninformative prior (Jeffrey's prior) has α parameters of $(.5, .5, .5, \ldots)$ and a uniform ("flat") distribution has $\alpha = (1, 1, 1, \ldots)$. As with the Beta distribution, all Dirichlets update in a simple way. If we have a Dirichlet prior over three types with parameter $\alpha = (\alpha_1, \alpha_2, \alpha_3)$ and we observe an outcome of type 1, for example, then the posterior distribution is also Dirichlet but now with parameter vector $\alpha' = (\alpha_1 + 1, \alpha_2, \alpha_3)$.

5.1.5 Moments: Mean and Variance

In what follows, we often refer to the "posterior mean" or the "posterior variance." These are simply summary statistics of the posterior distribution, or moments, and can be calculated easily once the posterior distribution is known (or approximated, see below) given data d.

The posterior mean, for instance for θ_1 – a component of θ – is $\int \theta_1 p(\theta|d)d\theta$. Similarly, the posterior variance is $\int (\theta_1 - (\bar{\theta}_1|d))^2 p(\theta|d)d\theta$. In the same way we we can imagine a query that is a function of multiple parameters, for instance $q(\theta) = \theta_3 - \theta_2$ and calculate the expected value of q using $\hat{q}(d) = \int q(\theta) p(\theta|d) d\theta$ and the variance as $V(q|d) = \int (q(\theta) - \hat{q}(d))^2 p(\theta|d) d\theta$.

Note that we calculate these quantities using the posterior distribution over the full parameter vector, θ. To put the point more intuitively, the most likely value of θ_1 will depend on which values of other parameters are most common and on which values of θ_1 are most likely in combination with the most common values of those other parameters. This is a point that particularly matters when the parameters of interest are dependent on each other in some way: For instance, if we are interested both in voter turnout and in the share of the vote that goes to a Democrat, and we think that these two phenomena are correlated with each other.

5.1.6 Learning

Bayesian updating is all about learning. We can see right away from Equation (5.2) whether we *learned* anything from data d. The simplest notion of learning is that our beliefs after seeing d are different than they were before we saw d. That is $\Pr(H|d) \neq \Pr(H)$. Or using Equation (5.2), we have learned something if:

$$\frac{\Pr(d|H)\Pr(H)}{\sum_{H'}(\Pr(d|H')\Pr(H'))} \neq \Pr(H). \tag{5.3}$$

So long as $\Pr(H) \in (0, 1)$, this can be written as:

$$\Pr(d|H) \neq \sum_{H' \neq H} \frac{\Pr(H')}{1 - \Pr(H)} \Pr(d|H')). \tag{5.4}$$

which simply means that the probability of d under the hypothesis is not the same as the probability of d averaged across all other hypotheses.

Two notions are useful for describing how much one can learn or is likely to learn from data: the probative value of data and the expected learning from data. We describe both here and pick up both ideas in later sections.[2]

To consider the simplest scenario, suppose there are two mutually exclusive and exhaustive hypotheses, H_0 and H_1 and that we place a prior probability

---

[2] In a footnote in Humphreys and Jacobs (2015), we describe a notion of probative value that made use of expected learning. We think, however, that it is better to keep these notions separate to avoid confusion and so adopt the definition used by Kaye (1986) and Fairfield and Charman (2017). As a practical matter, however, that work used the same concept of expected learning as presented here and varied probative value by varying the ϕ quantities directly.

of p on H_1. Imagine that the available evidence can take on two values, $K = 0$ or $K = 1$. Likelihoods are described by ϕ_0 and ϕ_1, where ϕ_0 denotes the probability $K = 1$ under H_0 and ϕ_1 denotes the probability $K = 1$ under H_1. Equation (5.2) then becomes:

$$\Pr(H_1|K = 1) = \frac{\phi_1 p}{\phi_1 p + \phi_0(1 - p)} \tag{5.5}$$

and the condition for learning (Equation 5.4) reduces to $\phi_1 \neq \phi_0$, so long as $p \in (0, 1)$.

More generally, the informativeness of evidence depends on how different ϕ_1 and ϕ_0 are from each other: how different the likelihood of seeing that evidence is under the two hypotheses. How best to measure that difference? There are many possibilities (see Kaye (1986) for a review), but a compelling approach is to use the log of the ratio of the likelihoods. This is a simple and elegant measure that corresponds to what Good (1950) proposes in multiple contributions, a measure of the "weight of evidence." Kaye (1986) refers to this as the most common measure of "probative value." Fairfield and Charman (2017) also use this measure, highlighting how it provides a useful way of characterizing the impact of, and of analyzing, evidence.

Definition 5.1. Probative value

Suppose that, if a hypothesis H is true, a clue K is observed with probability ϕ_1 (and otherwise is not observed). The probability that the clue is observed if the hypothesis is not true is denoted as ϕ_0. Let p refer to the prior that the hypothesis is true.

Then, the "probative value" of an observed clue K for H is:

$$\text{Probative value} := \log\left(\frac{\phi_1}{\phi_0}\right)$$

Some features of this measure of probative value are worth noting.

First, perhaps not immediately obvious, this notion of probative value should be thought of with respect to the *realized* value of the clue, not the possible data that might have been found. That is, it is about the data you have, not the data you might have. Thus, a clue (if found to be present) might have weak probative value if the clue is found, but strong probative value if it is *not* found. To illustrate, say $\phi_1 = \Pr(K = 1|H_1) = 0.999$ and $\phi_0 = \Pr(K = 1|H_0) = 0.333$. The probative value of the found clue is $\log(.999/.333) = 0.47$ – a piece of evidence "barely worth mentioning" according to Jeffreys (1998). Our beliefs will shift only a little toward H_1 if the clue is found. The *non*-appearance of the same clue, however, has strong probative value for H_0. In this case, probative value is $\log\left(\frac{\Pr(K=0|H_0)}{\Pr(K=0|H_1)}\right) = \log\left(\frac{1-\phi_0}{1-\phi_1}\right) = \log(.667/.001) = 2.82$ – "decisive" according to Jeffreys (1998).

An important implication here is that knowledge of the probative value of a clue, thus defined, is not necessarily a good guide to the *selection* of a clue to search for. When deciding on which evidence to go looking for, we do not know what we will find. Thus, knowing that the probative value of a clue is strong *if* we happen to find it – but that the clue's absence would be minimally informative – does not tell us whether it is worth expending resources looking for that clue.

Second, this measure of probative value makes no use of our priors on the hypotheses. In fact, Good's (1984) first desideratum of a measure of the weight of evidence is that it should be a function of ϕ_0 and ϕ_1 only. Kaye and Koehler (2003) also provide multiple arguments for the exclusion of information on priors from determinations of probative value. Yet, ignoring our prior confidence in the hypotheses when selecting clues to search for leaves us unable to tell whether we are setting ourselves up for a finding that is "decisive" or one that is "barely worth mentioning." If $K = 1$ constitutes strong evidence in favor of H_1 while $K = 0$ is weak evidence in favor of H_0, it may not be worth looking for the clue if we are highly confident *ex ante* that H_0 is right – since, under those beliefs, we are very unlikely to find $K = 1$, the evidence with high probative value.

Anticipating discussions in later chapters (especially Chapter 6 and the chapters in Part 3 of the book), we can think of a data strategy as a strategy that produces a probability distribution over the types of data that we might encounter. For instance, our data strategy might be to look for a particular clue K: So we then expect to find $K = 1$ with some probability and clue $K = 0$ with some probability. Our strategy might also be much more complex, involving random sampling of cases and a search for data in later stages conditional on what we find in earlier stages. Either way, our beliefs about what we are likely to find – and thus the value of a given data strategy – are shaped by our prior beliefs about the world.

In later analyses in this book, particularly when we turn to assessing research strategies, we use a measure of learning that takes prior confidence in the hypotheses fully into account: the expected reduction in uncertainty arising from a strategy. We can think of the expected reduction in uncertainty associated with a research strategy as the difference between the variance in our prior distribution on a query and the expected posterior variance on that query under the strategy. We can also (almost equivalently) conceptualize our uncertainty as "loss," or the (squared) errors arising from a strategy.[3] So then the expected gain from a research strategy can be thought of as the *reduction* in loss, or squared errors, that we expect to reap when we see new data (relative to the errors we make without the new data).

How can we assess expected reductions in loss under a research strategy? For any data strategy, D, we can imagine having seen different data patterns (d) that are *possible* under the strategy. We can then assess our beliefs about the errors we will likely make if we see and draw inferences from those possible data patterns. Finally, we can ask, prospectively, what errors we *expect* to make given our prior beliefs about the world and the kinds of data patterns that those beliefs imply we are most likely to observe.

Expected loss (equivalently, expected squared error or expected posterior variance) for query q and data strategy D can then be written:[4]

$$\mathcal{L}(q, D) = \mathbb{E}_\theta(\mathbb{E}_{d|\theta,D}(q(\theta) - \hat{q}(d))^2),$$

where $\hat{q}(d)$ is the expected value of the query after observing data d. To describe the *reduction in loss* that flows from strategy D, we need to calculate the loss metric a second time, this time using the prior distribution. Since our loss is defined as expected squared errors, this is simply the prior variance. We can then define the expected learning from a data strategy as follows.

Definition 5.2. Expected learning

Let $V(q) > 0$ denote prior variance on query q and $\mathcal{L}(q, D)$ the expected error on q from implementation of data strategy D. Then:

$$\text{Expected learning } (q, D) := 1 - \frac{\mathcal{L}(q, D)}{V(q)}$$

[3] We discuss the relationship between expected error and expected posterior variance more fully in Chapter 6.

[4] This quantity is given in Humphreys and Jacobs (2015; Equation 4). The idea behind this expression is that to assess loss, we need to specify our query q, which is itself a function of a set of underlying parameters, θ, that characterize the world. Suppose that θ correctly characterizes the world so that the true value of the query is $q(\theta)$. Then, the beliefs about the world in θ imply a probability distribution over the type of data we might see under a given data strategy. For any particular data realization d that we could potentially observe, we can derive an *estimate* of our query, $\hat{q}(d)$. We can then calculate the inaccuracy of that estimate relative to the truth, $q(\theta)$. We operationalize that inaccuracy, or loss, as a squared deviation, though any other metric could also be employed. We then calculate the expected loss over the different values of θ that we entertain – say, given a prior probability distribution over θ.

Note that expected learning ranges between 0 and 1. It is 1 when $\mathcal{L}(q, D) = 0$ – when we expect to end up with no uncertainty about the query after implementing the data strategy. And expected learning is 0 when $\mathcal{L}(q, D) = V(q)$ – when we expect no reduction in uncertainty.

Returning to our running illustration, suppose that if a hypothesis H_1 is true, then $K = 1$ is observed with probability ϕ_1 (and otherwise is not observed). If H_0 is true, then the clue is observed with probability ϕ_0. Let p denote the prior probability that H_1 is true. Then, the prior uncertainty is $V(H_1) = p(1 - p)$. The expected loss under the data strategy of looking for K is calculated by assessing (squared) errors in four situations – defined by whether H_1 or H_0 is true, and by whether or not we observe $K = 1$ when we go looking for it. We can use our priors and ϕ likelihoods to put a probability on each of these four situations, giving the expected loss as:

$$
\begin{aligned}
\mathcal{L} = p\phi_1 &\left(1 - \frac{\phi_1 p}{\phi_1 p + \phi_0(1 - p)} \right)^2 \\
&+ p(1 - \phi_1) \left(1 - \frac{(1 - \phi_1)p}{(1 - \phi_1)p + (1 - \phi_0)(1 - p)} \right)^2 \\
&+ (1 - p)\phi_0 \left(0 - \frac{\phi_1 p}{\phi_1 p + \phi_0(1 - p)} \right)^2 \\
&+ (1 - p)(1 - \phi_0) \left(0 - \frac{(1 - \phi_1)p}{(1 - \phi_1)p + (1 - \phi_0)(1 - p)} \right)^2.
\end{aligned} \tag{5.6}
$$

Putting these together (and simplifying), expected learning would then be:

$$
\text{Expected learning} = \frac{(\phi_1 - \phi_0)^2 p(1 - p)}{\phi_0(1 - \phi_0) - (\phi_1 - \phi_0)^2 p^2 - (\phi_1 - \phi_0)p(2\phi_0 - 1)}.
$$

This expression takes still simpler forms in special situations. For instance, in the situation in which $p = 0.5$ we have:

$$
\text{Expected learning} = \frac{(\phi_1 - \phi_0)^2}{2(\phi_1 + \phi_0) - (\phi_1 + \phi_0)^2}.
$$

Notably, this expression has some commonalities with probative value. Expected learning – like probative value – is clearly 0 when $\phi_1 = \phi_0$ – that is, when a clue is just as likely under an alternative hypothesis as under a given hypothesis (as we saw above already). In addition, expected learning is bounded by 0 and 1, and is largest when the probative value is greatest – when $\phi_1 = 1$ and $\phi_0 = 0$ (or vice versa).

But there nevertheless are disagreements. Compare, for instance, two clues we could go looking for, K_1 and K_2. For K_1, suppose that we have ($\phi_1 = 0.99$, $\phi_0 = 0.01$), while for K_2, we have ($\phi_1 = 0.099$, $\phi_0 = 0.001$). The probative value measure does not distinguish between these two clues: The probative value of finding the two clues is the same. However, with p=0.5, the Expected learning from searching for the two clues is very different: Expected learning from a search for K_1 is very large (an expected 95% reduction in variance), but expected learning for K_2 is small (5% reduction). This is because we do not *expect* to observe K_2 when we look for it, and we learn little if it is sought but not found.

We can also have clues for which the expected learning is the same but the probative value of a clue found differs greatly: For instance, still with $p = 0.5$, if we have K_3 with ($\phi_1 = 0.9$, $\phi_0 = 0.5$) and K_4 with ($\phi_1 = 0.5$, $\phi_0 = 0.1$).

A nice feature of the expected learning measure is that the concept generalizes easily to more complex research situations – for instance, to situations in which the decision to search for one clue depends on what we find when we search for a prior clue. Moreover, variants of the measure can be produced for different loss functions that reflect researcher desiderata when embarking on a research project.

5.1.7 Bayes Estimation in Practice

Although the principle of Bayesian inference is quite simple, in practice generating posteriors for continuous parameters is computationally complex. With continuous parameters, there is an infinity of possible parameter values, and there will rarely be an analytic solution – a way of *calculating* the posterior distribution. Instead, researchers use some form of sampling from the parameter "space" to generate an *approximation* of the posterior distribution.

Imagine, for instance, that you were interested in forming a posterior belief about the share of U.S. voters intending to vote Democrat, given polling data. (This is not truly continuous, but it might as well be with large elections.)

One approach would be to coarsen the parameter space: We could calculate the probability of observing the polling data given a discrete set of possible values, for example, $\theta = 0, \theta = 0.1, \theta = 0.2, \ldots, \theta = 1$. We could then apply Bayes' rule to calculate a posterior probability for each of these possible true values. The downside of this approach, however, is that, for a decent level of precision, it becomes computationally expensive to carry out with large parameter spaces – and parameter spaces get large quickly. For instance, if we are interested in vote shares, we might find 0.4, 0.5, and 0.6 too coarse and want posteriors for 0.51 or even 0.505. The latter would require a separate Bayesian calculation for each of 200 parameter values. And if we had *two* parameters that we wanted to slice up each into 200 possible values, we would then have 40,000 parameter pairs to worry about. What's more, *most* of those calculations would not be very informative if the plausible values lie within some small (though possibly unknown) range – such as between 0.4 and 0.6.

An alternative approach is to use variants of Markov Chain Monte Carlo (MCMC) sampling. Under MCMC approaches, parameter vectors – possible combinations of values for the parameters of interest – are sampled, and their likelihood is evaluated. If a sampled parameter vector is found to have a high likelihood, then new parameter vectors *near* it are drawn with a high probability in the next round. Based on the likelihood associated with these new draws, additional draws are then made in turn. We are thus sampling more from the parts of the posterior distribution that are closer to the most probable values of the parameters of interest, and the result is a chain of draws that build up to approximate the posterior distribution. The output from these procedures is not a set of probabilities for every possible parameter vector but rather a set of draws of parameter vectors from the underlying (but not directly observed) posterior distribution.

Many algorithms have been developed to achieve these tasks efficiently. In all of our applications using the `CausalQueries` software package, we rely on the `stan` procedures, which use MCMC methods: specifically, the Hamiltonian Monte Carlo algorithm and the no-U-turn sampler. Details on these approaches are given in the Stan Reference Manual (Stan et al., 2020).

5.2 Bayes Applied

5.2.1 Simple Bayesian Process Tracing

Process tracing, in its most basic form, seeks to use within-case evidence to draw inferences about a case. We first outline the logic of Bayesian process tracing *without* explicit reference to a causal model, and then introduce how Bayesian process tracing can be underpinned by a causal model.

To begin without a model: Suppose we want to know whether X caused Y in a case, and we use data on a within-case "clue," K, to make an inference about that question. We refer to the within-case evidence gathered during process tracing as *clues* in order to underline their probabilistic relationship to the causal relationship of interest. Readers familiar with the framework in Collier et al. (2010) can usefully think of "clues" as akin to causal process observations, although we highlight that there is no requirement that the clues be generated by the causal process connecting X to Y.

As we will show, we can think of our question – did X taking on the value it did in this case cause Y to take on the value it did – as a question about the case's nodal type for Y. So, to make inferences, the analyst looks for clues that will be observed with some probability if the case is of a given type and that will *not* be observed with some probability if the case is *not* of that type.

It is relatively straightforward to express the logic of process tracing in Bayesian terms. As noted by others (e.g., Beach and Pedersen, 2013; Bennett, 2008; Rohlfing, 2012), there is an evident connection between the use of evidence in process tracing and Bayesian inference. See Fairfield and Charman (2017) for a detailed treatment of a Bayesian approach to qualitative research. As we have shown elsewhere, translating process tracing into Bayesian terms can also aid the integration of qualitative with quantitative causal inferences (Humphreys and Jacobs, 2015).

To illustrate, suppose we are interested in economic crisis as a possible cause of regime collapse. We already have X, Y data on one authoritarian regime: We know that it suffered an economic crisis ($X = 1$) and collapsed ($Y = 1$). We want to know what caused the collapse: Was it the economic crisis or something else? To make progress, we will try to draw inferences given a "clue." Beliefs about the probabilities of observing clues for cases with different causal effects derive from theories of, or evidence about, the causal process connecting X and Y. Suppose we theorize that the mechanism through which economic crisis generates collapse runs via diminished regime capacity to reward its supporters during an economic downturn. A possible clue to the operation of a causal effect, then, might be the observation of diminishing rents flowing to regime supporters shortly after the crisis. If we believe the theory – and using the a, b, c, d notation for types from Chapter 2 – then this is a clue that we might believe to be highly probable for cases of type b that have experienced economic crisis (those for which the crisis in fact caused the collapse) but of low probability for cases of type d that have experienced crisis (those for which the collapse occurred for other reasons).

To make use of Bayes' rule we need to:

1. define our parameters
2. provide prior beliefs about the parameters
3. define a likelihood function – indicating the probability of observing different data patterns given stipulated parameters
4. provide the "probability of the data" – this can be calculated from 2 and 3
5. plug these into Bayes' rule to calculate a posterior on the parameters.

We can then calculate the posterior on any quantity of interest that can be formed by combining or transforming these parameters.

We discuss each of these steps in turn. We start with the simplest situation where we want to assess whether X caused Y.

Parameters. The inferential challenge is to determine whether the regime collapsed *because* of the crisis (it is a b type) or whether it would have collapsed even without it (d type). We do so using further information from the case – one or more clues.

Let $\theta \in \{a, b, c, d\}$ refer to the type of an individual case. In this initial setup, our hypothesis consists simply of a belief about θ for the case under examination: Specifically, whether the case is a b type ($\theta = b$). The parameter of interest is the causal type, θ.

We first assume that we know the likelihood and then walk through *deriving* the likelihood from a causal model.

5.2.1.1 Known Priors and Known Likelihood

We imagine first that the priors and the likelihood can simply be supplied by the researcher.

Prior. We let p denote a prior degree of confidence assigned to the hypothesis ($p = Pr(H)$). This is, here, our prior belief that an authoritarian regime that has experienced an economic crisis is a b.

Likelihood. We use the variable K to register the outcome of the search for a clue, with $K = 1$ indicating that a specific clue is searched for and found, and $K = 0$ indicating that the clue is searched for and not found. The likelihood, $Pr(K = 1|H)$ is the probability of observing the clue, when we look for it in our case, if the hypothesis is true – that is, here, if the case is a b type. The key feature of a clue is that the probability of observing the clue is believed to depend on the case's causal type. In order to calculate the probability of the data, we will in fact, need two such probabilities: We let ϕ_b denote the probability of observing the clue for a case of b type ($Pr(K = 1|\theta = b)$), and ϕ_d the probability of observing the clue for a case of d type ($Pr(K = 1|\theta = d)$). The key idea in many accounts of process tracing is that the *differences* between these probabilities provide clues with probative value, that is, the ability to generate learning about causal types. The likelihood, $Pr(K = 1|H)$, is simply ϕ_b.

Probability of the data. This is the probability of observing the clue when we look for it in a case, *regardless* of its type, ($Pr(K = 1)$). More specifically, it is the probability of the clue in an $X = 1$ case with a positive outcome ($Y = 1$). As such a case can only be a b or a d type, this probability can be calculated simply from ϕ_b and ϕ_d, together with our prior beliefs about how likely an $X = 1$, $Y = 1$ case is to be a b or a d type.

This probability aligns (inversely) with Van Evera's (1994) concept of "uniqueness."

Inference. We can now apply Bayes' rule to describe the learning that results from process tracing. If we observe the clue when we look for it in the case, then our *posterior* belief in the hypothesis that the case is of type b is:

$$\Pr(\theta = b|K = 1, X = Y = 1) = \frac{\phi_b p}{\phi_b p + \phi_d(1 - p)}.$$

In this exposition, we did not use a causal model in a meaningful way – we simply needed the priors and the clue probabilities.

5.2.1.2 Process Tracing with a Model: Derived Priors, Derived Likelihood

A central claim of this book is that the priors and likelihoods that we use in Bayesian process tracing do not need to be treated as primitives or raw inputs into our analysis: They can themselves be justified by an underlying – "lower level" – *causal model*. When we ground process tracing in a causal model, we can transparently derive our priors and the likelihoods of the evidence from a set of explicitly stated substantive beliefs about how the world works. As we elaborate below, grounding process tracing in a model also helpfully imposes a kind of logical consistency on our priors and likelihoods as they all emerge from the same underlying belief set.

We elaborate this point in much greater detail later, but we illustrate at a high level how Bayesian updating from a causal model works. Imagine a world in which an X, Y relationship is completely mediated by K: So we have the structural causal model $X \to K \to Y$. Moreover, suppose, from prior observations of the conditional distribution of outcomes given their causes, we mobilize background knowledge that:

- $\Pr(K = 1|X = 0) = 0$, $\Pr(K = 1|X = 1) = 0.5$
- $\Pr(Y = 1|K = 0) = 0.5$, $\Pr(Y = 1|K = 1) = 1$.

This background knowledge is consistent with a world in which units are equally split between b and c types in the first step (which we will write as b^K, c^K), and units are equally split between b and d types in the second step (b^Y, d^Y). To see this, note that these probabilities are inconsistent with adverse

Table 5.1 Worksheet to figure out implied "priors" ($\Pr(\theta = b|X = 1, Y = 1)$) and posteriors ($\Pr(\theta = b|X = 1, Y = 1, K = 1)$) from a chain model for a case with $X = 1$, $Y = 1$, given prior probabilities on each of the nodal-type combinations (rows)

θ^K	θ^Y	θ	$K|X = 1$	$Y|X = 1$	$\theta = b|X = Y = 1$	$\theta = b|X = Y = K = 1$
b^K	b^Y	b	1	1	TRUE	TRUE
b^K	d^Y	d	1	1	FALSE	FALSE
c^K	b^Y	c	0	0	–	–
c^K	d^Y	d	0	1	FALSE	–

effects at each stage. The differences in means then correspond to the share of types with positive effects.

We can calculate the types for the X causes Y relationship (θ) by combining types for each step. For instance, if a unit is a (b^K, b^Y) then it has type $\theta = b$ overall. If it is d^Y in the final step, then it is a d overall and so on.

Assume that the case at hand is sampled from this world.

Then, we can *calculate* that the prior probability, p, that X caused Y given $X = Y = 1$ is $p = \frac{1}{3}$. Given $X = 1$, the observation of $Y = 1$ is consistent with b types at both stages, a situation that our background knowledge tells us arises with probability 0.25; or with a d type in the second stage, which arises with probability 0.5. The conditional probability that X caused Y in this case is, therefore, $0.25/0.75 = 1/3$.

We can also use Table 5.1 to figure out the priors – where, to be clear, we mean beliefs prior to observing K albeit posterior to observing X and Y. Here, we represent the four combinations of types at the two stages that are consistent with our background knowledge. We place a prior on each combination, also based on this background knowledge. If the $X \to K$ effect is a b type 50% of the time and a c type 50% of the time, while the $K \to Y$ stage is half b's and half d's, then we will have each combination a quarter of the time.

We can then calculate the probability that $K = 1$ for a treated b and d case respectively as $\phi_b = 1$ and $\phi_d = 0.5$. We can work this out as well from Table 5.1. For ϕ_b, the probability of $K = 1$ for a b type, we take the average value for $K|X = 1$ in the rows for which $\theta = b$ – which in this case is just the first row, where the value of $K|X = 1$ is 1. For ϕ_d, we take the average value of $K|X = 1$ in the rows for which $\theta = d$: $(1 + 0)/2 = 0.5$. Note that, when we average across possible states of the world, we weight each state by its prior probability (though this weighting falls away here since the priors are the same for each row).

Then, using Bayes' rule (Equation 5.2), we can calculate the updated belief via:

$$\Pr(\theta = b | K = 1, X = Y = 1) = \frac{1 \times \frac{1}{3}}{1 \times \frac{1}{3} + \frac{1}{2} \times \frac{2}{3}}.$$

$$= \frac{1}{2}$$

We can also read the answer by simply taking the average value of the last column of Table 5.1, which has entries only for those cases in which we have $X = 1$, $Y = 1$ and $K = 1$. Counting *TRUE* as 1 and *FALSE* as 0, we get an average of 0.5. Thus, upon observing the clue $K = 1$ in an $X = 1$, $Y = 1$ case, we shift our beliefs that $X = 1$ caused $Y = 1$ from a prior of $\frac{1}{3}$ to a posterior of $\frac{1}{2}$. In contrast, had we observed $K = 0$, our posterior would have been 0.

One thing that these calculations demonstrate is that, as a practical matter, we do not have to go through the process of calculating a likelihood to engage in Bayesian updating. If we can directly calculate $\Pr(H, d)$ and $\Pr(d)$, then we can make direct use of Equation (5.1) instead of Equation (5.2).

A few broader lessons for Bayesian process tracing are worth highlighting.

First, we see that we can draw both our priors on a hypothesis and the probative value of the evidence from the same causal model. A model-free approach to Bayesian process tracing might encourage us to think of our priors and the probative values of the evidence as independent quantities. We might be tempted to engage in thought experiments examining how inferences change as priors change (as we did, e.g., in the treatment in Humphreys and Jacobs, 2015), keeping probative value fixed. But such a thought experiment may entertain values of the relevant probabilities that cannot be jointly justified by any single plausible underlying belief about how the world works. A model forces a kind of epistemic consistency on the beliefs entering into process tracing. If we altered the model used in the above illustration – for example, if we had a stronger first stage and so a larger value for $\Pr(K = 1 | X = 0)$ – this would alter *both* our prior, p, and our calculations of ϕ_d.

Second, we see that, when we use a causal model, our priors and the probative value of evidence can, in principle, be justified by prior data. For instance, in this case, we show how the relevant probabilities can be derived from patterns emerging from a series of experiments (and a belief that the case at hand is not different from – "exchangeable with" – those in the experiment). We can thus place a lighter burden on subjective beliefs.

Third, contrary to some advice (e.g., Fairfield and Charman, 2017, Table 3) we can get by without a full specification of all alternative causes for $Y = 1$.

Thinking through alternative hypotheses may be a very useful exercise for assessing subjective beliefs, but as a general matter, it is not necessary and may not be helpful. Our background model and data give enough information to figure out the probability that $K = 1$ if X did not cause Y. To be clear, we do not here assume that other causes do not exist; rather, we simply are not required to engage with them to engage with inference.

Fourth, this basic procedure can be used for many different types of queries, background models, and clue types. Nothing here is tied to a focus on the treatment effects emanating from a single cause for a single unit when researchers have access to a single mediator clue. The generalization is worked through in Chapter 7, but the core logic is all in this example already.

5.2.1.3 Connection with Classical Qualitative Tests

The example we discussed in the last section was of a "hoop test," one of the four classical tests ("smoking gun," "hoop," "straw in the wind," and "doubly decisive") described by Van Evera (1997) and Collier (2011). Seeing the clue led to a modest boost in confidence in the hypothesis, while not seeing the clue fully disconfirmed the hypothesis. In Chapter 15, we show how all these tests can be derived from more fundamental causal models in the same way.

The hoop test in this example makes use of an extreme probability – a probability of 0 of not seeing a clue if a hypothesis is true. But the core logic of process-tracing tests does not depend on such extreme probabilities. Rather, the logic described here allows for a simple generalization of Van Evera's typology of tests by conceiving of the certainty and uniqueness of clues as lying along a continuum. In this sense, the four tests might be thought of as special cases – particular regions that lie on the boundaries of a "probative-value space."

To illustrate the idea, we represent the range of combinations of possible probabilities for ϕ_b and ϕ_d as a square in Figure 5.2 and mark the spaces inhabited by Van Evera's tests. As can be seen, the type of test involved depends on both the probative value of the clue for the proposition that the unit is a b type (monotonic in ϕ_b/ϕ_d) and the probative value of the absence of the clue for the proposition that the units is a d type (monotonic in $(1 - \phi_d)/(1 - \phi_b)$). A clue acts as a smoking gun for proposition "b" (the proposition that the case is a b type) if it is highly unlikely to be observed if proposition b is false, and more likely to be observed if the proposition is true (bottom left, above diagonal). A clue acts as a "hoop" test if it is highly likely to be found if b is true, even if it is still quite likely to be found if it is false.

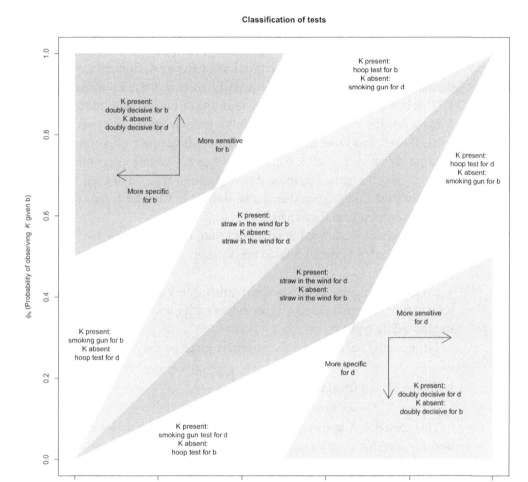

Figure 5.2   A mapping from the probability of observing a clue if the proposition that a case is a *b* type is true (ϕ_b) or false (ϕ_d) to a generalization of the tests described in Van Evera (1997)

Doubly decisive tests arise when a clue is very likely if *b* and very unlikely if not. It is, however, also easy to imagine clues with probative values lying in the large space between these extremes.[5]

---

[5] We thank Tasha Fairfield for discussions around this graph, which differs from that in Humphreys and Jacobs (2015) by placing tests more consistently on common rays (capturing ratios) originating from (0,0) and (1,1).

5.2.2 A Generalization: Bayesian Inference on Arbitrary Queries

In Chapter 4, we described queries of interest as queries over causal types.

Returning to our discussion of queries in Chapter 4, suppose we start with the model $X \rightarrow M \rightarrow Y$, and our query is whether X has a positive effect on Y. This is a query that is satisfied by four sets of causal types: those in which X has a positive effect on M and M has a positive effect on Y, with X being either 0 or 1; and those in which X has a negative effect on M and M has a negative effect on Y, with X being either 0 or 1. Our inferences on the query will thus involve gathering these different causal types, and their associated posterior probabilities, together. As we showed in Chapter 4, the same is true for very complex causal estimands.

Once queries are defined in terms of causal types, the formation of beliefs, given data d, about queries follows immediately from application of Equation (5.1).

Let $Q(q)$ define the set of types that satisfy query q, and let $D(d)$ denote the set of types that generate data d (recall that each causal type, if fully specified, implies a data type).

The updated beliefs about the query are given by the distribution:

$$p(q'|d) = \int_{Q(q')} p(\theta|d)d\theta = \frac{\int_{Q(q')\cap D(d)} p(\theta)d\theta}{\int_{D(d)} p(\theta')d\theta'}.$$

This expression gathers together all the causal types (combinations of nodal types) that satisfy a query and assesses how likely these are, collectively, given the data.[6]

Return now to Mr. Smith's puzzle from Section 5.1.1. We can think of the two "nodal types" here as the sexes of the two children, child A and child B. The query here is q: "Are both boys?" The statement "$q = 1$" is equivalent to the statement, "A is a boy & B is a boy." Thus, it takes the value $q = 1$ under just one causal type, when both nodes have been assigned to the value "boy." Statement $q = 0$ is the statement "'A is a boy & B is a girl' or 'A is a girl & B is a boy' or 'A is a girl & B is a girl'". Thus, $q = 0$ in three contexts. If we assume that each of the two children is equally likely to be a boy or a girl with independent probabilities, then each of the four contexts is equally likely. The result can then be figured out as $p(q = 1) = \frac{1 \times \frac{1}{4}}{1 \times \frac{1}{4} + 1 \times \frac{1}{4} + 1 \times \frac{1}{4} + 0 \times \frac{1}{4}} = \frac{1}{3}$. This answer requires summing over only one causal type. The quantity $p(q = 0)$ is

---

[6] For an abstract representation of the relations between assumptions, queries, data, and conclusions, see Figure 1 in Pearl (2012). For a treatment of the related idea of *abduction*, see Pearl (2009, p. 206).

of course, the complement of this, but using Bayes' formula, one can see that it can also be found by summing over the posterior probability of the three causal types for which the statement $q = 0$ is true.

5.3 Features of Bayesian Updating

Bayesian updating has implications that may not be obvious at first glance. These will matter for all forms of inference we examine in this book, but they can all be illustrated in simple settings.

5.3.1 Priors Matter

As we noted in the previous section, probative value does not depend upon priors. However, the amount of learning that results from a given piece of new data *can* depend strongly on prior beliefs. We have already seen this with the example of interpreting our test results above. Figure 5.3 illustrates the point for process tracing inferences.

In each subgraph of Figure 5.3 , we show how much learning occurs under different scenarios. The horizontal axis indicates the level of prior confidence in the hypothesis, and the curve indicates the posterior belief that arises if we do (or do not) observe the clue. We label the figures referencing classic tests that they approximate though, of course, there can be stronger or weaker versions of each of these tests.

As can be seen, the amount of learning that occurs – the shift in beliefs from prior to posterior – depends a good deal on what prior we start out with. For the smoking gun example (with probative value of just 0.9 – substantial, but not strong, according to Jeffreys (1998)), the amount of learning is highest for values around 0.25 – and then declines as we have more and more prior confidence in our hypothesis. For the hoop test (also with probative value of just 0.9), the amount of learning when the clue is *not* observed is greatest for hypotheses in which we have middling-high confidence (around 0.75), and minimal for hypotheses in which we have a very high or a very low level of confidence. At the maximum, beliefs change from 0.74 to 0.26 – a nearly two thirds down-weighting of the proposition.

The implication here is that our inferences with respect to a hypothesis must be based not just on the search for a clue predicted by the hypothesis but also on the *plausibility* of the hypothesis, based on other things we know.

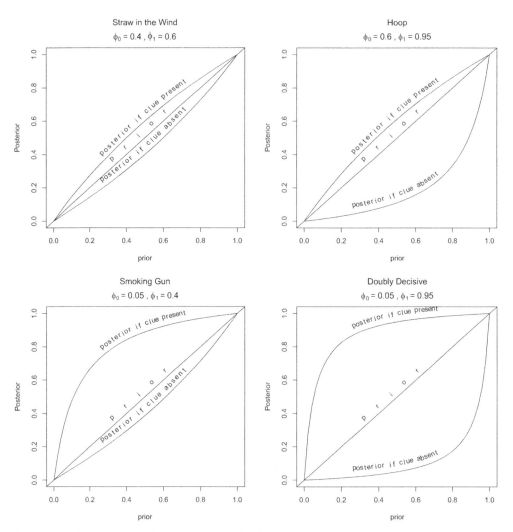

Figure 5.3 A smoking in which gun test with greatest impact on beliefs when priors are middling low and the clue is observed; a "hoop test" in which the greatest effects arise when priors are middling high and the clue is not observed

We emphasize two respects in which these implications depart from common intuitions.

First, we cannot make *general* statements about how decisive different categories of test, in Van Evera's framework, will be. It is commonly stated that hoop tests are devastating to a theory when they are failed, while smoking gun tests provide powerful evidence in favor of a hypothesis. But, in fact the amount learned depends not just on features of the clues but also on prior beliefs.

Second, although scholars frequently treat evidence that goes against the grain of the existing literature as especially enlightening, in the Bayesian framework the contribution of such evidence may sometimes be modest, precisely because received wisdom carries weight. Thus, although the discovery of *disconfirming* evidence – an observation thought to be strongly inconsistent with the hypothesis – for a hypothesis commonly believed to be true is more informative (has a larger impact on beliefs) than *confirming* evidence, this does not mean that we learn more than we would have if the prior were weaker. It is not true as a general proposition that we learn more the bigger the "surprise" a piece of evidence is. The effect of disconfirming evidence on a hypothesis about which we are highly confident can be *smaller* than it would be for a hypothesis about which we are only somewhat confident. When it comes to very strong hypotheses, the "discovery" of disconfirming evidence is very likely to be a false negative; likewise, the discovery of supporting evidence for a very implausible hypothesis is very likely to be a false positive. The Bayesian approach takes account of these features naturally.[7]

5.3.2 Simultaneous, Joint Updating

When we update, we often update over multiple quantities. When we see a smoking gun, for instance, we might update our beliefs that the butler did it, but we might also update our beliefs about how likely we are to see smoking guns – maybe they are not as rare as we thought.

Intuitively we might think of this updating as happening sequentially – first of all, we update over the general proposition, then we update over the particular claim. But in fact, it's simpler to update over both quantities at once. What we need to avoid is just updating over some of the unknown quantities while keeping others fixed.

As a simple illustration, say we thought there were a two-thirds chance that we were in World A in which K serves as a smoking gun test and a one-third chance that we were in world B in which K provides a hoop test. Specifically, we have:

World A:

- $\Pr(H = 0, K = 0|W = A) = \frac{1}{3}$
- $\Pr(H = 0, K = 1|W = A) = 0$

---

[7] We note, however, that one common intuition – that little is learned from disconfirming evidence on a low-plausibility hypothesis or from confirming evidence on a high-plausibility one – is correct.

- $\Pr(H = 1, K = 0 | W = A) = \frac{1}{3}$
- $\Pr(H = 1, K = 1 | W = A) = \frac{1}{3}$

World B:

- $\Pr(H = 0, K = 0 | W = B) = \frac{1}{3}$
- $\Pr(H = 0, K = 1 | W = B) = \frac{1}{3}$
- $\Pr(H = 1, K = 0 | W = B) = 0$
- $\Pr(H = 1, K = 1 | W = B) = \frac{1}{3}$

What should we infer when we see $K = 1$. If we knew we were in World A, then on learning $K = 1$ we would be sure that $H = 1$; whereas if we knew that we were in World B, then on learning K we would put the probability that $H = 1$ at 0.5. We might be tempted to infer that the expected probability that $H = 1$ is then $\frac{2}{3} \times 1 + \frac{1}{3} \times \frac{1}{2} = \frac{5}{6}$.

This is incorrect because when we observe $K = 1$, we need to update not just on our inferences *given* whatever world we are in, but also our beliefs *about* what world we are in. We might tackle the problem in three ways.

First, we might simplify. Integrating over worlds, the joint probabilities for H and K are:

Average World:

- $\Pr(H = 0, K = 0) = \frac{1}{3}$
- $\Pr(H = 0, K = 1) = \frac{1}{9}$
- $\Pr(H = 1, K = 0) = \frac{2}{9}$
- $\Pr(H = 1, K = 1) = \frac{1}{3}$

And from these numbers we can calculate the probability $H = 1$ given $K = 1$ as $\frac{\frac{1}{3}}{\frac{1}{3} + \frac{1}{9}} = \frac{3}{4}$.

This is the simplest approach. However, it gives no information about the learning over worlds. In practice, we might want to keep track of our beliefs about worlds. These might, for instance, be of theoretical interest and knowing which world we are in may be useful for the *next* case we look at.

So in approach 2 we update over the worlds and infer that we are in World A with probability $\frac{\frac{1}{3}\frac{2}{3}}{\frac{1}{3}\frac{2}{3} + \frac{1}{3}\frac{2}{3}} = \frac{1}{2}$. The numerator is the prior probability of being in World A times the probability of seeing $K = 1$ given we are in world A; the denominator is the probability of seeing $K = 1$. We can now do the correct calculation and infer probability $\frac{1}{2} \times 1 + \frac{1}{2} \times \frac{1}{2} = \frac{3}{4}$.

In a third approach, we imagine eight possible states and update directly over these eight states.

- $\Pr(H = 0, K = 0, W = A) = \frac{2}{9}$
- $\Pr(H = 0, K = 1, W = A) = 0$
- $\Pr(H = 1, K = 0, W = A) = \frac{2}{9}$
- $\Pr(H = 1, K = 1, W = A) = \frac{2}{9}$
- $\Pr(H = 0, K = 0, W = B) = \frac{1}{9}$
- $\Pr(H = 0, K = 1, W = B) = \frac{1}{9}$
- $\Pr(H = 1, K = 0, W = B) = 0$
- $\Pr(H = 1, K = 1, W = B) = \frac{1}{9}$

Then, applying Bayes' rule over these states yields the posterior probability: $\frac{\frac{2}{9}+\frac{1}{9}}{\frac{2}{9}+\frac{1}{9}+\frac{1}{9}} = \frac{3}{4}$. The numerator gathers the probability for all states in which $K = 1$ and $H = 1$, and the denominator gathers the probability for all states in which $K = 1$.

Thus, we have three ways to apply Bayes' rule in this simple setup.

More generally, we propose that researchers update over a causal model. As we explain later in this book, updating over a causal model allows us to learn across cases and levels of analysis: we can make inferences about the case at hand, about the population from which the case is drawn, and about other cases of interest, given data on those cases. In this example for instance, the inferences we would draw about future cases could be quite different if we believed W was the same for all units – and so our uncertainty represents what we might call "uncertainty about laws" – than if we believed that each unit was assigned W independently with a common probability – in which case we would think of the uncertainty as representing "uncertainty about units." Under the former belief, learning from one unit is informative for learning about another; under the second belief, it is not.

5.3.3 Posteriors Are Independent of the Ordering of Data

We often think of learning as a process in which we start off with some set of beliefs – our priors – we gather data, and update our beliefs, forming a posterior; we then observe new data, and we update again, forming a new posterior, having treated the previous posterior as a new prior. In such a scenario, it might seem natural that it would matter which data we saw first and which later.

In fact, however, Bayesian updating is blind to ordering. If we learn first that a card is a face card and second that it is black, our posteriors that the card is a Jack of Spades go from 1 in 52 to 1 in 12 to 1 in 6. If we learn first that the card is black and second that it is a face card, our posteriors that it is a Jack of Spades go from 1 in 52 to 1 in 26 to 1 in 6. We end up in the same place in both cases. And we would have had the same conclusion if we learned in one go that the card is a black face card.

The math here is easy enough. Our posterior given two sets of data D_1, D_2 can be written:

$$p(\theta|D_1, D_2) = \frac{p(\theta, D_1, D_2)}{p(D_1, D_2)} = \frac{p(\theta, D_1|D_2)p(D_2)}{p(D_1|D_2)p(D_2)} = \frac{p(\theta, D_1|D_2)}{p(D_1|D_2)}$$

or, equivalently:

$$p(\theta|D_1, D_2) = \frac{p(\theta, D_1, D_2)}{p(D_1, D_2)} = \frac{p(\theta, D_2|D_1)p(D_1)}{p(D_2|D_1)p(D_1)} = \frac{p(\theta, D_2|D_1)}{p(D_2|D_1)}.$$

In other words, our posteriors given both D_1 and D_2 can be thought of as the result of updating on D_2 given we already know D_1, or as the result of updating on D_1 given we already know D_2.

This fact will be useful in applications. Suppose that we are interested in X's effect on Y, starting with a flat prior. We might first encounter data on X and Y for a set of cases. Perhaps we subsequently observe additional data on (say) a moderator, K. It might seem natural to update once from the X, Y data and then a second time from the data on K. Rather than updating twice, however, the fact that updating is invariant to order means that we can start with a flat prior and update once with the data on X, Y, and K.

6 Theories as Causal Models

We embed the notion of a "theory" into the causal-models framework. We describe a conceptual hierarchy in which a theory is a "lower level" model that explains or justifies a "higher level" model. The approach has implications for the logical consistency of our inferences and for assessing when and how theory is useful for strengthening causal claims.

In Chapter 3, we described a set of theories and represented them as causal models. But so far we haven't been very explicit about what we mean by a theory or how theory maps onto a causal-model framework.

In this book, we will think of theory as a type of *explanation*: A theory provides an account of how or under what conditions a set of causal relationships operate. We generally express both a theory and the claims being theorized as causal models: A theory is a model that *implies* another model – possibly with the help of some data.

To fix ideas: a simple claim might be that "*A* caused *B* in case *j*." This claim is itself a model, albeit a very simple one. The theory that supports this model might, for instance, be of any of the following forms:

- "*A* always causes *B*"
- "*A* always causes *B* whenever *C*, and *C* holds in case *j*," or
- "*A* invariably causes *M* and *M* invariably causes *B*."

All of these theories have in common that they are arguments that could be provided to support the simple claim. In each case, if you believe the theory, you believe the implication.

We can also think about theoretical implications in probabilistic terms. Suppose that we start with a simple claim of the form "*A likely* caused *B* in case *j*." That probabilistic simple claim could follow from a theory that reflected uncertainty about causal processes, such as: "*A* usually causes *B*" or "*A* always causes *B* whenever *C*, and *C* probably holds in case *j*."[1]

The rest of this chapter builds out this logic and uses it to provide a way of characterizing when a theory is useful or not.

In the first section, we consider multiple senses in which one model might imply, and thus serve as a *theory of*, another model.

- First, we consider how one causal structure can imply (serve as a theory of) another causal structure, by including additional detail that explains how or when causal effects in the other model will unfold. If structural model *A* implies structural model *B*, then *A* is a theory of *B*.
- We then turn to logical relations between probabilistic models. We show how the distributions over nodal types in a simpler model structure can be underwritten by distributions over nodal types in a more detailed model structure. Here, a claim about the prevalence (or probability) of causal effects in a causal network is justified by claims about the prevalence or probability of causal effects in a more granular rendering of that causal network.
- Finally, we show how a probabilistic model plus *data* can provide a theoretical underpinning for a new, stronger model. The new model is again implied by another model, together with data.

In the second section, we consider how *models-as-theories-of* can be useful. In embedding theorization within the world of causal models, we ultimately have an empirical objective in mind. In our framework, theorizing a causal relationship of interest means elaborating our causal beliefs about the world in greater detail. As we show in later chapters, theorizing in the form of specifying underlying causal models allows us to generate research designs: to identify sources of inferential leverage and to explicitly and systematically link observations of components of a causal system to the causal questions we seek to answer. In this chapter, we point to ways in which the usefulness of theories can be assessed.

In the chapter's third and final section, we discuss the connection between the kinds of theories we focus on – what might be called empirical theories – and analytic theories of the kind developed for instance by formal theorists. Moving from one to the other requires a translation and we illustrate how

---

[1] The claim could also follow from a theory that reflected beliefs about heterogeneity of causal processes. For a review of rival approaches to scientific explanation, see Woodward (1973).

this might be done by showing how we can generate a causal model from a game-theoretic model.

6.1 Models as *Theories Of*

Let us say that a causal model, M', is a *theory of* M if M is implied by M'. It is a theory *because* it has implications. Otherwise, it is a conclusion, an inference, or a claim.

A theory, M', might itself sit atop – be supported by – another theory, M'', that implies M'. To help fix the idea of theory as "supporting" or "underlying" the model(s) it theorizes, we refer to the theory, M', as a *lower* level model relative to M and refer to M as a *higher* level model relative to its theorization, M'.[2]

Both structural models and probabilistic models – possibly in combination with data – imply other models.

6.1.1 Implications of Structural Causal Models

A structural model can imply multiple other simpler structural models. Similarly, a structural model can be implied *by* multiple more complex models.

Theorization often involves a refinement of causal types, implemented through the addition of nodes. Take the very simple model, M, represented in Figure 6.1a. The model simply states that X has (or *can* have) a causal effect on Y.

What theories might justify M? This question can be rephrased as "what models imply model M?" The figure points to two possibilities. Both models M' and M'' imply model M. They can be thought of as *theories*, or lower level models, of M.

Model M' differs from M by the addition of a node, K, in the causal chain between X and Y. We can say that M' is a *theory* of M for two reasons. First, it provides a *justification* – if you believe M' you should believe M. If X affects Y through K, then X affects Y. But as well as a justification, M' also provides an *explanation* of M. Suppose we already *know* that X affects Y but want to

---

[2] We note that our definition of theory differs somewhat from that given in Pearl (2009, p. 207): There a theory is a structural causal model and a restriction over the possible values of exogenous nodes but not a probability distribution over these nodes. Our definition also considers probabilistic models as theories, allowing statements such as "the average effect of X on Y in some domain is 0.5."

know *why*. If we ask, "Why does X affect Y?," M' provides an answer: X affects Y *because* X affects K, and K affects Y.

Model M'' differs from M by the addition of a node, C, that moderates the effect of X on Y. M'' justifies M in the sense that, if you believe M'', you should believe M. M'' provides an explanation of a kind also: If you believe model M'', then you likely believe that the relation between X and Y is what it is because of C's value. Had C been different, the causal relation between X and Y might have also been different.

Both of these models imply M but themselves constitute stronger – that is, more *specific* – claims about the world than does M. For instance, M' stipulates not only that X can affect Y but that such an effect *must* operate via K. For this reason, the two theories should be harder to accept than M – and so may themselves need to be defended, or theorized, by even lower level models.

Importantly, both M' and M'' involve a redefinition of θ^Y relative to model M. We see a change in the endogenous nodes as we go down a level (the addition of K or C) – and these changes, in turn, imply a change in the interpretation of the exogenous, θ nodes pointing into existing endogenous nodes (such as Y in this example).

As we move down a level, we can think of a part of θ^Y as being splintered off and captured by a new component of the more detailed model. Consider, for instance, the move from M down to M'. In moving from the higher to the lower level model, we have effectively *split* the nodal-type term θ^Y into two parts: $\theta^{Y_{lower}}$ and θ^K. Intuitively, in the higher level model, M, Y is a function of X and θ^Y, the latter representing all things other than X than can affect Y. Or, in the language of our nodal-type setup, θ^Y represents all of the (unspecified) sources of variation in X's effect on Y. When we insert K into the model, however, X now does not directly affect Y but only does so via K. Further, we model X as acting on K in a manner conditioned by θ^K; and θ^K represents all of the unspecified factors determining X's effect on K. The key thing to notice here is that θ^K now represents *a portion of the variance that θ^Y represented in the higher level graph*: Some of the variation in X's effect on Y now arises from variation in X's effect on K, which is captured by θ^K.

So, for instance, X might have no effect on Y because θ^K takes on the value θ^K_{00}, meaning that X has no effect on K. Put differently, any effect of X on Y must arise from an effect of X on K; so θ^K's value must be either θ^K_{01} or θ^K_{10} for X to affect Y.[3] What θ^K represents, then, is that part of the original θ^Y that

---

[3] As we emphasize further below, it is in fact only the random, unknown component of the $X \rightarrow K$ link that makes the addition of K potentially informative as a matter of research design: If K were a

arose from some force other than X operating at the *first* step of the causal chain from X to Y. So now θ^Y in the lower level graph is not quite the same entity as it was in the higher level graph. In the original graph, θ^Y represented *all* sources of variation in X's effect on Y. In the lower level model, with K as a mediator, θ^Y represents only the variation in K's effect on Y. In the move from model M down to model M', θ^Y has been expunged of any factors shaping the first stage of the causal process, which now reside in θ^K. We highlight this change in θ^Y's meaning by referring in the second model to $\theta^{Y_{lower}}$.

Consider next model M'' in Figure 6.1, which also supports (implies) the higher level model, M. The logical relationship between models M and M'', however, is somewhat different. Here, the lower level model *specifies* one of the conditions that determined the value of θ^Y in the higher level model. In specifying a moderator, C, we have extracted C from θ^Y, leaving $\theta^{Y_{lower}}$ to represent all factors *other than* C that condition Y's response to its parents. More precisely, $\theta^{Y_{lower}}$ now represents the set of nodal types defining how Y responds jointly to X and C. Again, the relabeling as $\theta^{Y_{lower}}$ reflects this change in the term's meaning. Whereas in Model M' we have extracted θ^K from θ^Y, in Model M'', it is C itself that we have extracted from θ^Y, specifying as a substantive variable what had been just a random disturbance.

6.1.2 Probabilistic Models Implied by Lower Level Probabilistic Models

We used Figure 6.1 to show how one structural model can be implied by another. In the same way, one *probabilistic* model can be implied by another. If a higher level probabilistic model is to be implied by a lower level probabilistic model, consistency requires that the probability distributions over exogenous nodes for the higher level model are those that are implied by the distributions over the exogenous nodes in the lower level model.

To illustrate, let us add a distribution over θ^K and θ^Y_{lower} to the structural model M' in Figure 6.1b. This gives us a probabilistic causal model. We will call this model M^p_{lower}. M^p_{lower}, in turn, implies a higher level probabilistic model, M^p_{higher}: M^p_{higher} is formed from the structure of Model (a) in Figure 6.1 together with a *particular* distribution over θ^Y. Specifically, θ^Y must have

---

deterministic function of X only, then knowledge of X would provide full knowledge of K, and nothing could be learned from observing K.

(a) A higher level model, M

(b) Lower level model, M': Disaggregating via mediation

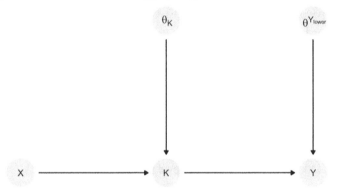

(c) Lower level model, M": Disaggregating via moderation

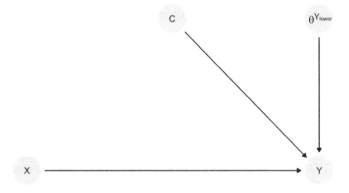

Figure 6.1 Two theories — lower level models — that explain a higher level model

the distribution that preserves the causal relations implied by the probabilistic beliefs in M^p_{lower}.

Recall that λ represents population-shares over causal types, and thus a probability distribution over θ. So for instance the probability that θ is θ^Y_{00} is simply λ^Y_{00}. So we have:

1. In M^p_{higher}, the probability that X has a positive effect on Y is λ^Y_{01}.
2. In M^p_{lower}, the probability that X has a positive effect on Y is $\lambda^{K_{\text{lower}}}_{01} \lambda^{Y_{\text{lower}}}_{01} + \lambda^{K_{\text{lower}}}_{10} \lambda^{Y_{\text{lower}}}_{10}$. That is, it is the probability that we have a chain of linked positive effects plus the probability that we have a chain of linked negative effects – the two ways in which we can get a positive total effect of X on Y in this model.

Consistency then requires a particular equality between the distributions (λs) at the two levels. Specifically, it requires that $\lambda^{Y_{\text{higher}}}_{01} = \lambda^{M_{\text{lower}}}_{01} \lambda^{Y_{\text{lower}}}_{01} + \lambda^{K_{\text{lower}}}_{10} \lambda^{Y_{\text{lower}}}_{10}$. So the value of $\lambda^{Y_{\text{higher}}}_{01}$ is *implied* by $\lambda^{K_{\text{lower}}}_{01}, \lambda^{Y_{\text{lower}}}_{01}, \lambda^{K_{\text{lower}}}_{10}, \lambda^{Y_{\text{lower}}}_{10}$.

In other words, the probability of a positive $X \rightarrow Y$ effect must be the same in M^p_{higher} as it is in M^p_{lower}. Otherwise, M^p_{higher} cannot be implied by M^p_{lower}, and the latter cannot serve as a *theory* of the former.

While the probability distributions in a lower level model must imply the probability distributions in the higher level model that it supports, the converse may not be true: Knowing the distribution over exogenous nodes of a higher level model does not provide sufficient information to recover distributions over exogenous nodes in the lower level model. So, for instance, knowing $\lambda^{Y_{\text{higher}}}$ does not give us enough information to determine the values of $\lambda^{Y_{\text{lower}}}$ and $\lambda^{K_{\text{lower}}}$. This is because there are many different combinations of $\lambda^{K_{\text{lower}}}_{01}, \lambda^{Y_{\text{lower}}}_{01}, \lambda^{K_{\text{lower}}}_{10}$, and $\lambda^{Y_{\text{lower}}}_{10}$ that will add up to any given value for $\lambda^{Y_{\text{higher}}}$.

6.1.3 Models Justified by Theory and Data

Finally, we can think of a higher level model as being supported by a lower level model combined with data. For this reason, we can fruitfully think of an initial model – when coupled with data – as constituting a *theory of* an updated model.

To see how this might work, imagine a scholar arguing: "M_1: X caused Y in country j." When pushed for a justification for the claim, they provide the lower level model: "M_0: X causes Y if and only if $C = 1$. Further, in this case, $C = 1$ and so X caused Y in this case."

Here, M_1 is implied by M_0 plus data $C = 1$.

We can take this further. If pushed now as to why M_0 is itself credible, the scholar might point to an even lower level model consisting of structural relations $X \rightarrow Y \leftarrow C$ plus flat priors over all nodal types – coupled with data on X, Y, and C, where the data *justify* the higher level belief about C's moderation of X's effect on Y.

As further justifications are sought, researchers seek acceptable lower models that, together with data, can justify higher level models. Note that, as we move down levels in this hierarchy of models, we may be – helpfully – moving from models that are *harder* to accept down to models that are *easier* to accept, because we are bringing data to bear. So, in the above example, it should be easier to accept $X \rightarrow Y \leftarrow C$ with flat priors than to accept the claim that "X causes Y if and only if $C = 1$." But the former works to justify the latter because we join it up with the data on X, Y, and C.

6.2 Gains from Theory

We now turn to consider how to think about whether a theory is *useful*. We are comfortable with the idea that theories, or models more generally, are wrong. Models are not full and faithful reflections of reality; they are maps designed for a particular purpose. We make use of them because we think that they *help* in some way.

But how do they actually help, and can we quantify the gains we get from using them?

We think we can.

6.2.1 Illustration: Gains from a Front-Door Theory

Here is an illustration with a theory that allows the use of the "front-door criterion" (Pearl, 2009). The key idea is that by invoking a theory for a model – which itself may require justification – one can draw inferences that would not have been possible without the theory.

Imagine we have a structural causal model M_0: $C \rightarrow X \rightarrow Y \leftarrow C$, as depicted in panel (a) of Figure 6.2. Here, C is a confound for the relationship between X and Y. Say we have data on three variables, X, Y, and K (a node that is not included in M_0). So we have data for two of the nodes in M_0 plus additional data on K, but we do not have data on C.

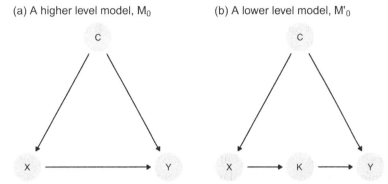

(a) A higher level model, M_0 (b) A lower level model, M'_0

Figure 6.2   A lower level model is invoked as a theory of a higher level model which in turn allows identification of the effects of X on Y

Now let's form a probabilistic causal model, M_0^p, by adding flat priors to M_0. Joining the X and Y data to probabilistic model M_0^p, we can then generate an updated model, M_1^p, with a probability distribution that reflects our learning from the data. Suppose that the data here display a strong correlation between X and Y. What kind of beliefs will M_1^p contain? From M_1^p, we would consider a causal connection between X and Y to be plausible – but quite uncertain. This uncertainty arises because we are aware that the correlation we see may be due to the unobserved confound C, and we currently have no leverage for distinguishing between a causal effect and confounding.

Suppose, however, that we now posit the lower level structural model M'_0: $C \to X \to K \to Y \leftarrow C$, as depicted in panel (b) of Figure 6.2. M'_0 implies M_0 in the structural sense discussed in Section 6.1.1.

M'_0 makes a stronger claim than M_0: M_0 presupposes a specific pathway between X and Y that M_0 does not. Critically, however, *if* we accept M'_0, then we can make use of our data on node, K, which was impossible when working with M_0.

Specifically, we can now:

- turn M'_0 into a probabilistic model $M_0^{'p}$;
- use data on X, Y, and K to move to an updated version, $M_1^{'p}$; notably, data on the mediator K may help us sort out whether the X, Y correlation is causal or a consequence of confounding;
- pose our causal question to $M_1^{'p}$, which has been informed by data on K.

This perhaps all seems a bit convoluted, so it is fair to ask: what are the gains? This depends on the data we observe, of course. If we observe, for instance, that X and K are strongly correlated and that K and Y are strongly correlated, then beliefs in $M_1'^P$ will reflect confidence that, in fact, X does cause Y – whereas with M_1^P we were very uncertain.

Thus, in return for specifying a theory of M_0, we may be able to make better use of data and form a more confident conclusion.

In other situations, we might imagine invoking a theory that does not necessarily involve new data, but that allows us to make different, perhaps tighter inferences using the same data. An example might be the invocation of theory that involves a monotonicity restriction or exclusion restriction that allows for the identification of a quantity that would not be identifiable without the theory.

Thus, one reason to theorize our models – develop lower level models that make stronger claims – is to be able to reap greater inferential leverage from the more elaborated theory when we go to the data.

6.2.2 Quantifying Gains

Can we quantify how much better off we are?

We need some evaluation criterion – some notion of "better off" – to answer this question. Two of the more intuitive criteria might be based on the following:

- Error: An error-based evaluation asks whether the theory helped reduce the (absolute) difference between an estimate and a target; similarly, we might focus on *squared* error – which essentially places more weight on bigger errors.
- Uncertainty: We might instead assess gains in terms of reduced uncertainty. We might measure uncertainty using the variance of our beliefs, or we might use relative entropy to assess reductions in uncertainty.

Other criteria (or loss functions) might focus on other features. For instance, we might ask whether the data we see are *explained* by the theory in the sense that they are more likely – less surprising – given the theory. Or we might want a criterion that takes account of the costs of collecting additional data or to the risks associated with false conclusions. For instance, in Heckerman et al. (1991), an objective function is generated using expected utility gains from diagnoses generated from new information over diagnoses based on what is believed already.

Table 6.1 Learning metrics

	Ex ante	Ex post
Subjective	Expected posterior variance	Posterior variance, change in beliefs, wisdom
Objective	Expected mean squared error	Error, squared error

Beyond specifying a criterion, we also can approach any criterion from a "subjective" or an "objective" position. Are we concerned with how uncertain we will be as researchers, or do we seek to benchmark our inferences against the true state of the world?

We can, further, distinguish between evaluation from an *ex ante* or an *ex post* perspective. Are we evaluating how we expect to do under a given theory before we have seen the data, or how we *have* done after we have drawn our inferences? Table 6.1 shows how these two dimensions might be crossed to generate four different approaches to evaluating learning.

So, for instance, in the top left quadrant (subjective/*ex ante*), we are interested in how uncertain we expect to be if we work with a given theory; in the bottom left quadrant (objective/*ex ante*), we are asking how far off we expect to be from some ground truth. In the second column, we are asking how uncertain we *are* about an inference we have made (subjective/*ex post*), or about how far off we have ended up from a ground truth (objective/*ex post*).

We now use this 2×2 structure to walk through possible metrics for gains from theory, focusing on a situation in which a theory lets us use additional data K to make inferences. Thus, when we speak of the gains from the theory, we mean the gains that come from the use of K in the ways *made possible by the theory*.

In this setup, we imagine that there is an unknown parameter, $q \in \{0, 1\}$, and we are interested in the value of q for a single unit drawn from some population. We have beliefs about the distribution of K, given q. Let $p(q, k)$ denote the joint distribution over q and k with marginal distributions $p(k)$ and $p(q)$. Let $p(q|k)$ denote a researcher's posterior given k, which we abbreviate to $\hat{q}_k$.

For the illustrations that follow, imagine that we start with a (subjective) prior that $q = 1$ of $p = 0.2$. And so our prior expectation for q is $\hat{q}_0 = p = 0.2$. We'll assume that that belief is correct in the sense that $q = 1$ for one-fifth of units in the population.

Now we have a theory under which we believe that $p(k = 1|q = 1) = 0.8$ and that $p(k = 1|q = 0) = 0.2$. Importantly, we will imagine that these two

Table 6.2 Possible events, event probabilities, and inferences

q (Unobserved)	k (Observable)	Event probability (subjective)	Event probability (objective)	Inference on q given k	Actual (squared) Error	Posterior variance
0	0	0.64	0.4	0.059	0.003	0.055
0	1	0.16	0.4	0.500	0.250	0.250
1	0	0.04	0.1	0.059	0.886	0.055
1	1	0.16	0.1	0.500	0.250	0.250

beliefs are *incorrect*, however: that, in fact, $p(k = 1|q = 1) = p(k = 1|q = 0) = 0.5$. Our theory, then, is wrong. We think K is informative, but in fact it is not. This difference between what our theory tells us and what the truth is will allow us to illustrate different conceptualizations of learning.

The key features of this example are summarized in Table 6.2. Each row here (or "event") represents a different situation we might end up in: A different combination of what the true answer to our query is (q is 0 or 1) and of what we observe when we examine K ($k = 1$ or $k = 0$). All four rows are *ex ante* possible.

Say, now, that we in fact observe $k = 1$ and update to $q_1 = p(q = 1|k = 1) = \frac{p(k=1|q=1)p(q=1)}{p(k=1|q=1)p(q=1)+p(k=1|q=0)p(q=0)} = \frac{0.8\times0.2}{0.8\times0.2+0.2\times0.8} = 0.5$. Suppose, however, that, unbeknownst to us, in reality $q = 0$. So we are in fact in row 2 of this table ($q = 0, k = 1$). But since we cannot observe q, we do not know whether we are in row 2, where $q = 0$, or row 4, where $q = 1$.

Let's now think about different ways of characterizing the gains from observing K, the piece of evidence made usable by our theory.

6.2.2.1 Objective, *ex post*

If we are willing to posit an external ground truth, then we can define "better" in objective terms. For instance, we might calculate the size of the error (or, more typically, the squared error) we make in our conclusions relative to the ground truth. We can then compare the error we make when we use the theory (and the clue that that theory makes usable) to draw an inference to the error that we make when we draw an inference without the aid of the theory (and its associated clue).

The difference in squared errors is given by $(q - \hat{q}_k)^2 - (q - \hat{q}_0)^2$.

In the numeric example, our objective *ex post* (squared) error is $(0 - 0.5)^2 = 0.25$ (using K), which compares unfavorably to our prior error

$(0 - 0.2)^2 = 0.04$ (without using K). Objectively, after the fact, we are worse off basing inferences on K than we were before. Note that we move in the wrong direction here not only because our theory about the informativeness of the clue is incorrect, but also because *in this instance* the clue realization that we happen upon points us in the wrong direction.

6.2.2.2 Objective, *ex ante*

Rather than asking how wrong we are given the data pattern we happened to observe, we can ask how wrong we are *expected* to be when we go looking for a clue that our theory makes usable (we say "are expected to be" rather than "we expect to be" because the evaluation may be made using beliefs that differ from the beliefs we bring with us when we draw inferences). An objective *ex ante* approach would ask what the *expected* error is from the conclusions that we will draw given a theory. For instance, how wrong are we likely to be if we base our best guess on our posterior mean, given the observation of a clue that the theory lets us make use of? "How wrong" might again be operationalized in different ways: for instance, in terms of expected squared error – the square of the distance between the truth and the posterior mean.

The *expected* squared error (see also Section 5.1.6) is:

$$\mathcal{L} := \int_q \int_k (\hat{q}_k - q)^2 p(k, q) dk dq.$$

This equation yields the error that one would expect to get with respect to any true value of the parameter (q), given the data one might see given q and the inferences one might draw. Note here that the joint distribution $p(k, q)$ is the objective (unknown) distribution, whereas the posterior $(\hat{q}_k)$ is calculated using the researcher's subjective beliefs. In principle, *ex ante* can be thought of with respect to the new information k or also with respect to the actual estimand q; we will work with the latter.

Returning to the numeric example, we can calculate the expected (actual) squared error with respect to the objective event probabilities in Table 6.2. This yields here 0.215. This might be compared (unfavorably) to the expected error if we just used the prior (0.2) on q, given the objective distribution of events. This would give expected (squared) error of 0.16.

We do badly in expectation not just because the theory is wrong, but because it is very wrong. We might have done better, and gained from the theory, in expectation, had the theory only been moderately wrong. To see this, imagine instead that in fact $p(k = 1 | q = 1) = 0.7, p(k = 1 | q = 0) = 0.3$ and so the probabilities of the four events are $(0.56, 0.24, 0.06, 0.14)$. Then, although we are overestimating the probative value of k, we are not wrong about k being informative. In this situation, where the theory is less wrong, our expected error would be 0.15 – an improvement relative to our prior.

6.2.2.3 Subjective, *ex post*

The problem, of course, with an objective approach is that we do not have the information – the true values of our queries – that we need to calculate objective errors.

A more subjective approach involves asking about the reduction in posterior variance. *Ex post* we can define "better" as the *reduction in posterior variance* from drawing an inference that makes use of a theory and its associated clue compared to an inference that does not.

A problem with this measure, however, is that posterior variance is not guaranteed to go down: Our uncertainty can increase as we gather more data. Importantly, however, that increase in uncertainty would not mean that we have not been learning. Rather, we have learned that things are not as simple as we thought – so we become less certain than we were before, in a manner justified by what we have observed.

One approach that addresses this issue asks: How much better are our guesses having observed K compared to what we would have guessed before, *given* what we know having observed K? This question captures the idea that, although we might be more uncertain than we were before, we think we are better off now because we are less naive. We might call this kind of improvement *wisdom* to reflect the idea that it values appreciation of justifiable uncertainty:

$$\text{Wisdom} = \frac{\int \left((\hat{q}_0 - q)^2 - (\hat{q}_k - q)^2\right) p(q|k)dq}{\int (\hat{q}_0 - q)^2 p(q)dq}.$$

The numerator in this expression captures how much better off we are with the guess we have made given current data ($\hat{q}_k$) compared to the guess we would have made if we had a theory that did not let us make use of it ($\hat{q}_0$), *all assessed knowing what we now know.* This can be interpreted simply as the subjective reduction in error (squared).[4] The denominator is simply the prior variance and is included here for scaling.

----

[4] The numerator simplifies according to:

$$\int \left((\hat{q}_0 - q)^2 - (\hat{q}_k - q)^2\right) p(q|k)dq = \int \left(\hat{q}_0^2 - 2q\hat{q}_0 - \hat{q}_k^2 + 2q\hat{q}_k\right) p(q|k)dq$$
$$= \left(\hat{q}_0^2 - 2\hat{q}_k\hat{q}_0 - \hat{q}_k^2 + 2\hat{q}_k^2\right)$$
$$= \left(\hat{q}_0 - \hat{q}_k\right)^2$$

Returning to the numeric example, our posterior variance after observing $k = 1$ is 0.25 compared to a prior variance of 0.16. So variance has increased. However, we have a gain in wisdom of $\frac{0.09}{0.16}$, reflecting how much better we believe our beliefs are compared to how they were before.

6.2.2.4 Subjective, *ex ante*

Finally, we might think about the contributions to learning that we *expect* from a theory before observing the data. We can conceptualize expected learning as the *reduction* in expected posterior variance: How certain do we expect we will be after we make use of new information? (See also our discussion in Section 5.1.6.)

For any k, we might write the posterior variance on $\hat{q}_k$ given observation k as $V(\hat{q}_k)$. Then, the expected posterior variance can be written:

$$EV := \int_k V(\hat{q}_k) p(k) dk.$$

This equation takes the posterior variance, given some data, over all the possible data that one might encounter given distribution $p(k)$. It is well known that whenever inferences are sensitive to the data, the expected posterior variance will be lower than the prior variance.[5] Interestingly, it is also the case that, if we assess expectations using the same priors that we use for forming posteriors, the expected posterior variance and squared error are equivalent (Scharf, 1991). To see this, we take advantage of the fact

From this we see that the measure does not depend on either prior or posterior variance (except through the denominator). Note also that wisdom, though non-negative, can exceed 1 in situations in which there is a radical re-evaluation of a prior theory, even if uncertainty rises. As an illustration, if our prior on some share is given by a Beta(2, 18) distribution, then our prior mean is 0.1, and our prior variance is very small, at 0.0043. If we observe another four positive cases, then our posterior mean becomes 1/4 and our posterior variance *increases* to 0.0075. We have shifted our beliefs upward and at the same time, become more uncertain. But we are also wiser since we are confident that our prior best guess of 0.1 is surely an underestimate. Our wisdom is 5.25 – a dramatic gain.

[5] This can be seen from the law of total variance which can be written as:

$$Var(Q|W) = E_{K|W}(Var(Q|K, W)) + Var_{K|W}(E(Q|K, W)).$$

The expression is written here to highlight the gains from observation of K, given what is already known from observation of W. See Raiffa and Schlaifer (1961). A similar expression can be given for the expected posterior variance from learning K in addition to W when W is not yet known. See, for example, Proposition 3 in Geweke and Amisano (2014). Note also that an implication is that the expected *reduction* in variance is then always positive, provided you are changing beliefs at all. In contrast, the (objective) expected error measure can be assessed under rival theoretical propositions, allowing for the real possibility that the gains of invoking a theory are negative.

that $p(q, k) = p(k)p(q|k) = p(q)p(k|q)$ and that $p(q|k)$ gives the posterior distribution of q given k. We then have:

$$\mathcal{L} = \int_q \int_k (\hat{q}_k - q)^2 p(q, k) dk dq$$

$$= \int_k \int_q (\hat{q}_k - q)^2 p(k)p(q|k) dq dk$$

$$= \int_k \left[\int_q (\hat{q}_k - q)^2 p(q|k) dq \right] p(k) dk$$

$$= \int_k V(\hat{q}_k) p(k) dk = EV.$$

The key move is in recognizing that $p(q|k)$ is in fact the posterior distribution on q given k. In using this, we assume that the same distribution is used for assessing error and for conducting analysis – that is we take the researcher's prior to be the relevant one for assessing error. Moreover, the reduction in expected posterior variance is also equal to *expected wisdom*.[6]

Returning to the numeric example in Table 6.2, the expected posterior variance (with expectations taken with respect to the subjective event probability distribution) is 0.118. Note that we would also get 0.118 if we took the expectation of the actual squared error with respect to subjective event probability distribution. The reduction in posterior variance over the prior variance of 0.16 is 26.47%.

We have described a set of possible metrics for gains from theory, but there is no single right metric. The right metric for assessing gains fundamentally depends on what the researcher values – whether that is making fewer errors, being confident in conclusions, avoiding overconfidence, or something else.

---

[6] That is, since:

$$\text{Wisdom} = \frac{\int \left((\hat{q}_0 - q)^2 - (\hat{q}_k - q)^2 \right) p(q|k) dq}{\int (\hat{q}_0 - q)^2 p(q) dq},$$

we have:

$$\text{Expected Wisdom} = \frac{\int (\hat{q}_0 - q)^2 p(q) dq - \int_k \int_q (\hat{q}_k - q)^2 p(q, k) dq dk}{\int (\hat{q}_0 - q)^2 p(q) dq}$$

and so:

$$\text{Expected Wisdom} = 1 - \frac{\text{Expected Posterior Variance}}{\text{Prior variance}}.$$

6.3 Formal Theories and Causal Models

It is relatively easy to see how the ideas above play out for what might be called empirical models. But in social sciences, "theory" is a term sometimes reserved for what might be called "analytic theories." In this last section, we work through how to use this framework when seeking to bring analytic theories to data.

As an example of an analytic theory, we might consider the existence of "Nash equilibria." Nash considered a class of settings ("normal form games") in which each player i can choose an action σ_i from set Σ_i and receives a payoff u_i that depends on the actions of all players. A particular game Γ is the collection of players, action sets, and payoffs.

Nash's theorem relates to the existence of a collection of strategies with the property that each strategy would produce the greatest utility for each player, given the strategies of the other players. Such a collection of strategies is called a Nash equilibrium.

The claim that such a collection of strategies exists in these settings is an analytic claim. Unless there are errors in the derivation of the result, the claim is true in the sense that the conclusions follow from the assumptions. There is no evidence that we could go looking for in the world to assess the claim. The same can be said of the theoretical claims of many formal models in social sciences; they are theoretical conclusions of the if – then variety (Clarke and Primo, 2012).

For this reason we will refer to theories of this form as "analytic theories."

When researchers refer to a theory of populism or a theory of democratization however, they often do not have such analytic theories in mind. Rather they have in mind what might be called "applied theories" (or perhaps more simply "scientific theories" or "empirical theories"): general claims about the relations between objects in the world. The distinction here corresponds to the distinction in Peressini (1999) between "pure mathematical theories" and "mathematized scientific theories."

Applied theory, in this sense, is a collection of claims with *empirical* content: An applied theory refers to a set of propositions regarding causal relations in the world that might or might not hold, and is susceptible to assessment using data. These theories might look formally a lot *like* analytic theories, but it is better to think of them as translations at most. The relations

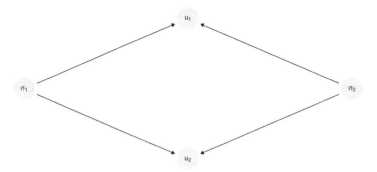

Figure 6.3   Formal structure of a normal form game

between nodes of an applied theory are a matter of conjecture, not a matter of necessity.[7]

Though it is not standard practice, formal models produced by game theorists can often be translated into applied theoretical analogs and then represented using the notation of structural causal models. Moreover, doing so may be fruitful. Using the approach described above, we can assess the utility of the applied theory, if not the analytic theory itself.

For two players, for instance, we might imagine a representation of a standard normal form game as shown in Figure 6.3.

The model includes all the primitives of a normal form game: we can read off the number of players, the strategy sets (the range of the strategy nodes) and the mapping from actions to utilities. Here, the only causal functions are the utility functions. In an analytic theory, these functions are known. In an applied translation of the theory these are a matter of conjecture: The functions capture the researcher's beliefs that actual actions will produce actual payoffs. So far the model does not capture any claims about behavior or expected behavior.

In contrast to Nash's theorem regarding the existence of equilibria, a behavioral theory might claim that in problems that can be represented as normal form games, players indeed *play* Nash equilibrium. This is a theory about how people act in the world. We might call it Nash's theory.

How might this theory be represented as a causal model? Figure 6.4 provides one representation.

Here, player beliefs about the game form (Γ) results in strategy choices by actors. If players play according to Nash's theory, *the causal functions for*

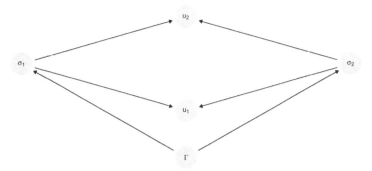

Figure 6.4   Normal form games with expectations and best responses

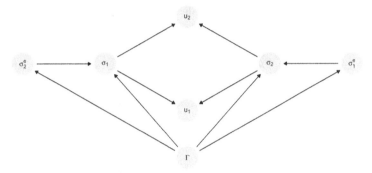

Figure 6.5   Normal form games with variation in player rationality

the strategy choices are given by the Nash equilibrium solution itself, with a refinement in case of multiplicity.

This model represents what we expect to happen in a game under Nash's theory and we can indeed see if the relations between nodes in the world look like what we expect under the theory. The relations are nevertheless a matter of conjecture, to be contrasted with the exact claims on strategy profiles that are produced by an analytic theory that assumes Nash equilibria are played.

So far the model does not provide much of an *explanation* for behavior. A lower level causal model might help. In Figure 6.5, the game form Γ determines the beliefs about what actions the other player would make (thus σ_2^e is 1's belief about 2's actions). The causal functions for σ_2^e and σ_1^e might, for instance, be the Nash equilibrium solution itself: that is, players expect other players to play according to the Nash equilibrium (or in the case of multiple equilibria, a particular equilibrium selected using some refinement). The beliefs, in turn, together with the game form (which contains u_1, u_2), are what

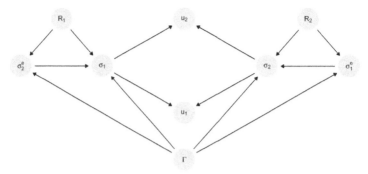

Figure 6.6   Formal structure of a normal form game (4)

cause the players to select a particular action. The causal function for σ_1 might thus be $\sigma_1 = \arg\max_\sigma u_1(\sigma, \sigma_2^e)$.

This representation implies a set of relations that can be compared against empirical patterns. Do players indeed hold these beliefs when playing a given game? Are actions indeed consistent with beliefs in ways specified by the theory? It provides a theory of beliefs and a theory of individual behavior as well as an explanation for social outcomes.

The model in Figure 6.5 provides a foundation of sorts for Nash's theory. It suggests that players play Nash equilibria *because* they expect others to and they are utility maximizers. But this is not the only explanation that can be provided; alternatively, behavior might line up with the theory without passing through beliefs at all, as suggested in some accounts from evolutionary game theory that show how processes might select for behavior that corresponds to Nash even if agents are unaware of the game they are playing.

One might step still further back and ask *why* would actors form these beliefs, or take these actions, and answer in terms of assumptions about actor rationality. Figure 6.6, for instance, is a model in which actor rationality might vary and might influence beliefs about the actions of others as well as reactions to those beliefs. Fully specified causal functions might specify not only how actors act when rational but also how they react when they are not. In this sense, the model in Figure 6.6 both nests Nash's theory and provides an explanation for why actors conform to the predictions of the theory.

In a final elaboration, we can represent a kind of underspecification of Nash's theory that makes it difficult to take the theory to data. In the above, we assume that players choose actions based on expectations that the other player would play the Nash equilibrium – or that the theory would specify which equilibrium in the case of multiplicity. But it is well known that

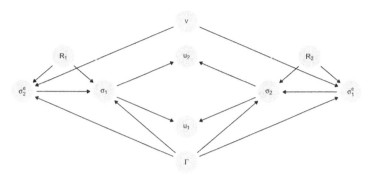

Figure 6.7   A normal form game with a representation of equilibrium selection norms

Nash's theory often does not provide a unique solution. This indeterminacy can be captured in the causal model shown in Figure 6.7, where a common shock – labeled v, and interpreted as norms – interacts with the game form to determine the expectations of other players.

The causal function for expectations can then allow for the possibility that (i) there is a particular equilibrium invariably chosen and played by both (ii) or a guarantee that players are playing one or other equilibrium together but uncertainty over which one is played, or (iii) the possibility that players are in fact out of sync, with each playing optimal strategies given beliefs but nevertheless not playing the same equilibria.

Nash's theory likely corresponds to position (ii). It can be captured by causal functions on beliefs given v but the theory does not specify v, in the same way that it does not specify Γ.

We highlight three points from this discussion.

First, the discussion highlights that thinking of theory as causal models does not force a sharp move away from abstract analytic theories; close analogs of these can often be incorporated in the same framework. This is true even for equilibrium analysis that seems to involve a kind of simultaneity at first blush.

Second, the discussion highlights how the causal modeling framework can make demands for specificity from formal theories. For instance, specifying a functional relation from game form to actions requires a specification of a selection criterion in the event of multiple equilibria. Including agent rationality as a justification for the theory invites a specification for what would happen absent rationality.

Third, the example shows a way of building a bridge from pure theory to empirical claims. One can think of Nash's theory as an entirely data-free set of claims. When translated into an applied theory – a set of propositions about the ways actual players *might* behave – and represented as a causal model, we are on a path to being able to use data to refine the theory. Thus, we might begin with a formal specification like that in Figure 6.7 but with initial uncertainty about player rationality, optimizing behavior, and equilibrium selection. This theory nests Nash but does not presume the theory to be a valid description of processes in the world. Combined with data, however, we shift to a more refined theory that might select Nash from the lower level model.

Finally, we can apply the ideas of Section 6.2 to formal theories and ask: Is the theory useful? For instance, does data on player rationality help us better understand the relationship between game structure and welfare?

Part II

Model-Based Causal Inference

7 Process Tracing with Causal Models

We show how process tracing can be implemented within a causal-model framework. The chapter outlines a model-based procedure for drawing case-level inferences from within-case evidence. We also show how a key result from the causal-models literature provides a condition for when the observation of a node in a causal model (a "clue") may be (or certainly will not be) informative, and we extract a set of implications for process-tracing strategies.

We now show how we can use causal models to address the kinds of problems of causal inference that social scientists frequently grapple with. We begin by demonstrating how we can use causal models to conduct confirmatory process tracing.

Going forward, we conceptualize process tracing somewhat more broadly than some previous treatments. Scholars have sometimes defined the method in terms of the parts of a causal system from which evidence is drawn or in terms of the kinds of questions being asked. For instance, George and Bennett (2005, p. 6) define process tracing, in part, as involving the use of evidence on "the sequence and values of the intervening variables" in a causal chain, while Bennett and Checkel (2015a, p. 7) specify the method as one undertaken "for the purposes of either developing or testing hypotheses about causal mechanisms that might causally explain" a case.

We take a slightly more ecumenical approach to thinking about the nature of the evidence that may be deployed or the inferential purposes being pursued in process tracing. We consider process tracing to be an approach that seeks to draw causal inferences *about a single case* using data *from* that case. The data used may be evidence on intervening steps, on features of context, or on any other potentially informative part of a causal system. Moreover, the causal question that one seeks to answer may be of any kind: whether about the cause of an outcome, the mechanism (or pathway) through which an effect unfolds, or any other query of interest to the analyst, as long as it is a question about the case at hand.

We deal in this chapter with confirmatory process tracing in the sense that our focus is on how to draw causal inferences *given* a set of background beliefs about how the world works, rather than how to inductively derive theoretical insights from the evidence. We note that other parts of the book – in particular, our treatments of population-level and mixed-data inference in Chapter 9, of model-justification in Chapter 15, and of model-evaluation in Chapter 16 – show how we can learn about theory from the data within a causal-model framework.

Our purpose in this chapter is to show how process tracing, defined in this manner, can be grounded in a causal model and implemented within a causal-model framework. In a nutshell, the procedure we describe here involves *the use of observable nodes on a causal graph to assess the value of one or more unobserved nodes on a causal graph* that are informative for our causal query.

There are a number of distinctive advantages to grounding process tracing in a causal model. First, process tracing from a model maximizes analytic transparency: It allows us to be fully explicit about the background beliefs informing our inferences, about the question we are asking, and about how precisely our answers follow from our prior beliefs and the new evidence that we are assessing. Research audiences and other scholars can then engage with and evaluate our inferences in ways uniquely enabled by formalization: They can scrutinize, call into question, and test for sensitivity to the model that we start with, the way we define our query, or the analytic steps we take upon observing the evidence. The approach also readily allows for the updating of inferences as additional case-level observations are brought to the table.

Second, grounding process tracing in a model enforces logical consistency on the set of beliefs entering into the analysis – such as between our priors on a causal question and our beliefs about the probative value of evidence – since all beliefs are derived from the same underlying model.

Third, as we show in this chapter and later in Chapter 12, embedding process tracing in a causal model offers a tool for making research design choices: It allows us to derive expectations about the kinds of new evidence that are potentially informative for our query, those that are likely to be *most* informative given what we have already observed, and the optimal sequence in which to search for within-case clues.

Finally, as we elaborate in Chapter 9, process tracing with a causal model opens an opportunity to integrate within-case and cross-case strategies of causal inference, allowing our inferences about individual cases to be informed by patterns observed across a larger set of cases.

7.1 The Intuition

When we undertake process tracing, we seek to answer a causal question about a given case. The key insight driving our approach is that the inference about a causal question for a case is a claim about *which causal types (collections of nodal types) are both likely* ex ante *(given prior knowledge) and consistent with the data.*[1]

The question of interest can be about any number of case-level causal features, including questions about a case-level causal effect, the pathway through which an effect operates, an actual cause, or causal attribution. We use observations from the case itself to address this query. We do so via a procedure in which we first encode prior knowledge in the form of a causal model, collect data on some nodes in the model from the case at hand, ask which causal possibilities (causal types) permitted by the model are consistent with the data, and then map those causal possibilities onto the specific causal query we seek to answer.

Given a causal model, we form posteriors over queries as follows:

1. **Specify all possible causal types for a model.** A causal type, recall, is a particular combination of nodal types for all nodes in a unit. That is, a single causal type specifies both a specific set of values of all exogenous variables in a model and the values that all endogenous variables *would* potentially take on for all possible values of the other endogenous variables. For a simple, binary $X \rightarrow Y$ model, the number of possible causal types will be 8; that is, 2 (the number of possible values X, the root node, can take on) times 4 (the number of possible nodal types for Y, the endogenous node). To illustrate, three of these causal types would be (writing them out here, rather than using our usual θ notation):

   - Type 1: $(X = 1)$ *and* $(Y = 1$ if $X = 1$, $Y = 0$ if $X = 0)$.
   - Type 2: $(X = 0)$ *and* $(Y = 1$ if $X = 1$, $Y = 0$ if $X = 0)$.
   - Type 3: $(X = 1)$ *and* $(Y = 1$ if $X = 1$, $Y = 1$ if $X = 0)$.

Whatever the model, we generate a complete set of all possible causal types.

---

[1] This differs from the task for mixed methods research that we will address in Chapter 9. There we will address questions about the distribution of causal types in populations.

2. **Specify priors over causal types.** We report how likely we think it is, ex ante, that a given unit is of a particular causal type. It is sometimes useful to conceive of the case at hand as having been randomly drawn from a broader population; thus, our prior beliefs about the case are equivalent to our beliefs about *how common* different causal types are in that population. In the simplest situation, we might place 0 weight on some causal types (those that are ruled out by background theory, for example) and equal weight on all others. More generally, we assign a lower probability to those causal types that we believe are relatively less common in the population and a higher probability to those causal types that we think are more common. Note that, in this critical step, we are *mobilizing our population-level beliefs* to allow us to draw *case-level* inferences.

3. **Specify the query in terms of causal types.** For instance, for the simple $X \rightarrow Y$ model, the query "Y responds positively to X" can be thought of as a collection of causal types: Q={Type 1, Type 2}, above.

4. **Once we observe the data, specify the set of causal types that are consistent with those data.** For instance, if we observe $X = 1$, $Y = 1$ we might specify the data-consistent set as {Type 1, Type 3}, excluding Type 2, with which these data are inconsistent.

5. **Update.** Updating is then done by adding up the prior probabilities on all causal types that are consistent with both the data and the query, and dividing this sum by the sum of prior probabilities on all causal types that are consistent with the data (whether or not they are consistent with the query).

This process is represented graphically in Figure 7.1, where we can think of probabilities as proportionate to areas. Our causal model defines the causal-type space. We then proceed by a process of elimination. Only some of the causal types in the model are consistent with prior knowledge. Only some are consistent with the data that we observe. Finally, any query itself maps onto a subset of the possible causal types. The causal types that remain in contention once we have observed the evidence are those at the intersection of consistency with priors and consistency with the data. *A* represents those types that are *also* consistent with a given answer to the query (say, X has a positive effect on Y).

　　Thus, our belief about the query before we have seen the data is the probability of all causal types consistent with our priors and with the query ($A+B$), as a proportion of the probability of all types consistent with our priors. Once we have seen the data, we have reduced the permissible types to $A + C$. Our posterior belief on the query is, then, the probability of those remaining types

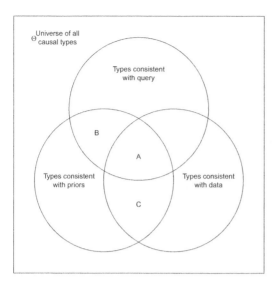

Figure 7.1   Logic of simple updating on arbitrary queries

that are also consistent with the query, as a share of the probability of *all* remaining types, or $A/(A + C)$.

We now turn to a formalization of these ideas.

7.2 A Formalization of the General Approach

The general approach to inference draws on the components we outlined in Chapters 2 to 4: causal models, queries, and priors. Coupled with data, these elements provide grounds for causal inferences. We continue to focus on a situation with binary variables, though we describe later how this can be extended. We walk through the procedure for simple models, though note that the approach outlined here can be applied to *any* causal model with discrete variables and to any queries defined over the model.

The process tracing procedure operates as follows.

7.2.1 The Model

First, we need a model.

A DAG

We begin with a DAG, or graphical causal model. As discussed in Chapter 2, a DAG identifies a set of variables and describes the parent–child relations between them, indicating for each variable which other variables are its direct (possible) causes. These relationship, in turn, tell us which (non-descendant) variables a given variable is *not* independent of given the other variables in the model.

Nodal Types

Once we have specified a DAG, we can determine the full set of possible nodal types: The types defining the value that a variable will take on given the values of its parents, which we have denoted with θ^j values for node j, as in θ_0^X or θ_{10}^Y. At each node, the range and number of possible nodal types is defined by the number of parents that that node has and the number of values the variables can take on. For instance, assuming all variables to be binary, if Y has parents X and Z, then there are $2^{(2^2)} = 16$) possible causal types for the Y node.

Causal Types

From the set of all possible nodal types for a DAG, we get the set of all possible causal types by simply elaborating all possible permutations of nodal types.

7.2.2 Priors

Our background beliefs about a causal domain will usually consist of more than just beliefs about which variables have causal connections; they will also typically contain beliefs about what *kinds* of effects operate between variables. That is, they will contain beliefs about which types are possible or, more generally, are more or less common in the world. We express these beliefs over causal effects as probability distributions over the nodal types. Generally, beliefs about causal types are implied by beliefs about nodal types. In cases with unobserved confounding, beliefs are defined over the joint distributions of nodal types.

For process tracing, our beliefs over nodal type θ^j, say, simply capture the subjective probability we have that the type takes on different values. We do not *need* to defend this belief to use the machinery. We use λ_x^j to denote the probability that $\theta^j = \theta_x^j$. Often, however, it helps with intuition to think of a given case of interest – the one we are studying and seek to learn about – as being drawn at random from a population and to think about our beliefs for the *single* case as stemming from our beliefs about the population from which it is drawn. In this sense, λ_x^j can be thought of as the *share* of cases in that population that we believe to be of type θ_x^j. So, for instance, our prior belief about the probability that inequality has a positive effect on democratization in Mexico in 1999 is our belief about how commonly inequality has a positive effect on democratization in the population of cases that are "like" Mexico in 1999.[2]

Vector λ^j is simply a set of numbers for each possible nodal type, with all numbers non-negative and summing to 1. So, for instance, λ^Y for our current example would be a vector with four values, each of which expresses a probability on one of the four nodal types at Y. So we might have $\lambda^Y_{01} = 0.1$, $\lambda^Y_{11} = 0.05$, and so on – with the λ^Y values summing to 1 because these values are defined over the full set of possible nodal types for Y. For the purposes of this chapter, we take λ as given – as the set of population-level beliefs we are operating with. In later chapters however, when we move beyond single cases, λ becomes quantity of interest, a parameter we want to learn about from the data.

Consider now beliefs over causal types. Let's start with a situation in which we assume that the nodal types are independent of one another. We can think of this as a situation in which there is no confounding that is not captured in the graph – no variable missing from the model that is a common ancestor of multiple nodes in the model. In this situation, our beliefs over causal types are simply the product of our beliefs over the component nodal types (since the joint probability of independent events is simply the product of their individual probabilities). For instance, one causal type might be "a unit in which $X = 1$ and in which $Y = 1$ no matter what value X takes." In this case, the probability that a case is of this causal type is $\Pr(\theta^X = \theta^X_1)\Pr(\theta^Y = \theta^Y_{11}) = \lambda^X_1 \lambda^Y_{11}$.

The simplest way in which we can express beliefs about the differential probabilities of different causal possibilities is by *eliminating* nodal types that we do not believe to be possible – setting their λ values to 0. Suppose, for instance, that we are examining the effect of ethnic diversity on civil war in a case. We might not know whether ethnic diversity causes civil war in this case, but we might have sufficient background knowledge to believe that ethnic diversity never has a *negative* effect on civil war: It never prevents a civil war from happening that would have happened in the absence of ethnic diversity. We would thus want to set the λ value for a negative causal effect to 0. If we then know nothing about the relative frequencies of the three remaining

---

[2] The reference population for a case is defined based on whatever we already know about the case. Thus, for instance, if we already know that the case has $Y = 1$ before we begin process tracing, then the relevant population for the formation of prior beliefs is all cases in which $Y = 1$.

nodal types for Y – a positive effect, a null effect with civil war destined to happen, and a null effect with civil war never going to happen – we may (following the principle of indifference) assign an equal weight of one-third to each of them.

In a situation of unobserved confounding, our beliefs over causal types are still well defined, though they are no longer the simple product of beliefs over nodal types. In this situation, we need to describe a joint distribution over nodal types. In practice, we can do this by specifying a probability for one nodal type and a conditional probability for another. Let us imagine for instance, in a simple $X \rightarrow Y$ model, that we believe that some unobserved factor both affects both the likelihood of $X = 1$ and also X's effect on Y: Maybe, for instance, X is more likely to be assigned to 1 where X has a positive effect. This is the same as saying that the probability distributions over θ^X and θ^Y are not independent. Now the probability of any combination of θ^X and θ^Y can be calculated using the joint probability formula, $\Pr(A, B) = \Pr(A)\Pr(B|A)$.[3] Thus, for instance, $\Pr(\theta^Y = \theta_{01}^Y, \theta^X = \theta_1^X) = \Pr(\theta^Y = \theta_{01}^Y)\Pr(\theta^X = \theta_1^X|\theta^Y = \theta_{01}^Y)$. To form priors over causal types in this situation, we need to posit beliefs about a set of more complex, conditional probabilities for X's type. Specifically, we need to posit, *for those cases* with a positive effect of X on Y, what are the chances a case is "assigned" to $X = 1$; *for those cases* with a negative effect, what are the chances a case is "assigned" to $X = 1$; and similarly for other nodal types.

In practice, we represent $\Pr(\theta_1^X, \theta_{01}^Y) = \Pr(\theta_1^X)\Pr(\theta_{01}^Y|\theta_1^X)$ using $\lambda_1^X \lambda_{01}^{Y|\theta_1^X}$. The notation is awkward but the key thing is that we have a well defined set of beliefs that we need to take into account to assess the probability of different causal types.

7.2.3 Possible Data Types

A *data type* is a particular pattern of data that we could potentially observe for a given case. More specifically, a data type is a set of values, one for each node in a model. For instance, in an $X \rightarrow Y \leftarrow Z$ model, $X = 1, Z = 0, Y = 0$ would be one data type; $X = 0, Z = 0, Y = 1$ another. We use X1Z0Y0 or X0Z0Y1, respectively, as shorthand for such data types.

Importantly, absent intervention, each possible causal type *maps deterministically into a single data type*. One intuitive way to think about why

---

[3] In words, the probability of A and B occurring is equal to the probability of A occurring times the probability of B occurring *given* that A occurs.

this is the case is that a causal type tells us (a) the values to which all root variables in a model are assigned and (b) how all other endogenous variables respond to their parents. Given these two components, only one set of node values is possible for a given causal type. For example, causal type $\theta = (\theta^X = \theta_1^X, \theta^Z = \theta_0^Z, \theta^Y = \theta_{0100}^Y)$ implies data $X = 1, Z = 0, Y = 1$ (the second digit in the subscript for θ^Y refers to the potential outcome for Y when $X = 1$ and $Z = 0$). Absent intervention, there is no other set of data that can be generated by this causal type.

Equally importantly, however, *the mapping from causal types to data types is not one-to-one.* More than one causal type can generate the same case-level data pattern. For instance, the causal type $\theta = (\theta^X = \theta_1^X, \theta^Z = \theta_0^Z, \theta^Y = \theta_{1101}^Y)$ will *also* generate the data type, $X = 1, Z = 0, Y = 1$. Thus, observing this data type leaves us with ambiguity about the causal type by which it was generated.

We can use an *ambiguities matrix* to summarize the mapping between causal types and data types. There is a row for each causal type and a column for each data type. An entry of 1 in a given cell indicates that the causal type generates the data type. Each row has a single 1 but each column can have many 1s – an indicator of the ambiguity we have about causal types when we observe a data type.

We illustrate with an ambiguities matrix for a simple $X \rightarrow Y$ model in Table 7.1. In the last column, we provide illustrative prior probabilities that could be placed on each causal type. As discussed above, each causal-type probability would be derived from beliefs about the λ^j probabilities for the component nodal types. Note how we can read the ambiguities off of the matrix. For instance, if we observe $X = 1, Y = 0$ in a case, we face an ambiguity about whether the case's causal type is $\theta_1^X, \theta_{00}^Y$ or $\theta_1^X, \theta_{10}^Y$: that is, about whether X has a negative effect on Y in this case or Y would be 0 in this case regardless of X's value.

As models get more complex, the numbers of causal and data types multiply, though generally the number of causal types increases faster than the number of data types. For a simple mediation model ($X \rightarrow M \rightarrow Y$), there are $2^3 = 8$ data types – possible combinations of values for X, M, Y – but $2 \times 4 \times 4$ causal types.

The ambiguities matrix tells us which causal types are consistent with the data we observe and, in doing so, shapes our inferences. Table 7.2 shows a portion of the ambiguities matrix for the $X \rightarrow M \rightarrow Y$ model, with priors on causal types appended in the final column. In this model, if we observe $X = 1, M = 0, Y = 0$, for instance, we have ambiguities over causal types.

Table 7.1 An ambiguities matrix, mapping from data types to causal types for a simple $X \rightarrow Y$ model

Data types →	X0Y0	X1Y0	X0Y1	X1Y1	Priors
Causal types ↓					
$\theta_0^X, \theta_{00}^Y$	1	0	0	0	0.125
$\theta_1^X, \theta_{00}^Y$	0	1	0	0	0.125
$\theta_0^X, \theta_{10}^Y$	0	0	1	0	0.125
$\theta_1^X, \theta_{10}^Y$	0	1	0	0	0.125
$\theta_0^X, \theta_{01}^Y$	1	0	0	0	0.125
$\theta_1^X, \theta_{01}^Y$	0	0	0	1	0.125
$\theta_0^X, \theta_{11}^Y$	0	0	1	0	0.125
$\theta_1^X, \theta_{11}^Y$	0	0	0	1	0.125

These data tell us that $\theta^X = \theta_1^X$. But they do not tell us whether M's type is such that X has a negative effect on M (θ_{10}^M) or X has no effect with M fixed at 0 (θ_{00}^M). Similarly, we do not know whether M has a positive effect on Y (θ_{01}^Y) or no effect with Y fixed at 0 (θ_{00}^Y). This leaves four combinations of nodal types – four causal types – that are consistent with the data. These types are picked out by the ambiguities matrix (two of these four can be seen in the second column of the excerpt of the ambiguities matrix displayed in Table 7.2).

7.2.4 Updating on Types Given the Data

Once we observe actual data in a case, we can then update on the probabilities assigned to each causal type. The logic is simple. When we observe a set of data from a case, we place 0 probability on all causal types that could not have produced these data; we then scale up the probabilities on all causal types that could have.

As a simple example, return to our $X \rightarrow Y$ model with equal prior weights (1/8) on each of the eight possible causal types, as in Table 7.1. Now suppose that we observe the data $X = 1$, $Y = 1$, that is, data type $X1Y1$. These data are consistent with some causal types but not others. Only two causal types are consistent with the data: $\theta_1^X, \theta_{01}^Y$ and $\theta_1^X, \theta_{11}^Y$. We therefore put 0 weight on all other causal types and scale up the remaining probabilities so that they sum to 1 (preserving the ratio between them). The result gives *posterior* probabilities on the causal types. We display an "updated" ambiguities matrix, with excluded data types and causal types removed, in Table 7.3.

Table 7.2 Excerpt from the ambiguities matrix for a simple mediation model. Rows are causal types, columns are data types. Last column shows possible priors over rows

Data types →	X0M0Y0	X1M0Y0	X0M1Y0	X1M1Y0	X0M0Y1	X1M0Y1	prior
Causal types ↓							
$\theta_0^X, \theta_{00}^M, \theta_{00}^Y$	1	0	0	0	0	0	0.02
$\theta_1^X, \theta_{00}^M, \theta_{00}^Y$	0	1	0	0	0	0	0.02
$\theta_0^X, \theta_{10}^M, \theta_{00}^Y$	0	0	1	0	0	0	0.02
$\theta_1^X, \theta_{10}^M, \theta_{00}^Y$	0	1	0	0	0	0	0.02
$\theta_0^X, \theta_{01}^M, \theta_{00}^Y$	1	0	0	0	0	0	0.04
$\theta_1^X, \theta_{01}^M, \theta_{00}^Y$	0	0	0	1	0	0	0.04
$\theta_0^X, \theta_{11}^M, \theta_{00}^Y$	0	0	1	0	0	0	0.02
$\theta_1^X, \theta_{11}^M, \theta_{00}^Y$	0	0	0	1	0	0	0.02
$\theta_0^X, \theta_{00}^M, \theta_{10}^Y$	0	0	0	0	1	0	0.02
$\theta_1^X, \theta_{00}^M, \theta_{10}^Y$	0	0	0	0	0	1	0.02
$\theta_0^X, \theta_{10}^M, \theta_{10}^Y$	0	0	1	0	0	0	0.02
$\theta_1^X, \theta_{10}^M, \theta_{10}^Y$	0	0	0	0	0	1	0.02
$\theta_0^X, \theta_{01}^M, \theta_{10}^Y$	0	0	0	0	1	0	0.04
$\theta_1^X, \theta_{01}^M, \theta_{10}^Y$	0	0	0	1	0	0	0.04
$\theta_0^X, \theta_{11}^M, \theta_{10}^Y$	0	0	1	0	0	0	0.02
$\theta_1^X, \theta_{11}^M, \theta_{10}^Y$	0	0	0	1	0	0	0.02

Table 7.3 Ambiguities in an $X \to Y$ model after observing $X = 1, Y = 1$ in a case

Data types →	X1Y1	Priors	Posteriors
Causal types ↓			
$\theta_1^X, \theta_{01}^Y$	1	1/8	1/2
$\theta_1^X, \theta_{11}^Y$	1	1/8	1/2

Before we see any data on the case at hand, then, we believe (based on our beliefs about the population to which the case belongs) that there is a 1/8 probability that the case is one in which X is assigned to 1 and has a positive effect on Y; and 1/8 probability that it's a case in which X gets assigned to 1 and has no effect on Y (and so Y is 1 regardless of X). Seeing the $X = 1, Y = 1$ data, we now believe that there is a 1/2 probability that the case is of the former type, and a 1/2 probability that it is of the latter type. Had our prior beliefs on types been different from each other, the posterior beliefs would have scaled up accordingly.

We now walk through how this works for the more complex $X \to M \to Y$ model, and the ambiguities matrix in Table 7.2. If we observe the data

Table 7.4 An updated version of the ambiguities matrix in Table 7.2, after observing $X = 1, M = 0$, $Y = 0$ in a case

Data types →	X1M0Y0	Priors	Posteriors
Causal types ↓			
$\theta_1^X, \theta_{00}^M, \theta_{00}^Y$	1	0.02	0.1667
$\theta_1^X, \theta_{10}^M, \theta_{00}^Y$	1	0.02	0.1667
$\theta_1^X, \theta_{00}^M, \theta_{01}^Y$	1	0.04	0.3333
$\theta_1^X, \theta_{10}^M, \theta_{01}^Y$	1	0.04	0.3333

$X = 1, M = 0, Y = 0$, for instance, this exercise would yield the updated ambiguities matrix in Table 7.4. Here, we have eliminated all rows (causal types) with a 0 in the relevant data-type column ($X1M0Y0$) and formed the posteriors by scaling up the priors in the retained rows.

A notable feature of the logic of single-case process tracing is that the relative probabilities on the retained causal types never change. If we start out believing that causal type A is twice as likely as causal type B, and both A and B are retained once we see the data, then A will be twice as likely as B in our posteriors. All updating occurs by *eliminating* causal types from consideration and zeroing in on those that remain.

A similar logic applies if partial data are observed: that is, if we do not collect data for all nodes in the model. The one difference is that, now, rather than reducing to one column we entertain the possibility of any data *type* consistent with the *observed data*. In general, more than one data type will be consistent with partial data. For instance, suppose that we observe $X = 1, Y = 0$ but do not observe M's value. These are data that are consistent with both the data type $X1M0Y0$ and the data type $X1M1Y0$ (since the unobserved M could be either 0 or 1). We thus retain both of these data-type columns as well as all causal types consistent with *either* of these data types. This gives the updated ambiguities matrix in Table 7.5. We note that, with these partial data, we are not able to update as strongly. For instance, for the causal type $\theta_1^X, \theta_{00}^M, \theta_{00}^Y$, instead of updating to a posterior probability of 0.1667, we update to a posterior of only 0.0833 – because there is a larger set of causal types with which these partial data are consistent.

7.2.5 Updating on Queries

We now have a posterior probability for each causal type for the case at hand. The causal question we are interested in answering, our query, may not be

Table 7.5 An updated version of the ambiguities matrix in Table 7.2, after observing partial data in case: $X = 1, Y = 0$, with M unobserved

Data types →	X1M0Y0	X1M1Y0	Priors	Posteriors
Causal types ↓				
$\theta_1^X, \theta_{00}^M, \theta_{00}^Y$	1	0	0.02	0.0833
$\theta_1^X, \theta_{10}^M, \theta_{00}^Y$	1	0	0.02	0.0833
$\theta_1^X, \theta_{01}^M, \theta_{00}^Y$	0	1	0.04	0.1667
$\theta_1^X, \theta_{11}^M, \theta_{00}^Y$	0	1	0.02	0.0833
$\theta_1^X, \theta_{01}^M, \theta_{10}^Y$	0	1	0.04	0.1667
$\theta_1^X, \theta_{11}^M, \theta_{10}^Y$	0	1	0.02	0.0833
$\theta_1^X, \theta_{00}^M, \theta_{01}^Y$	1	0	0.04	0.1667
$\theta_1^X, \theta_{10}^M, \theta_{01}^Y$	1	0	0.04	0.1667

about causal types *per se*. In general, any causal query can be defined as a *combination* of causal types, as described in Chapter 4.

For instance, suppose we are working with the model $X \rightarrow M \rightarrow Y$; and that our question is, "Did $X = 1$ cause $Y = 1$?." This question is asking both:

1. Does $X = 1$ in this case?
2. Does X have a positive effect on Y in this case?

The causal types that qualify are those, and only those, in which the answer to both is "yes."

Meeting condition (1) requires that $\theta^X = \theta_1^X$.

Meeting condition (2) requires that θ^M and θ^Y are such that X has an effect on M that yields a positive effect of X on Y. This could occur via a positive $X \rightarrow M$ effect linked to a positive $M \rightarrow Y$ effect or via a negative $X \rightarrow M$ effect linked to a negative $M \rightarrow Y$ effect.

Thus, the qualifying causal types in this model are:

- $\theta_1^X, \theta_{01}^M, \theta_{01}^Y$
- $\theta_1^X, \theta_{10}^M, \theta_{10}^Y$

Our *prior* on the query – what we believe before we collect data on the case at hand – is given simply by summing up the prior probabilities on each of the causal types that correspond to the query. Note that we must calculate the prior from the full ambiguities matrix, before excluding types for inconsistency with the data. Returning to the full ambiguities matrix in Table 7.2, we see that the priors on these two types (given the population parameters

Table 7.6 An updated version of the ambiguities matrix in Table 7.2, after observing $X = 1, M = 1, Y = 1$ in a case

Data types $\rightarrow$	X1M1Y1	Priors	Posteriors
Causal types $\downarrow$			
$\theta_1^X, \theta_{01}^M, \theta_{01}^Y$	1	0.08	0.4444
$\theta_1^X, \theta_{11}^M, \theta_{01}^Y$	1	0.04	0.2222
$\theta_1^X, \theta_{01}^M, \theta_{11}^Y$	1	0.04	0.2222
$\theta_1^X, \theta_{11}^M, \theta_{11}^Y$	1	0.02	0.1111

Table 7.7 An updated version of the ambiguities matrix in Table 7.2, after observing partial data in case: $X = 1, Y = 0$, with M unobserved

Data types $\rightarrow$	X1M0Y0	X1M1Y0	Priors	Posteriors
Causal types $\downarrow$				
$\theta_1^X, \theta_{00}^M, \theta_{10}^Y$	1	0	0.02	0.0769
$\theta_1^X, \theta_{10}^M, \theta_{10}^Y$	1	0	0.02	0.0769
$\theta_1^X, \theta_{01}^M, \theta_{01}^Y$	0	1	0.08	0.3077
$\theta_1^X, \theta_{11}^M, \theta_{01}^Y$	0	1	0.04	0.1538
$\theta_1^X, \theta_{00}^M, \theta_{11}^Y$	0	1	0.02	0.0769
$\theta_1^X, \theta_{10}^M, \theta_{11}^Y$	0	1	0.02	0.0769
$\theta_1^X, \theta_{01}^M, \theta_{11}^Y$	1	0	0.04	0.1538
$\theta_1^X, \theta_{11}^M, \theta_{11}^Y$	1	0	0.02	0.0769

assumed there) are 0.08 and 0.02, respectively, giving a prior for the query of 0.1.

The posterior on any query is, likewise, given by summing up the posterior probabilities on each of the causal types that correspond to the query, drawing of course from the updated ambiguities matrix. For instance, if we observe the data $X = 1, M = 1, Y = 1$, we update to the ambiguities matrix in Table 7.6. Our posterior on the query, "Did $X = 1$ cause $Y = 1$?" is the sum of the posteriors on the above two causal types. Since $\theta_1^X, \theta_{10}^M, \theta_{10}^Y$ is excluded by the data, this just leaves the posterior on $\theta_1^X, \theta_{01}^M, \theta_{01}^Y$, 0.4444, which is the posterior belief on our query.

If we observe only the partial data, $X = 1, Y = 1$, then we update to the ambiguities matrix in Table 7.7. Now both causal types satisfying the query are included, and we sum their posteriors to get the posterior on the query: $0.08 + 0.31 = 0.39$.

For more complex models and queries, it can be more difficult to eyeball the corresponding causal types. In practice, therefore, we use the get_query_types function in the CausalQueries package to do this for us.

7.3 Mapping from Models to Classic Qualitative Tests

The approach we have elaborated here appears different from that described in the literature on process-tracing tests – such as Collier (2011), Bennett (2008), or Humphreys and Jacobs (2015) – in which one seeks specific evidence that is directly informative about causal propositions: "clues" that arise with different probabilities if one proposition or another is true. In fact, however, the approaches are deeply connected. Specifically, we can think of causal models as providing a *justification* for the probative value that researchers assign to clues in the classic approach. One can use the predictive probabilities for queries from a model as the prior for the query before starting process tracing; and use the predictive probability of data given a query as likelihoods. In doing so, the priors and likelihoods are *justified* by the model (which of course implies that challenges to the model imply challenges to these quantities).

To see this, let's write down the probability of observing a given clue conditional on a unit's causal type using the ϕ notation from Humphreys and Jacobs (2015). Here, ϕ_{jx} refers to the probability of observing a clue, K, in a case of type j when $X = x$. Assuming an $X \rightarrow K \rightarrow Y$ model and a prior distribution over the lower level causal types (the λ's), we can derive, for an $X = 1$ case, the probability of seeing the clue if the case is of type b (positive effect) or of type d (no effect, and Y always 1):

$$\phi_{b1} = \frac{\lambda_{01}^K \lambda_{01}^Y}{\lambda_{01}^K \lambda_{01}^Y + \lambda_{10}^K \lambda_{10}^Y}$$

(7.1)

$$\phi_{d1} = \frac{\lambda_{11}^Y (\lambda_{01}^K + \lambda_{11}^K) + \lambda_{11}^K \lambda_{01}^Y}{\lambda_{11}^Y + \lambda_{00}^K \lambda_{10}^Y + \lambda_{11}^K \lambda_{01}^Y}.$$

These quantities allow for easy mapping between our prior beliefs about our causal query – as expressed in the lower level model – and the classic process-tracing tests in Van Evera (1997). Figure 7.2 illustrates this mapping. In each panel, we manipulate a prior for one or more of the lower level causal effects, keeping all other priors flat, relative to each other, and we see how probative value changes. As the curves for ϕ_b and ϕ_d diverge, probative value is increasing since there is an increasing difference between the probability of seeing the clue if X has a positive effect on Y and the probability of seeing the clue if X has no effect.

In the left panel, we see that as we place a lower prior probability on K's being negatively affected by X (that is, as we move left),[4] seeking $K = 1$ increasingly takes on the quality of a hoop test for X's having a positive effect on Y. The clue, that is, increasingly becomes something we must see if X positively affects Y, with the clue remaining moderately probable if there is no effect. Why? The less likely we believe it is that $K = 0$ was caused by $X = 1$, the less consistent the observation of $K = 0$ is with X having a positive causal effect on Y via K (since, to have such an effect, if $X = 1$ and $K = 0$, would precisely have to mean that $X = 1$ *caused* $K = 0$).

In the second graph, we simultaneously change the prior probabilities of zero effects at both stages in the sequence: of K and Y being 1 regardless of the values of X and K, respectively.[5] We see here that, as the probabilities of zero effects jointly diminish (again, moving left), seeking $K = 1$ increasingly becomes a smoking-gun test for a positive effect of X on Y: the probability of seeing the clue if the case is a d type diminishes. The reason is that, as zero effects at the lower level become less likely, it becomes increasingly unlikely that $K = 1$ could have occurred without a positive effect of X on K, and that $Y = 1$ could have occurred (given that we have seen $K = 1$) without a positive effect of K on Y.

In sum, when we undertake process tracing with a causal model, the probative value of the evidence derives in a systematic way from our prior beliefs about causal relations in the domain of interest – that is, from a lower-level model together with our beliefs about which causal effects are more or less likely to be operating in that model.

7.4 Assessing Probative Value from a Graph

As we have argued, causal queries can be expressed as collections of combinations of nodal types (i.e., as collections of causal types) in a causal model. A nodal type is itself represented as an unobservable node in a model – as a

---

[4] For a given value of λ_{01}^K, we hold the other λ^K values equal by assigning a value of $(1 - \lambda_{01}^K)/3$ to each.
[5] For a given value of λ_{11}^K, we hold the other λ^K's equal by assigning a value of $(1 - \lambda_{11}^K)/3$ to each; likewise for λ_{11}^Y and the other λ^Y values.

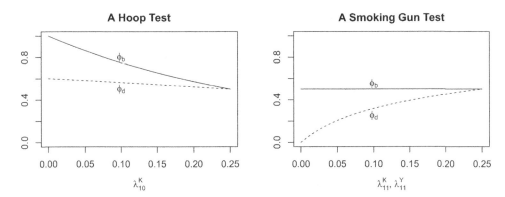

Figure 7.2   The probability of observing K given causal types for different beliefs on lower level causal effects

θ^j pointing into node j. Thus, causal inference in this framework is *the use of observable nodes on a causal graph to assess the value of one or more unobserved nodes on a causal graph.* Placing our queries on the graph together with the observable nodes has the important advantage of allowing us to graphically identify the possibilities for learning about these queries: that is, to figure out which observable nodes are potentially informative about a given query.

To think through the logic of potential probative value, it is useful to distinguish among three different features of the world, as represented in our causal model: there are the things we want to learn about; the things we have already observed; and the things we could observe. As notation going forward, we let:

- Q denote the *set* of θ^j nodes that define our *query*; usually Q cannot be directly observed so its values must be inferred;
- W denote a *set* of previously observed nodes in the causal model; and
- K denote a *set* of additional variables – clues – that we have not yet observed but could observe.

Now suppose that we seek to design a research project to investigate a causal question. How should the study be designed? Given that there are some features of the world that we have already observed, which additional clues should we seek to collect to shed new light on our question? In terms of the above notation, what we need to figure out is whether a given K might be informative about – might provide additional leverage on – Q given the prior observation of W.

To ask whether one variable (or set of variables) is informative about another is to ask whether the two (sets of) variables are, on average, related with one another, given whatever we already know. Conversely, if two variables' distributions are fully *independent* of one another (conditional on what else we have observed), then knowing the value of one variable can provide no new information about the value of the other.

Thus, asking whether a set of clues, K, is informative about Q given the prior observation of W, is equivalent to asking whether K and Q are conditionally independent given W. That is, K can be informative about Q given W only if K and Q are *not* conditionally independent of one another given W.

As our discussion of conditional independence in Chapter 2 implies, as long as we have built Q, K, and W into our causal model of the phenomenon of interest, we can answer this kind of question by inspecting the structure of the model's DAG. In particular, what we need to go looking for are relationships of *d-separation*. The following proposition, with only the names of the variable sets altered, is from Pearl (2009; Proposition 1.2.4):

Proposition 1: If sets Q and K are *d*-separated by W in a DAG, $\mathcal{G}$, then Q is independent of K conditional on W in every distribution compatible with $\mathcal{G}$. Conversely, if Q and K are *not* *d*-separated by W in $\mathcal{G}$, then Q and K are dependent conditional on W in at least one distribution compatible with $\mathcal{G}$.

We begin with a causal graph and a set of nodes on the graph (W) that we have already observed. Given what we have already observed, *a collection of clue nodes, K, will be uninformative about the query nodes, Q, if K is d-separated from Q by W on the graph.* (Equivalently, K, will be uninformative about Q, given that we have already observed W, if K and Q are conditionally independent given W.) When W *d*-separates K from Q, this means that what we have already observed already captures all information that the clues might yield about our query. On the other hand, if K and Q are *d*-connected (i.e., not *d*-separated) by W, then K is *possibly* informative about Q.[6] Note, moreover, that under quite general conditions (referred to in the literature as the *faithfulness* of a probability distribution), there are then at least *some* values of W for which K *will* be informative about Q.[7]

---

[6] This proposition is almost coextensive with the definition of a DAG. A DAG is a particular kind of dependency model ("graphoid") that is a summary of a collection of "independency statements," (I), over distinct subsets of $\mathcal{V}$ (Pearl and Verma, 1987), where $I(Q, W, K)$ means "we learn nothing about Q from K if we already know W." More formally: $I(K, W, Q) \leftrightarrow P(K, Q|W) = P(K|W)P(Q|W)$. A DAG dependency model is one where the set of independencies corresponds exactly to the relations that satisfy *d*-separation (Pearl and Verma, 1987, p376). Thus, on DAG $\mathcal{G}$, $I(K, W, Q)_\mathcal{G}$ implies that K and Q are *d*-separated by W.

[7] Put differently, there will not be any conditional independencies that are *not* captured in the DAG.

Simplest X, Y, graph

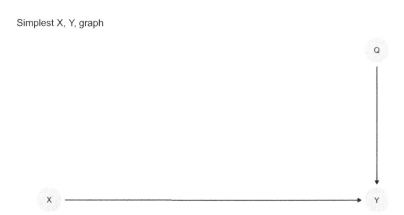

Figure 7.3   A simple causal model in which the effect of X on Y in a given case depends on the case's nodal type for Y (here marked Q to highlight that this quantity is the query of interest)

Let us examine Proposition 1 in practice. We begin with the simplest case possible, and then move on to more complex models.

The very simplest probabilistic causal graph, shown in Figure 7.3, has X influencing Y, with X determined by a coin flip. If we want to know X's effect on Y, this query is defined solely in terms of Y's nodal type, θ^Y. To help us conceptualize the more general point about informativeness for queries, we relabel θ^Y as Q to emphasize the fact that this node represents our query.

Let us assume that we have observed nothing yet in this case and then ask what clue(s) might be informative about Q, the node of interest. The other two nodes in the graph are X and Y: These are thus the possible clues that we might go looking for in our effort to learn about Q (i.e., they are the possible members of K).

First, can we learn about Q by observing X? We can answer this question by asking whether X is d-connected to Q on the graph given what we have already observed (which is nothing). We can see visually that there is no active path from X to Q: The only path between X and Q is blocked by colliding arrow heads. Thus, X and Q are d-separated, meaning that X will not be informative about Q: observing the value that a causal variable takes on in a case – having seen nothing else in the case – tells us nothing whatsoever about that variable's effect on the outcome. If we want to know whether a case is of a type in which the presence of natural resources would cause civil war, for instance, observing only that the case has natural resources does not help answer the question.

What, then, if we instead were to observe only Y? Is Y d-connected to Q given what we have already observed (which, again, is nothing)? It is: the arrow from Q to Y is an active path. Observing only the *outcome* in a case does tell us something about causal effects. Returning to the natural resources and civil war example, observing only that a country has had a civil war is informative about the case's causal type (the value of Q). In particular, it rules out the possibility that this is a case in which nothing could cause a civil war: that is, it excludes θ_{00}^Y (i.e., c-type) as a possible value of Q.

Suppose now, having observed Y, that we were to consider also observing X. Would we learn anything further about Q from doing so? We have already seen that observing X alone yields no information about Q because the two nodes are unconditionally d-separated, the path between them blocked by the colliding arrowheads at Y. However, as we have seen, observing a collider variable (or one of its descendants) *unblocks* the flow of information, generating relations of conditional dependence across the colliding arrowheads. Here, X and Q are d-connected by Y: Thus, if we have *already* observed Y, then observing X does confer additional information about Q. Knowing only that a country has natural resources tells us nothing about those resources' effect on civil war in that country. But if we already know that the country has a civil war, then learning that the country has natural resources helps narrow down the case's possible nodal types for Y. Having already used the observation of $Y = 1$ to rule out the possibility of θ_{00}^Y, observing $X = 1$ *together with* $Y = 1$ allows us to additionally rule out the possibility that natural resources *prevent* civil war, that is, that $Q = \theta_{10}^Y$.[8]

Finally, what if we observe X first and are considering whether to seek information about Y? Would doing so be informative? X does not d-separate Q from Y; thus, observing Y will be informative about Q. In fact, observing Y if we have already seen X is *more* informative than observing Y alone. The reasoning follows the logic of collision discussed just above. If we observe Y having already seen X, not only do we reap the information about Q provided by Y's correlation with Q; we simultaneously open up the path between X and Q, learning additionally from the conditional dependence between X and Q given Y.

We put Proposition 1 to work in a slightly more complex set of models in Figure 7.4. Here, we investigate the informativeness of a clue that is neither X nor Y. Each graph in Figure 7.4 has four variables: X; Y; a possible clue, K; and a node, Q, representing the query. It is probably most intuitive to think of

---

[8] That is, we can rule out that the case is an a type, or one with a negative causal effect.

Q in these graphs simply as θ^Y; but we leave the notation a bit more general to emphasize that any query can be composed of multiple nodal types.[9]

We draw all 34 possible graphs with variables X, Y, K, and Q for causal models in which (a) all variables are connected to at least one other variable, (b) X causes Y either directly or indirectly, and (c) Q is a direct cause of Y but is not caused by any other variable in the model. The title of each panel reports K's conditional informativeness using principles of d-separation: It tells us when K is possibly informative about Q depending on whether X, Y, both, or none are observed.[10]

The results show us not just what kinds of variables can be informative about the nodal types operating in a case but also what combinations of observations yield leverage on case-level causal effects. A number of features of the graphs are worth highlighting:

Clues at Many Stages

Process tracing has focused a great deal on observations that lie "along the path" between suspected causes and outcomes. What we see in Figure 7.4, however, is that observations at many different locations in a causal model can be informative about causal effects. We see here that K can be informative when it is pre-treatment (causally prior to X – e.g., panel (3)), post-treatment but pre-outcome (i.e., "between" X and Y as, e.g., in panel (20)), an auxiliary effect of X that itself has no effect on Y (e.g., in panel (19)), a post-outcome observation (after Y – e.g., in panel (15)), or a joint outcome of both the suspected cause and the main outcome of interest (e.g., panel (31)).

Mediator Clues

While clues that lie in between X and Y may be informative, how informative they are depends on what else is known. For instance, when a clue serves *only* as a mediator in our model (i.e., its only linkages are being caused by X and affecting Y) and Q points only into Y, as in panels (20) and (21), the clue is only informative about Q if we have also observed the outcome, Y. Of course, this condition may commonly be met – qualitative researchers usually engage in retrospective research and learn the outcome of the cases they are studying early on – but it is nonetheless worth noting why it matters: In this

---

[9] Recall, for instance, how a query about X's causal effect on Y in an $X \rightarrow M \rightarrow Y$ model is a question about the values of both θ^M and θ^Y.

[10] Note the "possibly" can be dropped under the assumption that the underlying probability model is "stable" (Pearl, 2009, Section 2.9.1) and with the interpretation that K is informative about Q for some, but not necessarily all, values of W.

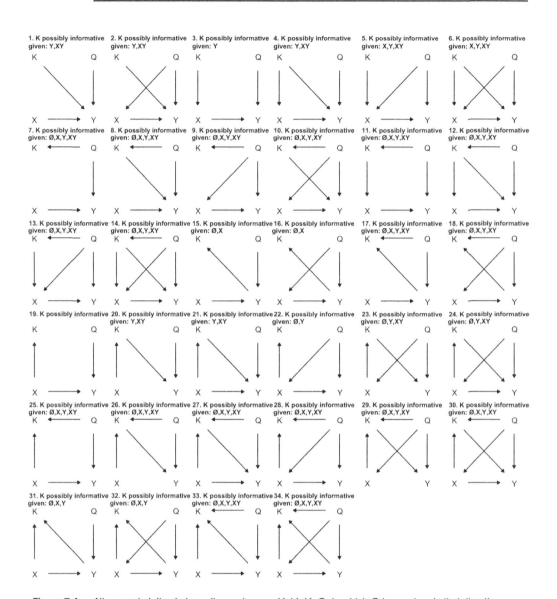

Figure 7.4 All connected directed acyclic graphs over X, Y, K, Q, in which Q is a root node that directly causes Y, and X is a direct or indirect cause of Y. Graph titles indicate conditions under which K can be informative about Q, given prior observation of X, Y, both, or neither ($\emptyset$)

setup, K is unconditionally *d*-separated from Q by the collision at Y; it is only by observing Y (the collider) that the path between K and Q becomes unblocked. (As we saw above, the very same is true for observing X; it is only when we know Y that X is informative about Q.)

In short, observations along causal paths are more helpful in identifying causal effects to the extent that we have measured the outcome. Importantly, this is not the same as saying that mediator clues are *only* informative about causal effects where we have observed the outcome. Observing Y is necessary for the mediator to be informative about a Q term that is connected only to Y. Observing a mediator without the outcome, however, could still be informative about the overall effect of X on Y by providing leverage on how the mediator responds to X, which is itself informative about X's effect on Y via the mediator.[11] Moreover, observing the mediator could be informative without the observation of Y if, for instance, Q also points into K itself or into a cause of K. As we discuss below, the clue then is informative as a "symptom" of one or more nodal types, generating learning that does not hinge on observing the outcome.

Symptoms as Clues

Some clues may themselves be affected by Q: that is to say, they may be symptoms of the same conditions that determine causal effects in a case. Imagine, for instance, a model of political corruption in which how politicians respond to institutional structures – whether institutions, X, curb their tendency to act corruptly, Y – depends on their underlying motives. Institutions that strengthen governmental transparency and accountability, for instance, might reduce corruption among those politicians who value long-term policy influence but not among those who value only short-run personal enrichment. In this model, politicians' motives essentially operate as an unobservable nodal type, in the position of Q, determining institutions' effects on corruption. While we cannot directly observe politicians' motives, however, there may be *consequences* of politicians' motives that are observable: for instance, whether politicians regularly make policy decisions with broad, long-run societal benefits. While such policy decisions would not be part of the causal chain generating institutions' effect on corruption, observing those policy decisions (or the lack of them) would be informative about that effect because these decisions are a symptom of the same conditions (politicians' motives) that enable or disable the effect.

We see that K is a child or descendant of Q in several of the graphs in Figure 7.4: Q directly causes K in panels (7) through (14), (17), (18), (25)–(30), (33), and (34); Q causes K only indirectly through X in panels (22) through

---

[11] In other words, the clue would then be providing leverage on the mediator's nodal type, that is, on a θ node pointing into the mediator itself.

(24); Q causes K only indirectly through Y in panels (15), (16), and (31); and Q causes K only indirectly through X and through Y in panel (32). We can then use the principle of d-separation to figure out when the symptom clue is potentially informative, given what we have already observed. It is easy to see that K is potentially informative, no matter what we have already observed, if K is directly affected by Q; there is nothing we could observe that would block the $Q \rightarrow K$ path. Thus, Q's "symptom" can, in this setup, contain information about type above and beyond that contained in the X and Y values. However, where Q affects K only through some other variable, observing that other variable renders K uninformative by blocking the Q-to-K path. For instance, where Q affects K indirectly through X, once we observe X, we already have all the information about Q that would be contained in K.

Surrogates as Clues

Clues may be consequences of the outcome, as in graphs (15) and (16). If K is a consequence *only* of Y, then it will contain no new information about Q when Y is already known. However, in situations where the outcome has not been observed, K can act as a "surrogate" for the outcome and thus yield leverage on Q (Frangakis and Rubin, 2002). A researcher might, for instance, want to understand causal effects on an outcome that is difficult to directly observe: consider, studies that seek to explain ideational change. Ideas themselves, the Y in such studies, are not directly observable. However, their consequences – such as statements by actors or policy decisions – will be observable and can thus serve as informative surrogates for the outcome of interest.

Clues may similarly serve as surrogates of a cause, as in graphs (19) and (22). Here, X causes K, but K plays no role in the causal process generating Y. K is of no help if we can directly measure X since the latter d-separates K from Q. But if an explanatory variable cannot be directly measured – consider, again, ideas or preferences as causes – then its consequences, including those that have no relationship to the outcome of interest, can provide leverage on the case-level causal effect.

Clues can also be a consequence of both our suspected cause and the outcome of interest, thus serving as what we might call "double surrogates," as in panels (31) and (32). Here, X is a direct cause of Y, and K is a joint product of X and Y. A double surrogate can be informative as long as we have not already observed both X and Y. Where data on either X or Y are missing, there is an open path between K and Q. If we have already observed both, however, then there is nothing left to be learned from K.

Instruments as Clues

Clues that are causally prior to an explanatory variable, and have no other effect on the outcome, can sometimes be informative. Consider, for instance, graph (3). Here, K is the only cause of X. It can thus serve as a proxy. If we have seen X, then X blocks the path between K and Q, and so K is unhelpful. K can be informative, though, if we have *not* observed X. Note that informativeness here still requires that we observe Y. Since Y is a collider for Q and the $K \rightarrow X \rightarrow Y$ chain, we need to observe Y in order to d-connect K to Q.

A rather different setup appears in graph (5), where both K and Q cause X. Now the conditions for K's informativeness are broader. Observing X still makes K uninformative as a proxy for X itself. However, because X is a collider for K and Q, observing X *opens up* a path from K to Q, rendering a dependency between them. Still, we have to observe at least one of X or Y for the instrument to be informative here. This is because both of K's paths to Q run through a collision that we need to unblock by observing the collider. For one path, the collider is X; for the other path, the collider is Y.[12]

Other patterns involving instrumentation are also imaginable, though not graphed here. For example, we might have a causal structure that combines instrumentation and surrogacy. Suppose that X is affected by Q and by an unobservable variable θ_X; and that θ_X has an observable consequence, K. Then, K, though not a cause of X, is a "surrogate instrument" (Hernán and Robins, 2006) as it is a descendant of an unobserved instrument, U, and thus allows us to extract inferences similar to those that we could draw from a true instrument.

Confounders as Clues

In several of the graphs, K is a confounder in that it is a direct cause of both X and Y (panels (4), (6), (12), and (14)). Let us focus on graph (4), which isolates K's role as a confounder. Here, K can be informative via two possible paths. First, if X is not observed but Y is, then K is d-connected to Q along the path $K \rightarrow X \rightarrow Y \leftarrow Q$. K is in this sense serving as a proxy for X, with its path to Q opened up by the observation of the collider, Y. Second, with

---

[12] As a simple example one might imagine a system in which $X = K$ if $q \in a, b$ and $X = 1 - K$ if $q \in c, d$. Then, if we observe, say, $X = Y = K = 1$, we can infer that $q = b$. Another way to think about what is happening in graph (5) is that K is providing information about the *assignment process*. In this graph, the causal effect (Y's potential outcomes, determined by Q) is also a partial determinant of the assignment of cases to values on X. In terms of cross-case correlational inference, then, we would think of this as a situation of confounding. Observing another cause of X, then, allows us to more fully characterize the process of assignment.

Y observed, K can provide information on Q via the more direct collision, $K \rightarrow Y \leftarrow Q$. If X *is* observed, then the first path is blocked, but the second still remains active. As with any pre-outcome variable, for a confounder clue to provide purchase on Y's nodal type, Y itself must be observed.

In a sense, then, the role of confounders as clues in case-level inference is the mirror image of the role of confounders as covariates in cross-case correlational inference. In a correlational inferential framework, controlling for a variable in K's position in graph (5) renders the X, Y correlation (which we assume to be observed) informative about X's average causal effect. When we use confounders as evidence in within-case inference, it is our observations of other variables that determine how informative the confounder *itself* will be about X's causal effect.

It is important to be precise about the kinds of claims that one can make from graphs like those in Figure 7.4. The graphs in this figure allow us to identify informativeness about an unobserved node Q that is a parent of Y. This setup does not, however, capture all the ways in which clues can be informative about the causal effect of X on Y or about other causal queries of interest. For instance, as noted above, even if a clue is uninformative about a Q node pointing into Y, it may still help establish whether X causes Y: The statement that X causes Y will for some graphs be a statement about a *collection* of nodes that comprise the query. This is the case, for instance, in any graph of the form $X \rightarrow M \rightarrow Y$, where we are interested not just in Y's response to M (the mediator) but also in M's response to X. Of interest, thus, are not just a θ^Y node pointing into Y but also a θ^M node pointing into M. Observations that provide leverage on either component of our query will thus aid an inference about the overall causal effect. A clue K that is d-separated from θ^Y may nevertheless be informative about X's effect on Y if it is *not* d-separated from θ^M. This opens up a broader range of variables as potentially informative clues.

Additionally, as our discussion in Chapter 2 makes clear, queries other than the case-level causal effect – such as average causal effects, actual causes, and causal paths – involve particular features of context: particular sets of θ^j nodes as members of our query set, Q. Thus, even for the same causal model, informativeness will be defined differently for each causal question that we seek to address. The broader point is that we can identify what kinds of observations may address our query if we can place that query on a causal graph and then assess the graph for relationships of d-separation and d-connection.

Further, we emphasize that a DAG can only tell us when a clue *may* be informative (perhaps conditional on some prior observation): thus, *d*-connectedness is necessary but not sufficient for informativeness. This fact follows directly from the rules for drawing a causal graph: The absence of an arrow between two variables implies that they are *not* directly causally related, while the presence of an arrow does not imply that they always are. Whether variables connected to one another by arrows are in fact causally related can depend on the values of other nodes. Likewise, whether a clue K is in fact informative may depend on particular values of W – the variables that have already been observed.

As a simple example, let $q = k_1 w + (1 - w)k_2$, where W is a variable that we have already observed and K_1 and K_2 are clues that we might choose to observe next. Here, if $w = 1$ then learning K_1 will be informative about Q, and learning K_2 will not; but if $w = 0$, then K_1 will be uninformative (and K_2 informative).

In general, then, graphical analysis alone can help us exclude unhelpful research designs, given our prior observations and a fairly minimal set of prior beliefs about causal linkages. This is no small feat. But identifying those empirical strategies that will yield the *greatest* leverage requires engaging more deeply with our causal model, as we show in detail in our discussion of clue-selection in Chapter 12.

7.5 Principles of Learning

While we can use software (such as `CausalQueries`) to implement process-tracing inference for us, it is helpful for researchers to be able to reason their way through what is happening "under the hood." We provide here some core principles and intuitions for thinking through the features of models and queries that influence whether and how much we can learn from within-case observations.

7.5.1 A DAG Alone Does Not Guarantee Probative Value for a Single Case

A DAG puts qualitative structure on causal relations, but quantitative implications depend on the beliefs over causal types. In general, learning from new data requires that, conditional on known data, the probability of a new data pattern is different depending on whether or not the query is true. With flat priors, this condition may not hold for many queries of interest.

To illustrate, suppose that we are interested in whether X caused Y and we posit a simple $X \rightarrow M \rightarrow Y$ model with flat priors over θ^M and θ^Y. Now we would like to conduct process tracing and observe M to tell us about the effect of X on Y in a case with $X = Y = 1$.

Does the observation of M provide leverage on whether $X = 1$ caused $Y = 1$?

It does not. We can learn nothing about X's effect on Y from observing M (again: when we have flat priors and we are examining a single case).

To see why, consider that there are two causal types that will satisfy the query, $X = 1$ caused $Y = 1$. Those are the types $\theta_1^X \theta_{01}^M \theta_{01}^Y$ and $\theta_1^X \theta_{10}^M \theta_{10}^Y$: Either linked positive effects or linked negative effects could generate an overall positive effect of X on Y. Moreover, with flat priors over nodal types, these causal types are equally likely. Now think about what we would conclude if we collected process data and observed $M = 1$ in the $X = Y = 1$ case. This observation would rule out various ways in which X did not cause Y but it also rules out one way in which the query could be satisfied: the causal type with linked negative effects. And what if we observed, instead, $M = 0$? This would have similar implications, this time ruling out the other way in which the query could be satisfied: linked positive effects. Intuitively, we would update the same way no matter what we find, which means we must not be updating at all.

More formally, conditional on observing $X = 1, Y = 1$ our prior that X caused Y is:

$$\frac{\lambda_{01}^M \lambda_{01}^Y + \lambda_{10}^M \lambda_{10}^Y}{(\lambda_{01}^M + \lambda_{11}^M)(\lambda_{01}^Y + \lambda_{11}^Y) + (\lambda_{10}^M + \lambda_{00}^M)(\lambda_{10}^Y + \lambda_{11}^Y)}.$$

Our posterior on observing $M = 1$ is:

$$\frac{\lambda_{01}^M \lambda_{01}^Y}{(\lambda_{01}^M + \lambda_{11}^M)(\lambda_{01}^Y + \lambda_{11}^Y)},$$

It is easy to see these are equal with flat priors ($\lambda_{ab}^j = \lambda^{j*}$ for all a, b). What we can see from the comparison is that when we observe data, we rule out half the types consistent with the data (denominator) but also rule out half the types consistent with the query *and* data (numerator).

However, informative priors on *either* θ^M or θ^Y would help here. For instance, if we believed that linked positive effects are more likely than linked negative effects, then observing M would be informative. Seeing $M = 1$ would then rule out the *less likely* way in which the query could be satisfied but rule in the more likely way, thus increasing our confidence that $X = 1$ caused $Y = 1$. Seeing $M = 0$ would reduce that confidence by ruling out the most likely way in which this effect could occur.

More generally, what we need at the level of priors depends on the query. Suppose that we start with the model, $X \rightarrow M \rightarrow Y$, and formulate the following query: Does X have a positive effect on Y that runs through a chain of positive effects via M? We can learn about this query without any informative priors over nodal types because of the way in which the query itself restricts the type space. Since the query is not satisfied if negative mediating effects are operating, we will update to probability 0 on the query for any observation that violates $X = M = Y$, and we will update upwards on the query for any observation of $X = M = Y$.

7.5.2 Learning Requires Uncertainty

While case-level inference from within-case evidence often requires informative priors about nodal types, there is also such a thing as *too much* information – or, put differently, as insufficient uncertainty about causal relations. Suppose, for instance, that our beliefs are such that X always has a positive effect on M in an $X \rightarrow M \rightarrow Y$ model. Consider, further, that we already know that $X = 1$ in a case. In that situation, nothing can be learned by observing M since the prior observation of X already reveals M's value given our prior beliefs.

To take a less extreme example, suppose that our priors put a *very high probability* on X's having a positive effect on M and that, again, we already know that $X = 1$ in a case. In that situation, we should *expect* to learn very little from observing M since we believe that we are very likely to see $M = 1$, given that we already know $X = 1$. It is true that our beliefs will shift *if* we look for M and find the unexpected value of $M = 0$. But because that data-realization is highly unlikely, we should expect the learning from observing M to be minimal.

We address the concept of expected learning more systematically in Chapters 12 and 13, but our general point here is that, we will learn more from process-tracing evidence, to the extent that (a) we know enough about causal relations in a domain to know how to make causal sense of the evidence we find, but (b) we do not know so much that that evidence can be largely predicted from what we have already observed.

7.5.3 Population-Level Uncertainty and Case-Level Causal Inference

In the procedure we described for process tracing in this chapter (and different to what we introduce in Chapter 8), we have assumed that λ is known and we do not place uncertainty around it.

This might appear somewhat heroic, but in fact for single case inference, if priors are defined directly over causal types, it is without loss of generality. The expected inferences we would make for any query accounting for uncertainty in priors over *causal types* is the same as the inferences we make if we use the expectation only.

With a little abuse of notation say that $\theta \in D$ if causal type θ produces data type D; let q denote a query and say $\theta \in Q$ if causal type θ satisfies the query.

Let $\pi(\theta|\lambda)$ denote the probability of causal type θ given λ and $p(\lambda)$ a prior distribution over λ. Then, the posterior on Q given data D is:

$$\Pr(Q|D) = \frac{\Pr(D, Q)}{\Pr(D)} = \frac{\int \sum_{\theta \in Q \cap D} \pi(\theta|\lambda)p(\lambda)d\lambda}{\int \sum_{\theta \in D} \pi(\theta|\lambda)p(\lambda)d\lambda} = \frac{\sum_{\theta \in Q \cap D} \overline{\pi}(\theta)}{\sum_{\theta \in D} \overline{\pi}(\theta)},$$

where $\overline{\pi}(\theta) = \int \pi(\theta|\lambda)p(\lambda)d\lambda$ is the expected value of λ under f and the last step involves swapping the summation and integral.

For intuition, in an $X \rightarrow Y$ model, if we observe $X = Y = 1$ then D consists of causal types $D = \{(\theta_1^X, \theta_{01}^Y), (\theta_1^X, \theta_{11}^Y)\}$ and the query set for "X has a positive effect on Y" consists of $Q = \{(\theta_1^X, \theta_{01}^Y), (\theta_0^X, \theta_{01}^Y)\}$. Then, $Q \cap D = \{(\theta_1^X, \theta_{01}^Y)\}$. Say we entertain two different values for the distribution of types: We believe with probability s that $\Pr(\theta = (\theta_1^X, \theta_{01}^Y)) = \lambda_b'$ and $\Pr(\theta = (\theta_1^X, \theta_{11}^Y)) = \lambda_d'$ and we believe with probability $1-s$ that $\Pr(\theta = (\theta_1^X, \theta_{01}^Y)) = \lambda_b''$ and $\Pr(\theta = (\theta_1^X, \theta_{11}^Y)) = \lambda_d''$. We then have:

$$\Pr(Q|D) = \frac{\Pr(D, Q)}{\Pr(D)} \tag{7.2}$$

$$= \frac{s\lambda_b' + (1-s)\lambda_b''}{s(\lambda_b' + \lambda_d') + (1-s)(\lambda_b'' + \lambda_d'')} \tag{7.3}$$

$$= \frac{s\lambda_b' + (1-s)\lambda_b''}{\left(s\lambda_b' + (1-s)\lambda_b''\right) + \left(s\lambda_d' + (1-s)(\lambda_d'')\right)} \tag{7.4}$$

$$= \frac{\overline{\lambda}_b}{\overline{\lambda}_b + \overline{\lambda}_d}. \tag{7.5}$$

Note, however, that the same cannot be said if priors are specified over nodal types rather than directly over causal types. One might imagine for instance being certain that X causes Y in a $X \rightarrow M \rightarrow Y$ model but uncertain as to whether the effect works through a sequence of two positive effects or a sequence of two negative effects. In this case the expected effect of X on M could be 0 as could the expected effect of M on Y. Using this information without retaining information about the joint distribution of beliefs over these relations would lead us astray.

7.6 Appendix: Process Tracing with `CausalQueries`

7.6.1 Example 1: Simple Model

Imagine a simple model in which $X \rightarrow M \rightarrow Y$. We can define the model thus:

```
model <- make_model("X -> M -> Y")
```

This model will be of limited use to us without some more specification of *how* processes work. We can make progress for instance if we have informative priors. Most simply, we can impose various monotonicity assumptions thus:

```
model <- model |>
  set_restrictions(decreasing("X", "M")) %>%
  set_restrictions(decreasing("M", "Y"))
```

From this model, we can draw a single case and examine parameter values (θ) and observed data for the case. See Table 7.8.

We can also start making inferences given a specified query given different clue patterns. Here, for instance we query the effect of X on Y for a case with $X = Y = 1$ given different possible observations on M (see Table 7.9).

```
queries <-
  query_model(model = model,
              query = c("Y[X=1] > Y[X=0]",
                        "Y==1 & X==1 & M==0",
                        "Y==1 & X==1 & M==1"),
              using = "priors",
              case_level = TRUE)
```

We see here that the monotonicity assumptions are enough to make observation of M into a hoop test for the proposition that $X = 1$ caused $Y = 1$.

Table 7.8 Nodal types and observed nodal values for a single hypothetical case given an $X \to M \to Y$ model

Node	Nodal_type	Observed
X	0	0
M	00	0
Y	01	0

Table 7.9 Inferences given different clue observations (simple model)

Query	Given	Using	Case.estimand	mean
Y[X=1] > Y[X=0]	X==1 & Y==1	priors	TRUE	0.205
Y[X=1] > Y[X=0]	X==1 & Y==1 & M==0	priors	TRUE	0.000
Y[X=1] > Y[X=0]	X==1 & Y==1 & M==1	priors	TRUE	0.256

7.6.2 Example 2: Many Clues

For a second example, we imagine a more complex process with three types of clues: A mediator clue ($K1$), a moderator clue ($K2$) and a post-treatment clue ($K3$) – which could, for instance, represent whether a case has been selected for study in the first place.

The model is constructed and graphed thus (see Figure 7.5):

```
model <- make_model("X -> K1 -> Y <- K2; Y -> K3; Y <-> K3")
```

```
plot(model)
```

We impose various monotonicity assumptions and set priors reflecting a belief that those cases in which $K1$ and $K2$ are likely to jointly produce Y are very likely to be selected for study ($K3 = 1$) regardless of the value of Y.

```
model <- make_model("X -> K1 -> Y <- K2; Y -> K3; Y <-> K3") %>%
    set_restrictions(decreasing("X", "K1")) %>%
    set_restrictions(decreasing("K1", "Y")) %>%
    set_restrictions(decreasing("K2", "Y")) %>%
    set_restrictions(decreasing("Y", "K3")) %>%
    set_priors(given = "Y.0001", nodal_type = "11", 10)
```

Table 7.10 gives an example of a single case drawn from this model, showing both nodal types (θ) and observed data for the case.

Table 7.10 A single case (causal type) drawn from the model shown in Figure 7.5

Node	Nodal_type	Observed
K1	00	0
K2	1	1
K3	11	1
X	1	1
Y	0000	0

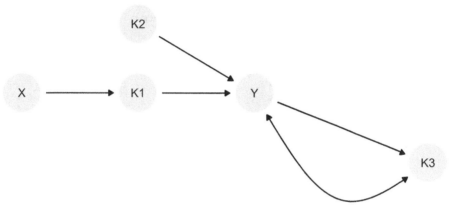

Figure 7.5   Three potentially informative clues for the effect of X on Y

The next code chunk generates inferences for a case in which $X = 1$ and $Y = 1$ depending on which clue pattern we observe (see Table 7.11 for output).

```
queries <-
  query_model(model = model,
             query = "Y[X=1] > Y[X=0]",
             given = c("Y==1 & X==1",
                       "Y==1 & X==1 & K1==1",
                       "Y==1 & X==1 & K2==1",
                       "Y==1 & X==1 & K3==1",
                       "Y==1 & X==1 & K1==1 & K2==1 & K3==1"),
             using = "priors",
             case_level = TRUE)
```

Table 7.11 Inferences given different clue observations

Given	Posterior
Y==1 & X==1	0.195
Y==1 & X==1 & K1==1	0.246
Y==1 & X==1 & K2==1	0.151
Y==1 & X==1 & K3==1	0.206
Y==1 & X==1 & K1==1 & K2==1 & K3==1	0.217

We see that positive data on $K1$ or $K3$ each increase confidence that X caused Y, with more learning from $K1$. Seeing $K2 = 1$ weakens confidence. Positive data on all three clues increases confidence.

8 Process-Tracing Applications

We apply the causal-model-based approach to process tracing to two major substantive issues in comparative politics: the relationship between inequality and democratization and the relationship between institutions and economic growth. Drawing on case-level data, we use restrictions on causal types together with flat priors to draw inferences about a range of causal queries. The applications are both very simple, but they are sufficiently complex to illustrate key features of process tracing with causal models: The different types of learning that can be gleaned from evidence on moderators and mediators, the dependence of inference from some clues on the values of other clues, and the scope for learning from more distal historical data when researchers have beliefs over confounding processes.

In this chapter, we illustrate how causal-model-based process tracing works using two substantive applications that have been of central interest to students of comparative politics for decades: the causes of democratization and the determinants of economic growth. In both cases, we develop simple models to demonstrate the logic of process tracing with causal models. In Chapter 10, we push the analysis further, illustrating the integration of process tracing with cross-case correlational analysis. The key difference is that, in this chapter, we assume – consistent with the process-tracing approach outlined in Chapter 7 – that the researcher comes to a case with a theoretical model in hand, including a set of beliefs about the shares of nodal types in the population. In Chapter 10, as we return to the same case-level queries, we use models that have been directly informed by data from that broader population of cases.

8.1 Inequality and Democratization

8.1.1 The Debate

Sociologists, economists, and political scientists have long theorized and empirically examined the relationship between inequality and democracy (e.g., Acemoglu and Robinson, 2005; Ansell and Samuels, 2014; Boix, 2003; Bollen and Jackman, 1985; Dahl, 1973). In recent years, the works of Boix (2003), Acemoglu and Robinson (2005), and Ansell and Samuels (2014) represent major theoretical advances in specifying when and how inequality might generate transitions to democracy (as well as its persistence, which we bracket here). The first and third of these books also provide large-n cross-national and historical tests of their theories' key correlational predictions. Haggard and Kaufman (2012), moreover, derive causal process observations from a large number of "Third Wave" cases of democratization in order to examine these theories' claims about the centrality of distributional issues to regime change.

We briefly summarize the core logics of and differences among these three sets of arguments here, bracketing many of their moving parts to focus on the basic theorized relationship between inequality and democracy. Both Boix's and Acemoglu and Robinson's theories operate within a Meltzer-Richard (Meltzer and Richard, 1981) framework in which, in a democracy, the median voter sets the level of taxation-and-transfer and, since mean income is higher than median income, benefits from and votes for redistribution from rich to poor. The poorer the median voter, the more redistribution they will prefer. Democracy thus implies greater redistribution than (right-wing) authoritarianism – a better material position for the poor at the expense of the rich elite. Thus, in each of these approaches, struggles over political regimes are conflicts over the distribution of material resources.

In Boix's model, the poor generally prefer democracy for its material benefits. When the poor mobilize to demand regime change, the rich face a choice as to whether to repress or concede, and they are more likely to repress as inequality is higher since, all else equal, they have more to lose from democracy. Thus, with the poor always preferring democracy over right-wing authoritarianism, inequality reduces the prospects for democratization.

In Acemoglu and Robinson's model, inequality simultaneously affects the expected net gains to democracy for both rich and poor. At low levels of inequality, democracy is relatively unthreatening to the elite, as in Boix, but likewise of little benefit to the poor. Since regime change is costly, the poor do not mobilize for democracy when inequality is low, and democratization does not occur. At high levels of inequality, democracy is of great benefit to the poor but has high expected costs for the elite; thus, democratization does not occur because the elite repress popular demands for regime change. In Acemoglu and Robinson's model, democracy emerges only when inequality is at middling levels: high enough for the poor to demand it and low enough for the rich to be willing to concede it.

Ansell and Samuels, finally, extend the distributive politics of regime change in three key ways. First, they allow for a two-sector economy, with a governing elite comprising the landed aristocracy and an urban industrial elite excluded from political power under authoritarian institutions. Total inequality in the economy is a function of inequality in the landed sector, inequality in the industrial sector, and the relative size of each. Second, authoritarian (landed) elites can tax the industrial bourgeoisie, thus giving the industrial elite an incentive to seek constraints on autocratic rule. Third, in Ansell and Samuels' model, rising industrial inequality means a rising industrial elite, generating a larger gap between them and industrial workers, though the industrial masses are richer than the peasantry. A number of results follow, of which we highlight just a couple. Rising land inequality reduces the likelihood of a bourgeois rebellion by giving the landed elite greater repressive capacities and increasing their expected losses under democracy. As industrial inequality rises, however, the industrial elite have more to lose to confiscatory taxation and thus greater incentive to push for partial democracy (in which they have the ability to constrain the government, while the poor remain politically excluded) as well as greater resources with which to mobilize and achieve it. Full democracy, brought on by joint mass and bourgeois rebellion, is most likely as the industrial sector grows in relative size, giving the urban masses more to lose to autocratic expropriation and more resources to mobilize and rebel.

These three theoretical frameworks thus posit rather differing relationships between inequality and democracy. Taking these theoretical logics as forms of background knowledge, we would consider it possible that inequality reduces the likelihood of democracy or that it increases the likelihood of democracy. Yet one feature that is consistent with all three theories is a claim that distributional grievances drive demands for regime change. Moreover, relative deprivation may cut both ways: While poorer groups may have more to gain from redistribution under democracy, better-off groups have more to fear from confiscatory taxation under autocracy. In all three frameworks, *mobilization* by groups with material grievances is critical to transitions to democracy: Elites do not voluntarily cede power.

In their qualitative analysis of "Third Wave" democratizations, Haggard and Kaufman point to additional factors, aside from inequality, that may generate transitions. Drawing on previous work on twentieth century democratic transitions (e.g., Huntington, 1993; Linz and Stepan, 1996), they pay particular attention to international pressures to democratize.

8.1.2 A Causal Model

We now treat these theories as a form of background knowledge and express them as a causal model. We begin with the structure. Suppose we are interested in the case-level causal effect of inequality on democratization of a previously autocratic political system. Suppose further, to simplify the illustration, that we conceptualize both variables in binary terms: Inequality is either high or low, and democratization either occurs or does not occur. This means that we want to know, for a given case of interest, whether high inequality (as opposed to low inequality) causes democracy to emerge, prevents democracy from emerging, or has no effect (i.e., with democratization either occurring or not occurring independent of inequality). We can represent this query in the simple, high-level causal model shown in Figure 8.1. Here, the question, "What is the causal effect of high inequality on democratization in this case?" is equivalent to asking what the value of θ^D is in the case, where the possible values are θ^D_{00}, θ^D_{01}, θ^D_{10}, and θ^D_{11}. We assume here that the case's nodal type, θ^D, is not itself observable, and thus we are in the position of having to make inferences about it.

Drawing on the logic of probative value discussed in Chapter 7, we can already identify possibilities for learning about θ^D from the other nodes represented in this high-level graph. Merely observing the level of inequality in a case will tell us nothing since I is not d-connected to θ^D if we have observed nothing else. On the other hand, only observing the outcome – regime type – in a case *can* give us information about θ^D since D *is* d-connected to θ^D. For instance, if we observe $D = 1$ (that a case democratized), then we can immediately rule out θ^D_{00} as a value of θ^D since this type does not permit democratization to occur. Further, conditional on observing D, I is now d-connected to θ^D: In other words, having observed the outcome, we can additionally learn about the case's type from observing the status of the causal

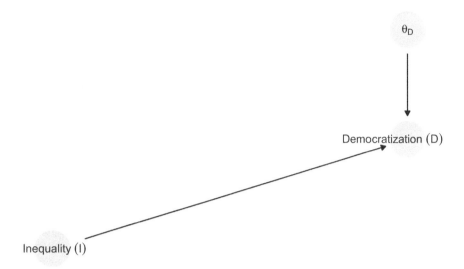

Figure 8.1   Simple higher level model of inequality and democratization

variable. For example, if $D = 1$, then observing $I = 1$ allows us additionally to rule out the value θ_{10}^D (a negative causal effect).

Now, observing just I and D alone will always leave two nodal types in contention. For instance, seeing $I = D = 1$ (the case had high inequality and democratized) would leave us unsure whether high inequality caused the democratization in this case ($\theta^D = \theta_{01}^D$) or the democratization would have happened anyway ($\theta^D = \theta_{11}^D$). This is a limitation of X, Y data that we refer to in Humphreys and Jacobs (2015) as the "fundamental problem of type ambiguity." Note that this does not mean that we will be left indifferent between the two remaining types. Learning from X, Y data alone – narrowing the types down to two – can be quite significant, depending on our priors over the distribution of types. For example, if we previously believed that a θ_{00}^D type (cases in which democracy will never occur, regardless of inequality) was much more likely than a θ_{11}^D type (democracy will always occur, regardless of inequality) and that positive and negative effects of inequality were about equally likely, then ruling out the θ_{00}^D and θ_{10}^D values for a case will shift us toward the belief that inequality caused democratization in the case. This is because we are ruling out both a negative effect and the type of null effect that we had considered the most likely, leaving a null effect that we consider relatively unlikely.

Nonetheless, we can increase the prospects for learning by *theorizing* the relationship between inequality and democratization. Given causal logics and

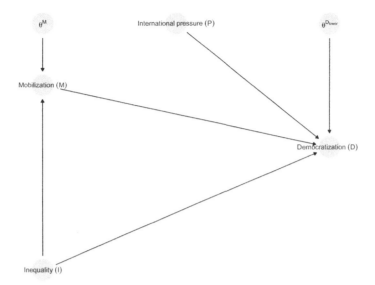

Figure 8.2   A lower level model of inequality and democratization in which inequality may affect regime type both directly and through mobilization of the lower classes, and international pressure may also affect regime type

empirical findings in the existing literature, we can say more than is contained in Figure 8.1 about the possible structure of the causal linkages between inequality and democratization. Moreover, we can embed this prior knowledge of the possible causal relations in this domain in a lower level model that is consistent with the high-level model that most simply represents our query.

If we were to seek to fully capture them, the models developed by Boix, Acemoglu, and Robinson, and Ansell and Samuels would, each individually, suggest causal graphs with a large number of nodes and edges connecting them. Representing all variables and relationships jointly contained in these three models would take an extremely complex graph. Yet there is no need to go down to the lowest possible level – to generate the *most* detailed graph – in order to increase our empirical leverage on the problem.

We represent in Figure 8.2 one possible lower level model consistent with our high-level model. Drawing on causal logics in the existing literature, we unpack the nodes in the high-level model in two ways:

1. We interpose a mediator between inequality and democratization: mobilization (M) by economically disadvantaged groups expressing material grievances. M is a function of both I and its nodal type, θ^M, which defines

its response to I. In inserting this mediator, we have extracted θ^M from θ^D, pulling out that part of D's response to I that depends on M's response to I.

2. We specify a second influence on democratization, international pressure (P). Like θ^M, P has also been extracted from θ^D; it represents that part of D's response to I that is conditioned by international pressures.

In representing the causal dependencies in this graph, we allow for inequality to have (in the language of mediation analysis) both an "indirect" effect on democratization via mobilization and a "direct" effect. The arrow running directly from I to D allows for effects of inequality on democratization beyond any effects running via mobilization of the poor, including effects that might run in the opposite direction. (For instance, it is possible that inequality has a positive effect on democratization via mobilization but a negative effect via any number of processes that are not explicitly specified in the model.) The graph also implies that there is no confounding: Since there is no arrow running from another variable in the graph to I, I is modeled as a root node.

The lower level graph thus has two exogenous, θ nodes that will be relevant to assessing causal effects: θ^M and $\theta^{D_{lower}}$. Node θ^M, capturing I's effect on M, ranges across the usual four values for a single-cause, binary setup: $\theta_{00}^M, \theta_{01}^M, \theta_{10}^M$, and θ_{11}^M.

Node $\theta^{D_{lower}}$ is considerably more complicated, however, because this node represents D's response to three causal variables: I, M, and P. One way to put this is that the values of $\theta^{D_{lower}}$ indicate how inequality's direct effect will depend on mobilization (and how mobilization's effect will depend on inequality), conditional on whether or not there is international pressure. Readers can find this more complex notation at work within the CausalQueries package, but for the sake of readability, we do not use it here in the text.

The result is $2^8 = 256$ possible nodal types for D. With four nodal types for M, we thus have 1024 possible combinations of causal effects between named variables in the lower level graph. How do these lower level nodal types map onto the higher level nodal types that are of interest? In other words, which combinations of lower level types represent a positive, negative, or zero causal effect of inequality on democratization? When working with the CausalQueries package, the software figures this out for us automatically once we define our model and our query, but we work through the logic "by hand" here to help convey the intuition.

Ignoring P for the moment, there are 16 ways that nodal types for M and nodal types for D can combine to create positive effects of I on D. These different types involve different combinations of direct and indirect effects. In Figure 4.5, for a similar model, we can see all 16 types in which there are overall effects, with some types producing direct effects, some indirect effects, and some both.

Another way to think of the different classes of causal types that generate a positive effect of I on D is to distinguish among types according to the ways that I affects M. This gives us three families of causal types: those in which overall effects are due to (or at least not disrupted by) a positive effect of I on M; those in which overall effects are due to (or not disrupted by) a negative effect of I on M; and those in which there is no effect of I on M at all.

To define a causal effect of I in this setup, we need to define the "joint effect" of I and M as being the effect of changing both variables simultaneously: when we both change I from 0 to 1 and change M in the manner in which it is changed by the change in I. Thus, for instance, the joint effect of I and M on D is positive if, when I has a positive effect on M, changing both I and M from 0 to 1 changes D from 0 to 1. Given this definition, a positive causal effect of inequality on democratization emerges for all of the following sets of causal types:

1. **Types where I has a positive effect on M:** I has a positive effect on M, and I and M have a *joint* positive effect on D, when P takes on whatever value it takes on in the case.
2. **Types where I has a negative effect on M:** I has a negative effect on M, and I and M have a *joint* negative effect on D, when P takes on whatever value it takes on in the case.
3. **Types where I has no effect on M:** I has no effect on M, and I has a positive effect on D, when we fix M's value (at 0 or at 1), and P at whatever value it takes on in the case.

If we start out with a case in which inequality is high and democratization has not occurred (or inequality is low and democratization *has* occurred), we will be interested in the possibility of a negative overall effect. A negative causal effect of inequality on democratization emerges for all of the following sets of causal types:

4. **Types where I has a positive effect on M:** I has a positive effect on M, and I and M have a *joint* negative effect on D, when P takes on whatever value it takes on in the case.

5. **Types where *I* has a negative effect on *M*:** *I* has a negative effect on *M*, and jointly increasing *I* while decreasing *M* generates a decrease in *D*, when *P* takes on whatever value it takes on in the case.
6. **Types where *I* has no effect on *M*:** *I* has no effect on *M*, and *I* has a negative effect on *D*, when we fix *M*'s value (at 0 or at 1), and *P* at whatever value it takes on in the case.

Finally, all other response patterns yield *no* effect of inequality on democratization.

Thus, for a case in which $I = D = 1$, our query amounts to assessing the probability that θ^M and $\theta^{D_{lower}}$ jointly take on values falling into conditions 1, 2, or 3. And for a case in which $I \neq D$, where we entertain the possibility of a negative effect, our query is an assessment of the probability of conditions 4, 5, or 6 arising.

8.1.2.1 Forming Priors

We now need to express prior beliefs about the probability distribution from which values of θ^M and $\theta^{D_{lower}}$ are drawn. We place structure on this problem by drawing a set of beliefs about the likelihood or monotonicity of effects and interactions among variables from the theories in Boix, Acemoglu and Robinson, and Ansell and Samuels. As a heuristic device, we weight more heavily those propositions that are more widely shared across the three works than those that are consistent with only one of the frameworks. We intend this part of the exercise to be merely illustrative of how one might go about forming priors from an existing base of knowledge; there are undoubtedly other ways in which one could do so from the inequality and democracy literature. Specifically, the belief that we embed in our priors about θ^M is:

- **Monotonicity of *I*'s effect on *M*: no negative effect.** In Acemoglu and Robinson, inequality should generally increase the chances of – and, in Boix, should never prevent – mobilization by the poor. Only in Ansell and Samuels' model does inequality have a partial downward effect on the poor's demand for democracy insofar as improved material welfare for the poor increases the chances of autocratic expropriation; and this effect is countervailed by the greater redistributive gains that the poor will enjoy under democracy as inequality rises.[1] Consistent with the weight of prior theory on this effect, in our initial run of the analysis, we rule out

---

[1] In addition, as the industrial bourgeoisie become richer, which increases the Gini, this group faces a greater risk of autocratic expropriation. If we consider the rising bourgeoisie's mobilization to be

negative effects of I on M. We are indifferent in our priors between positive and null effects and between the two types of null effects (mobilization always occurring or never occurring, regardless of the level of inequality). We thus set our prior on θ^M as: $p(\theta^M = \theta_{10}^M) = 0.0$, $p(\theta^M = \theta_{00}^M) = 0.25$, $p(\theta^M = \theta_{11}^M) = 0.25$, and $p(\theta^M = \theta_{01}^M) = 0.5$. We relax this monotonicity assumption to account for the Ansell and Samuels logic in a second run of the analysis.

For our prior on democracy's responses to inequality, mobilization, and international pressure $(\theta^{D_{lower}})$, we extract the following beliefs from the literature:

- **Monotonicity of direct I effect: no positive effect.** In none of the three theories does inequality promote democratization via a pathway *other than* via the poor's rising demand for it. In all three theories, inequality has a distinct negative effect on democratization via an increase in the elite's expected losses under democracy and, thus, its willingness to repress. In Ansell and Samuels, the distribution of resources also affects the probability of success of rebellion; thus higher inequality also reduces the prospects for democratization by strengthening the elite's hold on power. We thus set a zero prior probability on all types in which I's direct effect on D is positive for any value of P.
- **Monotonicity of M's effect: no negative effect.** In none of the three theories does mobilization reduce the prospects of democratization. We thus set a zero probability on all types in which M's effect on D is negative at any value of I or P.
- **Monotonicity of P's effect: no negative effect.** While international pressures are only discussed in Haggard and Kaufman's study, none of the studies considers the possibility that international pressures to democratize might prevent democratization that would otherwise have occurred. We thus set a zero probability on all types in which P's effect is negative at any value of I or M.

This reduces the number of nodal types for D from 256 to just 20. For all remaining allowable types, we set flat priors.

The remaining 20 allowable types involve a rich range of possible interactions among international pressure, inequality, and mobilization.

mobilization by a materially disadvantaged group, then this constitutes an additional positive effect of inequality on mobilization.

Since P conditions the effect of I, we must also establish a prior on the distribution of P. Here, we again set a flat prior by setting the prior probability of $P = 1$ to 0.5, implying that before observing the data, we think that international pressures to democratize are present half the time.

We show in Appendix (8.3) how to form this model using the `CausalQueries` package.

8.1.3 Results

We can now choose nodes in addition to I and D to observe from the lower level model. Recall that our query is about the joint values of θ^M and $\theta^{D_{\text{lower}}}$. By the logic of d-separation, we can immediately see that both M and P may be informative about these nodes when D has already been observed. Conditional on D, both M and P are d-connected to both θ^M and $\theta^{D_{\text{lower}}}$. Let us see what we learn if we search for either mobilization or international pressure or both, and find either clue present or absent.

We consider four distinct situations corresponding to four possible combinations of inequality and democratization values that we might be starting with. In each situation, the nature of the query changes. Where we start with a case with low inequality and no democratization, asking if the level of inequality caused the outcome is to ask if the lack of inequality caused the lack of democratization. Where we have high inequality and no democratization, we want to know if democratization was prevented by high inequality (as high inequality does in Boix's account). For cases in which democratization occurred, we want to know whether the lack or presence of inequality (whichever was the case) generated the democratization.

Inference is done by applying Bayes rule to the observed data given the priors. Different "causal types" are consistent or inconsistent with possible data observations. Conversely, the observation of data lets us shift weight toward causal types that are consistent with the data and away from those that are not. As a simple illustration: if we observe $D = 1$ in a case, then we would shift weight from types for which D is always 0, given the other observed data, to types for which D *can* be 1 given the other observed data.

In coding countries' level of inequality, we rely on Haggard and Kaufman's coding using the Gini coefficient from the Texas Inequality dataset and dichotomizing at the sample median. In coding cases for democratization, we use the codings in Cheibub et al. (2010), one of two measures used by Haggard and Kaufman. Our codings of the M and P clues come from close readings of the country-specific transition accounts in Haggard et al.

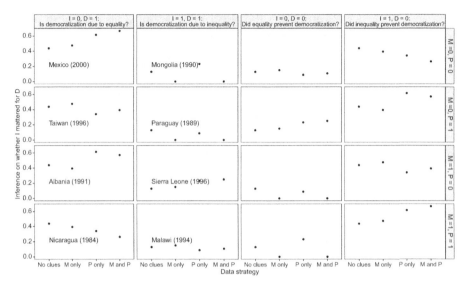

Figure 8.3   Case-level inferences for whether the level of inequality caused the democratization outcome, given possible observations of mobilization and pressure (untrained model)

(2012), the publicly shared qualitative dataset associated with Haggard and Kaufman (2012). We code M as 1 where the transition account refers to anti-government or anti-regime political mobilization by economically disadvantaged groups, and as 0 otherwise. For international pressure, we code $P = 0$ if international pressures to democratize are not mentioned in the transition account and $P = 1$ if they are.

We plot results for 16 types of cases in Figure 8.3. In the first two columns of the figure, we consider cases that democratized, first those with low inequality and then those with high inequality. In the second two columns, we consider cases that did not democratize, those with $I = 0$ and then those with $I = 1$. Within each column, each row represents a different realization of M and P values.

Since Haggard and Kaufman (2012) – from which we get our M and P data – includes only cases that democratized, we are only able to assign illustrative country names to the graphs in the $D = 1$ columns. In the $D = 0$ columns, we represent estimates we *would* arrive at if we observed the different M and/or D values in cases.

Within each country graph, we plot the inference we draw under different evidentiary conditions. We show how confident we would be that the level of inequality caused the democratization outcome if (a) we observed only the cause and the outcome (I and D); (b) we additionally observed either clue, the level of mobilization by disadvantaged classes or the level of international pressure; and (c) if we observed both of these clues.

We now discuss the four columns of Figure 8.3 in turn.

8.1.3.1 $I = 0, D = 1$: Low Inequality Countries that Democratized

In a case that had low inequality and had democratized, did low inequality cause democratization, as Boix's thesis would suggest? Results for cases with $I = 0, D = 1$ are shown in the first column of Figure 8.3. With the analyses in this column, we address the question: What is the probability that Mexico, Taiwan, Albania, and Nicaragua democratized *because* they had relatively low inequality? The first plotted point is our estimate of the probability that low inequality was a cause of democratization when we observed only I and D. Moving to the right, we then plot our inferences upon observing M only, upon observing P only, and upon observing M and P, respectively.

Upon observing only the level of inequality and the outcome of democratization in any of these cases, we would place a 0.438 probability of inequality having been a cause. With only these two pieces of information in hand, we reach identical inferences about the four cases since they take on the same I and D values.

How do our inferences change as we gather additional clues? Let us turn first to gathering information about mobilization. By comparing the "No clues" to the "M only" point, we can see that observing M changes our conclusions only modestly for all of the cases. Observing mobilization generally reduces our confidence in inequality's negative effect relative to observing no mobilization. If we observe the level of mobilization, our confidence that inequality mattered goes up slightly (to 0.475) in Mexico and Taiwan, where mobilization did not occur, and goes down slightly in Albania and Nicaragua (to 0.394) where mobilization did occur. M's limited informativeness derives from the nature of the question we are asking and the restrictions we have imposed on the model. Recall that we are looking here for a negative effect of I on D. Given the model restrictions (no negative $I \rightarrow M$ or $M \rightarrow D$ effects), this negative effect can only run via a direct effect, not through mobilization.

M can nonetheless still be informative as a *moderator* of I's direct effect. As we know, learning about moderators tells us something about (a) how a case's outcome responds to a causal variable under a given context (i.e., about the nodal types operating in the case) and (b) the context that the case is in. Thus, in the first instance, observing M together with I and D helps us eliminate types inconsistent with these three data points. For example, if we see $M = 0$, then we eliminate any type in which D is 0 when $M = 0$ and $I = 1$, under any value of P. Second, we learn from observing M about the value of M under which D will be responding to I. Now because M is itself potentially affected by I, the learning here is somewhat complicated. What we learn most directly from observing M is *the effect of I on M* in this case. If we observe $M = 1$, then we know that I has no effect on M in this case (since such an effect can only be positive in this model); whereas if we observe $M = 0$, I might or might not have a positive effect on M. Learning about this $I \rightarrow M$ effect then allows us to form a belief about how likely M would be to be 0 versus 1 if I changed from 0 to 1. That is, it allows us to learn about the moderating conditions under which D would be responding to this change in I (would mobilization be occurring or not)? This belief, in turn, allows us to form a belief about how D will respond to I given the values of $\theta^{D_{lower}}$ that are consistent with the I, M, and D observations. The sum total of this learning remains quite modest, as we can see by comparing the "M only" estimate in each $I = 0, D = 1$ graph to the "No clues" estimate.

As we see from the third estimate plotted on each graph, the international pressure clue is much more informative than the mobilization clue in an $I = 0, D = 1$ case. Observing the absence of international pressure makes us much more confident in low inequality's effect. The reason is that international pressure is an alternative cause of democratization – a condition that could have caused democratization regardless of the level of inequality. Observing the presence of international pressure in a case makes it less likely for low inequality to have caused the outcome. Once we bring this second clue into the analysis, Mexico and Taiwan sharply part ways: Seeing no international pressure in Mexico, we are now much more confident that inequality mattered for the Mexican transition (0.667); seeing international pressure in Taiwan, we are now substantially less confident that inequality mattered to the Taiwanese transition (0.393). Similarly, observing P sharply differentiates the Albanian and Nicaraguan cases: Seeing no international pressure in the Albanian transition considerably boosts our confidence in inequality's causal role there (0.571), while observing international pressure in the Nicaraguan transition strongly undermines our belief in an inequality effect there (0.263).

We can see from the fourth column that, if we have already observed P, then we gain further information from also observing M (and likewise going from only observing M to observing P as well), and they generally push our inferences in the same direction. For Mexico, where both mobilization and international pressure were absent, we become even more confident in low inequality's effect when we observe both than when we observe only one. In Nicaragua, meanwhile, where both are present, we believe it even less likely that low inequality mattered when we observe both than when we observe one. In Taiwan and Albania, where M and P take on different values, we see that we end up with inferences between the "M only" and the "P only" inferences when we observe both clues.

8.1.3.2 $I = 1, D = 1$: High Inequality Countries that Democratized

Where we see both high inequality and democratization, the question is whether high inequality caused democratization via a positive effect. Considering the second column of cases in Figure 8.3, did high inequality cause Mongolia, Sierra Leone, Paraguay, and Malawi to democratize?

Observing only the level of inequality and the democratization outcome, we would have fairly low confidence that inequality mattered, with a belief of 0.128. Let us see what we can learn if we also observe the level of mobilization, international pressure, or both.

M can now be highly informative since we are now looking for a *positive* effect of I on D, and a positive effect has to run through mobilization under the model restriction that rules out positive direct effects. The observation of a lack of mobilization is most telling: High inequality cannot have caused democratization, given our model, if inequality did not cause mobilization to occur. Thus, when we observe no mobilization by the masses in Mongolia and Paraguay, we can be certain (given our model) that high inequality did *not* cause democratization in these cases. Moreover, this result does not change if we also go and look for international pressure: Neither seeing pressure nor seeing its absence shifts our posterior away from 0. Observing P in these two cases only matters if we have *not* observed M.

If we look for mobilization and we do see it, on the other hand – as in Sierra Leone and Malawi – we are slightly more confident that high inequality was the cause of democratization (0.15). Moreover, if we first see $M = 1$, then observing international pressure can add much more information; and it substantially differentiates our conclusions about the causes of Sierra Leone's and Malawi's transitions. Just as in an $I = 0, D = 1$ case, it is the absence of international pressure that leaves the most "space" for inequality to have generated the democratization outcome. When we see the absence of pressure in Sierra Leone, our confidence that high inequality was a cause of the transition increases to 0.25; seeing pressure present in Malawi reduces our confidence in inequality's effect to 0.107.

We next examine causal relations for cases that did not democratize. These cases are not included in Haggard and Kaufman (2012), and so are not labeled in the figure. However, our model can tell us what we *would* believe if we also observed different clues in cases that did not democratize.

8.1.3.3 $I = 0, D = 0$: Low Inequality Countries that Did Not Democratize

To begin with $I = 0, D = 0$ cases, we would want to ask: Did the absence of high inequality prevent democratization that would have otherwise occurred (as, for instance, at the left-hand end of the Acemoglu and Robinson inverted U-curve)?

We start based on the I and D values and our model, believing that there is a 0.128 chance that low inequality prevented democratization. We then see that our beliefs shift most dramatically if we look for mobilization and find that it was present. The reason is the mirror image of the reason why $M = 0$ is so informative in an $I = 1, D = 1$ case: We are again looking for a positive effect of I on D, and such an effect has to run through the pathway mediated by M. So observing $M = 1$ when $I = 0$ must mean that I has no effect on M in this case, and thus I cannot have a positive effect on D. If we do *not* observe mobilization when we look for it, on the other hand, we now think it is somewhat more likely that $I = 0$ caused $D = 0$ since it is still possible that high inequality *could* cause mobilization.

We also see that observing whether there is international pressure has a substantial effect on our beliefs. When we observe $M = 0$ (or don't look for M at all), the presence of international pressure increases the likelihood that low inequality prevented democratization. Intuitively, this is because international pressure, on average across types, has a positive effect on democratization; so pressure's presence creates a greater opportunity for low inequality to counteract international pressure's effect and prevent democratization from occurring that otherwise would have (if there had been high inequality and the resulting mobilization).

In these cases, we see that observing $M = 0$ adds almost no information if we have already observed P, regardless of what value P takes on. However, seeing $M = 1$ dramatically shifts inferences even if we have already seen P – since, by the logic above, it tells us that low inequality could not have prevented democratization given our model. Likewise, if we have already observed $M = 1$, then there is no gain from observing P. It is only if we go looking for M and see $M = 0$ that P can be potentially informative.

We can see here the outlines of a conditional clue-selection logic – in which, the value of collecting information on a clue can depend on what we observe when seeking prior clues. We elaborate on this logic in greater depth in Chapter 12.

8.1.3.4 $I = 1, D = 0$: High Inequality Countries that Did Not Democratize

In cases with high inequality and no democratization, the question is whether high inequality prevented democratization via a negative effect, as theorized by Boix. That negative effect has to have operated via inequality's direct effect on democratization since our model's monotonicity restrictions allow only positive effects via mobilization. In an $I = 1, D = 0$ case, the consequence of observing P is similar in direction to, but greater in magnitude than, the consequence in the $I = 0, D = 0$ case: Seeing international pressure here greatly increases our confidence that high inequality prevented democratization, while seeing no international pressure moderately reduces that confidence. There is, returning to the same intuition, more opportunity for high inequality to exert a negative effect on democratization when international pressures are present and pushing toward democratization.

Here, however, looking for M has a more modest effect than it does in an $I = 0, D = 0$ case. This is because we learn nothing about the indirect pathway from I to D by observing M: As we have said, we already know from seeing high inequality and no democratization (given our monotonicity assumptions) that any effect could not have run through the presence or absence of mobilization. However, M provides some information given its role as a potential moderator for I's direct effect on D (since M is also pointing into D). Assuming that we have not observed P, we see a small downward shift in our confidence that inequality mattered if we see no mobilization, and a small upward shift if we see mobilization.

For this set of cases, we see that M and P's respective probative value is fairly independent of whether we have observed the other clue first or of what we found if we did.

8.1.4 Considerations: Theory Dependence

Haggard and Kaufman set out to use causal process observations to test inequality-based theories of democratization against the experiences of "Third Wave" democratizations. Their principal test is to examine whether they see evidence of distributive conflict in the process of democratization, defined largely as the presence or absence of mobilization prior to the transition. They secondarily look for other possible causes, specifically international pressure and splits in the elite.

In interpreting the evidence, Haggard and Kaufman generally treat the absence of mobilization as evidence against inequality-based theories of democratization as a whole (p. 7). They also see the *presence* of distributive mobilization in cases with high inequality and democratization as evidence against the causal role of inequality (p. 7). These inferences, however, seem only loosely connected to the logic of the causal theories under examination here. Haggard and Kaufman express concern that inequality-oriented arguments point to "cross-cutting effects" (p. 1) of inequality, but do not systematically work through the implications of these multiple pathways for empirical strategy.

Our analysis suggests that a systematic engagement with the underlying models can shift the interpretation of the evidence considerably. Under the model we have formulated, where inequality is *high*, the absence of mobilization in a country that democratized is damning to the notion that inequality mattered. However, where inequality is *low* – precisely the situation in which Boix's theory predicts that we will see democratization – things are more complicated. If we assume that inequality cannot prevent mobilization, then observing no mobilization (in a case with low inequality that democratized) does not work against the claim that inequality mattered for the transition; indeed, it slightly supports it, at least given what we think is a plausible model-representation of arguments in the literature. Observing the absence of mobilization in such a case can undercut an inequality-based explanation if (and only if) we believe it is possible that inequality might prevent mobilization that would otherwise have occurred, a belief inconsistent with our model. Further, in cases with high inequality and democratization, the *absence* of mobilization would be the observation least consistent with the claim that inequality mattered. Observing mobilization, in contrast, pushes in favor of an inequality-based explanation.

Moreover, it is striking that Haggard and Kaufman lean principally on a mediator clue, turning to evidence of international pressure and elite splits (moderators or alternative causes) largely as secondary clues to identify "ambiguous" cases. As we have shown, under a plausible model given prior theory, it is the moderator clue that is likely to be much more informative.

Of course, the model we have written down is only one possible interpretation of existing theoretical knowledge. It is possible that Haggard and Kaufman, and other scholars in this domain hold beliefs that diverge from those encoded in our working model. The larger point, however, is that our process-tracing inferences will inevitably *depend* – and could depend greatly – on our background knowledge of the domain under examination. Moreover, formalizing that knowledge as a causal model can help ensure that we take that prior knowledge into account – that the inferences we draw from new data are consistent with the knowledge we bring to the table.

The analysis also has insights regarding case selection. Haggard and Kaufman justify their choice of only $D = 1$ cases as a strategy "designed to test a particular theory and thus rests on the identification of the causal mechanism leading to regime change" (p. 4). Ultimately, however, the authors seem centrally concerned with assessing whether inequality, as opposed to some-thing else, played a key causal role in generating the outcome. As the results above demonstrate, however, there is nothing special about the $D = 1$ cases in generating leverage on this question. The tables for $D = 0$ show that, given the model, the same clues can shift beliefs about as much for $D = 0$ as for $D = 1$ cases. We leave a more detailed discussion of this kind of issue in model-based case-selection for Chapter 13.

Finally, we emphasize that all of the inferences in this chapter depend on a model that is constrained by theoretical insights but not systematically trained by data. Although we are able to make many inferences using this model, given observations from a case of interest, we have no empiri-cal grounds to justify these inferences. In Chapter 10, we show how this same model can be trained with broader data from multiple cases, and in Chapter 16 we illustrate how the model itself can be empirically evaluated.

8.2 Institutions and Growth

We now consider a second application, again connecting to a major debate in political economy. This time we use the application to illustrate inference given a focus on rival explanations, rather than mediation, and the scope for case level inference that arises specifically from beliefs regarding unobserved confounding.

8.2.1 The Debate

Just as there exists a long-running debate about the causes of democratiza-tion, a similar macro-level debate surrounds the causes of economic growth. Two main proposed explanations are geographic location and the quality of institutions. In a prominent geographic account, countries more distant from the equator experience cooler temperatures, climates less prone to disease, and other environmental benefits (Sachs, 2001). The institutional argument is also quite simple. Going back to Adam Smith, scholars have argued that protections against expropriation and state abuse are key to prosperity. An important contribution by Acemoglu et al. (2001) highlighted the difficulty of separating out cause and effect in studies of income and institutions and argued that a plausibly exogenous[2] feature – settler mortality – might usefully

---

[2] Our usage of the term "exogenous" here differs from the usage introduced in Chapter 2. Exogeneous is used here in the sense commonly employed by social scientists, to mean, essentially, that the variable is not a function of the outcome or of other factors that also cause the outcome.

help disentangle the causal effects of institutions. They argue, specifically, that colonizers constructed stronger institutions, with more robust rule of law and property rights protections, in places that posed lower risks to settlers' health.

Rodrik, Subramanian, and Trebbi (RST), (2004) pitted these ideas against each other (and against a third focused on trade policy) and concluded that "institutions rule" in the sense that they have a larger average effect. We use the RST 2004 data and couple it with a causal model in the hopes of being able to use case evidence to address case-level questions: Were good institutions plausibly a cause of wealth in a particular country? Does knowing about the location of a country make us more or less confident that institutions mattered?[3]

8.2.2 A Causal Model

We now construct the model. We are interested in a single outcome: economic productivity (Y) as measured by real per capita GDP in 1995.

We have two causes of interest: rule of law (R) and distance from the equator (D). We also include settler mortality as an *instrument* for institutional quality. In doing so we allow for the possibility that institutions are not exogenous in our model, but we assume that (lower) settler mortality has an effect on rule of law but is not related to wealth except via its effect on rule of law.

We show again in Appendix (8.3) how to form this model using the CausalQueries package.

The model includes two causes for Y (R and D), and one cause for R (M) that is otherwise unrelated to Y. In addition, it allows for arbitrary confounding between R and Y. The model is represented graphically in Figure 8.4.

To make case-level inferences on causal effects from this model, we need informative beliefs over causal relations. As with the last application, we will set priors based on three monotonicity assumptions. We return to these assumptions in Chapter 10, where we seek to use data to inform such beliefs.

We first adopt the monotonicity assumption built into RST's instrumental variables analysis: that M has a monotonic effect on R. More settler mortality never leads to greater institutional strength. From work on geography and growth (e.g., Sachs, 2001), we adopt the assumption that proximity to the equator does not bolster growth. The background logic is that geography determines climate, agricultural productivity, and the ease of diffusion of

---

[3] In what follows, we ignore that trade openness argument both for reasons of parsimony and because little evidence was found for its importance in Rodrik et al. (2004).

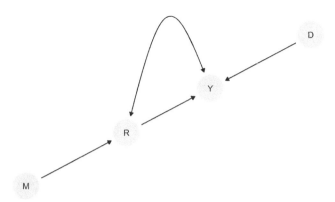

Figure 8.4   Institutions and growth DAG

important ideas and resources from other areas. We also suppose that strong institutions do not negatively affect national income. Few argue that weak protection of property rights is beneficial. For a discussion of "greasing" and "sanding" arguments, see Méon and Sekkat (2005).

These restrictions dramatically reduce the number of possible nodal types. In the base model, without any restrictions, there are 256 nodal types for Y, 4 for R, and 2 each for M and D. Following the restrictions, there are nine nodal types for Y and three for R. Allowing confounding, however, means that we have more parameters than nodal types; specifically, we now have $4 \times 9 = 36$ parameters for Y, allowing for possible dependence between the nine nodal types of Y and the four nodal types of R.

We highlight that we have imposed no assumption regarding whether R and M are substitutes or complements in producing Y.

8.2.3 Results

We first consider whether institutions caused good economic outcomes for different cases. We then adjust the model to show how inferences can change qualitatively when patterns of confounding are specified. Finally, we use the same model to demonstrate how a change in the query we pose can switch which node is the causal variable of interest and which is the clue.

8.2.3.1 Basic Results

We proceed in a similar manner as in the democratization example, focusing now on questions of the form "did good institutions cause high income" and assessing how our answer changes as we learn different facts about a case.

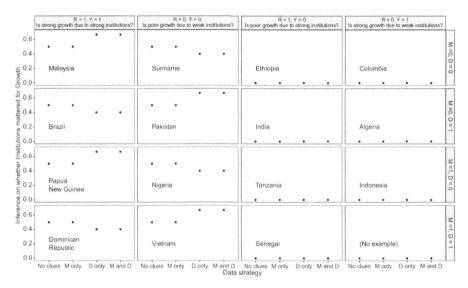

Figure 8.5   Case level inferences given possible observations of distance and mortality (untrained model)

We report results in Figure 8.5. Each column in the figure displays cases with a particular combination of economic growth and institutional quality. Within each combination, we then have the four possible permutations of settler mortality and distance from the equator. This makes for a total of 16 types of countries. There is a real-world example for fifteen of these, with the sole exception being when growth is high, institutional quality is low, settler mortality is high, and distance from the equator is high. As with the inequality and democratization application, we emphasize that the case-level inferences shown here are based purely on the observation of nodes in the model and the model itself, and do not incorporate richer information about cases that experts will surely have available to them.

Consider the cases with good growth and strong institutions, in the first column. Do good institutions explain good economic outcomes? The first thing we notice is that observing settler mortality rates (*M*) makes no difference to our answer to this question. What happens to our beliefs, however, when we observe *D*? As we see from comparing Brazil and the Dominican Republic to Malaysia and Papua New Guinea, observing that a case is distant from the equator makes us *less* likely to think that good economic outcomes are due to the institutions. As with democratization, evidence consistent with one explanation of the observed outcome results in less weight being placed on another explanation. Recall that we did not build into the model the specific idea that the causes are substitutes for one another.

Consider next the four $R = 0$, $Y = 0$ cases. For these cases, we ask: Did the lack of high quality institutions cause the lack of growth? We see here that we again learn nothing from M (regardless of distance from the equator). But, following the same alternative-cause logic that we discussed above, we are now more likely to think that the poor economic outcomes are due to weak institutions when we learn that a case is far from the equator – since being near the equator could have constituted an alternative cause of low growth. We are more confident that poor institutions were the culprit in Pakistan and Vietnam than in Suriname or Nigeria.

For the off-diagonal cases – those with $Y = 1$, $R = 0$ and those with $Y = 0$, $R = 1$ – we have nothing to learn from collecting additional clues since our monotonicity assumption implies, as an *a priori* matter, that R cannot have a negative effect on Y. No additional evidence can change our posterior beliefs about that question since the nodal types that would allow for a negative effect have been excluded from the model from the outset. This highlights just how strong a monotonicty assumption can be for an attribution query.

Notably, observing settler mortality makes no difference to inference for any type of case. Why is that? Looking to the graph, it is *not* that R d-separates M from Y. Without confounding, R would d-separate them; but with confounding, R is a collider for M and Y, meaning that observing R *connects* these two nodes. Thus, in principle, given the structure of the graph, M has the *potential* to be informative about θ^Y, that is, about R's effect on Y. The reason M is not informative in this instantiation of the model is that, although we have allowed for confounding, we have given no structure to this confounding. Building in more specific beliefs about the nature of the confounding would make a difference here.

8.2.3.2 Using Stronger Background Knowledge: Beliefs about Confounding

If we are willing to encode more specific beliefs about confounding in our model, then the instrument, M, can become informative about the case-level causal effect of R on Y. In the following example, we assume that there is a relation between the effect of M on R and the effect of R on Y: In particular, we imagine that $M = 0$ is more likely to have produced $R = 1$ in cases where $R = 1$ would make a difference to growth. Substantively, we might believe that – where settler mortality was low – settlers were more likely to create strong institutions in places where strong institutions would be likely to help. Thus, knowing that settlers plausibly caused the strong institutions we observe is itself informative about the effects of institutions on growth. In

Table 8.1 Learning from an instrument when patterns of confounding are specified: four $R = 1$, $Y = 1$ cases

Case	M	D	No clues	M only	D only	M and D
Malaysia	0	0	0.703	0.785	0.826	0.88
Brazil	0	1	0.703	0.785	0.612	0.709
Papua New Guinea	1	0	0.703	0.5	0.826	0.667
Dominican Republic	1	1	0.703	0.5	0.612	0.4

the language of the instrumental-variables literature, we can think of this as there being stronger effects for compliers.

Under these beliefs, observing $M = 0$ indicates that R is more likely to have been selected strategically on account of its economic effects. Conversely, learning that there was high mortality suggests that the good institutions we observe were not *due* to low mortality, and so – because selection effects are not in operation – observing the strength of institutions is less informative about the effectiveness of institutions.

In Table 8.1, we show the results of an analysis in which we build into our model the belief that it is very unlikely that institutions will have no effect on growth *if* settler mortality has a negative effect on institutional strength.[4] We report inferences here for four countries with strong institutions and high growth. The point to take away from the table is a simple one. Whereas M was completely uninformative in the analyses reported in Figure 8.5, we see that observing M *does* matter here. We see that where $M = 0$, observing M leads to a slight upward shift in the probability that R caused Y; where $M = 1$, observing M leads to a large downward shift in that probability. M remains informative for the query even if we have already observed D.

This analysis amplifies two general, closely related points we have made elsewhere. One is that whether or not a clue is informative for a given query cannot be read strictly from a DAG alone. We demonstrated in Chapter 7 that a clue's *potential* informativeness can be determined from a graph. However, whether the clue is in fact informative can depend, among other things, on the observed values of other nodes and the query we are trying to answer. We expand on clue informativeness in Chapter 12.

The second, connected point is that how much inferential leverage we can get out of process tracing will be shaped by the strength of the background knowledge we can bring to bear on the problem. As we saw, stipulating beliefs about the nature of the confounding turned an uninformative clue into an

---

[4] Specifically, we set a 0.01 probability on a null effect of R on Y given θ_{10}^R.

informative one. More generally, as we point out in Chapter 7, to undertake single-case process tracing, we need to begin with informative prior beliefs about which nodal types are more likely than others. If, for instance, we had begun both process-tracing exercises in this chapter with no restrictions and flat priors over all nodal types, none of the clues would have provided leverage on the problem. In the democratization model, if we had entered the analysis with no prior information about whether inequality more often had positive or negative effects on mobilization or whether mobilization more often had positive than negative effects on democratization, then observing $M = 1$ in an $I = 1, D = 1$ case would have provided no leverage on whether I had affected M or M had affected D in the case. We need not start with beliefs as strong as a monotonicity restriction. We can also set quantitative priors, such as stipulating that positive $I \rightarrow M$ effects are twice as common as negative ones. But for single-case process tracing to work, we have to bring to it thicker background knowledge than a DAG alone provides.

As we show in the next two chapters, a mixed-data approach opens up other possibilities. If we are working with a larger set of cases, then, we can begin with just a DAG, learn about the prevalence of different nodal types from the data itself, and then return to process-trace individual cases using this data-informed model.

8.2.3.3 Long-Run Effects

Finally, we note that although settler mortality is included in Acemoglu et al. (2001)'s and Rodrik et al. (2004)'s analyses as an instrument for studying the effect of recent institutions, the model can also be used to understand the effects of settler mortality itself on growth. Indeed, the title of Acemoglu et al. (2001)'s paper – "The Colonial Origins of Comparative Development" – suggests an interest in long-run processes. For a question about settler mortality's long-run effects on growth – using the same model – R can be thought of as a mediator of the effect of M on Y and so serve as a clue for answering the query.

In Table 8.2, we show the inferences we would draw about whether low mortality caused high growth in an $M = 0, Y = 1$ case, depending on what values of R and D we observe.

We see that the strong monotonicity assumption makes observing R a hoop test for the proposition that low mortality affected growth: We believe there is a positive probability that this is true if we observe $R = 1$ and 0 probability if $R = 0$. Inferences also depend on the case's distance from the equator. We again see a substitution logic in operation here: We have greater confidence

Table 8.2 Inferences on whether low mortality caused high growth in an $M = 0$, $Y = 1$ case given observations on distance and institutions

Distance (D)	Institutions (R)	Posterior
0	0	0.000
1	0	0.000
0	1	0.333
1	1	0.200

Table 8.3 Eight causal types generated by combinations of θ^Y and θ^{X_2}.

How Y is generated	$X_2 = 0$	$X_2 = 1$
X_1 alone ($\theta^Y = 0101$)	1	5
X_2 alone ($\theta^Y = 0011$)	2	6
Either X_1 or X_2 ($\theta^Y = 0111$)	3	7
X_1 and X_2 jointly ($\theta^Y = 0001$)	4	8

that low settler mortality caused high growth in countries where high growth cannot be explained by distance from the equator than we do in countries where distance is a viable explanation.

8.2.4 Considerations: Interactions between Clues

We saw in the last application that inferences from one clue were affected by data on another clue even though the model did not specify either complementarity or confounding. So where does this interaction come from?

The key idea is that observing $D = 1$ rules out some possible types we were entertaining in which R makes a difference when $D = 0$ (such as when either R or D would be sufficient) without ruling out types in which R does not make a difference when $D = 0$ (such as cases in which R and D are complements but $D = 0$).

To see the logic more explicitly, imagine we had a model with $X_1 \to Y \leftarrow X_2$ and flat priors over just four possible nodal types for Y (and two for X_2). We label the causal types as in Table 8.3.

We are interested in whether X_1 causes Y conditional perhaps on knowing X_1, X_2, and Y. Table 8.4 summarizes inferences. For instance, X_1 causes Y in cells 1, 3, 5, 8, and so our prior is 50%. If we learn that $X_2 = 1$ our prior remains at 50% (two possibilities, 5 and 8, from four, all equally weighted).

Table 8.4 Inferences from clue interactions

Information	Cases consistent with data	Subset consistent with $X = 1$ causes $Y - 1$	Belief
None (Prior)	1, 2, 3, 4, 5, 6, 7, 8	1, 3, 5, 8	1/2
$X_2 = 1$	5, 6, 7, 8	5, 8	1/2
$X_1 = 1, Y = 1$	1, 3, 5, 6, 7, 8	1, 3, 5, 8	2/3
$X_1 = 1, Y = 1, X_2 = 1$	5, 6, 7, 8	5, 8	1/2

Note that comparing the last line to the second to last line of Table 8.4, observation of $X_2 = 1$ rules out two types $(1, 3)$ in which X_1 could have had a causal effect, without ruling out any types that are consistent with the already available data, in which it does not (such as 6 or 7). The conclusion is that without information on X_1 and Y, X_2 can be uninformative for the effect of X_1 on Y (rows 1 and 2) but can still lead to a reduction in beliefs if X_1 and Y are known (rows 3 and 4). In some cases, it is even possible that $X_2 = 1$ could lead you to revise upward your belief that X_1 causes $Y = 1$ but downward your belief that X_1 caused $Y = 1$ in a case in which $X_1 = 1$ and $Y = 1$.[5]

8.3 Appendix: Forming Models in `CausalQueries`

The inequality and democratization model can be created in the `CausalQueries` package, along with monotonicity restrictions, like this:

```
model_id_pt <-

  make_model("I -> M -> D <- P; I -> D") |>
  set_restrictions(c(
    "(M[I=1] < M[I=0])",
    "(D[I=1] > D[I=0]) | (D[M=1] < D[M=0]) | (D[P=1] < D[P=0])"))
```

[5] Returning to the table, if we were quite sure that X_1 and X_2 were not substitutes (and so remove cases 3 and 7), the last column would be 1/2, 2/3, 3/4, 2/3 and so $X_2 = 1$ would lead you to increase your beliefs in the ATE but still reduce your beliefs in POC. If we were quite sure that they were not complements (and so remove cases 4 and 8) then $X_2 = 1$ would lead you to reduce your beliefs in both the ATE and the POC. Sometimes however, learning that cause X_2 is present can lead you to increase your beliefs that X_1 mattered even given $X_1 = 1$, $Y = 1$. For instance, say you were unsure whether a case was one in which $Y = 1$ regardless of X_1, X_2 or if $Y = 1$ only if both $X_1 = 1$ and $X_2 = 1$. Your prior on causal effect is 1/4. If you learn that $X_1 = 1$ and $Y = 1$, this increases to 1/3 (as you rule out the possibility of joint determination and $X_2 = 0$). However, if you just learn that $X_2 = 1$, then your belief goes up to 1/2 (for both cases where you do and do know $X_1 = 1$ and $Y = 1$).

Priors over the allowed (non-restricted) nodal types are set to be flat by default in the package. The model summary (found by typing `model_id_pt`) indicates that there is one restricted nodal type for M and 236 for D.

The institutions and growth model is formed like this:

```
model_rst_pt <- make_model("M -> R -> Y <- D; R <-> Y")  |>
  set_restrictions(c(
    "(R[M=1] > R[M=0])",
    "(Y[R=1] < Y[R=0]) | (Y[D=1] < Y[D=0])"))
```

Note that this model includes an unobserved confound. Monotonicity restrictions are again imposed (though we relax these when we return to the model in Chapter 10).

9 Integrated Inferences

We extend the analysis from Chapter 7 to multi-case settings and demonstrate how we can use the approach for mixed-method analysis. When analyzing multiple cases, we update our theory from the evidence and can then *use* our updated theory to draw both population- and case-level inferences. While single-case process tracing is entirely theory-informed, mixed-data inference is thus also *data*-informed. The approach can integrate information across any arbitrary mix of data structures, such as "thin" data on causes and outcomes in many cases and "thicker" process evidence on a subset of those cases.

We now extend the approach introduced in Chapter 7 to show how we can undertake causal-model-based causal inference using data on multiple cases.

In the single-case process-tracing setup, we start with a set of beliefs about causal effects at each node (i.e., about the distribution of nodal types in the population) and *apply* those beliefs, in combination with case-specific evidence, to the case at hand. The model itself remains static in single-case process tracing. When we draw on data from multiple cases, in contrast, we can use these data to *update* the model – to learn about the distribution of causal effects in the population. We can then use this updated, or trained, model to answer questions about causal relationships at the population level. We can also use this updated model at the *case* level – to undertake process-tracing on a given case with a model informed by observations of a wider set of cases. This means that, rather than the probative value of process-tracing evidence being supported only by our theoretical assumptions, probative value can emerge from the data itself.

Moreover, as we will show, causal models offer a powerful approach for *mixing* methods: that is, for integrating information drawn from different kinds of data strategies. We can readily update a causal model with a dataset that includes, for instance, data on only the explanatory variable and the outcome for a large set of cases and intensive data on causal processes for a subset of those cases.

We start the chapter with a conceptual point: As we demonstrate in the next section, the inferential logic introduced in Chapter 7 for single-case analysis can be used *as is* for multi-case analysis. Thus, the conceptual work for mixed-methods inference from causal models has, in a sense, been done already. We then show how we can deploy the same machinery, under assumptions regarding independence across cases, to learn about general causal processes. We explore the main payoffs of the approach: the ways in which it allows us to mix methods, integrate population- and case-level inference, and learn about causality in the absence of causal identification. And then, in the chapter's final section, we illustrate several ways in which the baseline approach can be extended – to the analysis of nonbinary data and to modeling measurement error and spillovers.

9.1 From One Unit to Many

Conceptualized correctly, there is no deep difference between the logic of inference used in single-case and in multi-case studies. To be clear, our claim here is not that any single "case" can be disaggregated into many "cases," thereby allowing for large-n analysis of single units (King et al., 1994). Our point is, rather, the opposite: Fundamentally, model-based inference always involves comparing *a* pattern of data with the logic of the model. Studies with multiple cases can, in fact, be conceptualized as single-case studies: We always draw our inferences from a single *collection* of clues, whether those clues have come from one or from many units.

In practice, when we move from a causal model with one observation to a causal model with multiple observations, we can use the structure we introduced in Chapter 7 by simply replacing nodes that have a single value (i.e., scalars) with nodes containing multiple values (i.e., vectors) drawn from multiple cases. We then make inferences about causal relations between nodes from observation of the values of multiple nodes' vectors.

To illustrate, consider the following situation. Suppose that our model includes a binary treatment, X, assigned to 1 with probability 0.5; an outcome, Y; and a third "clue" variable, K, all observable. We posit an unobserved variable θ^Y, representing Y's nodal type, with θ^Y taking on values in $\{a, b, c, d\}$ with equal probability. (We interpret the types in $\{a, b, c, d\}$ as defined in Section 2.1.) In addition to pointing into Y, moreover, θ^Y affects

K – in a rather convenient way. In particular, $K = 1$ whenever X has an effect on Y, while $K = 1$ with a 50% probability otherwise. In other words, our clue K is informative about θ^Y, a unit's nodal type for Y. As familiar from Chapters 7 and 8, when we observe K in a case, we can update on X's effect on Y within the case since that K value will have different likelihoods under different values of θ^Y.

So far, we have described the problem at the unit level. Let's now consider a two-case version of this setup. We do this by exchanging scalar nodes for vectors:

- We have a treatment node, $\mathbf{X}$, that can take on one of four values, $(0, 0)$, $(0, 1)$, $(1, 0)$, $(1, 1)$ with equal probability. The value $(0,0)$ simply means that $X = 0$ in both cases; the value $(0,1)$ means that X is 0 in the first case and 1 in the second case; and so on.
- θ^Y is now also a vector with two elements, one for each case. θ^Y can thus take on one of 16 values (a, a), (a, b), $\ldots$, (d, d). We interpret $\theta^Y = (a, b)$, for instance, to mean that Y's nodal type is a for the first case and b for the second case. Let us set a uniform prior distribution over these 16 possible values.
- $\mathbf{Y}$ is a vector that is generated by θ^Y and $\mathbf{X}$ in an obvious way. For instance, $\mathbf{X} = (0, 0)$, $\theta^Y = (a, b)$ generate outcomes $\mathbf{Y} = (1, 0)$.
- The vector $\mathbf{K}$ has the same domain as $\mathbf{X}$ and $\mathbf{Y}$. Consistent with the setup above, for any case j, the element $K_j = 1$ with probability 1 if $\theta_j^Y = b$ and with probability 0.5 if $\theta_j^Y \neq b$.

Now consider a causal estimand. In a single-case setup, we might ask whether X has an effect on Y in the case. For a multi-case setup, we might ask what the Sample Average Treatment Effect (SATE), τ, is. Note a subtle difference in the nature of the answers we seek in these two situations. In the first (single-case) instance, our estimand is binary – of the form: "Is the case a b type?" – and our answer is a probability. In multi-case estimation of the SATE, our estimand is categorical, and our answer will be a probability distribution: We are asking, "what is the probability that τ is 0?," "What is the probability that τ is 0.5?," and so on.

While the estimand shifts, we can use the tools introduced for single-case process tracing in Chapters 7 and 8 to analyze these data from multiple cases. Consider the probability that $\tau = 1$. A SATE of 1 would require that X have a positive effect on Y in both cases, that is, that $\theta^Y = (b, b)$. Under our uniform priors, this has just a 1 in 16 probability.

Table 9.1 Bayesian inferences for Sample Average Treatment Effects given different data patterns across two cases

X pattern	Y pattern	K pattern	$\tau = -1$	$\tau = -0.5$	$\tau = 0$	$\tau = 0.5$	$\tau = 1$
(1,1)	(1,1)	(1,1)	0	0	1/9	4/9	4/9
(1,1)	(1,1)	(1,0)	0	0	1/3	2/3	0
(1,1)	(1,1)	(0,0)	0	0	1	0	0

Now suppose that we observe that, for both units, $X = 1$ and $Y = 1$. This data pattern is consistent with only four possible θ vectors: (b, b), (d, d), (b, d), and (d, b). Moreover, each of these four is equally likely to produce the data pattern we see, though only one of them gets us $\tau = 1$. So our belief that $\tau = 1$ now shifts from 1 in 16 to 1 in 4.

Next, suppose that we further look at K in both cases and observe the data pattern $\mathbf{K} = (1, 1)$. The probability of this pattern for θ vector (b, b) $(\tau = 1)$ is 1. For the other three possible type vectors (d, d), (b, d), (d, b), the probability of this $\mathbf{K}$ pattern is 0.25, 0.5, and 0.5, respectively. We apply Bayes' rule now simply by dividing the probability of observing the K data pattern if the hypothesis $(\tau = 1)$ is true by the (unnormalized) sum of the probabilities of the K data pattern for *all* four θ vectors consistent with $X = 1, Y = 1$: so $1/(1 + 0.25 + 0.5 + 0.5) = 4/9$.

We can similarly figure out the posterior probability on any possible value of τ and build up a full posterior distribution. And we can do so given any K pattern (i.e., $\mathbf{K}$ realization) across the cases. Thus, if we observe $\mathbf{K} = (0, 1)$, the probability of this pattern for type vector (b, b) $(\tau = 1)$ is 0. For the type vectors (d, d), (b, d), (d, b), it is 0.25, 0, 0.5, respectively. Table 9.1 shows the posterior distribution over a set of discrete SATE values given different K patterns observed.

The conceptual point is that the general logic of inference with multiple units is the same as that with one unit. In both situations, we work out the likelihood of any given data *pattern* for each possible set of values of model parameters, and then update our beliefs about those parameters accordingly. From our posterior distribution over fundamental model parameters, we can then derive a posterior distribution over the possible answers to any causal query, such as the values of τ.

However, while conceptually simple, thinking of nodes on a DAG as representing outcomes for all units implies models of extraordinary complexity, whose complexity rises rapidly with the number of cases. For instance, consider the model in Figure 9.1 in which $X = (X_1, X_2)$ has a direct effect on

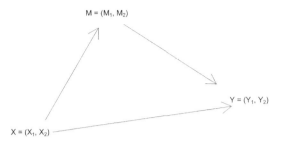

Figure 9.1   Multiple units as vector valued nodes on a single DAG

$Y = (Y_1, Y_2)$ as well as an indirect effect via $M = (M_1, M_2)$. The implied θ^X vector has four possible values. The θ^M vector has $4^4 = 256$ possibilities, and θ^Y has $4^{4 \times 4} = 4{,}294{,}967{,}296$. Together, this means about 5 billion causal types for just two binary units. The mind boggles.

Fortunately, we can use a different approach.

9.2 General Procedure

To illustrate the logical parallel between single-case and multi-case inference, we have worked through a problem of sample-level inference: In the last section, we imagined that we were trying to estimate the causal effect for the specific set of cases that we were observing. However, for the remainder of this chapter, and for the rest of the book, when we discuss multi-case analysis, we will set our sights primarily on learning about models that describe realizations of *general* processes. That is, we will seek to learn about *populations*. We will then use our updated, general models at two levels: To address queries about the population and to address queries about specific cases. This means that we will bracket sample-level inference: That is, studying a set of cases in order to estimate some causal quantity for that sample. It is entirely possible to pose sample-level queries within the framework, but this will not be our focus.

There are two reasons motivating our focus on general models applicable to a population. The first is that we are interested in learning across cases. Our strategy for learning across cases is to learn about population-level parameters. We will use data on a set of cases to update our beliefs about a general model that we think is of relevance for other cases drawn from the same population.

The second reason for structuring learning around populations is more practical. If we can think of units as draws from a large population, and then invoke independence assumptions across types, then we can greatly reduce the kind of complexity we discussed at the end of the last section. In the two-case example above, the vector θ^Y could take on any of 16 values $((a, a), (a, b), \ldots, (d, d))$. In any given case, however, θ^Y can take on only four possible values ($\{a, b, c, d\}$). So here is the simplifying move we make: Rather than trying to learn about the probabilities of 16 possible vector values for the two cases we're studying (or of the 1,048,576 values for 10 cases), we instead turn this into a problem of learning about how the population is divvied up among just four nodal types. And if we know about the relative proportions of these types in a population, we are then in a position to estimate the probability that any case drawn from this population is of a given type.

Thinking about inference in this way simplifies the problem by greatly reducing the parameter space, but we do not get this payoff for free. It requires invoking the assumption that (potential) outcomes in one unit are independent of (potential) outcomes in all other units. If we cannot stand by that assumption, then we will need to build independence failures into our models, in ways we discuss later in this chapter.

As we move to population-level inference, we will continue to use simple DAGs to describe causal structures. When working with populations, however, we will now think of a DAG as standing in for a more complex multi-case structure. We can think of each individual unit as having an identical unit-level DAG and as being connected to one another via nodes that are common across the population. Figure 9.2 illustrates (see also Figure 3 in Chickering and Pearl (1996) for an example of a similar graph for a DAG with unobserved confounding). Here, we replicate, twice, a simple unit-level DAG involving direct effects from X to Y as well as indirect effects via M. We now subscript the unit-level substantive nodes to indicate the different values they can take on for each of the two units. Each unit also has separate, subscripted θ terms, implying that nodal types can vary across units, too. The unit-level θ terms are linked, however, through dependence on common λs, representing for each node the population-level shares of its nodal types. Thus, since λ^X represents the population-level distribution of θ^X, λ^X matters for the values that both θ^{X_1} and θ^{X_2} will take on and in turn, for the values that X_1 and X_2 will take on. We conceptualize the relationships similarly for the other nodes.

Critically, we can deploy the principles of conditional independence on a DAG, explored in Chapter 7, to articulate how we can learn about one

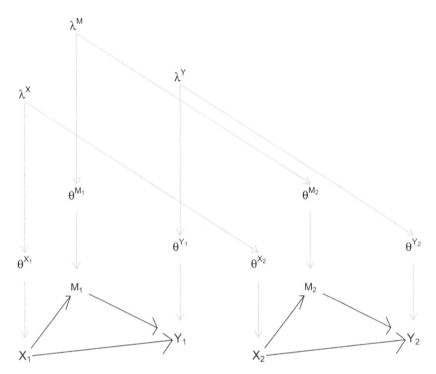

Figure 9.2   A population DAG with multiple units from the same population

case from another. We can learn about θ^{M_2} and about M_2 from observing M_1, for instance, because they are all descendants of the population-level node λ^M – and we know that information flows across a "forked path." The DAG elucidates less obvious possibilities, too. For instance, we can learn about θ^{Y_2} from observing M_1 if we also know Y_1, since Y_1 acts as a collider for M_1 and λ^Y; thus, observing Y_1 opens a path between M_1 and θ^{Y_2}.[1] Moreover, all of this cross-case learning depends on the λs being (at least somewhat) *unknown*: If the λs are known, then the path between unit DAGs is blocked, so there can be no learning across cases. Put more intuitively, we can transfer knowledge across cases if we can learn *from* (some) cases about a population to which other cases also belong – and this strategy depends on the fact that we don't already know all there is to know about the population.

---

[1] A final subtlety that we discuss later is that, with this larger structure, the DAG for a single case (e.g., $X_1 \rightarrow M_1 \rightarrow Y_1 \leftarrow M_1$) can be extracted *as is* from this larger DAG provided that we condition on the λs (or the θs) *or* the λs are independent of each other, as here. If the λs are not independent of each other then the DAG no longer captures all relations of conditional independence.

We now outline the general procedure for multi-case inference. The core steps in this procedure are:

- to figure out all possible causal types implied by a DAG
- to describe a set of distributions over these causal types
- for any distribution over causal types, figure out the likelihood of any data pattern.

With this likelihood in hand, we have enough to update our beliefs over distributions of causal types once we encounter the data. With updated beliefs about the distribution of causal types, we are ready, in turn, to pose any causal query of interest. This procedure can be seen as a generalization of the analysis used in Chickering and Pearl (1996) to study compliance. We use the same basic logic here, but now for arbitrary DAGs, data structures, and queries. Appendix shows how to implement all steps in code and provides a replication of the analysis in Chickering and Pearl (1996).

9.2.1 Setup

We now describe the procedure in more detail. The key steps are as follows.

1. **A DAG.** As with process tracing, we begin with a graphical causal model specifying possible causal linkages between nodes. Our "chain" model for instance has DAG: $X \rightarrow M \rightarrow Y$. As described above, we now imagine this DAG standing in for a larger ("extended") DAG in which this DAG is replicated for each unit and connected to other unit DAGs by population-level parameters (λs).
2. **Nodal types.** Just as in process tracing, the DAG and variable ranges define the set of possible nodal types in the model – the possible ways in which each variable is assigned (if a root node) or determined by its parents (otherwise). For the $X \rightarrow M \rightarrow Y$ model, there are two types for θ^X, four for θ^M, and four for θ^Y.
3. **Causal types.** A full set of nodal types gives rise to a full set of causal types, encompassing all possible combinations of nodal types across all nodes in the model. We let θ denote an arbitrary causal type. For an $X \rightarrow M \rightarrow Y$ model, one possible causal type would be $\theta = (\theta_1^X, \theta_{01}^M, \theta_{01}^Y)$.
4. **Parameters.** As before, we use λ^j to denote the population shares of the elements of θ^j (the nodal types) for a given node, j. Recall that in process tracing, we sought to learn about θ, and our priors were given by λ. When we shift to multi-case inference, λ becomes the parameter we want

to learn about: we seek to learn about the *shares* of types in a population (or, equivalently, about the probability of different types arising in cases drawn from that population).

5. **Priors.** In the process-tracing setup, we treat λ as given: We do not seek to learn about λ, and uncertainty over λ plays no role. When we get to observe data on multiple cases, however, we have the opportunity to learn *both* about the cases at hand *and* about the population. Moreover, our level of uncertainty about population-level parameters will shape our inferences. We thus want our parameters (the λ's) to be drawn from a prior *distribution* – a distribution that expresses our uncertainty and over which we can update once we see the data. While different distributions may be appropriate to the task in general, uncertainty over proportions (of cases, events, etc.) falling into a set of discrete categories is usefully described by a Dirichlet distribution, as discussed in Chapter 5. Recall that the parameters of a Dirichlet distribution (the α's) can be thought of as conveying both the relative expected proportions in each category and our degree of uncertainty.

With some abuse of graphical representation – we illustrate for only one replicate of the unit-level DAG – Figure 9.3 displays the relationship between the case and population levels, together with an indication of distributions on different quantities.

- θ denotes the case-level type with a categorical distribution. That distribution is described by the parameter vector λ.
- λ denotes the population-level shares of types. Uncertainty over λ itself is characterized by a Dirichlet distribution, described by parameter vector α.
- α captures our priors on the distribution of λ; in "multilevel" applications we might think of the α terms as parameters that we want to learn about, in which case we should provide a prior for α.[2]

9.2.2 Inference

Inference then works by figuring out the probability of the data given different possible parameter vectors, λs, and then applying Bayes rule. In practice, we proceed as follows.

---

[2] As discussed in Section 11.4, if we want to model heterogeneity across different populations we might use the Dirichlet distribution to capture the variation in λ across populations (rather than our uncertainty over λ). The α terms then become parameters that we want to learn about, and we need to provide a prior distribution for these, captured, perhaps, by an inverse Gamma distribution.

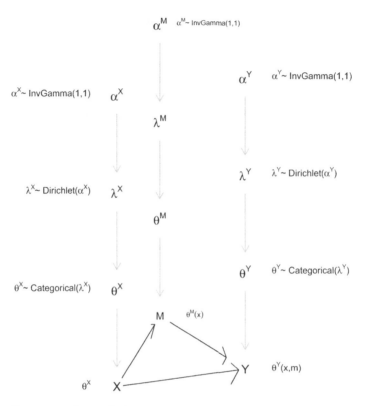

Figure 9.3   Types, parameters, and priors

9.2.2.1 Distributions over Causal Types

We first need to characterize our beliefs over causal types given any possible parameter vector, λ. Imagine a draw of one possible value of λ from the prior. This λ vector implies a set of nodal type shares for all nodes. That set of nodal type shares implies, in turn, a distribution over *causal* types (θ), which are just combinations of nodal types. If nodal types are independent of each other, then causal type shares are a simple matter of multiplying nodal-type shares. For instance, the probability of causal type $\theta = (\theta_1^X, \theta_{01}^M, \theta_{01}^Y)$ is simply $p(\theta|\lambda) = \lambda_1^X \lambda_{01}^M \lambda_{01}^Y$. More generally:

$$p(\theta|\lambda) = \prod_{k,j:\theta_k^j \in \theta} \lambda_k^j$$

9.2.2.2 Data Probabilities

Each causal type, in turn, implies a single data realization or data type. For instance, $\theta = (\theta_1^X, \theta_{01}^M, \theta_{01}^Y)$ implies data $X = 1, M = 1, Y = 1$

(and *only* that data type). Let $D(\theta)$ denote the data type implied by causal type θ.

A single data type, however, may be implied by multiple causal types. We use $\Theta(d)$ to denote the set of causal types that imply a given data type:

$$\Theta(d) = \{\theta | D(\theta) = d\}.$$

Let w_d be the probability of a given data type d (the "event probability"). The probability of a given data type is the sum of the probabilities of all causal types that imply it (given λ). So we have:

$$w_d = \sum_{\theta \in \Theta(d)} p(\theta | \lambda).$$

We use $\mathbf{w}$ to denote the vector of event probabilities over *all* possible data types.

To illustrate, a data type $d = (X = 1, M = 1, Y = 1)$ is consistent with four different causal types in the $X \to M \to Y$ model: $\Theta(d) = \{(\theta_0^X, \theta_{01}^M, \theta_{01}^Y), (\theta_0^X, \theta_{11}^M, \theta_{01}^Y), (\theta_0^X, \theta_{01}^M, \theta_{11}^Y), (\theta_0^X, \theta_{11}^M, \theta_{11}^Y)\}$. The probability of the data type is then calculated by summing up the probabilities of each causal type that implies the event. We can write this as: $w_{111} := \lambda_1^X (\lambda_{01}^M + \lambda_{11}^M)(\lambda_{01}^Y + \lambda_{11}^Y)$.

In practice, calculating the full $\mathbf{w}$ vector is made easier by the construction of an "ambiguities matrix," just as for process tracing, which tells us which causal types are consistent with a particular data type, as well as a "parameter matrix," which tells us which parameters determine the probability of a causal type.

We use Tables 9.2 and 9.3 to illustrate how to calculate the event probability for each data type for a given parameter vector λ, here using a simple $X \to Y$ model. Starting with data type $X = 0, Y = 0$ (first column of the ambiguities matrix), we see that the consistent causal types are $(\theta_0^X, \theta_{00}^Y)$ and $(\theta_0^X, \theta_{01}^Y)$, in rows 1 and 5. We then turn to columns 1 and 5 of the parameter matrix to read off the probability of each of these causal types – which, for each, is given by the probability of the nodal types out of which it is formed. So for $\theta_0^X, \theta_{00}^Y$, the probability is 0.4×0.3, and for $\theta_0^X, \theta_{01}^Y$, the probability is 0.4×0.2 – giving a total probability of 0.2 for the $X = 0, Y = 0$ data event. All four event probabilities, for the four possible data types, are then calculated in the same way.

In practice, within the `CausalQueries` package, these calculations are done using matrix operations.

Table 9.2 An ambiguities matrix for a simple
$X \rightarrow Y$ model (with no unobserved confounding).
Row labels indicate causal types, column labels
indicate data types

	X0Y0	X1Y0	X0Y1	X1Y1
X0Y00	1	0	0	0
X1Y00	0	1	0	0
X0Y10	0	0	1	0
X1Y10	0	1	0	0
X0Y01	1	0	0	0
X1Y01	0	0	0	1
X0Y11	0	0	1	0
X1Y11	0	0	0	1

Table 9.3 A parameter matrix for a simple $X \rightarrow Y$ model (with no unobserved confounding),
indicating a single draw of λ values from the prior distribution. Row labels indicate nodal types,
column labels indicate causal types

	X0.Y00	X1.Y00	X0.Y10	X1.Y10	X0.Y01	X1.Y01	X0.Y11	X1.Y11	λ
X.0	1	0	1	0	1	0	1	0	0.4
X.1	0	1	0	1	0	1	0	1	0.6
Y.00	1	1	0	0	0	0	0	0	0.3
Y.10	0	0	1	1	0	0	0	0	0.2
Y.01	0	0	0	0	1	1	0	0	0.2
Y.11	0	0	0	0	0	0	1	1	0.3

9.2.2.3 Likelihood

Now we know the probability of observing each data pattern in a *single* case
given λ. We can use these case-level event probabilities to aggregate up to the
likelihood of observing a data pattern across multiple cases (given λ). For this
aggregation, we make use of an independence assumption: that each unit is
independently drawn from a common population-level distribution. Doing
so lets us move from a categorical distribution that gives the probability that
a single case has a particular data type to a *multinomial* distribution that
gives the probability of seeing an arbitrary data pattern across any number
of cases.

Specifically, with discrete variables, we can think of a given multiple-case
data pattern simply as a set of counts across categories. This allows us to represent a multi-case data pattern in compact form. For, say, X, Y data, we

will observe a certain number of $X = 0, Y = 0$ cases (which we notate as n_{00}), a certain number of $X = 1, Y = 0$ cases (n_{10}), a certain number of $X = 0, Y = 1$ cases (n_{01}), and a certain number of $X = 1, Y = 1$ cases (n_{11}). A data pattern, given a particular set of variables observed (a search strategy), thus has a multinomial distribution. The likelihood of a data pattern under a given search strategy, in turn, takes the form of a multinomial distribution conditional on the number of cases observed, n, and the probability of each data type, given a particular λ. More formally, we write:

$$D \sim \text{Multinomial}(n, w(\lambda)).$$

To illustrate, for a three-node model, with X, Y, and M – all binary – let n_{XYM} denote an eight-element vector recording the number of cases in a sample displaying each possible combination of X, Y, M data. Thus, the data d can be summarized with a vector of counts of the form $\mathbf{n}_{XYM} :=$ $(n_{000}, n_{001}, n_{100}, \ldots, n_{111})$. The elements of n_{XYM} sum to n, the total number of cases studied. Likewise, let the event probabilities for data types given λ be registered in a vector, $w_{XYM} = (w_{000}, w_{001}, w_{100}, \ldots, w_{111})$. The likelihood of a data pattern, d, given λ is then:

$$p(d|\lambda) = p(n_{XYM}|\lambda) = \text{Multinom}\left(n_{XYM}\Big| \sum n_{XYM}, w_{XYM}(\lambda)\right).$$

9.2.2.4 Estimation

We now have all the components for updating on λ. Applying Bayes rule (see Chapter 5), we have:

$$p(\lambda|d) = \frac{p(d|\lambda)p(\lambda)}{\int_{\lambda'} p(d|\lambda')p(\lambda')}.$$

In the CausalQueries package this updating is implemented in stan, and the result of the updating is a dataframe that contains a collection of draws from the posterior distribution for λ. Table 9.4 illustrates what such a dataframe might look like for an $X \rightarrow M \rightarrow Y$ model. Each row represents a single draw from the posterior distribution, $p(\lambda|d)$. The 10 columns correspond to the model's 10 parameters: Each draw from λ's posterior distribution contains a set of population-level shares for each of the 10 nodal types in the model.

So, for instance, in the first row, we have one draw from our posterior distribution over λ. In this draw, we have a world in which the shares of cases with nodal types θ_0^X and θ_1^X are 47% and 53%, respectively; the shares with θ_{00}^M, θ_{10}^M, θ_{01}^M, and θ_{11}^M are 21%, 7%, 17%, and 55%, respectively; and the shares for θ_{00}^Y, θ_{10}^Y, θ_{01}^Y, and θ_{11}^Y are 20%, 23%, 15%, and 41%, respectively. For each

Table 9.4 An illustration of a posterior distribution for a $X \rightarrow M \rightarrow Y$ model. Each row is a draw from $p(\lambda|d)$. Such a posterior would typically have thousands of rows and capture the full joint posterior distribution over all parameters

X.0	X.1	M.00	M.10	M.01	M.11	Y.00	Y.10	Y.01	Y.11
0.47	0.53	0.21	0.07	0.17	0.55	0.20	0.23	0.15	0.41
0.68	0.32	0.02	0.41	0.38	0.19	0.12	0.20	0.07	0.61
0.33	0.67	0.16	0.45	0.27	0.12	0.08	0.02	0.81	0.09
0.68	0.32	0.15	0.10	0.70	0.05	0.03	0.07	0.00	0.90
0.17	0.83	0.02	0.11	0.64	0.22	0.44	0.06	0.30	0.20
0.83	0.17	0.16	0.08	0.02	0.73	0.49	0.28	0.12	0.11

draw of λ, these shares differ. Stan typically carries out thousands of draws to characterize the full joint posterior distribution over all parameters.

9.2.2.5 Querying

Once we have generated a posterior distribution for λ, we can then query that distribution. The simplest queries relate to values of λ itself. For instance, if we are interested in the probability that M has a positive effect on Y, given an updated $X \rightarrow M \rightarrow Y$ model, we want to know about the distribution of λ_{01}^Y. This distribution can be read directly from column 9 ($Y.01$) of Table 9.4.

More complex queries can all be described as summaries of combinations of these columns. For instance, the query, "What is the average effect of M on Y" is a question about the distribution of $\lambda_{01}^Y - \lambda_{10}^Y$, which is given by the difference between columns 9 and 8 of Table 9.4. This is a linear summary of parameters and is easily calculated.

Still more complex queries might ask about conditional quantities. Let $\pi(Q|D)$ denote the share of cases for which Q is true, *among* those that have features D. For instance, we could ask about the share of cases *among those that display $M = 1$, $Y = 1$* for which M causes Y. The condition D could even be a causal quantity and is not necessarily observable: For instance, we might be interested in the share of cases *among those for which M has a positive effect on Y* for which X also has a positive effect on M. Though more complex, we proceed in the same way for such "conditional queries," calculating the value of the query for each possible value of λ that we entertain and then taking the distribution over these values as given by our posterior of λ itself.

Let $\pi(Q|D, \lambda_i)$ denote the *share* of cases for which our query, Q, is satisfied, among those with condition D, given a specific parameter draw, λ_i. This could be, for instance, the share of cases with $M = 1$, $Y = 1$ for which M causes Y, under a single draw of λ from its posterior. Similarly, let $\pi(Q\&D|\lambda_i)$ denote the *share* of cases for which the query is satisfied and condition D is present, given λ_i. And let $\pi(D|\lambda_i)$ denote the *share* of cases with D given λ_i. Then, using the law of conditional probability, our conditional query under a single draw λ_i is:

$$\pi(Q|D, \lambda_i) = \frac{\pi(Q\&D|\lambda_i)}{\pi(D|\lambda_i)}.$$

For the conditional query about *the share of cases with $M = 1$, $Y = 1$ for which M causes Y*, we can read this from Table 9.4 as the ratio of the second-to-last column to the sum of the last two columns: $\frac{\lambda_{01}^Y}{\lambda_{01}^Y + \lambda_{11}^Y}$.[3]

We then have a posterior probability distribution over the query induced by our posterior distribution over λ, $p(\lambda)$. We can calculate the *expected value* of our query's posterior distribution as:

$$\hat{\pi}(Q|D, p) := \int \frac{\pi(Q\&D|\lambda_i)}{\pi(D|\lambda_i)} p(\lambda_i) d\lambda_i.$$

Here, we are essentially taking a weighted average of the different answers to our query across the different possible values of λ, weighting each answer by the probability of the λ_i from which it is derived.

Still more complex queries may require keeping some nodes constant while varying others. For instance, we might imagine the impact of a change in X on Y while keeping constant a mediator M that lies on a path from X to Y (where there is a second, direct path from X to Y). Complex as such queries might be, they too can be calculated as summaries of the combinations of columns of the posterior distribution, following the rules described in Chapter 4.

In all situations, once we have a distribution over the queries, we can calculate not just the expected value but also quantities such as the standard deviation of our posterior or the credibility intervals – a range of values over which 95% of our posterior probability mass lies.

9.2.2.6 Illustration

Figure 9.4 shows examples of a full mapping from data to posteriors for different data structures and queries. We begin with a simple chain model of the

---

[3] The calculation is simplified by the fact that the information on M is uninformative in this chain model. For the full calculation the denominator – the probability that $M = 1 \& Y = 1$ – is $(\lambda_0^X \lambda_{10}^M + \lambda_1^X \lambda_{01}^M \lambda_{11}^M)(\lambda_{01}^Y + \lambda_{11}^Y)$. The numerator – the probability that $(M = 1)\&(Y = 1)\&(M$ causes $Y) $ – is $(\lambda_0^X \lambda_{10}^M + \lambda_1^X \lambda_{01}^M \lambda_{11}^M)(\lambda_{01}^Y)$.

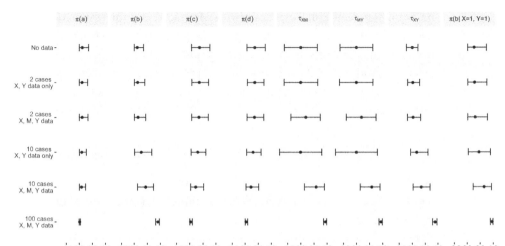

Figure 9.4   Posterior means and credibility intervals for a range of causal queries given different data, for a chain model

form $X \rightarrow M \rightarrow Y$, with flat priors over all nodal types.[4] In each column, we report inferences for a different query; and in each row, we report inferences for different data structures. For all data structures, we assume (for the sake of illustration) that we in fact observe a perfect positive correlation between X, Y, and M. However, across the rows, we vary for which nodes and for how many cases we observe data.

In the first four columns, we report queries about the shares of a, b, c, and d types in the population, referring to X's effect on Y. As we discussed in defining case-level causal-effect queries in Section 4.1, the mediation of this effect by M means that this query is asking a question about both λ^M and λ^Y. The next three columns ask about the average effect of X on M, M on Y, and X on Y. And the final column poses a conditional query, asking for what share of cases that display $X = 1$, $Y = 1$ does X have a positive effect on Y. As we can see, two features of our posterior beliefs shift as we add data: the expected value of the query and our degree of uncertainty.

For instance, as we go from 2 cases to 10 cases, and from just X, Y data to observing M as well, our beliefs about the proportion of positive-effect

---

[4] It is worth noting that the flat priors over nodal types in this chain model do *not* imply flat priors over the nodal types in a reduced $X \rightarrow Y$ model. For intuition: whereas in the simple model, flat priors imply that there is some causal effect (positive or negative) half the time, in the chain model, a causal effect occurs only if there are causal effects in *both* stages, and so, only one quarter of the time.

cases (including conditional on $X = 1, Y = 1$) go up, and our beliefs about the proportion of no-effect and negative-effect cases go down – sensibly, given the strong positive correlations in the data. Interestingly, more data does not necessarily generate less uncertainty; this is because, for some queries, the data and our priors are pulling in opposite directions, and when we are only analyzing 10 or fewer cases, there aren't enough data to overwhelm our priors. Also, movements from extreme values toward 0.5 can come with increased uncertainty. Ultimately, we can see in the last row that, with sufficiently large amounts of data, these credibility intervals shrink, and the mean of our posterior on the query approaches the "true" value.

9.2.3 Wrinkles

The basic procedure described above goes through with only minor adjustments when we have unobserved confounding or more complex sampling processes. We describe here how to take account of these features.

9.2.3.1 Unobserved Confounding

When there is unobserved confounding, we need parameter sets that allow for a joint distribution over nodal types. Unobserved confounding, put simply, means that there is confounding across nodes that is not captured by edges represented on the DAG. More formally, in the absence of unobserved confounding, we can treat the distribution of nodal types for a given node as independent of the distribution of nodal types for every other node. Unobserved confounding means that we believe that nodal types may be correlated across nodes. Thus, for instance, we might believe that those units assigned to $X = 1$ have different potential outcomes for Y than those assigned to $X = 0$ – that is, that the probability of $X = 1$ is not independent of whether or not X has an effect on Y. To allow for this, we have to allow θ^X and θ^Y to have a joint distribution. There are different ways to do this in practice, but a simple approach is to split the parameter set corresponding to the Y node into two: We specify one distribution for θ^Y when $X = 0$ and a separate distribution for θ^Y when $X = 1$. For each of these parameter sets, we specify four α parameters representing our priors. We can draw λ values for these conditional nodal types from the resulting Dirichlet distributions, as above, and can then calculate causal type probabilities in the usual way. Note that if we do this in an $X \rightarrow Y$ model, we have one two-dimensional Dirichlet distribution corresponding to X and two four-dimensional distributions corresponding to

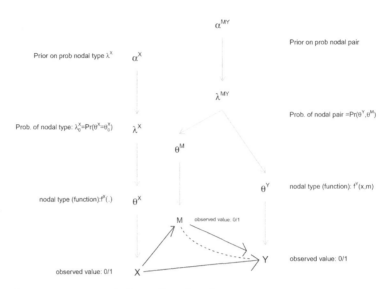

Figure 9.5   Types, parameters, and priors, with confounding

Y. In all, we have $1 + 3 + 3$ degrees of freedom: Exactly the number needed to represent a joint distribution over all eight θ^X, θ^Y combinations.

In Figure 9.5, we represent this confounding for a model with direct and indirect effects by indicating parameters values λ_{MY} that determine the joint distribution over θ_M and θ_Y.

9.2.3.2 Sampling and the Likelihood Principle

When we constructed the likelihood function – the probability of observing data given model parameters – we did not say much about how data were gathered. But surely *how* cases are sampled affects the probability of seeing different types of data and so affects the likelihood function. Ought we have different likelihood functions, for instance, if we decided to look for data on K only in places in which we have already observed $X = 1$ and $Y = 1$, or if we selected cases in which to examine K without taking into account known values of X and Y? Do we need to take account of such details when making inference?

The answer depends on whether and how details of sampling affect the likelihood of seeing different data patterns. In general, we can invoke the "likelihood principle," which is the principle that the relevant information for inference is contained in the likelihood. If sampling strategies don't alter the likelihood of observing data, then we can ignore them. In fact, since what matters is the relative likelihoods, we can treat two likelihood functions as equivalent if they are scalar multiples of each other. Thus, for instance, we can think of $\lambda^X \lambda^Y$ as equivalent to $2\lambda^X \lambda^Y$.

Here are two general rules of thumb:

- Strategies in which a unit's probability of selection into a sample is not related to its own potential outcomes can likely be ignored.
- Sampling strategies in which a unit's probability of selection into the sample is related to its own potential outcomes likely cannot be ignored.

To illustrate, let's consider a set of strategies that can be treated equivalently. We imagine an $X \rightarrow M \rightarrow Y$ model and suppose we have data on two cases: one case in which we see data on X and Y only, observing $X = 0, Y = 0$, and another in which in we have data on X, M, and Y, observing $X = 1, M = 0$, and $Y = 1$. Further, let $P(X = x, Y = y)$ denote the probability that we find $X = x$ and $Y = y$ when we seek data on X and Y.

Consider now three strategies that we might have used to gather these data.

Strategy 1: *Single multinomial draw.*
For each case, we could have randomly decided, with equal probability, whether or not to select data on X and Y only or on X, M, and Y. Each case then had 12 possible data types (4 possible X, Y data types and 8 possible X, M, Y data types). The probability of data type $X = 0, Y = 0$, for instance, is $0.5P(X = 0, Y = 0)$. The probability of observing the data we do observe is then:

$$2 \times \frac{1}{2}P(X = 0, Y = 0) \times \frac{1}{2}P(X = 1, M = 0, Y = 1).$$

Strategy 2: *Conditional (sequential) multinomial draws.*
We could have collected data on X and Y in two cases, and we then measured M in every case in which we observed $X = 1, Y = 1$. For this strategy, the probability of observing the data that we do observe is the probability of observing exactly one case with $X = 1, Y = 1$ and another with $X = 0, Y = 0$, times the probability of observing $M = 1$ in the case in which we observed $X = 1, Y = 1$.

$$2P(X = 0, Y = 0)P(X = 1, Y = 1)P(M = 0|X = 1, Y = 1)$$

which is equivalent to:

$$2P(X = 0, Y = 0)P(X = 1, M = 0, Y = 1).$$

Strategy 3: *Parallel multinomial draws.*
We could have sampled two cases and simultaneously examined X, Y in the first case and X, M, Y in the second case. The probability of seeing the data we see is then:

$$2P(X = 0, Y = 0)P(X = 1, M = 0, Y = 1).$$

We can readily see that, for all three strategies, the probability of observing the data we do in fact observe has the same form, albeit with possibly different constants. In other words, the differences in sampling across these strategies can be ignored.

Some differences in sampling procedures do have to be taken into account, however: in particular, sampling – or more generally missingness – that is related to potential outcomes. For a simple illustration, consider an $X \rightarrow Y$ model where data are only recorded in cases in which $Y = 1$. Thus, the observed data can have variation on X but not on Y. Naive updating that ignored the sampling process here would lead us to infer that $Y = 1$ regardless of X, and thus that X has no effect on Y. The problem here is that the likelihood is not taking account of the process through which cases enter our dataset.

In this situation, the correct likelihood would use event probabilities that consider the possible data types under the strategy. Let D^* denote the set of data types that are observable under the strategy (here D^* is the set of data types involving $Y = 1$). Then, event probabilities are:

$$w_d = \begin{cases} 0 & \text{if } d \notin D^* \\ \frac{x_d}{\sum_{d' \in D^*} x_{d'}} & \text{otherwise} \end{cases},$$

where $x_d = \sum_{\theta \in \Theta(d)} p(\theta | \lambda)$ is the uncensored data event probability.

An example of such sampling is the problem discussed in Knox et al. (2020) where reporting of police encounters depends on the outcome of those encounters.

While this kind of sampling can sometimes be handled relatively easily,[5] the general principle holds that sampling (missingness) that is related to potential outcomes is a part of the data-generating process and needs to be taken into account in the likelihood.[6]

---

[5] Such sampling is also implemented in the `CausalQueries` package.
[6] On strategies for addressing nonrandom sampling by blocking, see Bareinboim and Pearl (2016).

9.3 Payoffs

The most straightforward payoff to this approach is that we can learn about causal relationships in a population of interest from any number of cases drawn from that population. We can then use the updated model to ask causal questions about the population of interest or about individual cases within that population. In this section, we elaborate on three additional things that a causal-model-based approach to multi-case causal inference allows us to do: to integrate information from extensive and intensive data strategies; to empirically derive and justify the probative value of our process-tracing clues; and to learn about causal relationships even when they are not identified.

9.3.1 Mixing Methods

Having described the basic procedure, it is relatively straightforward now to explain what we mean when we say we can use this approach to mix methods. The notion of "mixing methods" can, of course, imply many things. What we mean in particular is that we can mix *evidence drawn from any combination of data strategies.* One common mixed-method research design in the social sciences involves combining (1) "extensive" data, meaning observations of a few variables for a large set of cases with (2) "intensive" data, meaning more in-depth observations for a small set of cases, usually a subset of the larger sample. The approach we have outlined can readily handle this kind of data mixture, and this is the kind of mixed strategy we will usually address in this book. More generally, though, as long as all data involve observations of nodes represented in our model, the framework can handle any arbitrary mixture of data structures.

The key features of the approach that allow for mixing are that we need neither data on *all* nodes nor data on the *same* nodes for all cases in order to implement the procedure. Whatever the data structure, we simply update our beliefs using whatever information we have.

The CausalQueries package will automatically perform updating on any arbitrary mixture of data structures we provide it with, but here is the basic idea. The logic is akin to that which we employ with partial process-tracing data (see Section 7.2.4). Suppose we have a data strategy s under which we gather data on n_s units for a subset of nodes, V_s. In calculating the probability of a pattern of partial data, we use all columns (data types) in the ambiguities matrix that are consistent with the partial data in order to calculate the event probability w_s. Our overall data strategy might involve multiple strategies like this.[7] If units are randomly assigned to data strategies and the observed number of units for each data type under each data strategy, s, is captured in the vector m_s,[8] then the likelihood is:

$$L = \prod_s \text{Multinom}(m_s | n_s, w_s).$$

That is, the likelihood of a given mixed data pattern is simply the product, across strategies, of the likelihood of observing the number of units that we observe of each possible data type for each strategy, given the number of cases observed under each strategy and the likelihood of each data type emerging under each strategy.

To illustrate, consider a model with nodes X, M, and Y. Suppose we have collected X, Y data for a set of cases, and have additionally collected data on M for a random subset of these – akin to conducting quantitative analysis on a large sample while conducting in-depth process tracing on part of the large-N sample. We can then summarize our data in two vectors, an eight-element n_{XYM} vector $(n_{000}, n_{001}, \ldots, n_{111})$ for the cases with process-tracing (M) observations, and a four-element vector $n_{XY*} = (n_{00*}, n_{10*}, n_{01*}, n_{11*})$ for the partial data on those cases on which we did not conduct process tracing. Likewise, we now have two sets of data probabilities: an eight-element vector for the set of cases with complete data, w_{XYM}, and a four-element vector for those with partial data, w_{XY*}.

Let n denote the total number of cases examined, and k the number for which we have data on M. Assuming that each observed case represents an independent, random draw from the population, we form the likelihood function quite simply as:

$$\Pr(d|\theta) = \text{Multinom}\,(n_{XY*}|n - k, w_{XY*}) \times \text{Multinom}\,(n_{XYM}|k, w_{XYM})\,.$$

That is, the likelihood of observing the mixed data pattern is the likelihood of observing the data we see in the non-process-traced cases (given the number of those cases and the event probability for each X, Y data type) times the likelihood of observing the data we see in the process-traced cases (given the number of those cases and the event probability for each X, M, Y data type).

---

[7] For example, data may be gathered through three strategies: S_1 in which data are gathered on nodes V_1 only in n_1 units for; S_2 in which data are gathered on nodes V_2 only in n_2 units; and S_3 in which data are gathered on nodes V_3 only in n_3 units.

[8] Specifically, m_s is a vector containing, for each strategy, s, the number of observed units that are of each data type that can possibly be observed under that strategy.

9.3.2 Deriving Probative Value from the Data

In Chapter 7, we discussed the fact that a DAG by itself is often insufficient to generate learning about causal effects from data on a single case. For many queries, a causal structure alone cannot make nodes on the graph informative as clues about causal relations. We also need to provide nonuniform prior beliefs about the population-level shares of nodal types.

When working with multiple cases, however, we can learn about causal relations starting with nothing more than the DAG and data. Learning about causal relations from the data can, in turn, *generate and justify the probative value of process-tracing clues* – that is, without the researcher having to *posit* any beliefs about nodal-type shares. In other words, we can simultaneously learn about population-level queries and empirically justify inferences we might make about new cases using case-level data.

For intuition, if we start with a simple model of the form $X \rightarrow Y \leftarrow K$, and have flat priors over causal types, then knowledge of K is uninformative about whether X caused Y in a case. But imagine that we observe data on X, K, and Y for multiple cases and find a strong correlation between X and Y only when $K = 1$. Now an inference that X mattered for Y in a case after seeing $K = 1$ can be justified by the updated model. That is, the model has *learned* that K is 1 more often in cases where it is likely that X affected Y. The data plus the DAG – without informative priors – have generated a probative value for our clue, K, which we can then leverage for process tracing. With real data, we show an example of this kind of learning in our multi-case analysis of the institutions and growth model in Chapter 10.

This represents a key integrative opportunity for model-based inference: A population-level model, updated on data from multiple cases, can allow us to empirically justify the causal inferences that we make about individual cases when we observe case-level data. To be clear, we imagine here that we first update our model using data from multiple cases, and then bring the updated model to an individual case – using the model to tell us what we should believe about the case given a set of observations from that case.

9.3.2.1 Two Types of Case-Level Conditional Inferences

We must be careful, however, about what we mean by case-level inference following model-updating. Generally speaking, case-level inference means asking about the probability that query Q is true for a unit with observed characteristics D. For instance, we might want to know about the probability that X caused Y in a case with $X = 1, Y = 1$, and $K = 1$. But there are two ways in which we might interpret this question and seek an answer from an updated model. We will refer to these two similar-but-distinct types of questions as an *uninformative*-case query and an *informative*-case query.

Uninformative-case query. With an updated model in hand, we can ask: What is the probability that Q is true for a case of interest that has characteristics D? In this setup, we have selected the case for inference *because* it has characteristics D – for example, we have randomly drawn the case from among those that have D – and we have a question about this kind of case. If we can treat this case as undifferentiated in expectation from other units with D in the population, then we can treat the *share* of cases in the population with D for which the query is satisfied as the *probability* with which Q is true for the case of interest. Thus, if our updated model tells us that X causes Y for 80% of cases in the population with $X = 1$, $Y = 1$, and $K = 1$, then our best guess for any case with these observed features, absent other data, is that there is an 80% probability that X causes Y in this case.

Informative-case query. Say that instead of randomly sampling a case *from among the cases that have D*, we were to randomly select a case from the population and *observe* that this new case has characteristics D. Then, what should we believe about Q? Things are different now because the observation of D in a randomly sampled case is now new information, and this additional data may lead us to update our causal model, even as we query it.

To calculate *uninformative-case queries*, we make use of our posterior beliefs about the *share* of units in a population that satisfy the conditional query. This is quantity $\pi(Q|D, p)$ that we discussed in Section 9.2.2.5, where p now is our posterior distribution over λ. We use the *expected value* of this posterior distribution over the conditional query to answer the uninformative-case query:

$$\hat{\pi}(Q|D, p) := \int \frac{\pi(Q \& D|\lambda_i)}{\pi(D|\lambda_i)} p(\lambda_i) d\lambda_i.$$

For the informative-case query – what should we believe about Q for a randomly selected case in which we *observe D* – we need to take into account the new information that D's observation represents. That is, we need to allow for updating on our posterior distribution over λ given the new observation. We thus use the law of conditional probability to calculate:

$$\hat{\phi}(Q|D, p) := \frac{\int \Pr(Q \& D|\lambda_i) p(\lambda_i) d\lambda_i}{\int \Pr(D|\lambda_i) p(\lambda_i) d\lambda_i} = \frac{\int \pi(Q \& D|\lambda_i) p(\lambda_i) d\lambda_i}{\int \pi(D|\lambda_i) p(\lambda_i) d\lambda_i}.$$

Note we have made use of the fact that for a single case $\Pr(Q\&D|\lambda_i) = \pi(Q\&D|\lambda_i)$.

In this calculation, we have a value for $\pi(Q\&D)$ for each possible λ_i, as in the uninformative-case query. The key difference is that observing D can now lead us to shift probability toward those λ_i's under which the observation of D was more likely to occur – and in turn toward those answers to our query (those $\pi(Q\&D)$ values) implied by those now-more-probable λ_i's. Put differently, in an informative-case query, the case-level data do not just give us information about the kind of case we're examining; they can also provide new information about the way causal relations operate in the world we're in (i.e., about λ), informing how we interpret the evidence we see in the case.

Formally, $\hat{\phi}$ and $\hat{\pi}$ look quite similar, and the differences between them are somewhat subtle. They relate to each other in a simple way, however. If we let $p'(\lambda_i)$ denote the posterior on λ after seeing data D on a new case, then:

$$p'(\lambda_i) = \frac{\Pr(D|\lambda_i)p(\lambda_i)}{\int \Pr(D|\lambda_i')p(\lambda_i')d\lambda_i'}.$$

And then:

$$\hat{\phi}(Q|D, p) = \frac{\int \Pr(Q\&D|\lambda_i)p(\lambda_i)d\lambda_i}{\int \Pr(D|\lambda_i)p(\lambda_i)d\lambda_i} \tag{9.1}$$

$$= \int \frac{\Pr(Q\&D|\lambda_i)}{\Pr(D|\lambda_i)} \frac{\Pr(D|\lambda_i)p(\lambda_i)}{\int \Pr(D|\lambda_i')p(\lambda_i')d\lambda_i'} d\lambda_i \tag{9.2}$$

$$= \int \frac{\Pr(Q\&D|\lambda_i)}{\Pr(D|\lambda_i)} p'(\lambda_i)d\lambda_i \tag{9.3}$$

$$= \hat{\pi}(Q|D, p'). \tag{9.4}$$

In other words, posing a $\hat{\phi}$ query about a new "informative" case is equivalent to first using that new case to update λ and then posing a $\hat{\pi}$ query about the case using the posterior distribution on λ. The one thing we have to be sure *not* to do is to first use the new case to update on λ and then pose a $\hat{\phi}$ query about the same case – since that would effectively be updating λ twice from the same case data.

9.3.2.2 When New Cases Carry New Information

The difference between uninformative- and informative-case queries turns on the nature of uncertainty over the conditioning information, D. When undertaking an uninformative-case query, we have no uncertainty about whether we will observe D in the case: The case of interest has been selected *for* its display of D. In an informative-case query, because we don't condition selection on D, we don't know whether we will observe D in the case before we select it: Thus, observing D can potentially tell us something about the world (about λ).

By the same token, if the likelihood of observing D in a randomly selected case is the same under all beliefs we might have about the world, then we will *not* update those beliefs when we observe D. The informative-case query then collapses into an uninformative one. In fact, comparing expressions $\hat{\pi}(Q|D)$ and $\hat{\phi}(Q|D)$ above, we can see that if $\Pr(D)$ is constant over λ_i, then $\hat{\pi}(Q|D) = \hat{\phi}(Q|D)$.

For instance, we will not update on λ from observing D in a randomly selected case if D's distribution in the population is *known*. Suppose that we are interested in a subgroup effect – for instance, the conditional average treatment effect of X on Y for democracies and for non-democracies – and that the relative sizes of these two subgroups are already known. Then, when we randomly draw a case and observe that it is a democracy, we do not learn anything about the world: The likelihood of having observed a democracy in a randomly drawn case is the same under all values of λ_i. So $\hat{\pi}(Q|D)$ and $\hat{\phi}(Q|D)$ are the same. Thus, if we think there is a positive effect in 50% of democracies in the population and in 30% of the non-democracies, then we think that the probability that there is an effect in a new random case is 0.5 if it is a democracy and 0.3 if it is a non-democracy.

While this seems like a straightforward equivalence, it depends crucially on the fact that we *know* the share of democracies and non-democracies in the population in advance of drawing the case. If we didn't, then observing democracy in the new case *could* alter our beliefs about λ.

Similarly, $\hat{\pi}(Q|D)$ and $\hat{\phi}(Q|D)$ will be the same for any case-level query for which D is the empty set – that is, for which we condition on no observed characteristic. For instance, if our query is simply the probability that X has a positive effect on Y in a case, then $\hat{\pi}(Q|D)$ will simply be the share of cases in the population with a positive effect. For $\hat{\phi}(Q|D)$, we are not making use of any information from the newly drawn case and so will not update on λ; we will just use the very same population share used for $\hat{\pi}(Q|D)$.

Conversely, if $\Pr(D)$ is not constant over λ_i then $\hat{\phi}(Q|D)$ can differ from $\hat{\pi}(Q|D)$: That is, our case-level inference may differ depending on whether we selected the case *because* it displayed D or we discovered D after randomly drawing the case. For this reason, it is in principle possible to arrive at two *seemingly* contradictory inferences at the same time: We can simultaneously

Table 9.5 Beliefs over two states of the world, where information on a new case leads to updating about the state of the world

λ	$p(\lambda)$	λ_1^Y	λ_2^Y	λ_0^K	λ_1^K
λ_1	0.01	1	0	0.001	0.999
λ_2	0.99	0	1	0.999	0.001

figure that $\hat{\pi}(X$ causes $Y|K = 1, p)$ is very small and that $\hat{\phi}(X$ causes $Y|K = 1, p)$ is very large. In other words, you could believe that among units for which $K = 1$, it is unlikely that there is an effect of X on Y, while at the same time observing $K = 1$ in a new case could be enough to convince you that X caused Y for the case.

A quite stark example can illustrate how this can be possible. Imagine that we have a model in which Y is a function of both X and K: $X \rightarrow Y \leftarrow K$. Suppose, further, we entertained just two possible nodal types for θ^Y:

1. θ_1^Y: $Y = 1$ if and only if both $X = 1$ and $K = 1$; we let λ_1^Y denote the share of cases with $\theta^Y = \theta_1^Y$
2. θ_2^Y: $Y = 0$ regardless of X and K; we let λ_2^Y denote the share of cases with $\theta^Y = \theta_2^Y$.

We also let λ_1^K denote the share of cases in which $K = 1$.

We then imagine two possible worlds that we might be in, λ_1 and λ_2, described in Table 9.5.

Note that we start out believing there is a 0.01 probability that we are in λ_1 and a 0.99 probability that we are in λ_2.

For the query $\hat{\pi}(X$ causes $Y|K = 1)$, we ask: *What is the probability that X causes Y in a case with $K = 1$?* This is the same as asking for what share of $K = 1$ cases in the population X does cause Y. The answer is 100% if $\lambda = \lambda_1$ and 0% if $\lambda = \lambda_2$. So, given the probability our model places on the two worlds, the expected share is $p(\lambda_1) = 0.01$. Thus, if we were to present you with a case randomly selected from those with $K = 1$, you would say it is very unlikely that X causes Y for that case.

For the query $\hat{\phi}(X$ causes $Y|K = 1)$, we ask: *What is the probability that X causes Y in a randomly drawn case in which we then observe $K = 1$?* The likelihoods of observing $K = 1$ or $K = 0$ for a randomly drawn case, given different beliefs about X's effect, are shown in Table 9.6.

We can read $\hat{\phi}(X$ causes $Y|K = 1)$ off of this table: The probability that X causes Y given the observation of $K = 1$ is $0.01/(0.01 + 0.001) = 0.91$.

Table 9.6 Joint distribution of λ and K

	$K = 0$	$K = 1$
λ_1 (X causes Y)	0	0.01
λ_2 (X doesn't cause Y)	0.989	0.001

So, we think that the typical $K = 1$ case has a very low probability of being one in which X causes Y because our model tells us we're very likely in a world (that of λ_2) in which X never causes Y. Yet the likely world (where λ_2) is *also* a world in which we should almost never observe $K = 1$. Thus, *finding out* that $K = 1$ in a randomly drawn case allows us to update to a belief that we are more likely in the world of λ_1 – where X indeed causes Y whenever $K = 1$. In other words, our prior beliefs about the world can be upended by what we see in new cases, in turn changing how we understand those cases.

9.3.3 Learning without Identification

A third payoff of this approach is that it allows us to engage in inference even when causal queries are not *identified*. When a query is identified, each true value for the query is associated with a unique distribution of data types. Thus, as we gather more and more data, our posterior on the query should converge on the true value. When a query is not identified, multiple true values of the query will be associated with the same distribution of data types. With a non-identified query, our posterior will never converge on a unique value regardless of how much data we collect since multiple answers will be equally consistent with the data. A key advantage of a causal model framework, however, is that we can *learn* about queries that are not identified but are still "partially identified," even if we cannot remove all uncertainty over such queries.

We can illustrate the difference between identified and non-identified causal questions by comparing an ATE query to a probability of causation (PC) query for a simple $X \rightarrow Y$ model. When asking about the ATE, we are asking about the average effect of X on Y, or the difference between λ_{01}^Y (the share of units with positive effects) and λ_{10}^Y (share with negative effects). When asking about the PC, we are asking, for a case with given values of X and Y, about the probability that X caused Y in that case. This PC query is defined by a different set of parameters. For, say, an $X = 1, Y = 1$ case and a $X \rightarrow Y$ model, the probability of causation is given by just $\lambda_{01}^Y/(\lambda_{01}^Y + \lambda_{11}^Y)$.

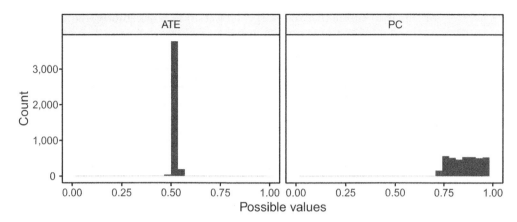

Figure 9.6   Posterior distributions. ATE is identified, PC is not identified but has informative bounds

Let us assume a "true" set of parameters, unknown to the researcher, such that $\lambda^Y_{01} = 0.6$ and $\lambda^Y_{10} = 0.1$ while we set $\lambda^Y_{00} = 0.2$ and $\lambda^Y_{11} = 0.1$. Thus, the true average causal effect is 0.5. We now use these parameters and the model to simulate a large amount of data ($N = 10{,}000$). We then return to the model, set flat priors over nodal types, and update the model using the simulated data. We graph the posterior on our two queries, the ATE and the probability of positive causation in an $X = 1$, $Y = 1$ case, in Figure 9.6.

The figure nicely illustrates the difference between an identified and non-identified query. While the ATE converges on the right answer, the probability of causation fails to converge even with a massive amount of data. We see instead a range of values for this query on which our updated model places roughly equal posterior probability.

Importantly, however, we see that we *do* learn about the probability of causation. Despite the lack of convergence, our posterior rules out a wide range of values. While our prior on the query was 0.5, we have correctly updated toward a range of values that includes (and happens to be fairly well centered over) the true value (≈ 0.86).

A distinctive feature of updating a causal model is that it lets us learn about non-identified quantities in this manner. We might end up with "ridges" in our posterior distributions: ranges or combinations of parameter values that are equally likely given the data. But our posterior weight can nonetheless shift toward the right answer.

At the same time, for non-identified queries, we have to be cautious about the impact of our priors. As N becomes large, the remaining curvature we see in our posteriors may simply be a function of those priors. One way to inspect for this is to simulate a very large dataset and see whether variance shrinks. A second approach is to do sensitivity analyses by updating the model on the same data with different sets of priors to see how this affects the shape of the posterior.

Finally, we note a nontrivial practical payoff. Whether quantities are identified or not, we calculate answers to queries in the same way: by defining a model, then updating it and querying it. We do not have to figure out the particular estimating equation that works to return a good estimate of an estimand. To illustrate the point, in a beautiful contribution, Angrist and Imbens (1995) show that, under a small set of conditions, average treatment effects for compliers (or "CACE" for "complier average causal effects") are identifiable, and then figure out what procedure one can use for estimating them (instrumental variables). Yet a researcher who believed that the conditions Angrist and Imbens stipulate held in their causal model, updated their model with a large amount of data, and queried for the complier average effect would get to the right answer with a low posterior variance. And they would get there even if they had never read Angrist and Imbens (1995), did not know beforehand that their quantity of interest was identified, and did not know what estimating equation they would need to estimate it consistently.

9.4 Extensions

In our presentation of the baseline approach so far, we have assumed that we are analyzing binary data on a set of cases with independent (potential) outcomes for the central purpose of estimating causal relationships. In this last section, we consider four extensions of this basic approach: a procedure for handling nonbinary data and applications of the framework to modeling and learning about measurement error and spillovers between units.

9.4.1 Beyond Binary Data

The approach we have described readily generalizes to nonbinary data. Moving beyond binary nodes allows for considerably greater flexibility in response functions. For instance, moving from binary to merely three-level ordinal X and Y variables allows us to represent nonlinear and even non-monotonic relationships. It also allows us to pose more complex queries, such as, "What is the probability that Y is linear in X?," "What is the probability that Y is concave in X?" or "What is the probability that Y is monotonic in X?"

Table 9.7 Posteriors on potential outcomes for nonbinary model

Q	Using	True value	Mean	SD
$Y(0)$	Posteriors	0	0.38	0.09
$Y(1)$	Posteriors	1	0.98	0.07
$Y(2)$	Posteriors	3	2.61	0.09
$Y(3)$	Posteriors	2	2.02	0.07

To move to nonbinary nodes, we need to be able to expand the nodal-type space to accommodate the richer range of possible relations between nodes that can take on more than two possible values. Suppose, for instance, that we want to operate with variables with four ordinal categories. In an $X \rightarrow Y$ model, Y's nodal types have to accommodate four possible values that X can take on, and four possible values that Y can take on for any value of X. This yields $4^4 = 256$ nodal types for Y and 1024 causal types (compared to just 8 in a binary setup).

The CausalQueries package, set up to work most naturally with binary nodes, can in principle, be used to represent nonbinary data as well.[9]

In the illustration below with two four-level variables, we generate data ($N = 100$) from a non-monotonic process with the following potential outcomes: $Y(0) = 0$, $Y(1) = 1$, $Y(2) = 3$, and $Y(3) = 2$. We then update and report on posteriors on potential outcomes.

Updating and querying are done in the usual way. In Table 9.7, we show results for a simple set of queries in which we ask what Y's expected outcome is for each value of X. We report the mean and standard deviation for the posterior on each query and as a benchmark, also show the "true" parameter value that we used to generate the data.

We see that the model performs well. As in the binary setup, the posterior reflects both the data and the priors. And, as usual, we have access to a full posterior distribution over all nodal types and can thus ask arbitrary queries of the updated model.

---

[9] The trick, as it were, is to express integers in base-2 and then represent the integer as a series of 0's and 1's on multiple nodes. In base-2 counting we would represent four integer values for X (say, 0, 1, 2, 3) using 00, 01, 10, 11. If we use one binary node, X_1 to represent the first digit, and a second node X_2 to represent the second, we have enough information to capture the four values of X. The mapping then is: $X_1 = 0, X_2 = 0$ represents $X = 0$; $X_1 = 0, X_2 = 1$ represents $X = 1$; $X_1 = 1, X_2 = 0$ represents $X = 2$; and $X_1 = 1, X_2 = 1$ represents $X = 3$. We construct Y in the same way. We can then represent a simple $X \rightarrow Y$ relation as a model with two X nodes each pointing into two Y nodes: $Y_1 \leftarrow X_1 \rightarrow Y_2, Y_1 \leftarrow X_2 \rightarrow Y_2$. To allow for the full range of nodal types we need to allow a joint distribution over θ^{X_1} and θ^{X_2} and over θ^{Y_1} and θ^{Y_2}, which results in three degrees of freedom for X and 255 for Y, as required.

The greatest challenge posed by the move to nonbinary data is computational. If Y takes on m possible values and has k parents, each taking on r possible values, we then have $m^{(r^k)}$ nodal types for Y. Thus, the cost of more granular measurement is complexity – an explosion of the parameter space – as the nodal type space expands rapidly with the granularity of measurement and the number of explanatory variables. With three-level ordinal variables pointing into the same outcome, for instance, we have $3^{27} = 7.6$ *trillion* nodal types.

We expect that, as measurement becomes more granular, researchers will want to manage the complexity by placing structure onto the possible patterns of causal effects. Structure, imposed through model restrictions, can quite rapidly tame the complexity. For some substantive problems, one form of structure we might be willing to impose is monotonicity. In a $X \rightarrow Y$ model with three-level variables, excluding non-monotonic effects brings down the number of nodal types from 27 to 17. Alternatively, we may have a strong reason to rule out effects in one direction: Disallowing negative effects, for instance, brings us down to 10 nodal types. If we are willing to assume linearity, the number of nodal types falls further to 5.

9.4.2 Measurement Error

One potential application of the approach we have described in this chapter to integrating differing forms of data is to address the problem of measurement error. The conceptual move to address measurement error in a causal model setup is quite simple: We incorporate the error-generating process into our model.

Consider, for instance, a model in which we build in a process generating measurement error on the dependent variable.

$X \rightarrow Y \rightarrow Y_{\text{measured}} \leftarrow$ source of measurement error.

Here, X has an effect on the true value of our outcome of interest, Y. The true value of Y, in turn, has an effect on the value of Y that we measure, but so too does a potential problem with our coding process. Thus, the measured value of Y is a function of both the true value and error.

To motivate the setup, imagine that we are interested in the effect of a rule restricting long-term care staff to working at a single site (X) on outbreaks of the novel coronavirus in long-term care facilities (Y), defined as infections among two or more staff or residents. We do not directly observe infections, however; rather, we observe positive results of PCR tests. We also know that testing is neither comprehensive nor uniform. For some units, regular random testing is carried out on staff and residents, while in others, only symptomatic individuals are tested. It is the latter arrangement that potentially introduces measurement error.

If we approach the problem naively, ignoring measurement error and treating $Y_{measured}$ as though it were identical to Y, a differences-in-means approach might produce attenuation bias – insofar as we are averaging between the true relationship and 0.

We can do better with a causal model, however. Without any additional data, we can update on both λ^Y and $\lambda^{Y_{measured}}$, and our posterior uncertainty would reflect uncertainty in measurement. We could go further if, for instance, we could reasonably exclude negative effects of Y on $Y_{measured}$. Then, if we observe (say) a negative correlation between X and $Y_{measured}$, we can update on the substantive effect of interest – λ^Y – in the direction of a larger share of negative effects: It is only *via* negative effects of X on Y that a negative correlation between X and $Y_{measured}$ could emerge. At the same time, we learn about the measure itself as we update on $\lambda^{Y_{measured}}$: The negative observed correlation between X and $Y_{measured}$ is an indicator of the degree to which $Y_{measured}$ is picking up true Y.

We can do better still if we can collect more detailed information on at least some units. One data strategy would be to invest in observing Y, the true outbreak status of each unit, for a subset of units for which we already have data on X and $Y_{measured}$ – perhaps by implementing a random-testing protocol at a subset of facilities. Getting better measures of Y for some cases will allow us to update more directly on λ^Y, and so the true effect of X on Y, for those cases. But just as importantly, observing true Y will allow us to update on measurement *quality*, $\lambda^{Y_{measured}}$, and thus help us make better use of the data we have for those cases where we only observe $Y_{measured}$. This strategy, of course, parallels a commonly prescribed use of mixed methods, in which qualitative research takes place in a small set of units to generate more credible measures for large-n analysis (see, e.g., Seawright, 2016).

To illustrate, we posit a true average effect of X on Y of 0.6. We also posit an average "effect" of Y on measured Y of just 0.7, allowing for measurement error.

In this setup, with a large amount of data, we would arrive at a differences-in-means estimate of the effect of X on *measured* Y of about 0.42. Importantly, this would be the effect of X on $Y_{measured}$ – not the effect of X on Y – but if we were not thinking about the possibility of measurement error, we might conflate the two, arriving at an estimate far from the true value.

Table 9.8 Inferences on effects on true Y given measurement error
(true ATE = 0.6)

Data	Using	Mean	SD
Data on Y measured only	Posteriors	0.64	0.09
Data on true Y for 20% of units	Posteriors	0.63	0.03
Data on true Y	Posteriors	0.61	0.02

We can improve on this "naive" estimate in a number of ways using a causal model, as shown in Table 9.8. First, we can do much better simply by undertaking the estimation within a causal model framework, even if we simply make use of the exact same data. We write down the following simple model $X \rightarrow Y \rightarrow Y_{\text{measured}}$, and we build in a monotonicity restriction that disallows negative effects of Y on Y_{measured}. As we can see from the first row in Table 9.8, our mean estimate of the ATE moves much closer to the true value of 0.6, and it has an appropriately larger posterior standard deviation.

Second, we can add data by gathering measures of "true" Y for 20% of our sample. As we can see from the second row in the table, this investment in additional data does not change our posterior mean much but yields a dramatic increase in precision. In fact, as we can see by comparison to the third row, partial data on "true" Y yields an estimate that is almost the same and almost as precise as the one we would arrive at with data on "true" Y for *all* cases.

An alternative strategy might involve gathering multiple measures of Y, each with its own independent source of error. Consider the model, $X \rightarrow Y \rightarrow Y_{\text{measured}[1]}$; $Y \rightarrow Y_{\text{measured}[2]}$. Assume again a true ATE of X on Y of 0.6, that Y has an average effect of 0.7 on both $Y_{\text{measured}[1]}$ and $Y_{\text{measured}[2]}$, and no negative effects of true Y on the measures.[10] In this setup, updating the true Y can be thought of as a Bayesian version of "triangulation," or factor analysis. The results in Table 9.9 are based on the same data as in the previous example but are now augmented with the second noisy measure for Y.

As we can see, two noisy measures perform in this example about as well as access to full data on the true Y (as in Table 9.8).

The main point here is that measurement error matters for inference and can be taken directly into account within a causal model framework.

[10] Importantly, this model assumes nodal types for $Y_{\text{measured}[1]}$ and $Y_{\text{measured}[2]}$ are independent of one another (no unobserved confounding), implying independent sources of measurement error in this setup.

Table 9.9 Inferences on effects on true Y given two noisy measures (true ATE = 0.6)

Data	Using	Mean	SD
Two noisy measures	Posteriors	0.61	0.02

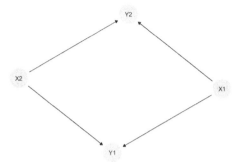

Figure 9.7   Model with spillovers: The treatment status of two units each affects the outcomes for both

Confusing measured variables for variables of interest will obviously lead to false conclusions. But if measurement concerns loom large, we can respond by making them part of our model and learning about them. We have illustrated this point for simple setups, but more complex structures could be just as well envisioned, such as those where the error is related to X or, more perniciously, to the effects of X on Y.

9.4.3 Spillovers

A common threat to causal inference is the possibility of spillovers: a given unit's outcome being affected by the treatment status of another (e.g., possibly neighboring) unit. We can readily set up a causal model to allow for the estimation of various quantities related to spillovers.

Consider, for instance, the causal model represented in Figure 9.7. We consider here groupings of pairs of units across which spillovers might occur. We might imagine, for instance, geographically proximate villages separated from other groups such that spillovers might occur between neighboring villages but can be ruled out across more distal villages. Here, X_i and Y_i represent village i's treatment status and outcome, respectively. The pattern of directed edges indicates that each village's outcome might be affected both by its own and by its neighbors' treatment status.

Table 9.10 Spillover queries

Query	Using	Mean	SD
only_self_treated	Posteriors	0.37	0.05
only_other_treated	Posteriors	0.00	0.04
one_treated	Posteriors	0.19	0.04
both_treated	Posteriors	0.75	0.05

We now simulate data that allow for spillovers. Specifically, while independently assigning X_1 and X_2 to treatment 50% of the time, we (a) set Y_1 equal to X_1, meaning that Unit 1 is affected only by its own treatment status and (b) set Y_2 equal to $X_1 \times X_2$, meaning that Unit 2 is equally affected by its own treatment status and that of its neighbor, such that $Y_2 = 1$ only if both Unit 2 and its neighbor are assigned to treatment.

We simulate 100 observations from this data-generating process and then update a model (with flat priors over all nodal types). Results are presented in Table 9.10.

Now we can extract a number of spillover-relevant causal quantities from the updated model. First, we ask: What is the average effect of exposing a unit *directly* to treatment ("only_self_treated") when the neighboring unit is untreated? Under the data-generating process that we have posited, we know that this effect will be 1 for Unit 1 (which always has a positive treatment effect) and 0 for Unit 2 (which sees a positive effect of X_2 only when $X_1 = 1$), yielding an average across the two units of 0.5. In Table 9.10, see that we update, given our 100 observations, from a prior of 0 to a posterior mean of 0.371, approaching the right answer.

A second question we can ask is about the spillover itself: What is the average treatment effect for a unit of its neighbor being assigned to treatment when the unit itself is not assigned to treatment ("only_other_treated")? We know that the correct answer is 0 since Unit 1 responds only to its own treatment status, and Unit 2 requires that both units be assigned to treatment to see an effect. Our posterior estimate of this effect is right on target, at 0.

We can then ask about the average effect of *any* one unit being treated, as compared to no units being treated ("one_treated"). This is a more complex quantity. To estimate it, we have to consider what happens to the outcome in Unit 1 when only X_1 shifts from control to treatment, with X_2 at control (the true effect is 1); what happens to Unit 1 when only X_2 shifts from control to treatment, with X_1 at control (the true effect is 0); and the same two effects for Unit 2 (both true effects are 0). We then average across both the treatment conditions and units. We arrive at a posterior mean of 0.186, not far from the true value of 0.25.

Finally, we can ask about the average effect of both treatments going from control to treatment ("both_treated"). The true value of this effect is 1 for both units, and the posterior has shifted quite far in the direction of this value.

Obviously, more complex setups are possible. The main idea however is that spillovers, often seen as a threat to inference, can just as well been seen as an opportunity to learn about an array of causal processes.

9.5 Appendix: Mixing Methods with CausalQueries

9.5.1 An Illustration in Code

We now demonstrate how to do model updating in CausalQueries when you have X and Y data for many cases but "causal process observations" for only a smaller number of cases.

Imagine a simple model in which X has a possible direct or indirect effect via M. We can define the model thus:

```
model <- make_model("X -> M -> Y <- X")
```

We do not provide any structure to priors or impose any monotonicity constraints. But we do imagine that we can access some data and update using these data. For this illustration, the data are consistent with effects running through M; moreover, X, Y data are available for all units, but M is available for some units only. We now input the data and update the model.

```
data <- data.frame(
    X = c(0,0,0,0,1,1,1,1),
    M = c(NA,0,0,1,0,1,1,NA),
    Y = c(0,0,0,1,0,1,1,1)) %>%
    uncount(10)


model <- update_model(model, data)
```

We can now query the updated model to figure out how our inferences for a case depend on M:

```
query_model(model,
            query = "Y[X=1]> Y[X=0]",
```

Table 9.11 Querying an updated model

Given	Estimate
$X{==}1 \,\&\, Y{==}1$	0.718
$X{==}1 \,\&\, Y{==}1 \,\&\, M{==}0$	0.580
$X{==}1 \,\&\, Y{==}1 \,\&\, M{==}1$	0.734

Table 9.12 Lipid study data from Chickering and Pearl (1996). Note data are reported in compact form with counts of events, assuming a data strategy in which data are sought on all nodes (ZXY)

Event	Strategy	Count
Z0X0Y0	ZXY	158
Z1X0Y0	ZXY	52
Z0X1Y0	ZXY	0
Z1X1Y0	ZXY	23
Z0X0Y1	ZXY	14
Z1X0Y1	ZXY	12
Z0X1Y1	ZXY	0
Z1X1Y1	ZXY	78

```
given = c("X==1 & Y==1",
          "X==1 & Y==1 & M==1",
          "X==1 & Y==1 & M==0"),
     using = "posteriors",
     case_level = TRUE)
```

Results are shown in Table 9.11. We see that M is informative (particularly when $M = 0$) about causal effects in a new case, given our observation of processes in previous cases. The key thing here is that the informativeness of M for the new case is justified by the updating of the original model – a model that itself contained no assumptions about whether or how effects passed through M.

9.5.2 Replication of Chickering and Pearl (1996) Lipid Analysis

Chickering and Pearl (1996) assess the problem of drawing inferences in the presence of imperfect compliance. They use data that look like those in Table 9.12.

Table 9.13 Replication of Chickering and Pearl (1996)

Query	Given	Using	Mean	SD	Cred low	Cred high
Q 1	–	Posteriors	0.556	0.1	0.375	0.733

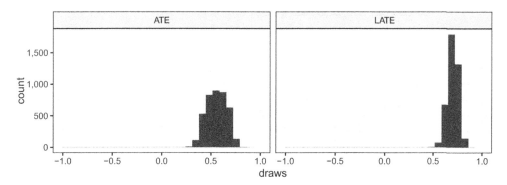

Figure 9.8 Posterior distributions on average treatment effects and treatment effects for compliers. Left panel replicates Chickering and Pearl (1996)

Chickering and Pearl (1996) use a Gibbs sampler to update over 16 response types (and so 15 degrees of freedom). The parameterization in CausalQueries has four nodal types for X and four parameters capturing the conditional distribution of the four nodal types for Y given each nodal type for X, giving $3 + 4 \times 3 = 15$ degrees of freedom.

In CausalQueries the complete code for model specification, updating, and querying is quite compact:

```
results <-
```

```
  make_model("Z -> X -> Y; X <-> Y") |>
  update_model(data, data_type = "compact") |>
  query_model(query = "Y[X=1] - Y[X=0]", using = "posteriors")
```

Table 9.13 reports the results while Figure 9.8 shows the full posterior distribution for this query.

The results agree with the findings in Chickering and Pearl (1996). We also show the posterior distribution for the average effects *among the compliers* – those for whom Z has a positive effect on X – which is tighter thanks to identification for this query.

Chickering and Pearl (1996) also assess probabilities of counterfactual events for single cases. For instance, would there be a positive effect for

Table 9.14 Case level counterfactual inference following model
updating (replication of Chickering and Pearl, 1996)

Case level	Mean	SD	Cred low	Cred high
FALSE	0.641	0.153	0.374	0.898
TRUE	0.640		0.640	0.640

someone with $X = 0$, and $Y = 0$? Our answers to this query, shown in
Table 9.14, also agree with Chickering and Pearl's. Note that when we calculate inferences for a single "new" case ("Case level") our conclusion is a single
number, a probability, and it does not have a confidence interval around it.

```
make_model("Z -> X -> Y; X <-> Y") |>
  update_model(data, data_type = "compact") |>
  query_model(
    query = "Y[X=1] - Y[X=0]",
    given = "X==0 & Y==0",
    case_level = c(FALSE, TRUE)
    using = "posteriors")
```

9.5.3 Probative Value Arising from Correlations in the Posterior Distribution over Parameters

In Chapter 7, we showed how you can use rules of d-separation to assess
whether data on a node has probative value for a query given a case-level
DAG. In that discussion, we were conditioning on λ (or assuming that non-
independencies arising from the joint distribution of λ were already captured
by the DAG). How do things change when we update over the distribution
of λ?

In that case, it is possible that when we update over λ we have dependencies in our beliefs that call for a reassessment of the case-level DAG and so a
reassessment of when case-level data have probative value for a query.

Thus, we may have a case-level DAG where two nodes, A and B are d-
separated given C conditional on λ. In other words, we are convinced that in
the data generating process, whatever it is, A and B are d-separated given C
and so A has no probative value for learning about B given C. We might even
specify prior beliefs over λ such that beliefs over λ^A and λ^B are independent
and so A and B are also d-separated for each case in the population DAG
(Figure 9.2). However, after updating, beliefs over λ^A and λ^B may no longer

Table 9.15 Probability distribution over two parameter vectors

λ	$p(\lambda)$	λ_0^X	λ_1^X	λ_{01}^M	λ_{10}^M	λ_{01}^Y	λ_{10}^Y
λ_1	0.5	0.5	0.5	0.01	0.99	0.01	0.99
λ_2	0.5	0.5	0.5	0.99	0.01	0.99	0.01

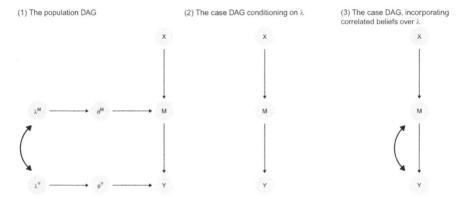

Figure 9.9 d-connectedness via correlations in beliefs over λ

be independent and, in consequence, A and B may no longer be d-separated given C.

We illustrate by imagining a chain model of the form $X \to M \to Y$. Note that as written X is d-separated from Y given M. Say, however, that we have the following (Table 9.15) joint distribution of beliefs over model parameters (where, as before, subscript 01 indicates a positive effect and 10 a negative effect):

Beliefs like this might arise if you observe a lot of strongly correlated data on X and Y but never get to observe M.

Say we now ask about $\hat{\pi}(X = 0 | M = 1, Y = 1)$. This is given by $\frac{\lambda_0^X \lambda_{10}^M \lambda_{01}^Y}{\lambda_0^X \lambda_{10}^M \lambda_{01}^Y + \lambda_1^X \lambda_{01}^M \lambda_{01}^Y} = \lambda_{01}^M$ which has expected value $0.5 \times 0.01 + 0.5 \times 0.99 = 0.5$. Similarly $\hat{\pi}(X = 1 | M = 1, Y = 0) = 0.5$. The reason is that in the model, *conditional on λ*, Y is d-separated from X by M.

However, when we now ask about $\hat{\phi}(X = 0 | M = 1, Y = 1)$ we are not conditioning on λ. We have

$\hat{\phi}(X = 1 | M = 1, Y = 0) = 0.02$ and $\hat{\phi}(X = 1 | M = 1, Y = 1) = 0.98$. Thus, we do not have conditional independence. Referring back to Figure 9.2, if we were to include double-headed arrows between the λ^M and λ^Y terms and then focus on the DAG for unit 1, we would then have to include double-headed arrows between M and Y.

For this reason, when drawing DAGs we need to be careful to specify either that the DAG represents the independence of θ terms *given* λ or make sure that the DAG is faithful to violations of independence that arise from correlated beliefs over λ. Figure 9.9 illustrates. If we mean only the former, then we cannot use the rules of d-separation to determine whether a clue has probative value for our beliefs on causal quantities.

10 Integrated Inferences Applications

Parallel to the single-case process-tracing analyses in Chapter 8, we show how we can use data from multiple cases to update our models of inequality and democratization and of institutions and growth. We then use the updated models to draw both population-level and case-level inferences. These applications illustrate situations in which learning is minimal and in which it is more substantial, and demonstrate how the probative value of process-tracing clues can be empirically established through model-updating.

In Chapter 8, we undertook single-case process tracing from causal models about inequality and democratization and about institutions and growth. In that chapter, we took the model as given and sought to draw inferences about individual cases given data on those cases. In this chapter, which applies the multi-case setup in Chapter 9 to the same two substantive problems, the models become objects that we both learn from and learn about. We use data on a large set of cases to update our beliefs about the general model and then use this "trained" model to make inferences about causal questions posed at both the population and the case level.

In the process-tracing applications, we had to posit beliefs about the distribution (or population-level share) of nodal types for each node in the model. For multi-case process tracing, in contrast, we posit a prior distribution *over the distribution* of nodal types – that is, a distribution over λ. Because we set a prior distribution over distributions of nodal types (rather than fixing proportions), we can now update on these population-level distributions as the model confronts data.

The same applies to beliefs about confounding. Recall that we allow for unobserved confounding by allowing λ to include beliefs about the *joint* distributions of nodal types; we set priors on these joint distributions as well. In the inequality and democratization application, we allow for unobserved confounding between inequality and mobilization: The possibility that inequality may be more or less likely in places where inequality would induce mobilization. In the institutions and growth application, we allow for unobserved confounding between institutions and growth. In both examples, we refrain from expressing informed prior beliefs about the direction or magnitude of the confounding; we merely allow for the possibility of confounding and set a flat prior over its direction and magnitude. Furthermore, in the institutions and growth example, we show how we can usefully *learn* about the confounding directly from the data.

10.1 Inequality and Democratization

We begin with the same basic model that we used in Chapter 8, with inequality (I) potentially affecting democratization (D) both through a direct pathway and through an indirect pathway mediated by mobilization (M). International pressure (P) is also a "parent" of democratization.

Further, we impose the same set of monotonicity restrictions, ruling out a negative effect of inequality on mobilization, a direct positive effect of inequality on democratization, a negative effect of mobilization on democracy, and a negative effect of pressure on democratization. Note that this setup allows for inequality to have a positive (through mobilization) effect on democratization, a negative (direct) effect on democratization, or no effect at all.

Finally, we allow for confounding. The theoretical intuition we want to capture in the model is that the level of inequality could be endogenous to inequality's effect on mobilization. In particular, in places where inequality would pose a mobilizational threat, governments may work harder to reduce inequality. To allow for this possibility, we need to create distinct elements of λ representing the conditional distribution of I's nodal types given M's: One parameter for θ^I's distribution when M's nodal type is θ_{01}^M, and another parameter for θ^I's distribution when M's nodal type is something else.

This model, with confounding, is represented graphically as in Figure 10.1. The possibility of confounding is represented with the bidirected edge, connecting I and M.

10.1.1 Data

To train the model, we add data.

As in Chapter 8, we will confront the model with data drawn from our coding of the case narratives in the Supplementary Material for Haggard and

Table 10.1 Data (snippet) derived from Haggard and Kaufman (2012)

Case	P	I	M	D
Afghanistan		1		0
Albania	0	0	1	1
Algeria		0		0
Angola		1		0
Argentina	0	0	1	1
Bangladesh	0	0	0	1

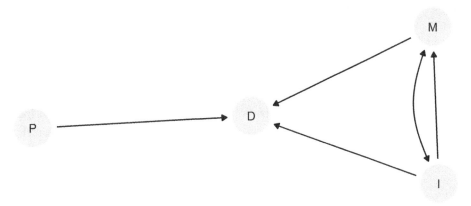

Figure 10.1   Democracy and inequality model

Kaufman (2012). However, rather than implementing the analysis case-by-case, we now derive leverage from the joint distribution of the data available across all cases.

Table 10.1 gives a snippet of the data.

Note that this dataset takes a non-rectangular form common to much multi-method research. While we have data on the main causal variable of interest (I) and the outcome (D) for all cases, Haggard and Kaufman's collection of more detailed case evidence was conditional on a case's outcome, $D = 1$: They gathered qualitative data on the presence of international pressure and the presence of mass-mobilization *only* for those cases that democratized. This is not uncommon when selecting cases for process tracing from a larger population. The analyst often reasons that more can be learned about how an outcome arises by focusing on cases where the outcome of interest has in fact occurred. (We assess this case-selection intuition, in

Table 10.2 Pairwise correlations in the democracy-inequality (PIMD) data. P = Pressure, I = Inequality, M = Mobilization, D = Democratization

	P	I	M	D
P	1.000	0.157	−0.177	
I	0.157	1.000	0.114	−0.154
M	−0.177	0.114	1.000	
D		−0.154		1.000

the context of model-based inferences, in Chapter 13.) The result is a nested mixed design in which we have "thin" (I and D) data on a large set of cases and "thicker" data on a subset of those cases.

The raw correlations between variables are shown in Table 10.2. Some correlations are missing because, as just noted, data on some variables were only gathered conditional on the values of others. The correlations we do see are not very strong. There is, in particular, a weak overall relationship between inequality and democratization – though this is consistent with inequality having heterogeneous effects across the sample. The strongest correlation in the data is between P and M, which are assumed to be uncorrelated in the model, though this correlation is also quite weak.

10.1.2 Case-Level Queries

With data and model in hand, we can now update our model using the procedure described in Chapter 9 to get a posterior distribution over λ. From this posterior over λ, we can then generate posterior beliefs over all causal relations in the model.

We then use our posterior over λ to make claims about the probability that inequality mattered for democratization in cases with different I, D, and potentially M and/or D values. This is similar to the question we posed when we undertook process tracing in Chapter 8, but we are now using a model that has been trained on data. In other words, we are using knowledge of observed relationships across a large number of cases to inform our beliefs about what we should conclude when we observe *particular* evidentiary patterns in a *specific* case.

Our results are graphed in Figure 10.2. In the first two columns of the figure, we consider what we would conclude in a case that democratized. In the first column, we ask about the probability that *low* inequality caused

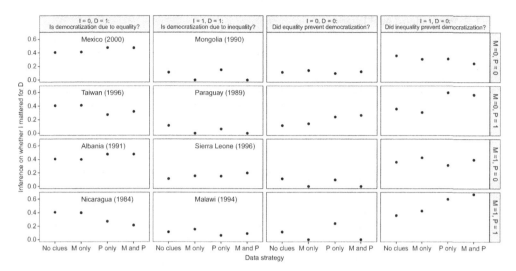

Figure 10.2　Case-level inferences given inequality and democratization values and possible observations of mobilization and pressure

democratization in an $I = 0, D = 1$ case. In the second column, we ask about the probability that *high* inequality caused democratization in an $(I = 1, D = 1)$ case. In each column, we assess how our answers would differ based on potential observations of mobilization and international pressure in the case at hand. We note that, for all results here, we are calculating $\hat{\pi}(Q|D)$ as defined in Chapter 9: That is, we are drawing inferences about case-level probabilities from population shares, treating the case about which we want to draw an inference as "uninformative" about those population shares.

Overall, we find that the results are remarkably similar to those derived from the untrained model in Chapter 8: This is clear from a comparison of the patterns in Figure 10.2 here to those in Figure 8.3. There are some cases, especially in the $I = 0, D = 1$ column, for which M appears to be slightly less informative under the trained model than under the untrained model. But the main takeaway is that the observed data here do not seem to substantially shift our beliefs from those implied by the theoretical assumptions that we originally built into the model.

This comparison does not tell us definitively how much we have learned from the data. It is possible, for instance, that while our beliefs about these queries shift little, there could be (possibly countervailing) shifts in the underlying beliefs about type shares out of which the queries are composed. We examine in more detail in Section 10.1.4 below whether the multi-case data in this application yield updating about underlying type shares.

10.1.3 Population-Level Queries

We can also pose questions to the model at the population level. One set of questions we can ask of the updated model is about the share of cases for which inequality has a positive effect or has a negative effect on democratization. We can pose this question at different levels of conditioning. For instance, we can ask:

1. **For all cases.** For what proportion of all cases in the population does inequality have a positive effect on democratization? For what proportion a negative effect?
2. **For all cases with a given causal state and outcome.** Among those cases that in fact had high inequality and democratized, for what proportion was the high inequality a cause of democratization? Among those cases that in fact had high inequality and did not democratize, for what proportion did the high inequality prevent democratization?
3. **For cases with a given causal state and outcome, and with or without mobilization and pressure.** We can also drill down to make inferences about smaller subgroups of the population. For what share of high-inequality, democratizing cases *with* mobilization did inequality cause the outcome? For what proportion *without* mobilization? Likewise, for the presence or absence of international pressure?

For each of these population-level questions, we can generate a posterior distribution that describes our beliefs, by building from our posterior over λ. We can define each query quite simply in terms of the causal types that correspond to the effect of interest and then calculate the share of the subgroup in question that has a causal type that satisfies the query. For instance, for query 2 above as applied to the $I = 1, D = 1$ subgroup: We add up the population share of those causal types that give us both $I = 1, D = 1$ *and* a positive effect of I on D, and divide that by the sum of the shares of all causal types that give us $I = 1, D = 1$.

In Figure 10.3, we graph posterior distributions for the full set of queries. In the first column, we are concerned with positive effects of I on D, and in the second column with negative effects.

Starting with the first column, in the first row we are simply asking for what proportion of cases in the population does I have a positive effect. We can see that the share of cases with positive effects is estimated to be very low, with a good deal of confidence. In the next row–where the attribution question presupposes we know the values of I and D – we see that the expected share of

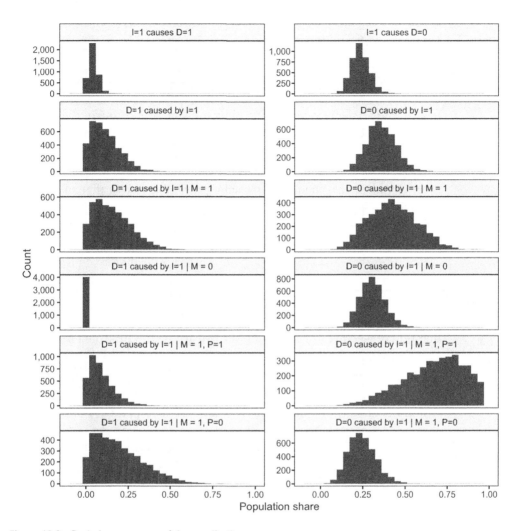

Figure 10.3 Posteriors on causes of democratization

positive effects is considerably higher for the subgroup of the population that in fact experienced high inequality and democratization, though uncertainty about this share is relatively high. The expected proportion of positive causal effects is believed to be even higher among those $I = 1, D = 1$ cases in which mobilization occurred – and higher again when an alternative cause (international pressure) is absent. Again, however, our uncertainty about these shares is also great.

We also see that we believe that democratization is not caused by inequality in those $I = 1, D = 1$ cases in which mobilization is absent. Interestingly this result derives purely from the model restrictions, rather than from the data: Under the restrictions we imposed, a positive effect of inequality can operate *only* through mobilization.

Turning now to the cases in which democratization did not occur, the second column of Figure 10.3 asks for what proportion of cases overall inequality has a negative effect on democratization; for what proportion of $I = 1, D = 0$ cases inequality prevented democratization; and this latter query conditional on different clue realizations. We see that inequality appears, overall, more commonly to prevent democratization than to cause it. We are, moreover, most confident that inequality played a preventive role in that subgroup in which there was both mobilization and international pressure – both of which *could* have generated democratization – but still no democratization occurred (second-to-last plot in the second column).

10.1.4 Explorations: How Much Do We Get from the Model versus the Data?

The lack of movement in our case-level queries, in Section 10.1.2, raises the question of whether or how much we are learning from the data in this analysis, as compared to the beliefs that we built into the model at the outset, including through the monotonicity restrictions that we imposed. To examine this in greater detail, in Figure 10.4 we plot posteriors on parameter values within each family of parameters. The families correspond to nodal types for each node except M. For M, to reflect the confounding that we have allowed for between I and M, we have one family for nodal types for M conditional on $I = 0$ and another for nodal types for M conditional on $I = 1$.

Recall that we had eliminated nodal types that violated monotonicity (e.g., those representing negative effects of I on M or of M or P on D) and then placed flat priors on the remaining nodal types within each family. In other words, in our priors the plotted points in each graph would simply fall along a vertical line. The question now is whether we see a significant divergence from the vertical alignment within each set.

From inspection of Figure 10.4, we see that we do. For the root nodes, P and I we see that we have adjusted to expect $P = 0$ and $I = 1$ to be relatively more common. For M, we have adjusted to expect that $M = 1$ regardless of I for cases assigned to $I = 0$, and to expect that $M = 0$ regardless of I, for cases assigned to $I = 1$. Thus, we expect mobilization to be negatively correlated with inequality. For D, the most dramatic movement is in favor of the null effect represented by the top nodal type: As compared to our priors, we now more strongly believe that democratization will occur regardless of

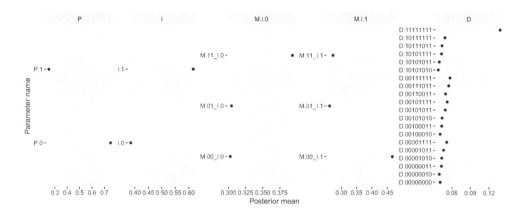

Figure 10.4 Posterior means of parameters from the democracy model

inequality, mobilization, or international pressure (the interpretation of the other nodal types is given in this footnote).[1]

In all, we can see quite clearly that we have learned from the data about the shares of types in the population, and that the direction of movement is overall toward putting *less* weight on causal effects among nodes than our flat priors had implied.

10.2 Institutions and Growth

We now return to our model of institutions and growth from Chapter 8. Rather than presupposing the probability of different nodal types, however, we seek to build up those beliefs from data from a large set of cases, using the trained model to then answer a set of both population- and case-level queries.

The structural causal model that we use (shown in Figure 10.5) is the same model that we used in Chapter 8. However, we build in weaker assumptions, given that we aim to learn about our model from the data. Specifically, we drop two of the monotonicity assumptions: We no longer assume that growth (Y) is monotonic in institutions or in mortality. The only

---

[1] Each digit indicates the potential value of D for particular values of I, P, and D; specifically, the first digit corresponds to the value of D when $I = 0$, $P = 0$, and $M = 0$, the subsequent digits give the value for D when I, P, and M take values $(1, 0, 0)$, $(0, 1, 0)$, $(1, 1, 0)$, $(0, 0, 1)$, $(1, 0, 1)$, $(0, 1, 1)$, and $(1, 1, 1)$, respectively.

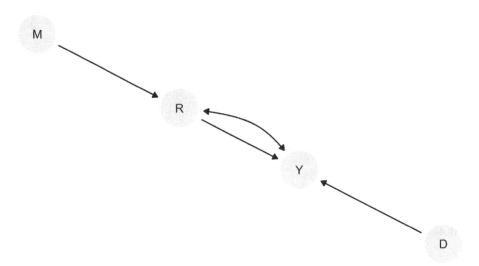

Figure 10.5 Institutions and growth model

monotonicity assumption that we retain is with respect to the instrument, mortality (M): Its effect on institutions (R) cannot be positive. Otherwise, we form flat priors over all nodal types in the model – building in no assumptions other than the causal structure and monotonicity of M's effects. Moreover, as in Chapter 8, we allow for confounding between institutions and growth, allowing for other unobserved common causes of these variables.

10.2.1 Data

We draw our data from the supplementary material for Rodrik et al.'s (2004) paper on the long-run economic effects of institutions. We dichotomize all variables at their sample median, and so are working with somewhat coarser data than used in the original paper. Table 10.3 provides a snippet of the dataset.

Unlike in the inequality application, the data here form a rectangular dataset: Rodrik et al. (2004) collected measures for all variables for all cases, rather than gathering more detailed evidence only on a subset of cases (as Haggard and Kaufman (2012) did in process tracing only the democratizing cases).

The raw correlations between variables are shown in Table 10.4. We note that these bivariate relationships are, in general, much stronger (despite the coarsening) than in the data used in the inequality and democracy application. One thing to notice is that M is, in fact, more strongly correlated with

Table 10.3 Data (snippet) derived from Rodrik et al. (2004)

Country	Distance (D)	Mortality (M)	Institutions (R)	Growth (Y)
Angola	0	1	0	0
Argentina	1	0	1	1
Australia	1	0	1	1
Burundi	0	1	0	0
Benin	0	1	0	0
Burkina Faso	0	1	0	0

Table 10.4 Pairwise correlations in the growth-institutions data. D = Distance from the Equator, M = Settler Mortality, R = Institutional Rule of Law, Y = Growth

	D	M	R	Y
D	1.000	−0.373	0.240	0.291
M	−0.373	1.000	−0.369	−0.572
R	0.240	−0.369	1.000	0.494
Y	0.291	−0.572	0.494	1.000

Y than R is – which might give pause about the exclusion restriction, which assumes that M's effect on Y runs only through R. Also, M and D – which are, by assumption, independent in our model – are quite strongly correlated. We will return to these apparent tensions between our DAG and the data when we consider model evaluation in Chapter 16.

10.2.2 Queries

With the data in hand, we now update our model to derive posteriors on the distribution of model parameters, from which we can then answer any causal query about the model.[2]

Before looking at the more specific case- and population-level queries, we first ask whether the data have changed our beliefs, using our priors as a baseline, about the effect of institutions on growth (possibly conditional on mortality and distance from the equator). The results in Table 10.5 indicate that they have: whereas our priors implied that R has a zero average effect on Y, our posterior belief is that R has a positive average effect on Y, raising the

---

[2] With CausalQueries this is done using update_model(model, data).

Table 10.5 Posterior beliefs about the average effect of R on Y given M and D. Cred low and Cred high indicate the 95% credibility interval

Using	Given	Mean	SD	Cred low	Cred high
Priors	–	0.00	0.10	−0.20	0.19
Posteriors	–	0.15	0.07	0.01	0.30
Posteriors	M == 0	0.15	0.07	0.01	0.30
Posteriors	M == 1	0.15	0.07	0.01	0.30
Posteriors	D == 0	0.13	0.10	−0.06	0.31
Posteriors	D == 1	0.18	0.10	−0.01	0.36

probability of good development outcomes by around 15 percentage points. Our belief about this average effect is the same for cases with high and low settler mortality.[3] We do have different beliefs about institutions' effects on the subgroups of the population closer to and further from the equator, however, with R's effect stronger for those countries that are more distant from the equator. In this sense, D and R are complements – a feature that can also be seen immediately from regression analysis.

10.2.2.1 Case-Level Queries

We now turn to case-level inference. Similar to our procedure in the democratization example, we do so by considering cases with four different possible combinations of growth outcomes and institutional quality. For each type of case, we ask whether the cause plausibly explains the outcome – and how beliefs about that effect would change if we learned about settler mortality (M), distance from the equator (D), or both. This gives us 16 possible combinations of underlying values of the four variables, with four possible evidentiary situations: We observe only R and Y; we additionally observe M only; we additionally observe D; or we additionally observe both M and D. We plot our beliefs about the query for each evidentiary situation and case type. By comparing inferences across evidentiary situations, we can see how informative our M and D clues are about case-level causation.

In Figure 10.6, we plot our beliefs both as derived from the untrained model (using priors) and as derived from the model trained by the data (using posteriors). (Recall also that the model here is different from the one we used in Chapter 8 in that we now do not impose monotonicity restrictions other than that between M and R, so the inferences using priors here will not be

---

[3] This makes sense since the ATE query does not condition on R, and so M is d-separated from Y in the model.

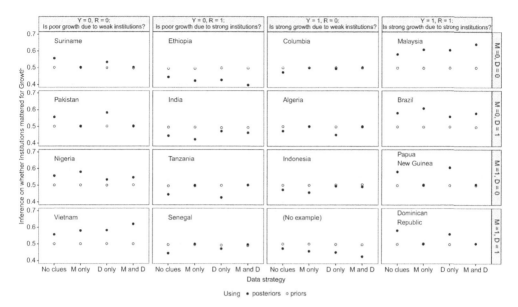

Figure 10.6   Case-level inferences given possible observations of distance and mortality

the same as they were in the process-tracing exercise in that chapter.) Because we have built so little prior knowledge into our model, the M and D clues are always uninformative in the untrained model; regardless of what we observe, we believe there is a 0.5 probability that R mattered for Y in every case. But we plot these inferences to throw into sharp relief the fact that, in this application, the probative value of the clues derives entirely from data rather than from theoretical assumptions.

We can see that when we encounter a case with weak institutions and low growth (first column), using the trained model will lead us to believe it likely that the former caused the latter. We see a parallel result for cases with strong institutions and growth (last column). We can also see in both columns, by comparing the posterior to the prior, that these inferences are heavily grounded in the data we have used to update the model, rather than in prior assumptions. When we turn to the cases with weak institutions and high growth, and vice versa, we see that the updated model leads us to believe it *less* likely that institutions generated the outcome.

Moreover, if we want to collect more information about a given case, both settler mortality (M) and distance from the equator D are informative. Turning first to distance, consider an $R = 0$, $Y = 0$ state. When we additionally observe that this state is close to the equator ($D = 0$), we become less confident institutions were the culprit in this case; but we become more confident

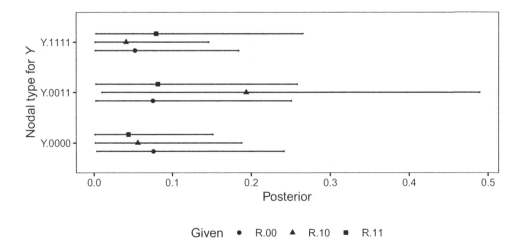

Figure 10.7 A selection of posterior distributions (with 95% credibility intervals) on nodal types for Y given nodal types for R (selected types)

that institutions were the problem if we observe the state to be far from the equator ($D = 1$). Likewise, for an $R = 1, Y = 1$ case, proximity to the equator makes us more confident that the strong institutions helped while distance from the equator makes us less so. This last result may seem surprising given our beliefs that R and D are complements. R and D may well be complements for the average treatment effect, but, *conditional* on $R = 1$ (and $Y = 1$) knowing that $D = 1$ reduces confidence that R did the work.

Second, unlike in the untrained process-tracing model, settler mortality is informative in the updated model (even though it is not for average treatment effects). Strong institutions are now believed to be more likely to have caused high growth in places with lower mortality (see, e.g., Malaysia and Brazil). This result is in line with the confounding logic we discussed in Section 8.2.3.2 of Chapter 8 in the context of process tracing, where we stipulated beliefs about selection effects. Note, however, that we have *not* imposed beliefs about confounding in the present analysis. Rather, here, we have learned about the confounding from the data. Put differently, correlations in our beliefs about nodal types have emerged from updating. Figure 10.7 shows posteriors for our beliefs about the *conditional* probability of θ^Y given θ^R. Recall that we began with flat expectations across the shares represented in this figure. While credibility intervals are large, we can see that we now expect a type for which Y responds positively to R regardless of M to be more common among cases in which institutions respond negatively to settler mortality. This is consistent with a world in which settlers responded to

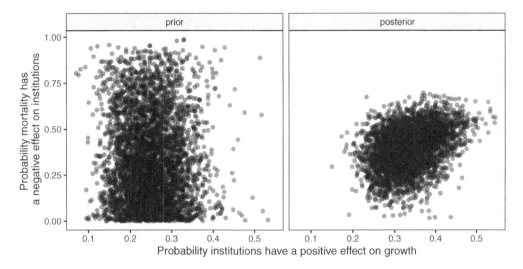

Figure 10.8 Correlated posteriors

low mortality by building strong institutions *specifically* in those places where they rationally expected strong institutions to help.

We can see the learning about this confounding more starkly in Figure 10.8. In each panel of the figure, we plot a summary of our beliefs about the probability that institutional strength has a positive effect on growth against our beliefs that settler mortality has a negative effect on institutional strength. In the left panel, we plot this relationship for our priors, with each point representing one draw from our prior over λ. As we can see, the two sets of beliefs about effects are completely uncorrelated in our priors. In the right panel, we plot our joint posterior for these two effects: Each point represents our belief about both effects under a single draw from our posterior over λ. We can see here that the two sets of beliefs are correlated in the updated model: The more strongly we believe that strong institutions are helpful for growth, the more strongly we also believe that low settler mortality causes strong institutions.

10.2.2.2 Population-Level Queries

Again the updated model can be used not just to inform inferences about cases but also to make population-level claims. In Figure 10.9, we graph the posteriors for a set of queries, conditional on observed data on institutional quality, distance, and settler mortality. The queries plotted here are parallel to the population-level queries that we answered for the inequality and

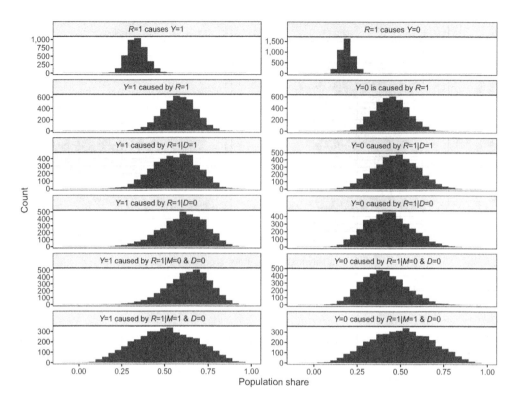

Figure 10.9   Posteriors on causes of growth

democracy model, with the attibution questions presupposing knowledge of R and Y.

In the first row of graphs, we can see that we estimate both positive effects and negative effects of institutions on growth to be somewhat common in the population. However, we believe positive effects to be more common than negative effects. Similarly, in the second row we can see that we think that strong institutions caused the high growth in a higher share of $R = 1, Y = 1$ cases as compared to the share of $R = 1, Y = 0$ cases in which we think strong institutions caused the weak growth.

Looking within more refined subgroups, we see some variation in beliefs about the shares of cases with causal effects, albeit with quite wide credibility intervals. The largest difference is, among those cases close to the equator, between those with high and with low settler mortality. Within the $R = 1, Y = 1, D = 0$ subgroup, we think positive effects are more common among those cases that experienced low mortality than among those that experienced high mortality, consistent with the learning about confounding that we have discussed above. Parallel to this result, and in keeping with the notion of strategic institutional choice by settlers, we find that the low-mortality cases are also ones in which we think it less likely that institutions had an adverse effect on growth in the $R = 1, Y = 0, D = 0$ subgroup.

10.2.3 Explorations: Direct and Indirect Paths from M to Y

Our glance at the raw data suggested a strong negative correlation between mortality and growth, even stronger than the positive correlation between institutions and growth. This might lead us to wonder whether our model is correct – in particular, whether we should allow for a direct path from M to Y. In this subsection, we make and update a model in which we allow for a direct arrow from M to Y, as well as the mediated path that runs from mortality to institutions to growth. We can then pose queries about *how* settler mortality affects long-run growth, asking how much of the effect runs through institutions and how much of this effect runs through all other channels (i.e., "directly").

To maintain simplicity here, we exclude D from the new model and work with a DAG of the form:

$$M \rightarrow R \rightarrow Y \leftarrow M; Y \leftrightarrow R.$$

So we now have both a direct path from M to Y and the mediated path from M to Y that runs through R. We maintain the possibility of unobserved confounding between R and Y. Note that dropping D represents a permissible reduction of the original model since D was a parent to only one node in that model.

In our pathway analysis, we will distinguish between the "indirect" and "direct" effects of settler mortality on growth. We define these quantities more formally below, but first, we give a basic intuition for the difference. By an "indirect" effect, we mean an effect that runs along the $M \rightarrow R \rightarrow Y$ pathway: an effect that, for its operation, depends both on mortality's effect on institutions and on institutions' effect on growth. By a "direct" effect, we mean an effect that operates via the direct $M \rightarrow Y$ pathway. Importantly, labeling this effect "direct" does not imply that there are no mediating steps in this causal pathway. It means only that we have not *included* any of this pathway's mediating steps in the DAG. Thus, the "direct" effect does not represent a specific alternative mechanism to the institutional one. Rather, it captures

Table 10.6 Direct and indirect effects of settler mortality on growth

Effect	Query	Mean	SD	Cred low	Cred high
Total	`Y[M = 0] - Y[M=1]`	0.27	0.08	0.12	0.42
Direct 0	`Y[M = 0, R = R[M=0]]`				
	`- Y[M=1, R = R[M=0]]`	0.19	0.09	0.02	0.37
Direct 1	`Y[M = 0, R = R[M=1]]`				
	`- Y[M=1, R = R[M=1]]`	0.21	0.09	0.04	0.38
Indirect 0	`Y[M = 0, R = R[M=0]]`				
	`- Y[M=0, R = R[M=1]]`	0.06	0.07	−0.05	0.22
Indirect 1	`Y[M = 1, R = R[M=0]]`				
	`- Y[M=1, R = R[M=1]]`	0.08	0.07	−0.03	0.25

a residual: the effect of settler mortality on long-run growth that operates through all mechanisms *other* than the one mediated by institutions.

In Table 10.6, we report results for a pathway analysis at the population level. First, we report our posterior belief about the total average effect of settler mortality on long-run growth, with a posterior mean of 0.272. Then, we report the portion of these effects that run through each pathway.

First, we pose two versions of the direct-effects query, intended to get at the effect of settler mortality that does *not* run through mortality's effect on institutions. To frame a direct-effects query, we need to imagine a manipulation in which the mortality level is changed, but institutions remain fixed. There are two versions of such a query, however. In the first version, labeled "Direct 0," we report the expected change in long-run growth under an imagined manipulation in which we change mortality from 0 to 1 while fixing institutions at the value they would take on *if settler mortality were set to 0*. In the second version ("Direct 1"), we imagine the same change in mortality but fix institutions at the value they would take on *if settler mortality were set to 1*. The difference between these queries is potentially important since mortality's direct effect might *depend* on institutional conditions. As we can see, we get quite similar posterior means from these two direct-effect queries (0.195 versus 0.211).

We turn then to estimating the effect that is operating through institutions. This indirect-effects query asks the following: What change in growth occurs if we change institutions as they *would* change *if* there were a change in settler mortality but with settler mortality in fact held constant (so that no direct effect can be operating). Again, there are two versions of this query: The first ("Indirect 0") holds mortality fixed at 0 while the second ("Indirect 1") holds

Table 10.7 Direct and indirect effects of settler mortality on growth for a case with high mortality, weak institutions, and low growth

Query	ATE	Direct	Indirect
Formula	Y[M=0] > Y[M=1]	Y[M=0, R=R[M=1]] > Y[M=1, R=R[M=1]]	Y[M=1, R=R[M=0]]> Y[M=1, R=R[M=1]]
Given	M==1 & Y==0 & R==0	M==1 & Y==0 & R==0	M==1 & Y==0 & R==0
Estimate	0.64	0.54	0.25

mortality fixed at 1. For both, we posit the change in institutions that would happen if mortality were changed from 0 to 1. As we can see from the fourth and fifth rows of Table 10.6, we get similar estimates of this indirect effect from the two queries (0.061 and 0.077).

Overall, Table 10.6 suggests that both causal pathways are in operation. Yet direct effects appear far stronger than indirect effects. That is to say, we estimate that more of settler mortality's effect on long-run growth runs through channels *other* than the institutional mechanism, than runs through that mechanism. The strongest effect is estimated to be the direct effect with institutions fixed at whatever they would take on if mortality were high. We estimate the weakest pathway to be the indirect effect in places with low mortality. Note that the first query, the total effect, is equal to the sum of "Direct 0" and "Indirect 1" and (equivalently) to the sum of "Direct 1" and "Indirect 0"; this decomposition is documented, for instance, in Imai et al. (2010).

With our updated model of the population in hand, we can now ask similar questions at the case level. Suppose, for instance, that we see a case that had high settler mortality and low growth; we also observe a suspected mediator of mortality's effect, seeing that the case has weak institutions. One question we can ask about this case is the total case-level effect: What is the probability that high settler mortality caused low growth, through any mechanism, in this case, given our observations in this case? We can then delve further to ask about the pathway operating in the case: about the probability that settler mortality caused low growth through institutions or through an alternative pathway.

The results of these case-level pathway queries – drawn from a model informed by the large-N data – are reported in Table 10.7. In the top row, we see that the probability that high mortality was a cause of low growth in the case is estimated to be 0.648. We estimate the probability that high settler mortality caused the low growth through a noninstitutions pathway to be somewhat lower, at 0.542. And the probability that high settler mortality caused low growth, specifically via the institutional pathway, is much lower, at 0.252.

This result is quite striking: Even when institutions take precisely the form, we *expect* them to take if the institutional mechanism is operating (i.e., they are weak in a high-mortality, low-growth case), our trained model tells us that we should still believe it to be about twice as likely that high mortality mattered through a noninstitutional mechanism than that it mattered via institutions. The results in Table 10.7 also have implications for the effects of alternative hypothetical manipulations. They suggest that changing mortality in this kind of case from high to low – while keeping institutions weak – would be more likely to improve outcomes than would keeping mortality high but changing institutions to whatever value they *would* take on if mortality were low.

Overall, these results suggest that any analysis of the long-run effects of settler mortality on economic growth that constrains such effects to run through institutions will likely get the story wrong. Notably, these findings also pose a challenge to the instrumental-variable strategy underlying Rodrik et al. (2004) and Acemoglu et al. (2001) analyses, which (via the exclusion restriction) involve the assumption that settler mortality affects growth only via institutions.

10.3 Conclusion

We close with a few substantive and methodological conclusions from the analyses in this chapter.

Turning first to substantive conclusions from the inequality and democratization analysis, we saw in Figure 10.4 that most movements in our beliefs on nodal types went in the direction of reduced confidence in causal effects. We saw in particular a sharp increase in our posterior on the share of cases for which I has no effect on M, and in the share of cases that would have democratized regardless of the values of all other nodes in the model. These findings tilt, above all, against strong confidence that inequality affects mass mobilization or that inequality, mobilization, or international pressure affected democratization during the period under examination. *Something* generated the Third Wave of democratization in the 1980s and 1990s, but these findings suggest that the democratizations we see are not well explained by patterns of inequality, either at the population or case level.

We see two primary takeaways from our updating of the institutions and growth model. First, the analysis lends support to the basic claim that rule-of-law institutions matter for post-colonial countries' rates of economic growth. More interestingly, we think, the analysis yields evidence of a selection effect in which the places that had strong rule-of-law institutions imposed on them by colonizing powers were on average places in which such institutions were more likely to spur higher rates of long-run growth. If true, the policy implications are potentially quite stark: It suggests that creating "strong" institutions in places that do not currently have them would be unlikely to generate the same positive effects that we see in the cases that *do* have them.

The analyses in this chapter also illustrate a number of integrative payoffs to multi-case causal-model-based inference. For one thing, we have seen how readily the approach can handle data drawn from a mix of data-collection strategies, such as the collection of data on a small number of nodes for a large number of cases together with more intensive data collection on a subset of these. We have shown how, from a single process of updating, we can then answer causal questions of any kind at either the population or the case level: For both applications, we updated our model with the data just once, and then simply posed the query of interest to the same posterior distribution over λ.

Further, the institutions and growth application nicely demonstrates how the approach allows for inferences at one level of analysis to be *informed* by learning at another level. In particular, we saw how the probative value of a given node observation (a clue) could be shaped by learning from multi-case data about population-level relationships. Indeed, for the Institutions and Growth application, beginning with a model in which no node would have had probative value for R's effect on Y, we *generated* probative value for D and M from the data. The approach thus provides a way of empirically *justifying* process-tracing inferences. By the same token the analysis of the democracy model poses a *challenge* to claims about the probative value of data on mobilization and international pressure for understanding democratization.

Finally, we see that in this framework, confounding is not just something we have to worry about, but also something we can usefully *learn* about. Confounding becomes just another set of model parameters (nodal type shares conditional on other nodes' values); and because the possible values of these parameters imply different likelihoods for different data patterns, we can update on confounding from the data – even when we cannot observe the source of confounding itself (which is left unobserved in the institutions and growth model). What's more, the institutions and growth example illustrates how learning about confounding can be helpful in nonobvious ways: Recall how updating on confounding between M and Y made M an informative clue about R's effect on Y, where it had not been before.

The findings presented here also make clear that even a large amount of data will not always move our beliefs about a query of interest. As we saw in the democracy model, the case-level conclusions we draw about I's effect on D do not change after updating with a substantial amount of data. This is simply because the patterns in the data do not happen to pull against our starting beliefs about the relationship between these two variables. In the institutions and growth model, we see a very different picture, with the data substantially moving our inferences.

11 Mixing Models

We show how we can integrate inferences across models. We provide four examples of situations in which, by combining models, researchers can learn more than they could from any single model. Examples include situations in which researchers seek to integrate inferences from experimental and observational data, seek to learn across settings, or seek to integrate inferences from multiple studies.

In Chapters 9 and 10, we described one form of integration that causal models can enable: the systematic combination of (what we typically think of as) qualitative and quantitative evidence for the purposes of drawing population- and case-level causal inferences. One feature of the analyses we have been considering so far is that the integration is essentially integration of inferences in the context of a single study. We are, for instance, integrating quantitative evidence for a large set of cases with qualitative evidence for a *subset* of those cases. We are, moreover, drawing inferences from the set of cases we observe to a population *within which* that sample of cases is situated.

In this chapter, we examine how we can use causal models to integrate across studies or settings that are, in a sense, more disjointed from one another: across studies that examine different causal relationships altogether; study designs that require different assumptions about exogeneity; and contexts across which the causal quantities of interest may vary.

1. **Integrating across a model.** Often, individual studies in a substantive domain examine distinct segments of a broader web of causal relationships. For instance, while one study might examine the effect of X on Y, another might examine the effect of Z on Y, and yet another might examine the effect of Z on K. We show in this chapter how we can, under some conditions, integrate across such studies in ways that yield learning that we could not achieve by taking each study on its own terms.

2. **Integrating between experimental and observational studies.** One form of multi-method research that has become increasingly common is the use

of both observational and experimental methods to study the same basic causal relationships. While an experiment can offer causal identification in a usually local or highly controlled setting, an observational analysis can often shed light on how the same relationships operate "in the wild," if with a greater risk of confounding. Often, observational and experimental results are presented in parallel, as separate sources of support for a causal claim. We show how, in a causal model setup, we can use experimental and observational data *jointly* to address questions that cannot be answered when the designs are considered separately.

3. **Transporting knowledge across contexts.** Researchers are sometimes in a situation where they can identify causal quantities in a particular setting – say, from a randomized controlled trial implemented in a specific local context – but want to know how those inferences travel to other settings. Would the intervention work differently in other countries or regions? As we will explain, we can draw inferences about causal relationships in other contexts with an appropriately specified causal model and the right data from the original context.

4. **Models in hierarchies.** Sometimes, researchers learn about the same types of processes in different settings. By thinking of the processes in each setting as deriving from a family of processes, researchers can learn from observations in one setting about causal processes in another and also learn about the nature of heterogeneity between settings.

Before delving into the details of these strategies, we make one key qualification explicit: each of these approaches requires us to believe that setting- or study-specific causal model can be nested within a lower level, "encompassing," model that operates across the multiple settings that we are learning from and want to draw inferences about. Encompassing models, of course, can specifically take heterogeneity across settings into account by including in the model moderators that condition the effects of interest. But we have to believe that we have indeed captured in the model any ways in which relationships vary across the set of contexts across which we are integrating evidence or transporting inferences.

Put differently, and perhaps more positively, we see social scientists commonly seeking to transport knowledge or combine information informally across studies and settings. Often such efforts are motivated, sometimes implicitly, by an interest in or reliance on general theoretical propositions. The approaches that we describe below ask the researcher to be *explicit* about the underlying causal beliefs that warrant that integration while also ensuring that the integration proceeds in a way that is logically consistent with stated beliefs.

11.1 A Jigsaw Puzzle: Integrating across a Model

Generating knowledge about a causal domain often involves cumulating learning across studies that each focus on some specific part of the domain. For instance, scholars interested in the political economy of democratization might undertake studies focused on the relationship between inequality and mass protests; studies on the role of mass mobilization in generating regime change; pathways other than mass mobilization through which inequality might affect democratization; studies of the effect of international sanctions on the likelihood that autocracies will democratize; and studies of the effects of democratization on other things, such as growth or the distribution of resources.

We can think of these studies as each analyzing data on a particular part of a broader, more encompassing causal model. In an informal way, *if* findings "hold together" reasonably intuitively, we might be able to piece together an impression of the overall relations among variables in this domain. Yet an informal approach becomes more difficult for complex models or data patterns and, more importantly, will leave opportunities for learning unexploited.

Consider the simple DAG in Figure 11.1, in which both X and Z are causes of Y, and Z also causes K.

Now imagine three studies, all conducted in contexts in which we believe this model to hold:

1. Study 1 is an RCT in which X is randomized, with data collected on both Y and K. Z is not observed.
2. Study 2 is a factorial experiment, in which X and Z are independently randomized, allowing an examination of the joint effects of X and Z on Y. K is not observed.
3. Study 3 is an experiment randomizing Z, with only K observed as an outcome. X and Y are not observed.

Now, let's say that our primary interest is in the relationship between X and Y. Obviously, Study 1 will, with a sufficiently large sample, perform just fine in estimating the average treatment effect of X on Y. However, what if we are

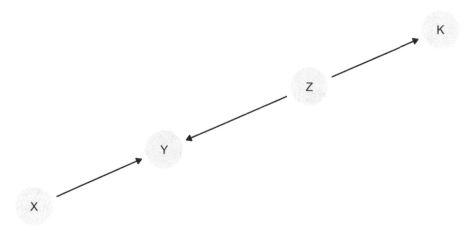

Figure 11.1   A DAG containing nodes that feature in different studies

interested in a case-oriented query, such as the probability of causation: the probability, say, that $X = 1$ caused $Y = 1$ in a given $X = 1$, $Y = 1$ case?

We know that within-case, process-tracing clues can sometimes provide probative value on case-level estimands like the probability of causation, and we have observed K in the Study 1 cases. So what if we combine the X, Y, and K data?

A simple analysis of the graph tells us that K cannot help us learn about Y's potential outcomes since K and Y are d-separated by Z, and we have not observed Z in Study 1. We see this confirmed in Table 11.1.

In the first pair of rows, we show the results of analyses in which we have simulated data from the whole model, then updated using the Study 1 observations. We give here the posterior mean on the probability of causation for an $X = Y = 1$ case, conditional on each possible value that K might take on. As we can see, our beliefs about the estimand remain essentially unaffected by K's value, meaning that it contains no information about X's effect in the case.

We see that the same thing is true for the other studies. In Study 2, we have not used K to update the model, and so have not learned anything from the data about K's relationship to the other variables. Thus, we have no foundation on which to ground the probative value of K. In Study 3, we understand the Z, K relationship well, but know nothing quantitatively about how Z and X relate to Y. Thus, we have learned nothing from Study 3 about what observing K might tell us about the effect of X on Y.

Table 11.1 Clue K is uninformative in all three studies for the query that $X = 1$ caused $Y = 1$ in a given case

Study	Given	Mean	SD	Conf low	Conf high
1	X == 1 & Y == 1 & K == 1	0.585	0.110	0.358	0.784
	X == 1 & Y == 1 & K == 0	0.574	0.112	0.342	0.785
2	X == 1 & Y == 1 & K == 1	0.722	0.114	0.472	0.898
	X == 1 & Y == 1 & K == 0	0.719	0.114	0.457	0.893
3	X == 1 & Y == 1 & K == 1	0.497	0.152	0.209	0.796
	X == 1 & Y == 1 & K == 0	0.501	0.131	0.250	0.751

Table 11.2 Clue K is informative after combining studies linking K to Z and Z to Y

Given	Mean	SD	Conf low	Conf high
X == 1 & Y == 1 & K == 1	0.82	0.08	0.62	0.93
X == 1 & Y == 1 & K == 0	0.61	0.13	0.35	0.84
X == 1 & Y == 1 & K == 1 & Z == 1	0.84	0.08	0.64	0.96
X == 1 & Y == 1 & K == 0 & Z == 1	0.84	0.08	0.64	0.96

However, we can do much better if we combine the data and update *jointly* across all model parameters. The results are shown in Table 11.2. Updating simultaneously across the studies allows us, in a sense, to bridge across inferences. In particular, inferences from Study 2 make Z informative about Y's potential outcomes under different values of X. Meanwhile, inferences from the data in Study 3 allow us to use information on K to update on values for Z. As we now see in rows 1 and 2, having updated the model in an integrated fashion, K now *is* informative about the probability of causation, with our posterior mean on this query changing substantially depending on the value of K that we observe in a case.

Rows 3–4 highlight that the updating works through inferences that K allows us to make about Z: We see that if Z is already known (we show this for $Z = 1$, but it holds for $Z = 0$ as well), then there are no additional gains from the knowledge of K.

We devote Chapter 15 to a discussion of how we justify a model. However, we note already that in this example, we have a form of model justification. We have seen an instance in which a researcher (examining a case in Study 1) might wish to draw inferences using K, but does not have anything in their study that justifies using K for inference. However, with access to additional data from other studies and making use of a lower level model, the researcher now has a justification for a process tracing strategy.

11.2 Combining Observational and Experimental Data

Experimental studies are often understood as the "gold standard" for causal inference. This is, in particular, because of the ability of a randomized trial (given certain assumptions, such as "no spillovers") to eliminate sources of confounding. By design, an experiment removes from the situation processes that, in nature, would generate a correlation between selection into treatment and potential outcomes. An experiment thereby allows for an unbiased estimate of the average causal effect of the treatment on the outcome.

At the same time, an interesting weakness of experimental studies is that, by dealing so effectively with selection into treatment, they limit our ability to learn about selection and its implications in the real world. Often, however, we want to know what causal effects would be specifically for units that *would* in fact, take up a treatment in a real-world, nonexperimental setting. This kind of problem is studied, for example, by Knox et al. (2019).

Consider, for instance, a policy that would make schooling subsidies available to parents, with the aim of improving educational outcomes for children. How would we know if the policy was effective? A source of confounding in an observational setting might be that those parents who apply for and take up the subsidy might also be those who are investing more in their children's education in other ways, as compared to those parents who do not apply for the subsidy. The result is that when we compare those in treatment against those not in treatment we can expect to see a gap even if the subsidies are ineffective. To eliminate this problem, we might design an experiment in which parents are randomly assigned to receive (or not receive) the subsidy and compare outcomes between children in the treatment and control groups. With a no-spillovers assumption, we can extract the ATE of the receipt of subsidies.

What this experiment cannot tell us, however, is how much the policy will boost educational outcomes outside the experiment. That is because the causal quantity of interest, for answering that question, is *not* the ATE: It is the average treatment effect for the *treated* (ATT), given real-world selection effects. That is, the policymaker wants to know what the effect of the subsidy will be for the children of parents who *select into* treatment. One could imagine the real-world ATT being higher than the ATE if, for instance, those parents who are informed and interested enough to take up the subsidy also put the subsidy to more effective use. One could also imagine the ATT being lower than the ATE if, for instance, there are diminishing marginal returns to educational investments, and the self-selecting parents are already investing quite a lot.

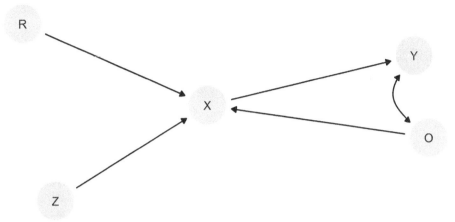

Figure 11.2 A model that nests an observational and an experimental study. The treatment X either takes on the observational value O, or the assigned values Z, depending on whether or not the case has been randomized, R

Even outside a policy context, we may be interested in the effect of a causal condition *where* that causal condition emerges. To return to our inequality and democracy example, we may want to know what would have happened to autocracies with low inequality *if* they had had high inequality – the standard average-treatment effect question. But we might also be interested in knowing how much of a difference high inequality makes *in the kinds of cases* where high inequality tends to occur – where the effect could be very different.

With such questions, we are in a sort of bind. The experiment cannot tell us *who* would naturally select into treatment and what the effects would be for them. Yet an observational study faces the challenge of confounding. Ideally, we would like to be able to combine the best features of both: use an experiment to deal with confounding and use observational data to learn about those whom nature assigns to treatment.

We can achieve this form of integration with a causal model. We do so by creating a model in which random assignment is nested within a broader set of assignment processes. We plot the model in Figure 11.2.

At the substantive core of this model is the $X \rightarrow Y$ relationship. However, we give X a parent that is an unconfounded root node, Z, to capture a random-assignment process. We give X a second parent, O, that is confounded with Y: O here represents the observational scenario. Finally, we include a "switch" variable, R, that determines whether X is randomly assigned or not. So when $R = 1$, X is determined solely by Z, with $X = Z$. When $R = 0$, we are in an observational setting, and X is determined solely by the confounded O, with $X = O$.

Table 11.3 Estimands conditional on assignment scheme

Query	Given	Using	Mean	SD	Cred low	Cred high
ATE	–	truth	0.2		0.20	0.20
ATE	–	priors	0.0	0.26	−0.52	0.51
ATE	R == 0	truth	0.2		0.20	0.20
ATE	R == 0	priors	0.0	0.26	−0.52	0.51
ATE	R == 1	truth	0.2		0.20	0.20
ATE	R == 1	priors	0.0	0.26	−0.52	0.51

Table 11.4 Inferences on the ATE from differences in means with only observational data

Estimate	Std. Error	t value	Pr($>|t|$)	CI Lower	CI Upper	DF
0.828	0.029	28.82	0	0.771	0.884	173

A few notes on the parameter space: Parameters allow for complete confounding between O and Y, but Z and Y are unconfounded. X has only one causal type since its job is to operate as a conveyor belt, simply inheriting the value of Z or O, depending on R.

Note also that this model assumes the exclusion restriction that entering the experimental sample (R) is not related to Y other than through the assignment of X.

Now let us imagine true parameter values such that X has a 0.2 average effect on Y. However, the effect is different for those who are selected into treatment in an observational setting: it is positive (0.6) for cases in which $X = 1$ under observational assignment, but negative (−0.2) for cases in which $X = 0$ under observational assignment. (See Supplementary Material for complete specification.)

When we use the model to analyze the data, we will start with flat priors on the causal types.

The implied true values for the estimands of interest, and our priors on those estimands, are displayed in Table 11.3.

Now we generate data from the model and then update the model using these data.

We begin by analyzing just the observational data (cases where $R = 0$) and display the results in Table 11.4. Recall that the true average effect of X on Y is 0.2. Naive analysis of the observational data, taking a simple difference in means between the $X = 0$ and $X = 1$ cases, yields a strongly upwardly biased estimate of that effect, of 0.83.

Table 11.5 Estimates on the ATE for observational ($R = 0$) and experimental
($R = 1$) set

Query	Given	Using	Mean	SD	Cred low	Cred high
ATE	–	posteriors	0.203	0.032	0.141	0.265
ATE	R == 0	posteriors	0.203	0.032	0.141	0.265
ATE	R == 1	posteriors	0.203	0.032	0.141	0.265

In contrast, when we update on the full causal model and use both the
experimental and observational data, we get the much more accurate results
shown in Table 11.5. Moving down the rows, we show here the estimate of
the unconditional ATE, the estimate for the observational context ($R = 0$),
and the estimate for the experimental context ($R = 1$). Unsurprisingly, the
estimates are identical across all three settings since, in the model, R is d-
separated from Y by X, which is observed. And, as we see, the posterior means
are very close to the right answer of 0.2.

Since the model used both the experimental and the observational data,
we might wonder from where the leverage was derived: Did the observational data improve our estimates of the average treatment effect, or do our
inferences emerge strictly from the experimental data? In the book's Supplementary Material, we show the results that we get when we update using
experimental data only. Comparing the two sets of results, we find there that
we do indeed get a tightening of posterior variance and a more accurate result
when we use both the observational and experimental data, but the experimental data alone are quite powerful, as we should expect for an estimate of
the ATE. The observational data do not add a great deal to an ATE estimate,
and the gains from observational data would be smaller still (and the experimental results even more accurate) if the experimental sample were larger.

However, what we can learn about uniquely from this model and the
combined observational and experimental data is *heterogeneity* in effects
between those in treatment and those in control *in the observational* setting.
In Table 11.6, we display the results of ATT and average treatment effect for
the control (ATC) queries of the updated model. To estimate the ATT we pose
an ATE query while conditioning on $X = 1$, while for an ATC query we pose
the ATE query while conditioning on $X = 0$. In the first two rows, we see
that, in the experimental setting (conditioning on $R = 1$), the average effect
of X on Y is the same in both the treated and control groups, exactly as we
would expect under random assignment. In the third row, we see the estimate
of X's average effect for those assigned "by nature" to the control group in the

Table 11.6 Effects of X conditional on X for units that were randomly assigned or not. Effects of X do not depend on X in the experimental group, but they do in the observational group because of self-selection

Query	Given	Using	Mean	SD	Cred low	Cred high
ATE	R == 1 & X == 0	posteriors	0.203	0.032	0.141	0.265
ATE	R == 1 & X == 1	posteriors	0.203	0.032	0.141	0.265
ATE	R == 0 & X == 0	posteriors	−0.169	0.027	−0.222	−0.114
ATE	R == 0 & X == 1	posteriors	0.534	0.050	0.433	0.628

observational setting, extracting a result close to the "true" value of −0.2. The final row shows our estimate of the treatment effect for those who are selected into treatment in the observational setting, again getting close to the answer implied by the underlying data-generating process (0.6).

In sum, we can learn nothing about the observational ATT or ATC from the experimental data alone, where the ATT and ATC are the same quantity. And in the observational data alone, we are hobbled by confounding of unknown direction and size. What the mixed model and data, in effect, are able to do is to let us (a) learn about the ATE from experimental data, (b) use experimental inferences on the ATE to separate true effects from confounding in the observational data and thus learn about the direction and size of the confounding in those data, and (c) estimate the treatment effect for the $X = 0$ group and for the $X = 1$ group, respectively, in the observational data *using* knowledge about confounding in these data. By mixing the experimental and observational data, we can learn about how the treatment has affected those units that, in the "real" world of the observational setting, selected into treatment *and* about how the treatment *would* affect those that selected into control.

It is not hard to see why the observational ATT and ATC might be of great interest to decision-makers where strong causal heterogeneity is a possibility. Imagine a situation, for instance, in which the ATE was the same as in our previous example, but with the negative effects arising in the group that naturally selects into treatment and a positive effect for those that naturally do not. Based on the experimental data alone, we might conclude that the policy that makes $X = 1$ available is a good bet, given its positive ATE (assuming, of course, that $Y = 1$ is a valued outcome). And, of course, the observational data alone would not allow us to confidently conclude otherwise. What the integrated analysis can reveal, however, is that X in fact has a *negative* mean effect on those who would be most likely to take up the treatment. The strong positive effect for the control strongly shapes the experimental results but will go unrealized in the real world. In a similar vein, these estimates can aid causal explanations. Seeing the positive ATE might lead us to infer that most of the $X = 1$, $Y = 1$ cases we observe in the world are ones in which $X = 1$ caused $Y = 1$. The observational ATT estimates would point in a very different direction, however, indicating that these are actually the cases in which X is least likely to have a positive effect and, thus, where $Y = 1$ was most likely generated by some other cause.

We note that the results here relate to the LATE theorem (Angrist and Imbens, 1995). Imagine using data only on (a) the experimental group in control and (b) the observational group, some of whom are in treatment. We can conceptualize our design as one in which the observational group is "encouraged" to take up treatment, allowing us to estimate the effect for the "compliers" in the observational setting: those that self-select into treatment. Conversely, we could use data only on (a) the experimental group in treatment and (b) the observational group, some of whom are in control. This is a design in which the observational group is "encouraged" to take up the control condition, allowing us to estimate the effect for the "compliers" in this group (those that self-select into control).

11.3 Transportation of Findings across Contexts

Sometimes, we study the effect of X on Y in one context (a country, region, or time period, for instance) and then want to make inferences about these effects in another context (say, another country, region, or time period). We may face the challenge that effects are heterogeneous, and that conditions that vary across contexts may be related to treatment assignment, outcomes, and selection into the sample. For example, we might study the relationship between inequality and democratization in low-income countries and then want to know how those effects travel to middle-income settings. However, the level of income may have implications jointly for the level of inequality and for how likely inequality is to generate regime change, meaning that causal effects uncovered in the first context cannot be assumed to operate in the same way in the second context.

This is the problem studied by Pearl and Bareinboim (2014). In particular, Pearl and Bareinboim (2014) identify the nodes for which data are needed to "license" external claims, given a model.

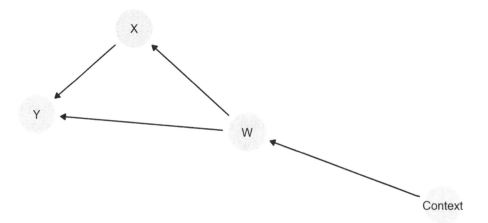

Figure 11.3   Extrapolation when confounders have different distributions across contexts

We illustrate with a simple model in which an observable confounder has a different distribution across contexts. In the model drawn in Figure 11.3, *Context* determines the distribution of the confounder, W. We set a restriction such that the value of W in Context 1 is never less than the value of W in Context 0; our priors are otherwise flat over the remaining nodal types in the model.

We show priors and true values for the estimands, drawn from a "true" set of parameter values that we have posited,) in Figure 11.4. We see that the incidence of $W = 1$ is higher in Context 1 than in Context 0, both in our priors and in the "truth" posited by the assigned parameter values. The "true" ATE of X on Y is also higher in Context 1, though this is not reflected in our priors. The average treatment effect conditional on W is the same in both contexts, whether we work from priors or assigned parameter values, as it must be given the model. That is, in this model the ATE varies conditional on W – and it varies conditional *only* on W.

We now update the model using data from one context and then see if we can transport those findings to the other context. Specifically, we update using data on X, Y, and W from Context 0. We then use the updated beliefs to draw inferences about Context 1, using data *only* on W from Context 1. In Figure 11.5, we show our posteriors on the queries of interest as compared to the truth, given the "true" parameter values we have posited.

We see that we have done well in recovering the effects, *both* for the context we studied (i.e., in which we observed X and Y) and for the context we did not study. We can think of the learning here as akin to post-stratification. We

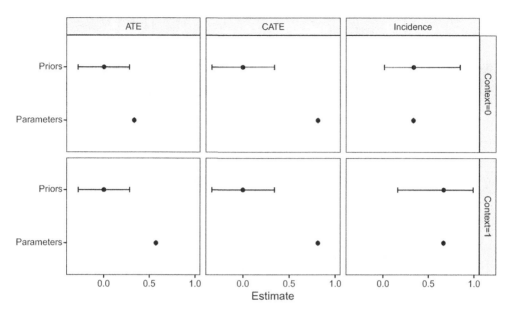

Figure 11.4 Priors and true values (parameters) for three estimands: the effect of X on Y (ATE), the effect conditional on $W = 1$ (CATE), and the frequency of W (Incidence)

have learned from observing X, Y, and W in Context 0 how X's effect depends on W. Then we use those updated beliefs when confronted with a new value of W in Context 1 to form a belief about X's effect in this second context. Of course, getting the right answer from this procedure depends, as always, on starting with a good model.

We can also see, in Figure 11.5, what would have happened if we had attempted to make the extrapolation to Context 1 without data on W in that context. We see a very large posterior variance. The high posterior variance here captures the fact that we know things could be different in Context 1, but we don't know in what way they are different. So we don't learn much, but at least we know that we don't.

11.4 Multilevel Models, Meta-analysis

A key idea in Bayesian meta-analysis is that when we analyze multiple studies together, not only do we learn about common processes that give rise to the different results seen in different sites, but we also learn more about each study from seeing the other studies.

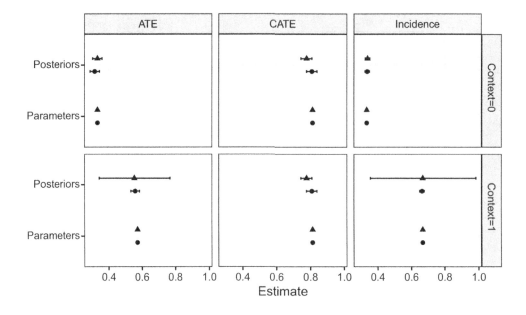

Figure 11.5 Extrapolation when two contexts differ on W and W is not observable in target context. Posteriors and true values (parameters), for the average effect, the average effect conditional on W (CATE), and the incidence of W, for two contexts

A classic setup is provided in Gelman et al. (2013), in which we have access to estimates of effects and uncertainty in eight sites (schools), $(b_j, se_j)_{j \in \{1,2,\ldots,8\}}$. To integrate learning across these studies, we employ a "hierarchical model" that treats each b_j as a draw from distribution $N(\beta_j, se_j)$ (and, in turn treats each β_j is a draw from distribution $N(\beta, \sigma)$). In that setup we want to learn about the superpopulation parameters β, σ, but we also get to learn more about the study-level effects $(\beta_j)_{j \in \{1,2,\ldots,8\}}$ by studying them jointly.

A hierarchical model like this allows us to think about the populations in our study sites as themselves drawn from a larger population ("superpopulation") of settings. And, crucially, it allows us, in turn to use data in the study sites to learn about that broader superpopulation of settings.

Although often used in the context of linear models with parameters for average causal effects, this logic works just as well with the kinds of causal models we have been using in this book.

Let's review how our analytic setup has worked so far. At each node in a causal model, we conceptualize a given case as having a particular nodal type. The case's nodal type is drawn from a distribution of nodal types in the population of cases from which this case has been drawn. When we do process tracing, we consider that population-level distribution to be a set of fixed shares of nodal types in the population: Say, for node Y, we might believe that half the cases in the population are λ_{01}^Y, a quarter are λ_{00}^Y, and a quarter are λ_{11}^Y. We then use data from the case to update on the case's nodal types (or on the combination of nodal types that correspond to some case-level query), given the population-level shares.

When we engage in population-level inference, we begin with *uncertainty* about the population-level shares of types, and we express our prior beliefs about those shares as a Dirichlet *distribution*. So, for instance, our beliefs might be centered around a $\lambda_{01}^Y = 0.5$, $\lambda_{00}^Y = 0.25$, $\lambda_{11}^Y = 0.25$ breakdown of shares in the population; and we also express some degree of uncertainty about what the breakdown is. Now when we analyze data on some number of cases, we can update both on those cases' types and on our beliefs about the distribution of types in the population – perhaps shifting toward a higher share of λ_{01}^Y's (and with a change in the distribution's variance).

As in the last section, we can also build a model in which there are multiple settings, possibly differing on some population-level characteristics. Fundamentally, however, the setup in the last section still involved population-level inference in that we were assuming that the *type shares* (λ values) are the same across settings. The settings might differ in the value of a moderating variable, but they do not differ in the shares of cases that *would* respond in any given way to the moderator (and other causal conditions). The data allow us to update on what those common, cross-setting type proportions are.

When we build a hierarchical model, each case is still understood as being embedded within a population: our cases might be citizens, say, each embedded within a country. The key difference from population-level inference is that we now conceive of there being *multiple* populations – say, multiple countries – each drawn from a population of populations, or superpopulation. Now we think of each population (country) as having its own set of type shares for each node. In practice we think of each country's type shares as being drawn from a Dirichlet distribution of type shares (for each node) that lives at the superpopulation level. Moreover, we are *uncertain* about what that distribution at the superpopulation level *is*. We are uncertain about what type proportions the superpopulation-level distribution is centered around, and we are uncertain about how dispersed this distribution is. While the distribution's central tendency will be related to the mean type shares for countries, its variance will determine the degree of *heterogeneity* across countries in their type shares.

To summarize, in population-level inference, we express uncertainty about the population's type shares with a Dirichlet prior, at the population level, on which we update. In the hierarchical setting, we are uncertain about the population-level type shares and the superpopulation Dirichlet from which each node's type shares are drawn. We express our uncertainty about each superpopulation Dirichlet by positing a prior distribution over the Dirichlet's α parameters.

Now when we observe data on citizens within countries, we can update our beliefs about the types for the particular citizens we observe, about type shares in the population of citizens within each country that we study, *and* on the parameters of the Dirichlet distribution from which population shares have been drawn. In updating on the last of these, we are learning not just about the countries we observe but also about those we do not directly observe.

We illustrate with a simulation using a simple $X \rightarrow Y$ model. We imagine that we are studying the $X \rightarrow Y$ effect in 10 countries. Each country has a parameter distribution drawn from a common Dirichlet distribution.

We assign a particular true set of superpopulation parameter values that, for the analytic exercise, are treated as unknown and that we would like to recover. In this true world, the probability of assignment to $X = 1$ is distributed Beta(6, 4), meaning that on average, 40% of units are assigned to treatment, though there is variation in this proportion across countries (or study sites). Nodal types on Y are distributed Dirichlet with parameter $\alpha^Y = (3, 4, 10, 3)$, meaning that in the average country, the treatment effect is 0.3 (i.e. $\frac{10}{20} - \frac{4}{20}$), though this also varies across countries. Using these true parameter values, we simulate X, Y data for 50 observations for $n = 10$ countries.

We now need to specify uncertainty over the (α) parameters of the Dirichlet distribution at the superpopulation level. In practice, we use an inverse gamma distribution for this, the critical feature being that we presuppose positive numbers but otherwise keep priors on these parameters dispersed. When we update now, we update simultaneously over the α parameters and the λ parameters *for each country*.

In Figure 11.6 we plot the results. We focus on the average treatment effects and show a comparison of three values for each country: the unpooled estimate, or the estimate we get for each country using only data from that country; the pooled estimate, or the estimate we get for each country using data from *all* countries to inform that country's parameter estimate; and the truth as posited for this simulation. As we can see, the pooled estimates are

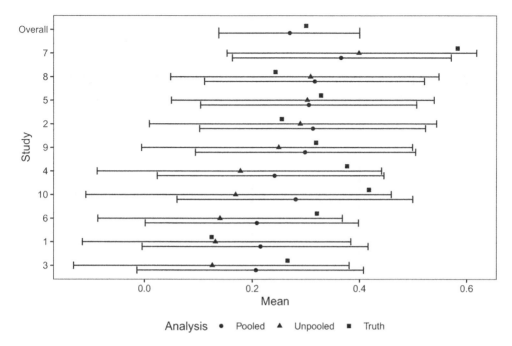

Figure 11.6   Updating on study-level parameters from integrated analyses. Error bars indicate 95% credibility intervals. Studies are ordered by the size of the estimates from the unpooled analysis

generally closer to the center than the unpooled estimates: this is because we are effectively using data from all countries to discount extreme features of the data observed in a given country. Put differently, the pooled data serve somewhat like a prior when it comes to drawing inferences about a single country: our inference is a compromise between the data from that country and the beliefs we have formed from the pooled data. We can also see that, for most countries, the pooling helps: The regularization provided by the pooling often (but not always) gives us an estimate closer to the truth for most of the settings. This is especially true when the unpooled estimates are unusually low. Across cases we have a reduction in root-mean-squared error of 64%.

Of course, we also get an estimate for the meta-estimand, the average effect in the superpopulation. This lies close to the correct answer and has a relatively tight credibility interval.

Finally, we can extract estimates of the *variation* in treatment effects across cases – a quantity distinct from our *uncertainty* about average effects. We can, for instance, think of a concentration parameter, operationalized as the sum of the α^j terms for a node, with a higher value representing lower overall heterogeneity. In this example, the "true" α^Y terms that we assigned summed to 20. This "true" α^Y vector implies that treatment effects lie, 95% of the time, between −0.06 and 0.61. Our estimate of this concentration parameter is 26.39. With this particular data draw, we thus underestimate heterogeneity. Though this concentration parameter estimate still implies considerable heterogeneity in effects:[1] Our posteriors imply that we expect treatment effects to lie, with 95% probability, between −0.01 and 0.54.[2]

---

[1] There is of course also posterior variation around this estimate.
[2] Implied variation at the mean estimates of α.

Part III

Design Choices

12 Clue Selection as a Decision Problem

> With this chapter, we begin to turn our attention to how causal models can inform research design. In the present chapter, we draw out the implications of the causal model approach for clue-selection strategies: for figuring out which pieces of evidence are likely to be most informative about a question of interest. We demonstrate procedures for assessing which clues minimize expected posterior variance and how to construct an optimal decision tree for determining a dynamic clue-gathering strategy.

The causal models framework can be used not just for analysis but also for guiding research design. This is the topic of the next three chapters. We start here by addressing the problem of clue selection: determining which qualitative data to gather on a case when conducting process tracing.

Evidently, it makes sense to gather clues that have large probative value, but whether or not a given clue will have probative value depends on the model we are working with and the question we are asking. As we will see, a clue's informativeness can also depend on what other clues have already been collected. Finding out that the butler had no motive may be informative for the claim that he is innocent, but it will not be useful if we already know that he had no opportunity.

We have already provided some insight into the problem in Chapter 7, where we showed how relations of d-connection can tell us when a clue is *possibly* informative about a query. In this chapter, we go further to show how we can use our causal model to figure out which clues and clue-selection strategies are likely to be *most* informative about the query we seek to address.

12.1 A Model-Informed Approach to Clue Selection

The representation of inference problems as one of querying a Bayesian model points to a relatively simple method for selecting the most informative clues for collection. Consider, first, a situation in which one can invest in collecting various forms of evidence on a case and wants to know the expected gains from all possible collections of evidence that one could gather.

We can assess alternative strategies through the following procedure:

1. Define the model.
2. Define a query on the model.
3. Define a data strategy: a set of clues for which one might search (e.g., observe the value of Y).
4. Given prior data, figure out the probability of different possible realizations of the new data.
5. For each possible realization, calculate the posterior variance we would have if we observed that realization.
6. Calculate the *expected* posterior variance for the data strategy by taking a weighted average of the variances arising from the different data realizations, with weights given by the probability of observing the data realization in question.

If repeated for different sets of clues, this procedure then allows us to choose the clue strategy with the lowest expected posterior variance.

A still more sophisticated approach would, for multiple clues, take sequence into account: It would tell us which clues to search for later in the process given the realization of clues sought earlier. The path dependence of clue selection arises from the possibility that the informativeness of a clue may depend on the value of other nodes in the model. A given clue K_2, for instance, may be informative if another clue K_1 has the value of 1 but not if it has the value 0.

We provide tools for both of these approaches and illustrate them below for a simple model of government survival as well as for our democratization model from Chapter 8.

12.1.1 Clue Selection with a Simple Example

Consider a model of government survival in office in which retaining office depends on not being perceived as corrupt by the public. We show a DAG for this model in Figure 12.1. We take two conditions as root nodes in this model. First, a country may or may not have a free press (X). Second, the country's government may or may not be sensitive to public opinion (S).[1]

---

[1] Government sensitivity here can be thought of as government sophistication (Does it take the actions of others into account when making decisions?) or as a matter of preferences (Does it have an overriding incentive to engage in corruption?).

Free press and government survival

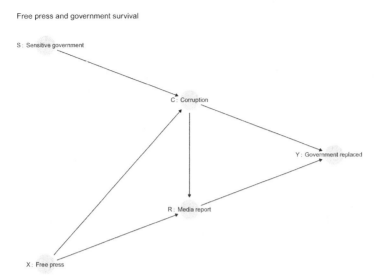

Figure 12.1 Causal model in which S and X are stochastic, C and R have only two possible nodal types each, $Y = 1$ if and only if C and R are both 1

We set equal prior probabilities on the two values of X and on the two values of S. In terms of causal relations, we then allow that the government's decision about whether to engage in corruption $(C = 1)$ may depend on whether the government is sensitive to public opinion and whether there is a free press (that might reveal that corruption). Moreover, we allow that whether the press will report on the corruption $(R = 1)$ may depend on whether there is government corruption and whether the press is free. Finally, whether the government will be removed from office $(Y = 1)$ may depend on whether it has acted corruptly and whether this gets reported in the press.

We work with a highly restricted version of this model to simplify the illustration. We will call this version the base survival model and later also consider two variants that have the same DAG but different nodal types permitted. At node C, we allow only two types: either corruption is always present (θ^C_{1111}) or corruption is always present except when there is both a free press $(X = 1)$ and sensitivity to public opinion $(S = 1)$ (θ^C_{1110}). At R, we allow only for θ^R_{0001} and θ^R_{0000}: the possibility that there is reporting on corruption if and only if there is corruption and a free press, and the possibility that there is never reporting on corruption. For both C and R, we put equal prior probabilities on all permitted nodal types. Finally, at Y, we restrict to just one nodal type, θ^Y_{0001}: The government will remain in office unless there is both corruption $(C = 1)$ and reporting on corruption $(R = 1)$.

To summarize the intuition, governments will only fall if there is both corruption and reporting on corruption. We are uncertain whether or not corruption is always present; but if corruption is ever absent, it can only be because there exist both a free press and a government that cares about public opinion. We are also uncertain whether or not media reporting on corruption is always absent; but if it is ever present, it can only be because there is both corruption and a free press. One implication is that governments that are sensitive to public opinion will never fall because they will always eschew corruption when a free press – the only mechanism that can generate reporting on corruption – is present. In turn, the presence of a free press can only matter for government survival if governments are *not* sensitive and thus do not strategically adjust their behavior in response to the risk of reporting.

Suppose now that our query is whether X has a positive effect on Y, and we want to know which clues will be most helpful in answering this question. Using the model, we can ask how likely different data realizations are under each possible clue strategy and what we would infer about our query from each possible data realization, given existing data. We illustrate for a situation in which we already know that $Y = 0$.

Table 12.1 shows results for each possible clue strategy. The S, X, C, R, Y columns of Table 12.1 define the data realizations. The matrix includes all combinations of possible realized values for all available clue strategies, given that we have already observed $Y = 0$. Note that since we can already infer that $R = 0$ from $Y = 0$, we omit strategies that seek data on R. A "0" or "1" represents the observed value for a node that we have chosen to observe while "?" indicates that a node is not observed under the given strategy. Thus, for instance, in the first five rows, we are collecting data on all nodes. In the next three rows, we have sought data on all nodes except S.

We also indicate the probability of each realization given the strategy, the inference we would make from each data realization – that is, the posterior probability that X has a positive effect on Y, given that $Y = 0$ – and the posterior variance.

Since each inference, under each data realization, has an associated posterior variance, or level of uncertainty, it is easy to assess the *expected* posterior variance from a given clue strategy. We calculate the expected posterior variance from a given strategy as a weighted average of the posterior variances associated with each possible data-realization under the strategy, with weights given by the probability of each data-realization arising. We then operationalize expected learning from a strategy using the expected *reduction* in variance

Table 12.1 Inferences on whether X has a positive effect on Y, given different data patterns under different clue strategies

Strategy	S	X	C	R	Y	Prob	Posterior mean	Posterior Variance
SXC	1	1	0	0	0	0.154	0.000	0.000
	0	0	1	0	0	0.308	0.500	0.250
	1	0	1	0	0	0.308	0.250	0.188
	0	1	1	0	0	0.154	0.000	0.000
	1	1	1	0	0	0.077	0.000	0.000
XC	?	1	0	0	0	0.154	0.000	0.000
	?	0	1	0	0	0.615	0.375	0.234
	?	1	1	0	0	0.231	0.000	0.000
SC	1	?	0	0	0	0.154	0.000	0.000
	0	?	1	0	0	0.462	0.333	0.222
	1	?	1	0	0	0.385	0.200	0.160
SX	0	0	?	0	0	0.308	0.500	0.250
	1	0	?	0	0	0.308	0.250	0.188
	0	1	?	0	0	0.154	0.000	0.000
	1	1	?	0	0	0.231	0.000	0.000
C	?	?	0	0	0	0.154	0.000	0.000
	?	?	1	0	0	0.846	0.273	0.198
X	?	0	?	0	0	0.615	0.375	0.234
	?	1	?	0	0	0.385	0.000	0.000
S	0	?	?	0	0	0.462	0.333	0.222
	1	?	?	0	0	0.538	0.143	0.122
Prior	?	?	?	0	0	1.000	0.231	0.178

upon observing the data. We present the expected reduction in posterior variance for each possible clue strategy, given the prior observation of Y, in the upper panel of Figure 12.2 (ignore the lower panels for the moment). We can see a couple of patterns here:

- By far, the biggest gains in expected learning come from observing X. We can see this most readily by comparing the one-clue strategies to one another. But in general, any strategy that includes observing X always does substantially better than the comparable strategy that excludes X. The intuition here is fairly straightforward: If we want to know whether $Y = 0$ was caused by $X = 0$, and start out very uncertain about X's value, we should expect to learn a good deal from figuring out whether X is in fact equal to 0.

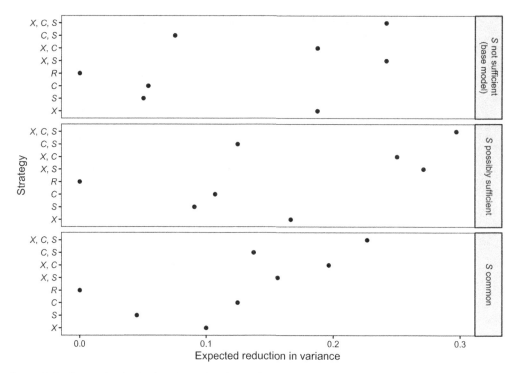

Figure 12.2   Expected reduction in variance for different data strategies for the base survival model and two variants of the model

- There are also considerable gains from observing S or C by themselves. Consider, first, why observing S is informative. S is potentially informative because it tells us something about whether X can affect Y by affecting R. Remember that a government is removed only if there is both corruption ($C = 1$) and reporting on corruption ($R = 1$). Moreover, there is only reporting on corruption (if ever) if $C = 1$. Thus, for both of these reasons, X can only have a positive effect on government removal (by causing reporting on corruption) if $C = 1$: That is, if there is corruption. And S (government sensitivity) tells us something about what C's value is likely to be if X were set to 1, i.e., if there is a free press.

   Specifically, if we observe $S = 0$, then we know for sure that $C = 1$, regardless of X, since C is always 1 when $S = 0$ under both permitted nodal types for C. If $S = 1$, on the other hand, there is a lower chance that C would be equal to 1 if X were set to 1: For one of C's permitted nodal types, there is always corruption; but for the other type, sensitive governments avoid corruption when there is a free press, so X moving to 1 would give us $C = 0$. Recall that we have put equal prior probabilities on these two nodal types. Thus, if we observe $S = 1$, we conclude that there is a lower probability that C will take on the value necessary for X to exert a positive effect on Y than if we observe $S = 0$.

Why, then, is C informative? If we observe $C = 0$, then we know that X must be equal to 1 since, under permitted nodal types for C, there is an absence of corruption *only* in the presence of a free press and sensitive governments. And if $X = 1$ with $Y = 0$, a positive effect is ruled out with certainty. If we observe $C = 1$, then there remains some possibility that $X = 0$ as well as some possibility C would remain at 1 if X were set to 1 (depending on C's unknown nodal type), allowing X to yield a positive effect on Y through R.

- There are no gains from observing R if $Y = 0$. This result follows from our table of data possibilities consistent with $Y = 0$ (Table 12.1). As we can see, there is no possibility of observing anything other than $R = 0$ if we have already seen $Y = 0$. We can see why by thinking, jointly, about how Y is determined and how R is determined. Y can be 0 either because $C = 0$ or because $R = 0$. So if R were equal to 1, this must mean that C was 0. However, a necessary condition for R to be 1, under R's permitted nodal types, is $C = 1$ and $X = 1$. In other words, the condition under which R could be 1 is a condition under which Y would not be 0. Thus, if we already know $Y = 0$, we know $R = 0$, and there is no gain from actually looking for R.

- Once we observe X, the next-most informative clue to add to our research design is S: X, S has the greatest expected reduction in posterior variance of any of the two-clue strategies. And, in fact, there are no gains to adding C to X, relative to observing X by itself.

  Let us develop the intuition underlying this result.

  Imagine that we have already observed X's value. If $X = 1$, then (given $Y = 0$) a positive effect is immediately ruled out with certainty, rendering any further observations of no value. If we observe $X = 0$, however, then (under this causal model) we know for certain that $C = 1$, simply because $C = 1$ for both of C's permitted nodal types when $X = 0$ (there is always corruption when there is no free press). Thus, there is nothing to be gained by observing C. (We have already seen why there is nothing to be gained from observing R.)

  Why are there possible gains to observing S even if we're going to observe X? S is informative because it tells us something about whether X can affect Y by affecting R. The potential gains from observing S with

X arise from the possibility that we may see $X = 0$ (since $X = 1$ would decide the matter by itself). If $X = 0$, then we still need to know whether Y *would* be 1 if we changed X to 1. As discussed above, *that* depends on whether C would be 1 if X were set to 1, and (as, again, explained above) S is informative on that matter.

- We also see – and it follows from the above logic – that we cannot improve on an X, S strategy by gathering more data. Thus, if the search for information is costly, looking only for X and S dominates all three- and four-clue strategies.

- Clues can be more informative jointly than separately, and the expected gains from observing one clue can depend on which other clues we plan to observe. To see this, observe that, among the one-clue strategies, observing C by itself is slightly *more* informative than observing S by itself. However, if we are planning to observe X, then the gains flip, and it is only S that offers additional useful information. As we have discussed, observing X makes observing C uninformative while S remains informative as a moderator of X's effect.

We would add that the pattern here forms part of a broader point that we wish to emphasize in this chapter: While process tracing often focuses on examining steps along causal pathways, it will often be the case that we learn more from *moderators*, like S in this model, than from mediators, like C and R. We return to this point below.

12.1.2 Dependence on Prior Beliefs

Optimal clue strategies can depend on our prior beliefs about causal relationships among the variables in the model. We illustrate this point here, examining how the evaluation of clue strategies shift as we relax restrictions on nodal types and set informative priors over nodal types.

Relaxing restrictions. In the analysis above, we allowed for just two (of 16 possible) nodal types at both C and R, effectively expressing strong beliefs about how C's and R's values are determined. But what if we are less certain than this?

Suppose we are not sure that corruption can be prevented only through a combination of a free press and government sensitivity. We think it possible that government sensitivity might be sufficient: That S might negatively affect C regardless of X's value. (Perhaps, for instance, there are means other than via a free press through which the public might learn of government corruption.) We allow for this causal possibility by expanding the set of nodal types for C to include θ^C_{1010}.

The evaluation of strategies under this adjusted set of beliefs, for the same query (whether X has a positive effect on Y) and prior data ($Y = 0$) as before, is displayed in the middle panel of Figure 12.2.

We see that, among one-clue strategies, observing X is still the best choice. The best two-clue strategy is also still X, S. Where things change most significantly, however, is among three-clue strategies: Now we can do even better by additionally observing C. The reason is that, with greater uncertainty about its nodal types, C's value is no longer known when $X = 0$: It is now possible that $C = 0$ when $X = 0$ since we think it possible that C's nodal type is θ^C_{1010}. Since C's value bears on whether X can have an effect via R, we can thus, potentially learn something by observing C even if we have already seen X and S.

We can also see C's enhanced informational value in other places. Among one-clue strategies, observing C alone generates greater learning here than it does under the base model. More strikingly, among two-clue strategies, we see that observing C can now generate learning even if we have *already* observed X (whereas there was no gain from strategy X, C relative to X under the base model). While X, S is still a better strategy than X, C, the change in diagnosis could matter if, for instance, we cannot observe S for some reason or if observing S is much more costly than observing C.

Moreover, the expected variance reduction from observing S is also greater under the new model, for most one- and two-clue strategies. For the informal intuition here, note that S is potentially informative about C's value as a parent of C. And we now believe (with the added nodal type for C) that there may be an additional way in which S could matter for C, and thus provide information about its value. Moreover, since the added nodal type has S exerting a negative effect on C regardless of X's value, S can now be informative even if we have already observed $X = 0$.

Finally, we can see that nothing has changed in regard to R, about whose nodal types we have retained the same beliefs. It is still uniformly unprofitable to observe R because we still know R's value whenever $X = 0$.

Changing probabilities. We can also see what happens when, rather than permitting new nodal types, we have more informative beliefs about the prevalence of permitted types. Suppose we believe most governments to be sensitive to public opinion. This would imply that we should put greater weight on θ^S_1 than on θ^S_0.

The third panel of Figure 12.2 shows the evaluation of strategies for a model in which we put a 90% prior probability on $S = 1$. A number of features stand out. First is the lower reduction in variance from most strategies under the new model: Having a more extreme belief about S's value gives us stronger prior beliefs about whether X could have caused Y since such an effect *depends* on S's value. A second striking difference is that searching for S is expected to be much less informative in this model. The reason is simple: We now have a strong prior belief about what we are likely to find when we search for S. We *could* be surprised, but we should not *expect* to be. In the original model, in contrast, we were maximally uncertain about S's value – believing it had a 0.5 chance of being 1 – and so there was much more to be gained by looking. Finally, we see that a search for C becomes more fruitful than before; the reason is that with $S = 1$ likely, C is now more sensitive to (and informative about) X's value.

The highest level lesson from this discussion is that even for a very simple model, assessing which clues are most information – in combination with which other clues – is relatively complex. It becomes more complex as models become more complex. Even still, there is a relatively simple procedure that can be applied to answer the question that can be used once a causal model has been fully specified.

12.1.3 Clue Selection for the Democratization Model

We now apply this approach to the model of democratization that we worked with in Chapters 8 and 10.

We start by specifying the democratization model, with negative effects ruled out for $I \rightarrow M$, $M \rightarrow D$, and $P \rightarrow D$ and a positive direct effect ruled out for $I \rightarrow D$. We set flat priors over all remaining nodal types. We will call this our "base" model. We then examine how optimal clue-selection strategies change as we modify the model and the query.

12.1.3.1 Base Model

Let's assume that we have already observed both levels of inequality and the outcome of democratization in a case, and we want to know whether inequality caused democratization in that case. The decision we confront is what combination of the other nodes – mobilization or international pressure – we should select to collect data on: The available strategies are to observe nothing further; to observe P only; to observe M only; or to observe both P and M.

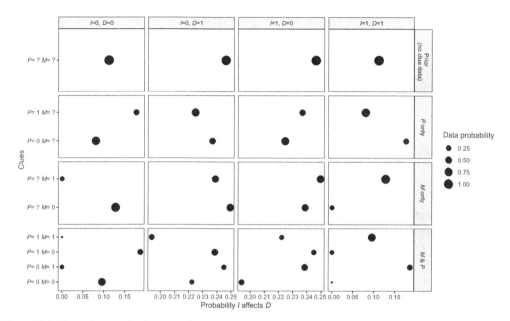

Figure 12.3   Base democratization model: What we expect to find and what we expect to learn from different clue strategies. Size of each dot indicates the probability of observing the data pattern given the search strategy

We illustrate the consequences of these options for our query in two ways. First, in Figure 12.3, we show the possible inferences we could draw from different clue strategies. This figure displays all data realizations that might result from all possible clue-selection strategies, the inference we would draw about our query from each realization of the data, and the probability of each realization occurring under each strategy. In each column of the figure, we show these quantities for a different combination of I, D values observed in a case prior to clue selection. Within each graph in the figure, the size of the plotted point corresponding to each data realization is scaled to the *probability* of that data realization occurring given the model and the case's I and D values. These data probabilities constitute key information for evaluating a clue strategy: A given strategy might allow for a potential data realization that *would* shift our inferences by a large amount *if* observed, but that data realization might be highly unlikely to occur.

In reading Figure 12.3, we want to examine how much inferences shift to the left or right relative to our "prior" belief shown in the top row of graphs – that is, what we infer from only having observed I and D. In an $I = 0, D = 0$ case, for instance, we can see that if we search only for P, our inference about the probability that I mattered for D will shift down slightly if we observe

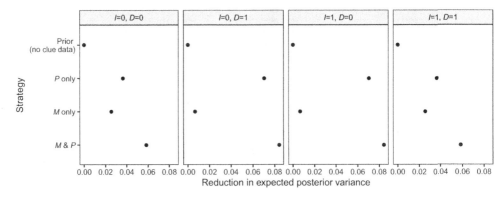

Figure 12.4 Reduction in expected variance from different data strategies for different kinds of cases (base democratization model)

$P = 0$ but will shift up substantially if we observe $P = 1$. If we look for M only, we see that the more impactful potential observation ($M = 1$) is much less likely to be observed, given our model and $I = 0, D = 0$, than the less impactful observation ($M = 0$). This will necessarily limit how fruitful we expect a strategy of searching for M alone to be.

In Figure 12.4, we average across the possible ways that each clue-selection strategy might turn out to calculate the reduction in uncertainty (i.e., in variance) that we *expect* to achieve under each strategy. We can think of expected uncertainty reduction, our measure of expected learning, as a summary assessment of a strategy's value. Again, we plot this uncertainty reduction separately by column for each I, D combination. Thus, strategies that shift us further to the right, toward a larger reduction in uncertainty, are those from which we expect to learn the most.

One clear message emerging from Figure 12.4 is that, if we have to choose one of the two clues to go looking for, then we should choose P. Given our model (including our restrictions of and priors on the types), we expect to reduce our uncertainty more by learning about an alternative cause of democratization (international pressure) than by learning about a mediator (mobilization), regardless of the I and D values in the case.

We also see differences depending on the case's I and D values. In particular, we see that the mediator, M, is much more informative for $I = D$ cases (first and fourth columns). This is because, given the restrictions on nodal types in our model, these are cases in which the causal effect we are looking for is one that *could* have operated via the mediator – that is, because any $I \rightarrow D$ effect in such cases has to be positive. In contrast, M is informative

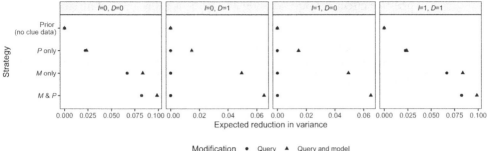

Figure 12.5   Revised query and/or model: Expected reduction in posterior variance from different data strategies for cases with different *I* and *D* values

only as a moderator of the cause's direct effects when the $I \rightarrow D$ effect can only be negative (second and third columns, where $I \neq D$). This finding illustrates an important, more general point: The process-tracing evidence that will be most informative to go looking for can depend on what it is we have already observed.

12.1.3.2 Revised Model, Revised Query

We can also see how the comparison across clue strategies changes if we revise the model or change the query. To illustrate, let's first revise the query: imagine that we are interested in understanding whether inequality plausibly mattered for democratization *via* mobilization.

The model revision that we contemplate removes a restriction, allowing the possibility of a negative effect of inequality on mobilization. We now set the probability of a negative $I \rightarrow M$ effect at 0.1 instead of 0. Our new, pathway-related query is defined as follows: *If we could keep I constant but vary M over the values that it would take as I changes from 0 to 1, would D then change, (given the observed values of I and D)?*[2]

Figure 12.5 shows how our uncertainty would change, in expectation, under different clue-selection strategies, comparing a scenario in which we alter the query only, without changing the model, to a scenario in which we alter both the query and the model.

Looking first at the scenario in which we change the query only, we always learn from observing M or P in an $I = 0, D = 0$ or an $I = 1, D = 1$ case. However, the relative values on M and P are reversed from what they were for our first query. Whereas P was more informative for assessing whether I had

---

[2] Formally this query is $D(I = 0, M = M(I = 1)) \neg D(I = 0, M = M(I = 0))$.

a positive effect on D, observing M's value is more important, in expectation, for learning whether I had a positive effect on D *through* the M-mediated pathway. For the cases where $I = 0, D = 1$ or $I = 1, D = 0$, on the other hand, we learn nothing because we already know (or have assumed in the model) that negative effects cannot operate through M.

However, if we change the model, M becomes still more important for the pathway query. As we can see, we now expect to learn from M both in $I \neq D$ and in $I = D$ cases – the patterns of learning are very similar, though note that the degree of learning is still lower for the $I \neq D$ cases. Consider an $I = 0, D = 1$ case. When negative $I \rightarrow M$ effects were excluded, I could not have a negative effect on D through M. M was informative about this type of case only as a moderator of I's direct negative effect on D, but there was nothing to learn about mediated effects. An observation of $M = 1$ counted as evidence against $I = 0$ being the cause of $D = 1$ only because $M = 1$ could be the cause (given that M could have a positive effect on D); but again, there was no question of effects going through M. Once we relax the monotonicity restriction and allow negative effects of I on M, M is additionally informative as a potential *mediator* of a negative $I \rightarrow D$ effect and thus informative for our new query.

12.2 Dynamic Strategies

The clue-collection strategies described above assume that researchers select the full set of clues to be gathered in advance and do not alter their strategies as they go along. However, the expected informativeness of a given clue may depend on the values of *other* clues that we could observe first. Thus, if we have the flexibility to adjust clue selection procedures as we observe data, then we can select an optimal strategy in a dynamic sense, taking into account earlier observations when selecting later ones.

Given n nodes, a dynamic data collection strategy will be of the form:

$$\sigma = \{K_1, (K_2|K_1 = 1), (K_2|K_1 = 0), (K_3|K_1 = 1, K_2 = 0), \dots\}$$

where each K_j is an element of the nodes on the graph or is the empty set. Thus, we start with observing K_1; then, whether we choose to observe K_2 depends on the value of K_1; whether we choose to observe K_3 depends on the value of K_1 and (if we observed it) K_2; and so on. A strategy *vector* specifies a series of conditional clue-search actions: It identifies the first clue sought and

Table 12.2 Illustration of three (of many) possible two-step strategies

Strategy	Step 1	Step 2 if 0	Step 2 if 1	Expected variance	Expected cost
1	S	None	None	0.167	1
2	S	X	X	0	2
3	S	None	X	0	1.5

then which clues are sought conditional on the realization of all prior clues sought.

Each possible strategy has an associated expected reduction in variance. We can also build in an expected cost associated with each clue, allowing us to treat clue selection as a problem of optimizing over informativeness and cost.

Let's illustrate with the government survival example from before, using the base model (in which we allow for only two nodal types at C and at R and only one nodal type at Y). Imagine a situation in which we know that $Y = 0$ and are interested in whether $Y = 0$ because of S (the value of which we have not observed). We consider strategies in which we first seek information on one node and then, conditional on what we find, look or do not look for data on one other node. With five nodes, one already known, there are 4×4^2 strategies of this form (that is 4 first-clue choices, and then 16 possible *pairs* of responses to whatever value is found on the first clue).

To consider the simplest subset of these, consider the strategies that involve looking first at S. If we learn here that the government was not sophisticated, then this answers the query in the negative: The government could not have remained in power because it was sophisticated. If we learn that the government *was* sophisticated, then it might have been the cause, but we do not yet know that with certainty. Our next move might be to examine whether there was a free press (X): learning that there was or was not a free press will settle the matter since sophistication will have caused the government's survival if and only if there is a free press.

We represent each of these three two-step strategies (three of many possible ones) in Table 12.2, along with the expected variance reduction associated with each. In addition, we indicate each strategy's expected cost. Here, we assume, for simplicity, that each clue has a cost of 1. We can see that we expect to learn the same amount from Strategies 2 and 3, but that Strategy 3 comes at a lower expected cost because we have a 50% chance of only having to collect one observation, depending on what we observe.

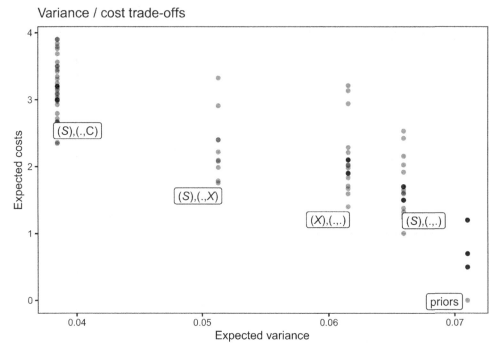

Figure 12.6   Cost-variance trade-offs for all dynamic strategies involving up to two clues, under base government-survival model, with undominated strategies labeled. In each label, the term in first set of parentheses indicates which clue is observed first. The two elements in the second set of parentheses indicate which clue or none (.) is to be observed if the first clue realization is 0 and if it is 1, respectively

We can, of course, also calculate the expected costs of different strategies while allowing different clues to come at different costs. Figure 12.6 plots all dynamic strategies involving up to two clues, assuming $Y = 0$ has already been observed, showing expected variance-reduction for the query, "Did S cause Y?" and expected cost. For this exercise, we set differential clue prices such that X is the most costly clue to collect, followed by C, then S, then Y, then R. We have labeled the strategies that lie along the frontier of optimal strategies. The optimal choice then depends on how we want to trade-off cost against learning. Among the notable points along this frontier, we see that the cheapest strategy among those that minimize variance involves gathering S and then gathering C if and only if we observe $S=1$. We can also see that the lowest-variance strategy that minimizes costs involves gathering S only and then stopping.

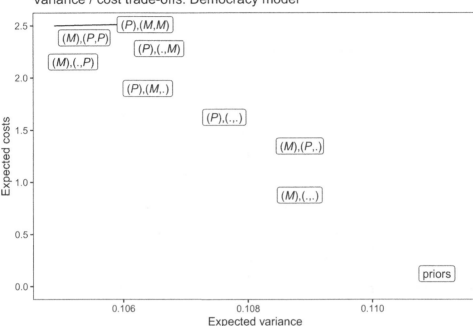

Figure 12.7 Cost-variance tradeoffs for all dynamic strategies involving up to two clues, under the base democratization model

We also implement this exercise for the basic inequality and democratization model. We illustrate (Figure 12.7) for a situation in which we know there is high inequality and democratization has occurred, and we want to know if high inequality caused the democratization. We will assume here that mobilization is easy to observe (low-cost), but pressure is difficult (high-cost).

We can see here that four strategies are non-dominated by any alternative. These are, in order of increasing cost:

1. Observe M first, then stop. This strategy has relatively high expected uncertainty but minimizes costs relative to any other strategy: We observe just one clue, and it's the cheaper one.
2. Observe P first, then stop. We'll learn more from this strategy than from Strategy 1, though at a higher cost. Still, no other strategy allows us to reduce costs without increasing variance.
3. Observe P first; if $P = 0$, observe M; otherwise stop. We, again, get uncertainty reduction here, relative to Strategy 2, but again at a higher cost.

4. Observe M first; if $M = 0$, stop; if $M = 1$, observe P. This strategy gets us the lowest expected posterior variance of any strategy. Moreover, it is not the highest-cost strategy, which would be to observe both clues no matter what. Once we've observed $M = 0$, we get nothing from the additional investment in P since $M = 0$ already tells us that I could not have had a positive effect on D.

Note also that both Strategies 3 and 4 are *conditional* two-clue strategies: They involve first seeking one clue and seeking a second clue only under one of the possible realizations of the first clue. But they have different outcomes. Perhaps most interestingly, we don't expect to learn the most by starting with the most probative clue. If we start with the more informative clue, P, observing M only if $P = 0$, we expect to end up with *more* uncertainty than if we start with the less informative clue, M, and observe P only if $M = 1$.

12.3 Conclusion

In this chapter, we have sought to show how clue-selection strategies for process-tracing can be guided by a causal model. An explicit statement of a causal model allows one to assess what will be inferred given all possible observations over all nodes on a graph. This opens the way for simple strategies for assessing which case-level data are most valuable for what query, and in what order these should be gathered. A key takeaway from this chapter's analysis is that there is no one-size-fits-all approach to deciding where in a case to look for probative value. The most useful clue will not always be a step along a causal chain or in any other particular location. Which clue strategy we should expect to be most informative will depend on features of the research situation: on the prior beliefs we have embedded in our model, on the question we are asking, and on what data we have already observed. The procedures outlined in this chapter give the researcher a systematic, transparent way of reasoning from a model, a query, and a set of prior observations to a choice among the available clue strategies. Strategies may be fixed in advance or dynamic, and information about the costliness of clues can readily be incorporated into the analysis.

The procedures that we describe in this chapter may not always be practicable. Researchers may find it difficult to describe a model in advance and place prior beliefs on nodal types. Moreover, the collection of new data could easily give rise to possibilities and logics that were not previously contemplated. Nothing here seeks to deny these potential challenges. Our claim here is a modest one: Insofar as one can specify a model before engaging in data gathering, the model provides a powerful tool to assess what data it will be most useful to gather.

13 Case Selection

We show how to use causal models to inform the selection of cases
for intensive analysis. We outline a procedure in which we predict the
inferences that will be made when future data are found and use these predictions to inform case-selection strategies. We ask: Given a set of cases on
which we already have data on X and Y, which of these cases will it be most
advantageous to choose for more in-depth investigation? We show that the
optimal case-selection strategy depends jointly on the model we start with
and the causal question we seek to answer, and we draw out the implication
that researchers should be wary of generic case-selection principles.

Very often, researchers start out with access to X, Y data on many cases and
then want to select a subset of cases – case studies – to examine more carefully
in order to draw stronger conclusions either about general processes or about
likely effects in specific cases. A key design decision is to determine which
cases are most likely to be informative about the question at hand. This chapter shows how we can use a causal-model-based approach to inform this key
research-design decision.

13.1 Common Case-Selection Strategies

A host of different strategies have been proposed for selecting cases for in-
depth study based on the observed values of X and Y data. Perhaps the most
common strategy is to select cases in which $X = 1$ and $Y = 1$ and look to see
whether in fact X caused Y in the chosen cases, using some approach to inferring causality from within-case evidence. But many other selection strategies
have been proposed, including strategies to select cases "on the regression
line" or, for some purposes, cases "off the regression line" (e.g., Lieberman,
2005). Some scholars suggest ensuring variation in X (most prominently,

King et al., 1994), while others have proposed various kinds of matching principles. Still, others have pointed to the advantages of a random sampling of cases, either stratified or unstratified by values on X or Y (Fearon and Laitin, 2008; Herron and Quinn, 2016).

One reason why case-selection strategies might differ is that we might be using the case studies in quite different ways.

A matching strategy, for instance – selecting cases that are comparable on many features but that differ on X – can replicate on a small scale the kind of inference done by matching estimators with large-n data. Such a strategy can draw leverage from X, Y variation even if researchers have matched on other within-case characteristics. xw

Other strategies seek to use qualitative information to check assumptions made in cross-case X, Y analysis: For example, is the measurement of X and Y reliable in critical cases? For addressing such questions, given limited resources, it might make sense to focus on cases for which validation plausibly makes a difference to the X, Y inferences: For example, we might focus on influential cases that have unusually extreme values on X and Y. Similar arguments are made for checking assumptions on selection processes, though we consider this a more complex desideratum since this requires making case-level causal inferences and not simply measurement claims (Dunning, 2012). Seawright (2016) advocates for selecting extreme and deviant cases for purposes such as the discovery of measurement error or omitted variables that might have consequences for inferences drawn from cross-case X, Y correlations.

A third purpose is to use a case to generate alternative or richer theories of causal processes, as in Lieberman's "model-building" mode of "nested analysis" (Lieberman, 2005). Lieberman suggests that cases "off the regression" line will typically be of greatest interest for this purpose. Weller and Barnes (2014) also focus on both X, Y relations and whether the cases are useful for hypothesis generation.

In what follows, we focus on a simpler and more general way of thinking about the purpose of gathering more detailed evidence on a subset of cases: The richer evidence gathered in our chosen cases will feed directly into model-updating and, in turn, help answer our query. We can thus frame the case-selection task as follows: Given existing X, Y data for a set of cases and a given clue (or set of clues) that we can go looking for in a more intensive analysis (i.e., process tracing) of some subset of these cases, we want to figure out *which cases* to select for intensive analysis so that we maximize expected learning about some well specified question of interest.

The basic insight of this chapter is simple enough: *The optimal strategy for case selection for a model-based analysis is a function of the model we start with and the query we seek to address*, just as we saw for the optimal clue-selection strategy in Chapter 12. This insight yields guidance that is consistent with some common advice but at odds with other advice. But the most general message of this chapter is about the overall approach: That is, have clear goals – know what question you are asking and whether you are posing it at the case level, the population level, or both – think through in advance what you might find in cases you could select for inquiry, think through how what you might find addresses your goals, and then choose accordingly. More specifically, we show how researchers can use a causal model to formalize this analysis: To tell them what types of cases are likely to yield the greatest learning given their model and the query that they seek to answer.

The broad injunction to select cases to maximize learning is in line with the general recommendations of Fairfield and Charman (2022), though the strategy for maximizing learning differs here, particularly in its grounding in a causal model. Most closely related to our analysis in this chapter is the contribution of Herron and Quinn (2016), who build on Seawright and Gerring (2008). While Seawright and Gerring provide a taxonomy of approaches to case selection, they do not provide a general strategy for assessing the relative merits of these different approaches. As we do, Herron and Quinn (2016) focus on a situation with binary X, Y data and assess the gains from learning about causal type in a set of cases. (Interestingly, in their treatment, the causal type, Z_i is called a confounder rather than being an estimand of direct interest; in our setup, confounding as normally understood arises because of different probabilities of different causal types of being assigned to "treatment," or an $X = 1$ value.)

Our setup differs from that in Herron and Quinn (2016) in a few ways. Herron and Quinn (2016) parameterize differently, though this difference is not important.[1] Perhaps the most important difference between our analysis and that in Herron and Quinn (2016) is that we connect the inference strategy to process-tracing approaches. Whereas Herron and Quinn (2016) assume

---

[1] Herron and Quinn (2016) have a parameter θ that governs the distribution of data over X and Y and then, conditional on X, Y values, a set of parameters ψ_{xy} that describe the probability of a case's being of a given causal type. We take both θ and ψ_{xy} to derive from the fundamental distribution of causal types and assignment probabilities. The difference in parameterization does have implications for interpretations of the priors. For example, flat priors over θ and ψ imply a tighter distribution than a uniform prior over the causal types. In fact, Herron and Quinn (2016) use priors with greater variance than uniform.

that causal types can be read directly, we assume that these are inferred *imperfectly* from evidence and we endogenize the informativeness of the evidence to features of the inquiries.[2] Despite these various differences, our results will agree in key ways with those in Herron and Quinn (2016).

13.2 No General Rules

Case selection is about choosing in which cases we will seek further information. We want to look for evidence in cases where that evidence is likely to be most informative. And the informativeness of a case depends, in turn, on our model and our query.

We start in this section by illustrating how simple rules – like choosing cases where $X = 1$ and $Y = 1$ or choosing the cases we most care about – may sometimes lead us astray. Rather, we will argue that there is a general procedure for determining how to select cases, and this procedure requires a specification of the learning we expect to achieve, given different data patterns we might find.

13.2.1 Any Cell Might Do

Although it might be tempting to seek general case-selection rules of the form "examine cases in which $X = 1$ and $Y = 1$" or "ignore cases in which $X = 0$ and $Y = 1$," it is easily demonstrated that which cases will be (in expectation) more informative depends on models and queries.

Suppose that we know that processes in some population can be represented by the model $X \to Y \leftarrow K$, and, moreover:

- $\Pr(Y = 1 | X = 0, K = 0) = 1$
- $\Pr(Y = 1 | X = 1, K = 0) = 0.5$

---

[2] There are differences in addition to these. Here, we assume that the case-selection decision is made after observing the XY distribution and we explore a range of different possible contingency tables. In Herron and Quinn (2016), the distribution from which the contingency tables are drawn is fixed, though set to exhibit an expected observed difference in means (though not necessarily a true treatment effect) of 0.2. They assume large X, Y datasets (with 10,000 units) and case-selection strategies ranging from 1 to 20 cases. Another important difference, is that in many of their analyses, Herron and Quinn (2016) take the perspective of an outside analyst who knows the true treatment effect; they then assess the expected bias generated by a research strategy over the possible data realizations. We, instead, take the perspective of a researcher who has *beliefs* about the true treatment effect that correspond to their priors, and for whom there is, therefore, no *expected* bias.

- $\Pr(Y = 1 | X = 0, K = 1) = 0$
- $\Pr(Y = 1 | X = 1, K = 1) = 0.9$

One way to read this set of statements is that X's causal effect on Y varies with K. Say we know that in the population, the share of $X = 1$ cases, λ_1^X is 0.5. But we do not know how common K is. Nor do we know the joint distribution of X and Y. Thus, we do not know either the average effect of X or the probability that X caused Y either in the population or for a case with particular X, Y values. We will let κ denote the unknown quantity $\Pr(K = 1) = \lambda_1^K$.

What do the above statements tell us about K's *informativeness*? The beliefs above imply that if we were given a case with $X = Y = 1$, then K is a "doubly decisive" clue for assessing whether, in this case, X causes Y. In particular, we see that for an $X = Y = 1$ case, observing $K = 1$ implies that X caused Y: This is because, if X were 0 Y would have been 0. We also see that $K = 0$ in an $X = 1$, $Y = 1$ case implies that X did not cause Y since Y would have still been 1 even if X were 0. So an $X = Y = 1$ case would be a highly informative place to go looking for K.

However, if we had a case in which $X = Y = 0$, then learning K would be entirely uninformative for the case. In particular, we already *know* that $K = 1$ in this case as the statements above exclude the possibility of a case in which $X = Y = 0$ and $K = 0$. So there would be nothing gained by "looking" to see what K's value is in the case.

For the same reason, we can learn nothing from K in an $X = 0$, $Y = 1$ case since we know that $K = 0$ in such a case.

On the other hand, if we chose an $X = 1$, $Y = 0$ case, then K would again be doubly decisive, with $K = 0$ implying that $X = 1$ caused $Y = 0$ (because the counterfactual of $X = 0$ would have resulted in $Y = 1$ when K is 0), and $K = 1$ implying that $X = 1$ did not cause $Y = 0$ (because the counterfactual of $X = 0$ would still result in $Y = 0$ since there is zero likelihood that $Y = 1$ when X is 0 and K is 1).

We have chosen extreme values for this illustration – our beliefs could, of course, allow for gradations of informativeness, rather than all-or-nothing identification – but the larger point is that beliefs about the way the world works can have a powerful effect on the kind of case from which learning is possible. And note that in this example, there is nothing special about where a case lies relative to a (notional) regression line: Informativeness in this setup happens to depend on X's value entirely. Though again, this is a particular feature of this particular set of beliefs about the world.

There are two further considerations we might take into account when deciding whether to choose an $X = 1, Y = 0$ case or an $X = 1, Y = 1$ case. In both cases, the clue will be doubly decisive, so we will learn about the case. However, the cases may still differ with respect to:

- How great our prior uncertainty is about the case?
- What we can learn from the case for the population?

13.2.1.1 Case-Level Prior Uncertainty

Prior uncertainty in our example reduces to the prior that $K = 1$ in the case. We have:

$$Pr(K = 1 | X = Y = 1) = \frac{Pr(K = 1, X = 1, Y = 1)}{Pr(X = 1, Y = 1)}.$$

Making use of the fact that $Pr(X = x, K = 1) = 0.5\kappa$ and $Pr(X = x, K = 0) = 0.5(1 - \kappa)$ this can be written:

$$Pr(K = 1 | X = Y = 1)$$
$$= \frac{Pr(Y = 1 | K = 1, X = 1)\kappa}{Pr(Y = 1 | K = 1, X = 1)\kappa + Pr(Y = 1 | K = 0, X = 1)(1 - \kappa)}. \quad (13.1)$$

From what we know about the population, we then have:

$$Pr(K = 1 | X = Y = 1) = \frac{0.9\kappa}{0.9\kappa + 0.5(1 - \kappa)}.$$

So if we had a case prior that $\kappa = .5$ (and so each K, X combination is equally likely) we would have $Pr(K = 1 | X = 1, Y = 1) = \frac{0.9}{0.9+0.5} = 0.64$.

For an $X = 1, Y = 0$ case, the same calculation would yield $Pr(K = 1 | X = 1, Y = 0) = \frac{0.1}{0.5+0.1} = 0.17$.

In other words, with these priors, we are more uncertain about the value of K in the $X = 1, Y = 1$ case than in the $X = 1, Y = 0$ case and expect to learn more from the first kind of case than from the second.

13.2.1.2 Population Inference

Suppose, now, that we were interested in a population query: the average effect of X on Y. We can see that this is equal to $\kappa \times 0.9 + (1 - \kappa) \times (-0.5)) = 1.4 \times Pr(K = 1) - 0.5$. For this query, we need only determine the prevalence of $K = 1$ in the population. It might seem that this means that it is irrelevant what type of case we choose: why not use pure random sampling to determine K's prevalence? As we saw above, however, we have more information about the likely value of K in some kinds of cases than in others. Thus,

Table 13.1 Beliefs about data outcomes for two different values of λ_1^K values ($X = 0$ cases omitted)

λ_1^K	K	X	Y	$Pr(X, Y, K \vert \lambda_1^K)$	$Pr(X, Y \vert \lambda_1^K)$	$Pr(K \vert X, Y, \lambda_1^K)$
0.33	0	1	0	0.17	0.18	0.91
0.67	0	1	0	0.08	0.12	0.71
0.33	1	1	0	0.02	0.18	0.09
0.67	1	1	0	0.03	0.12	0.29
0.33	0	1	1	0.17	0.32	0.53
0.67	0	1	1	0.08	0.38	0.22
0.33	1	1	1	0.15	0.32	0.47
0.67	1	1	1	0.30	0.38	0.78

for this population-level estimand as well, selecting an $X = 1$ case will be informative, while selecting an $X = 0$ case will not be informative.

We also expect different inferences in the two kinds of cases for the population share of $K = 1$ cases, λ_1^K.

For illustration, say we entertain two equally likely possibilities about λ_1^K: either $\lambda_1^K = \kappa^H = 2/3$ or $\lambda_1^K = \kappa^L = 1/3$. We can request a case with any X, Y combination to inspect and then draw an inference about λ_1^K. Note that since we request a case with particular X, Y features *we do not learn from the values of X and Y* in the case we examine (except perhaps if we were told that no such case existed). We have, after all, requested a case like this to look at.

Table 13.1 shows the implied probabilities put on different data patterns for the different values of λ_1^K we entertain. For instance, looking at the last row, if $\lambda_1^K = 0.67$ we expect $X = 1, K = 1$ with probability 0.5×0.67 and expect $Y = 1$ with probability 0.9 given $X = 1, K = 1$, meaning $Pr(X = 1, K = 1, Y = 1 \vert \lambda_1^K = 0.67) = 0.5 \times 0.67 \times 0.9 \approx 0.30$. Quantity $Pr(X = 1, Y = 1 \vert \lambda_1^K = 0.67)$ is calculated similarly. The last column is the ratio of these two, which has the same form as Equation 13.1:

$$Pr(K = 1 \vert X = 1, Y = 1, \lambda_1^K = 0.67) = \frac{0.9\lambda_1^K}{0.9\lambda_1^K + 0.5(1 - \lambda_1^K)} \approx 0.78.$$

We omit the $X = 0$ cases from the table since there is nothing to learn from K for these and so our beliefs about λ_1^K would in such a case not change given whatever we find.

From this table, we can calculate what we are likely to find and then what we will infer when we find it, in an $X = 1, Y = 1$ case:

- $\Pr(K = 1 | X = 1, Y = 1) = 0.63$
- $\Pr(\lambda_1^K = \frac{2}{3} | X = 1, Y = 1, K = 1) = 0.62$
- $\Pr(\lambda_1^K = \frac{2}{3} | X = 1, Y = 1, K = 0) = 0.29.$

We can now calculate the expected posterior *variance* as 0.224.[3] This is an improvement on the prior variance of 0.25.

Similarly, we can calculate:

- $\Pr(K = 1 | X = 1, Y = 0) = 0.19$
- $\Pr(\lambda_1^K = \frac{2}{3} | X = 1, Y = 0, K = 1) = 0.76$
- $\Pr(\lambda_1^K = \frac{2}{3} | X = 1, Y = 0, K = 0) = 0.44.$

Now the expected posterior variance, while still an improvement over the prior, is higher than what we expect if we choose a $X = 1, Y = 1$ case, at 0.234.

In summary, under the stipulated beliefs about the world, we can learn most about the population ATE by selecting an $X = Y = 1$ for study. We learn something from an $X = 1, Y = 0$ case, and nothing at all from a case with $X = 0$. We can also learn about the case-level effects for cases with $X = 1$ and $Y = 0$. If we are interested in the case-level effect for an $X = 0$ case, then there are no gains from any case-selection strategy since we know K's value based on X and Y's value.

But here's the thing. While we have demonstrated specific gains from a $X = 1, Y = 1$ case in this example, there is nothing *generally* preferable about such a case. Under a different set of beliefs about the world, we would expect to learn more from an $X = Y = 0$ case than from an $X = Y = 1$ case. Suppose, for instance, that we have a model in which:

- $X \rightarrow Y \leftarrow K$
- $\Pr(Y = 1 | X = 0, K = 0) = 0.5$
- $\Pr(Y = 1 | X = 1, K = 0) = 0$
- $\Pr(Y = 1 | X = 0, K = 1) = 0.5$
- $\Pr(Y = 1 | X = 1, K = 1) = 1$

In this world, we learn nothing from observing a case in which $X = 1, Y = 1$ since we already know that $K = 1$. In contrast, if $X = Y = 0$, then if we learn that $K = 1$, we know that, were $X = 1$, Y would have been 1; and if instead, we observe $K = 0$, we know that Y would have (still) been 0 if X were 1. Now K is doubly decisive for an $X = Y = 0$ case but unhelpful for an

---

[3] We use the fact that variance for a Bernoulli with parameter p is $p(1 - p)$; here, $\Pr\left(\lambda_1^K = \frac{2}{3}\right)\left(1 - \Pr\left(\lambda_1^K = \frac{2}{3}\right)\right).$

Table 13.2 The data we start with. If we are interested in whether X caused Y in case A, are we better gathering data on M in case A or on K in case B?

Case	X	Y	K	M
A	1	1	1	
B	0	0		1

$X = Y = 1$ case. Our lessons for case selection get turned on their head with this new background model. We can easily mix things up again to construct a situation in which the off-diagonal cases are the informative ones.

In summary: beware of simple rules for case selection. Depending on the model, our priors, and the query, any type of case can be optimal.

13.2.2 Interest in a Case Might Not Justify Selecting that Case

It seems obvious that if your query of interest is *defined* at the case level – not at the population level – then the choice of cases is determined trivially by the query. Just study the case you have a question about.

This is not correct, however.

Sometimes we might be interested in effects in case A but still be better off gathering more information about case B instead of digging deeper into case A. We illustrate this phenomenon for a situation in which the learning from cases operates via updating on a general model (and subsequent application of that model to the case of interest) rather than via direct *application* of a prior, informative general model to the case of interest.

We imagine a world in which we have causal model $X \to M \to Y \leftarrow K$, flat priors on all nodal types, and start with data as in Table 13.2.
In other words, we start out with data only on clue K in case A and only on clue M in case B. We are interested specifically in whether X mattered for Y in case A. We now want to figure out in which case to focus our further data-collection efforts: Are we better off gathering data on M for case A or on K for case B?

Given the model, we can work out what we might find under each strategy and what we might then infer for our query about A. These potential inferences and the associated (case-level) uncertainty are detailed in Table 13.3. Note that the probability of finding $K = 1$ in case B or $M = 1$ in case A is calculated *after* taking account of the data we already have on A and B.

Table 13.3 Probability of the data and inferences, given different data realizations, on a query, Q: What is the probability that $X = 1$ caused $Y = 1$ in case A?

Quantity	Best guess	Uncertainty
Prior on Q	0.258	0.191
Probability $K = 1$ for B	0.660	
Posterior on Q if we find $K = 0$ for B:	0.249	0.187
Posterior on Q if we find $K = 1$ for B:	0.261	0.193
Probability $M = 1$ for A	0.489	
Posterior on Q if we find $M = 0$ for A:	0.312	0.215
Posterior on Q if we find $M = 1$ for A:	0.200	0.160

This table then gives us enough to calculate the *expected* uncertainty under each strategy.

- The baseline uncertainty for case A is 0.191.
- Under a strategy in which we gather data on K in case B, the expected uncertainty for effects in A is 0.191 (that is, identical up to rounding error).
- The expected uncertainty (about effects in A) from gathering data on M in case A is 0.188.

These numbers are all very similar – highlighting the difficulty of drawing inferences without a strong prior model based on just two cases. This is one (negative) lesson of this exercise.

Nevertheless, the expected uncertainties do diverge. Intuitively, when we investigate causal effects in case B we in principle benefit from a Millian logic: Finding that the cases are *similar* on K – the moderator – makes us think it more likely that variation in X is explaining outcomes. At least K is not explaining the outcome. The gain is however quantitatively small. When we investigate case A we are more likely to be convinced that X mattered in case A when we find that *differences* in M – the mediator – are in line with differences in X and Y. M is the path through which any effect needs to operate, and if M is similar in both cases this knocks confidence that X was making a difference.

So here to learn about case A, we do well by finding out more about case A, as intuition would suggest.

Suppose, however, that we are interested in making an inference about case B. Now which strategy would be better?

Details of the inferences we would draw about X's effect on Y in case B for each possible data strategy are given in Table 13.4.

This table looks familiar (we explain why soon). We see here again that updating on case B is also best achieved by observation of M in case A, rather

Table 13.4 Probability of the data and inferences, given different data realizations, on a query, Q': What is the probability that $X = 0$ caused $Y = 0$ in case B?

Quantity	Best guess	Uncertainty
Prior on Q'	0.258	0.191
Probability $K = 1$ for B	0.660	
Posterior on Q' if you find $K = 0$ for B:	0.249	0.187
Posterior on Q' if you find $K = 1$ for B:	0.263	0.194
Probability $M = 1$ for A	0.489	
Posterior on Q' if you find $M = 0$ for A:	0.312	0.215
Posterior on Q' if you find $M = 1$ for A:	0.200	0.160

than K in case B. In other words tightening inferences on B is best done by investigating A further. In particular:

- The baseline uncertainty for case B is 0.191.
- Under a strategy in which we gather data on K for case B, the expected uncertainty for effects in B is 0.192.
- The expected uncertainty (for effects in B) from gathering data on M in case A is 0.188.

Note that Tables 13.3 and 13.4 are in fact identical (up to simulation error beyond the third digit), even though they are asking about different cases. The reason is that, regardless of which case we are interested in, the learning takes place by updating the *same* population-level model, and then applying those population-level beliefs to a case. (This is the $\hat{\pi}$ calculation we introduced in Chapter 9.) So for both queries, the decision about which case to choose for further study comes down to the same criterion: In which case is the clue to be observed likely to be most informative about the effect of X on Y in the population? The answer is case A, where we can observe M: This is because observing cross-case variation in the mediator M in this model, which we can do only by collecting more evidence on case A, is more informative about X's effect on Y than is observing cross-case variation in the moderator K (which is what we get from selecting case B).

This example provides a reminder that we can learn about a case by updating a general causal model rather than by simply *applying* a prior model to the case data. It confirms the possibility of this learning, even as it highlights the possibly limited scope of learning from very few cases. And it points to a counterintuitive implication for case selection: Sometimes (as here, where our initial model does not imply strong probative value for clues) we can learn the most about a case by learning as much as we can about our model, which may or may not imply collecting additional information about the case of interest.

13.3 General Strategy

We now introduce a flexible approach to comparing the prospective learning from alternative case-selection strategies. To help explore the intuition behind this strategy, we start by walking through a simplified setup and then implement the approach for a range of models, strategies, and causal queries.

13.3.1 Walk through of the General Strategy

Consider a situation in which our model is $X \to M \to Y$. Suppose, further, that we restrict the nodal types so that X cannot have a negative effect on M, and M cannot have a negative effect on Y, with flat priors over all remaining nodal types. Imagine then that we begin by collecting only X, Y data on six cases and obtain the data pattern shown in Table 13.5. We can see that the data display a modest positive correlation between X and Y, evidence weakly suggestive of a positive average effect of X on Y given the model.

These X, Y data already give us some information about the causal effect of X on Y. Yet, we want to learn more by examining some subset of these cases more deeply – and, specifically, by collecting data on M for two of these cases. Which cases should we select? We consider three strategies, each conditional on X and Y values:

- Strategy A chooses two cases on the "regression line," implied by the data pattern, one randomly drawn from the $X = Y = 0$ cell and one randomly drawn from the $X = Y = 1$ cell

Table 13.5 Observed data prior to case selection

Data type	Count
X0Y0	2
X1Y0	1
X0Y1	1
X1Y1	2

- Strategy B chooses off the regression line, one randomly drawn from the $X = 1$, $Y = 0$ cell and one randomly drawn from the $X = 0$, $Y = 1$ cell
- Strategy C chooses two cases, both from the $X = 1$, $Y = 1$ cell

How can we evaluate these strategies prospectively?

We recognize that different strategies yield different *possible* data patterns. For instance, Strategy A (on the line) could possibly give us a data pattern that includes the observation $X = 0$, $M = 0$, $Y = 0$. Yet Strategy A cannot possibly yield a data pattern that includes the observation $X = 1$, $M = 0$, $Y = 0$ – because it does not involve the inspection of M in an $X = 1$, $Y = 0$ case – whereas Strategy B (off the line) *can* yield a pattern that includes this observation. And none of the three strategies can possibly yield a pattern that includes both $X = 1$, $M = 0$, $Y = 0$ and $X = 0$, $M = 1$, $Y = 0$.

In Table 13.6, we represent the full set of possible data patterns that can arise from each strategy, with the possible data patterns for strategy A or B labeled $A1$, $A2$, etc. or $B1$, $B2$, etc., respectively. For instance, A is a strategy in which we look for M in one $X = 0$, $Y = 0$ case and one $X = 1$, $Y = 1$ case. $A1$, then, is a realization in which we observe $M = 0$ in both cases. As we can see, there are four possible data patterns from strategies A and B, representing the four different combinations of M values we might find across the two cases selected for deeper investigation. There are three possible outcomes from strategy C. In the comparison presented here, none of the possible data patterns overlap across strategies.

The next step is to grapple with the fact that not all possible data realizations for a given strategy are equally *likely* to emerge. We represent the data probabilities near the bottom of the table. How likely a data pattern is to emerge will depend on the model, any restrictions or priors we have built into the model, and any updating of beliefs that arises from the pure X, Y data. Note, for instance, that data pattern $A3$ is much more likely to emerge than the other data patterns possible under Strategy A. This is for two reasons. One is that $A3$ involves M co-varying with X and Y, a pattern consistent with X having an effect on Y – since, in this model, X can only affect Y if it affects M and if M effects Y. Data patterns $A1$ and $A4$ have M constant between the two cases, even as X and Y vary; this is a pattern inconsistent with X having an effect on Y. $A3$, then, is more likely than $A1$ or $A4$ because the restrictions on the model plus the evidence from the X, Y data make us believe that X *does* have an average effect on Y. Second, we believe $A3$ is more probable than $A2$ because of the model's restrictions: The model allows positive effects of X on M and of M on Y (a way of generating $A3$), but rules out negative intermediate effects (a way of generating $A2$).

Table 13.6 Each column shows a possible distribution of data that can be generated from a given case-selection strategy, for strategies A, B, and C. We calculate the probability of each data possibility, given the data seen so far, and the posterior variance associated with each one

Data type	A1	A2	A3	A4	B1	B2	B3	B4	C1	C2	C3
X0M0Y0	1	0	1	0	0	0	0	0	0	0	0
X0M0Y1	0	0	0	0	1	0	1	0	0	0	0
X0M1Y0	0	1	0	1	0	0	0	0	0	0	0
X0M1Y1	0	0	0	0	0	1	0	1	0	0	0
X0Y0	1	1	1	1	2	2	2	2	2	2	2
X0Y1	1	1	1	1	0	0	0	0	1	1	1
X1M0Y0	0	0	0	0	1	1	0	0	0	0	0
X1M0Y1	1	1	0	0	0	0	0	0	2	1	0
X1M1Y0	0	0	0	0	0	0	1	1	0	0	0
X1M1Y1	0	0	1	1	0	0	0	0	0	1	2
X1Y0	1	1	1	1	0	0	0	0	1	1	1
X1Y1	1	1	1	1	2	2	2	2	0	0	0
Probability	0.17	0.029	0.634	0.167	0.265	0.237	0.234	0.264	0.079	0.239	0.681
Posterior mean	0.077	0.041	0.171	0.077	0.13	0.14	0.14	0.129	0.047	0.09	0.162
Posterior variance	0.007	0.003	0.02	0.007	0.017	0.018	0.017	0.017	0.003	0.009	0.02

Table 13.7 Expected posterior variances

Strategy	Variance
Offline	0.0172
Online	0.0152
Two $X = 1, Y = 1$ cases	0.0159

Finally, each possible data realization will (if realized) generate (possible) updating of our beliefs about the query of interest. In the second-to-last row of Table 13.6, we can see the mean of the posterior distribution (for the ATE of X on Y) under each data pattern.

How do we now evaluate the different strategies? This is the same as asking what our loss function is (or utility function or objective function). As in Chapter 12 we will focus on posterior variance and in particular, *expected* posterior variance, though we emphasize that the same procedure can be used with other loss functions (a natural candidate from the study of experimental design is the expected *information gain* (Lindley, 1956)[4]).

The posterior variance on the ATE, for each data pattern, is represented in the table's final row. We can see that our level of posterior uncertainty varies across possible data realizations. We operationalize the expected learning under each case-selection strategy as the *expected* reduction in posterior variance.

From the probability of each data type (given the model and the X, Y data seen so far) and the posterior variance given each data realization, the implied *expected* variance is easily calculated as a weighted average. The expected posterior variances for our three strategies are summarized in Table 13.7.

In this example, we see that we would expect to be better off – in the sense of having less posterior uncertainty – by focusing our process-tracing efforts on the regression line than off the regression line. We only do marginally better by spreading over the line than by concentrating on positive cases. We save an account of the intuition underlying this result for the discussion of our more extensive simulations below.

The key takeaway here is the procedure for assessing case-selection strategies:

---

[4] Lindley (1956, Equation (7)) defines the average gain from an experiment as $E_x(I_1(x) - I_0)]$ where x is the data that might be observed, given the design, and $I_1(x) = \int p(\theta|x) \log(p(\theta|x)) d\theta$ and $I_0 = \int p(\theta) \log(p(\theta)) d\theta$.

1. Derive from the model the full set of possible data patterns under each case-selection strategy being assessed.
2. Calculate the probability of each data pattern given the model (with any priors or restrictions), the prior X, Y data, and the strategy.
3. Generate a posterior distribution on the query of interest for each data pattern.
4. Use the probability of different data patterns together with the posterior variance under each data pattern to calculate the expected posterior variance on the query of interest for each strategy.

13.3.2 Simulation Strategy

In this section, we generalize the model-based approach by applying it to a wide range of models, queries, and case-selection strategies.

In all scenarios examined here, we imagine a situation in which we have already observed some data (the values of some nodes from the causal model in some set of cases) and must now decide in which cases we should gather additional data. We will assume throughout that we are considering gathering additional observations in cases for which we already have *some* data. In other words, we are deciding which subset of the cases – among those we have already gathered some data on – we should investigate more *deeply*. (This is distinct from the question of "wide vs. deep," examined in Chapter 14, where we might decide to observe cases we have not yet seen at all.)

The general intuition of the case-selection approach that we develop here is that we can use our causal model and any previously observed data to estimate what observations we are more or less likely to make under a given case-selection strategy, and then figure out how uncertain we can expect to end up being under the strategy, given whatever causal question we seek to answer.

We proceed as follows:

DAG. We start, as always, with a DAG representing our beliefs about which variables we believe to be direct causes of other variables. For the current illustrations, we consider four different structures:

- Chain model: an $X \to M \to Y$ model, where M is a mediator
- Confounded model: a model with $X \to Y$ and with M as a confounder, pointing into both X and Y
- Moderator model: an $X \to Y \leftarrow M$ model, where M is a moderator

- Two-path model: a model in which $X \rightarrow M \rightarrow Y \leftarrow X$, meaning that X can affect Y both through a direct path and indirectly via M

Restrictions or priors. We can augment the models to allow for informative priors or restrictions on nodal types. Here, for each model, we examine a version with no restrictions and a version with monotonicity restrictions.

Given data. If we have already made observations of any of the model's nodes in some set of cases, we can use this information to condition our strategy for searching for further information. For instance, if we have observed X's and Y's values in a set of cases, we might select cases for process tracing based on their values of X and/or Y. And, importantly, what we have already observed in the cases will affect the inferences we will draw when we observe additional data, including how *informative* a particular new observation is likely to be.

For the simulations, we assume that we have already observed X and Y in a set of cases and found a positive correlation. Specifically, for all simulations, we assume prior X, Y data of $N = 6$, with a weak positive relationship ($2\ X = 1, Y = 1$ cases, $2\ X = 0, Y = 0$ cases, and 1 case in each off-diagonal cell). And it is *from* these original six cases that we are selecting our cases for process tracing. In the experiments below, we do not examine how the prior data itself might affect the choice of case-selection strategies (as we do, for instance, with clue-selection in Chapter 12), but we invite the reader to explore these relationships by adjusting the code we provide in Supplementary Material.

Query. We define our query. This could, for instance, be X's average effect on Y or it might be the probability that X has a negative effect on Y in an $X = 1, Y = 0$ case. We can use the general procedure to identify case-selection strategies for any causal query that can be defined on a DAG. And, importantly, the optimal case-selection strategy may depend on the query. The best case-selection strategy for answering one query may not be the best case-selection strategy for another query.

In the simulations, we examine four common queries:

- ATE: What is the average effect of X on Y for the population?
- Probability of positive causation: What is the probability that $Y = 1$ because $X = 1$ for a case randomly drawn from the population of $X = 1, Y = 1$ cases?
- Probability of negative causation: What is the probability that $Y = 1$ is due to $X = 0$ for a case randomly drawn from the population of $X = 0, Y = 1$ cases?

- Probability of an indirect effect: Defined only for the two-path models, we estimate the probability that the effect of X on Y operates through the indirect path. More precisely, we ask, for an $X = 1$, $Y = 1$ case in which $X = 1$ caused $Y = 1$, what the probability is that that effect would have occurred if M were held fixed at the value it takes on when $X = 1$.[5]

Define one or more strategies. A strategy is defined, generically, as the search for data on a given set of *nodes*, in a given *number* of cases that are randomly selected *conditional* on some information we already have about potential cases. In the simulations below, our strategy will always involve uncovering M's value in one or two cases. What we are wondering is how to choose these one or two cases for deeper analysis.

Specifically, for our simulations, we assess the contributions of eight strategies, with inferences from the X, Y data alone serving as our baseline. In the figures below, the strategies run along the X-axis of each graph and can be interpreted as follows:

- **Prior**: conduct no intensive analysis, with beliefs based on X, Y data only
- **1 off**: data on M is sought in one case in the $X = 1$, $Y = 0$ cell
- **1 on**: data on M is sought in one case in the $X = 1$, $Y = 1$ cell
- **2 off**: data on M is sought in one $X = 0$, $Y = 1$ case and one $X = 1$, $Y = 0$ case
- **2 pos**: data on M is sought for two cases in the $X = 1$, $Y = 1$ cell
- **2 on**: data on M is sought in one $X = 1$, $Y = 1$ case and one $X = 0$, $Y = 0$ case
- **fix X**: a strategy in which we seek M in two cases in which a causal condition was present, with X fixed at 1, one with $Y = 0$ and one with $Y = 1$
- **fix Y**: a strategy in which we seek M in two cases in which a positive outcome was observed, with Y fixed at 1, one with $X = 0$ and one with $X = 1$

These are all "pure" strategies in the sense that the number of units for which data on M is sought in each cell is fixed. One could also imagine random strategies in which a researcher chooses at random in which cells to look. For example, if we choose one case at random, we are randomly choosing between a case on the regression line and a case off the line. The performance

---

[5] In code, this somewhat complicated query is expressed as "Y[X=0, M=M[X=1]]==Y[X=1, M=M[X=1]]", given "(X == 1 & Y == 1) & (Y[X=1]>Y[X=0])".

of a random strategy will be a weighted average of the pure strategies over which the random strategy is randomizing.

Possible data. For each strategy, there are multiple possible sets of data that we could end up observing. In particular, the data we could end up with will be the X, Y patterns we have already observed, plus some pattern of M observations.

Probability of the data. We then calculate a probability of each possible data realization, given the model (with any restrictions or priors) and any data that we have already observed. Starting with the model together with our priors, we update our beliefs about λ based on the previously observed data. This posterior now represents our *prior* for the purposes of the process tracing. In the analyses below, we use the already-observed X, Y correlation to update our beliefs about causal-type share allocations in the population. We then use this posterior to draw a series of λ values.

Given that the ambiguities matrix gives us the mapping from causal types to data realizations, we can calculate for each λ draw, the probability of each data possibility given that particular λ and the strategy. We then average across repeated λ draws to get the probability of each possible data realization.

Posterior on estimate given the data. For each data possibility, we can then ask what inference we would get from each data possibility, given whatever query we seek to answer, as well as the variance of that posterior. Examining the inferences from possible data realizations, as we do below, can help us understand how the learning unfolds for different strategies.

Expected posterior variance under each strategy. The quantity of ultimate interest is the posterior variance that we expect to end up with under each strategy. The expected posterior variance is simply an average of the posterior variances under each data possibility, weighted by the probability of each data possibility. We operationalize the expected learning under a strategy as the expected *reduction* in posterior variance arising from that strategy.

13.3.3 Results

The main results are shown in Figures 13.1 and 13.2.

The two figures take two different approaches to representing the value of alternative strategies. In Figure 13.1, we examine the informativeness of strategies by showing how much our inferences depend on what we observe

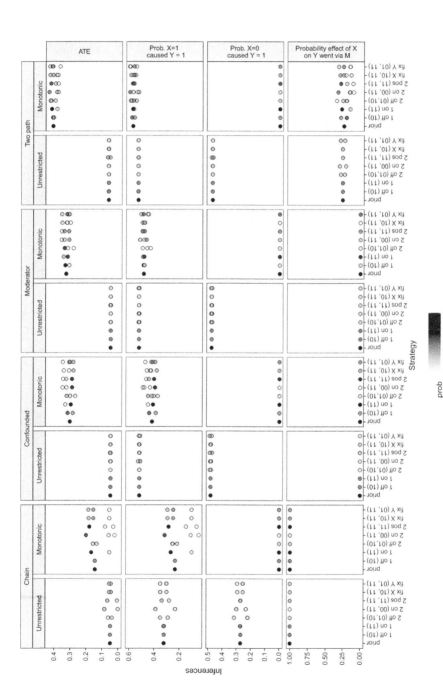

Figure 13.1 Inferences on four different queries given possible observations under different case-selection strategies, for four different causal models. For each model, we analyze both an unrestricted model and a model with monotonicity restrictions

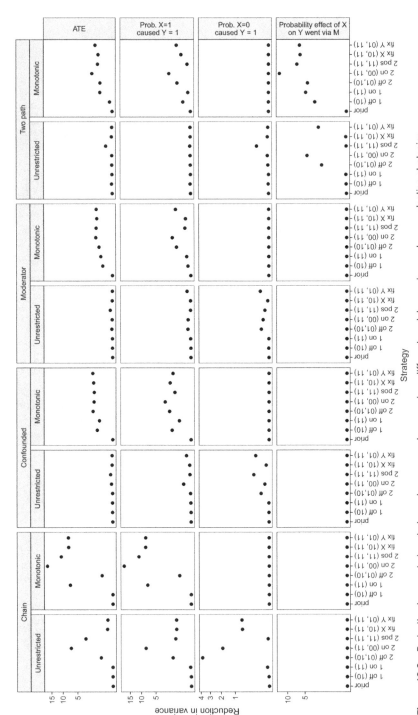

Figure 13.2 Reduction in expected posterior variance on each query given different models, queries, and case-selection strategies

within the cases. For a given model, query, and case-selection strategy, we plot the inferences we would draw from each of the possible data-realizations under the strategy. (Where inferences do not depend on the observed data, the multiple points are superimposed upon one another.) Generally, a larger spread across points (for a given model-query-strategy combination) represents a greater opportunity for learning from the data. However, as expected learning is also a function of how likely each data realization is, we represent the probability of each potential inference via shading of the points. In Figure 13.2, we directly plot expected learning, operationalized as the expected reduction in posterior variance.

In the remainder of this section, we walk through the results and suggest, often tentatively, interpretations of some of the more striking patterns. We caution that reasoning one's way through expected learning for different model-query-strategy combinations, given a particular pattern in the prior data, can be tricky – hence, our recommendation that researchers simulate their way to research-design guidance, rather than relying on intuition.

13.3.3.1 $N=1$ Strategies, Unrestricted Models

Suppose we can only conduct process tracing (observe M) for a single case drawn from our sample of six X, Y cases. Should we choose a case from on or off the regression line implied by the X, Y pattern? In Figure 13.1, we can see that for all unrestricted models, our inferences are completely unaffected by the observation of M in a single case, regardless of which case-selection strategy we choose and regardless of the query of interest. We see only one point plotted for the two $N = 1$ strategies for all unrestricted models and all queries because the inference is the same regardless of the realized value of M. In Figure 13.2, we see, in the same vein, that we expect 0 reduction in expected posterior variance from these $N = 1$ strategies: They cannot make us any less uncertain about our estimates because the observations we glean cannot affect our beliefs.

To see why, let's first consider the on-the-line strategy. Not having observed M previously, we still have flat priors over the nodal types governing X's effect on M and M's effect on Y. That is to say, we still have no idea whether X's positive effect on Y (if present) more commonly operates through a chain of positive effects or a chain of negative effects. Thus, the observation of, say, $M = 1$ in an $X = 1$, $Y = 1$ case is equally consistent with a positive $X \rightarrow Y$ effect (to the extent that effect operates via linked positive effects) and with no $X \rightarrow Y$ effect (to the extent positive effects operate through linked negative effects). Observing $M = 1$ in an $X = 1$, $Y = 1$ case, therefore, tells us nothing about the causal effect in that case and, thus, nothing about the average effect either.

Similarly, we have no idea whether X's negative effect on Y (if present) operates through a positive-negative chain or a negative-positive chain, making $M = 1$ or $M = 0$ in an $X = 1$, $Y = 0$ case both equally consistent with a negative or null $X \to Y$ effect, yielding no information about causation in the case. By a similar logic, observing $M = 1$ in the $X = 1$, $Y = 1$ case is uninformative about negative effects in an $X = 0$, $Y = 1$ case, and observing $M = 1$ in an $X = 1$, $Y = 0$ case tells us nothing about positive effects in an $X = 1$, $Y = 1$ case.

The same logic applies to drawing inferences from M as a moderator or to learning from M about indirect effects. In the absence of prior information about effects, one case is not enough. For more intuition about this finding, see Section 7.5.1.

13.3.3.2 $N=1$ Strategies, Monotonic Models

The situation changes, however, when we operate with models with monotonicity restrictions (as it would more generally for models with informative, rather than flat, priors). Now we can see that our inferences on the queries do generally depend on M's realization in a single case and that we expect to learn. For many model-query combinations, the two $N = 1$ strategies perform comparably, but there are situations in which we see substantial differences.

Most notably, in a chain model with negative effects ruled out by assumption, we learn almost nothing from choosing an off-the-line case: This is because we already know from the model itself that there can be no $X \to Y$ effect in such a case since such an effect would require a negative effect at one stage. The only learning that can occur in such a case is about the prevalence of positive effects (relative to null effects) at individual stages ($X \to M$ and $M \to Y$), which in turn has implications for the prevalence of positive effects (relative to null effects) of X on Y. Likely for similar reasons, in the monotonic two-path model, an on-the-line case is much more informative than an off-the-line case about the ATE and about the probability that the effect runs via the indirect path.

Interestingly, however, the on-the-line strategy is not uniformly superior for an $N = 1$ process-tracing design. We appear to learn significantly more from an off-the-line case than an on-the-line case when estimating the share of positive effects in the population of $X = 1$, $Y = 1$ cases and operating with a monotonic confounded or two-path model. At first, this seems surprising:

Why would we not want to choose an $X = 1$, $Y = 1$ case for learning about the population of $X = 1$, $Y = 1$ cases? One possible reason is that, in the on-the-line case, one data realization is much more likely than the other, while we are more uncertain about what we will find in the off-the-line case. For instance, in the confounding model with monotonicity, in an $X = 1$, $Y = 1$ case we would learn about the prevalence of confounding from seeing $M = 0$ (where confounding cannot be operating since negative effects are excluded) as opposed to $M = 1$; but we do not *expect to see* $M = 0$ when both of its children (X and Y) take a value of 1 while negative effects are excluded. In an $X = 1$, $Y = 0$ case, however, $M = 0$ and $M = 1$ are about equally likely to be observed, and we can learn about confounding from each realization. We can see these differences in relative data probabilities from the shadings in the graphs, where we have more even shading for the possible inferences from the one-off strategy than for the one-on strategy.

The general point here is that we expect to learn more from seeking a clue the more uncertain we are about what we will find, and some case-selection strategies will give us better opportunities to resolve uncertainty than others.

13.3.3.3 $N=2$ Strategies, Unrestricted Models

Next, we consider the selection of *two* of our six cases. Now, because we are observing M in two cases, we can learn from the variation in M across these cases – or, more specifically, from its covariation with X and with Y. This should matter especially for unrestricted models, where we start out with no information about intermediate causal effects (e.g., whether they are more often positive or more often negative). Thus, when we only process trace one case, we cannot learn about causal effects in the cases we process trace since we don't know how to interpret the clue. In contrast, if we observe M in two or more cases, we *do* learn about causal effects for those cases because of the leverage provided by observing covariation between the process-tracing clue and other variables.

We assess the expected gains from five $N = 2$ strategies: examine two off-the line cases, one $X = 1$, $Y = 0$ case and one $X = 0$, $Y = 1$ case; examine two on-the-line cases, an $X = Y = 0$ case and an $X = Y = 1$ case; examine two treated, positive outcome ($X = Y = 1$) cases; select on X by examining two $X = 1$ cases with different Y values; and select on Y by examining two $Y = 1$ cases with different X values.

A key message of these results is that each strategy's performance depends quite heavily on the model we start with and what we want to learn. For instance, when estimating the ATE, the on-the-line strategy in which we disperse the cases across cells (two-on) clearly outperforms both the dispersed off-the-line strategy (two-off) and an on-the-line strategy in which we concentrate on one cell (two-pos) *if* we are working with an unrestricted chain model, and the off-the-line strategy is clearly the worst-performing of the three. The differences in learning about the ATE are more muted, however, for an unrestricted confounded model, and the two-pos strategy does *better* than the other two for a two-path model.

If we seek to learn about the probability of positive causation in an $X = 1, Y = 1$ case, then there is little difference between two-off and two-pos, with two-on performing best. We also see that two-pos has lost its edge in an unrestricted two-path model, with no strategy offering leverage. When estimating the probability of a *negative* effect for an $X = 0, Y = 1$ case, we see that the two-off strategy performs best for the chain model, *but* that the two-pos strategy offers the greatest leverage in a two-path model. Finally, when estimating the probability of an indirect positive effect in an unrestricted two-path model, we get the most from a two-on strategy, though the two-off strategy does moderately well.

In general, selecting conditional on a fixed value of X or Y (while dispersing on the other variable) does not do particularly well in unrestricted models, and it does not usually matter much which variable we fix on. There are exceptions, however. Perhaps most strikingly, in a two-path unrestricted model, we do relatively well in estimating the probability of an indirect positive effect when we fix Y but stand to learn nothing if we fix X. Interestingly, fixing Y generally does better than fixing X across all model-query combinations shown, given the prior data pattern we are working with.

This pattern is particularly interesting in light of canonical advice in the qualitative methods literature. King et al. (1994) advise selecting for variation on the explanatory variable and, as a second-best approach, on the dependent variable. And they warn sternly against selection for variation on both at the same time. But note what happens if we follow their advice. Suppose we start with an unrestricted chain model, hoping to learn about the ATE or probability of positive causation, and decide to select for variation on X, ignoring Y. We might get lucky and end up with a pair of highly informative on-the-line cases. But, depending on the joint X, Y distribution in the population, we might just as easily end up with a fairly uninformative off-the-line case or $X = 0, Y = 1, X = 1, Y = 1$ pair. We do better if we intentionally select on *both* X and Y in this setup. This is equally true if we want to learn about the probability of negative effects in this model, in which case we want to choose an off-the-line case, or if we want to learn about positive indirect effects in a two-path model, where we want both X and Y to be 1. King, Keohane, and Verba's advice makes sense if all we are interested in is examining covariation between X and the Y: Then we can learn from forcing X to vary and letting Y's values fall where they may. However, seeking leverage from the observation of a third variable is a different matter. As our simulations indicate, the strategy from which we stand to learn the most will depend on how we think the world works and what we want to learn.

13.3.3.4 $N=2$ Strategies, Monotonic Models

Generally speaking, we get more leverage across strategies, models, and queries if we are willing to rule out negative effects by assumption. The most dramatic illustration of this is in a comparison of the unrestricted to a monotonic moderator and two-path models, where we face bleak prospects of learning about the ATE and the probability of positive effects in an unrestricted model, regardless of strategy. Imposing monotonicity assumptions on these two models makes for relatively similar ATE-learning opportunities across $N = 2$ strategies while boosting the relative performance of two-on (best) and two-off (second-best) strategies for learning about the probability of positive causation.

The relative performance also flips in some places. For instance, whereas two-pos gives us the most leverage for estimating the ATE in an unrestricted two-path model, the two-on strategy is optimal once we impose monotonicity. And two-pos leapfrogs two-off for estimating positive indirect effects when we go from an unrestricted to a monotonic two-path model. The opposite seems to be true for estimating the ATE or the probability of positive causation in a confounded model, where two-off does relatively better when we introduce monotonicity restrictions.

13.4 Conclusion

A small number of summary conclusions stand out.

First, case selection, in general, depends on the purpose of an investigation, captured here by the query. Considerations differ depending on whether your interest in a case is in learning about the specific case you select or in using the case to learn about a population. Clarity on that overarching purpose is critical, though sometimes absent from discussions of case selection in the existing literature. More generally, although we often focus on simple queries like case-level or average causal effects, the set of queries that might motivate you may be endless. You might focus on estimating effects for units with particular characteristics, on figuring out which interventions have the biggest impact at the lowest cost, on identifying the interventions that have the most equal impact across units, or on learning about likely effects in a *new* population that has different characteristics from the one that data have been drawn from. Each of these goals might imply a different case-selection strategy.

Second, we see lessons here specifically for population-level inference. One case, we find, generally will not help unless our model already presupposes probative value – for instance, if we build in monotonicity assumptions. Two cases *can* be enough to generate probative value where we had none before. What is learned from a particular case depends on what other cases we have selected. For instance, we very often do better when we choose cases with different X, Y values – yet even this possibility depends on the model and the query.

A more pessimistic set of implications of these simulations points to the limits to learning about populations from in-depth investigation of a set of cases. For one thing, studying a small number of cases will, in general, yield quite modest learning about the population they are drawn from. In addition, we find that learning about some queries can be very difficult in the context of some models. For instance, we found it especially hard to get traction on the ATE and the probability of positive causal effects from a mediator clue in an unrestricted two-path model – though we do much better when our query shifts to figuring out the path through which effects operate. In short, a research strategy that combines extensive X, Y-style analysis with drilling down on a subset of cases can, but is not guaranteed to, provide leverage on the population of interest.

The highest-level lesson from this exercise is the sensitivity of case-selection strategy to models and queries; these determine when different case-level findings will be informative and in which combinations they are most informative. This finding calls for skepticism about broad rules for case selection that provide guidance without taking account of background beliefs about how the world works or the specific question being asked. More positively, as we show in action here, if you can describe your model, your priors, and the data you already have, there is a fairly simple procedure for figuring out where to go next.

14 Going Wide, Going Deep

We turn to the problem of choosing between going "wide" and going "deep": between seeking a little bit of information on a large number of cases versus studying a smaller number of cases intensively. We outline a simulation-based approach to identifying the optimal mix of breadth and depth. Simulations suggest that going deep is especially valuable where confounding is a concern, for queries about causal pathways, and where models embed strong beliefs about causal effects. We also find that there are diminishing marginal returns to each strategy, and that depth often provides the greatest gains when we have cross-case evidence on only a modest number of cases.

We continue exploring how we can leverage causal models in making research-design choices by thinking about the tradeoff between intensive (deep) and extensive (wide) analysis.

Suppose that we have identified those clues that will be most informative and those cases in which it would be most valuable to conduct process tracing, given our beliefs about the world. A further question that we face is the classic challenge of methods *mixing*: What mixture of quantitative and qualitative evidence is optimal? We argued in Chapter 9 that the distinction between quantitative and qualitative inference is, in a causal-model framework, without much of a difference. But here we frame a more precise question: Given finite resources, how should we trade-off between studying a larger number of cases at a given level of intensiveness, on the one hand, and drilling down to learn more intensively about some subset of the cases in our sample? How should we decide between going "wide" and going "deep"?

Just as with the selection of clues and cases examined in Chapters 12 and 13, how much we should expect to learn from going wide versus going deep will depend on our queries as well as on how we think the world works, as expressed in the causal model with which we start and as shaped by the data that we have seen at the point of making the wide-versus-deep decision.

We examine here queries commonly associated with large-N, quantitative strategies of analysis (such as average treatment effects), as well as queries commonly associated with more case-oriented, qualitative approaches (queries about causal pathways and about causal effects at the case level). The analysis in this chapter makes clear the opportunities for integration across these lines of inquiry. We show that investing in in-depth process tracing will sometimes make sense even when one aims to learn about average effects in a population. Likewise, collecting X, Y data can sometimes help us draw inferences that will aid in case-level explanation.

14.1 Walk-Through of a Simple Comparison

To build up our intuitions about how the optimal mix of strategies might depend on how the world works, let us explore a simple comparison of wide and deep strategies.

Imagine a world in which we have a large amount of data on X and Y (2,000 observations), and we see that X and Y are perfectly correlated. We might be tempted to infer that X causes Y. If X were randomly assigned, then we might be able to justify that inference. Suppose, however, that our data are observational and, in particular, we are aware of an observable confound, M, that might determine both X and Y. In that situation, the effect of X on Y is not identified. As shown by Manski (1995), this data pattern could be produced even if X had no effect but all those cases that were destined to have $Y = 1$ were assigned to $X = 1$ while all those who would have had $Y = 0$ regardless were assigned to $X = 0$. Indeed, different priors could support beliefs about the average effect lying anywhere between 0 and 1.

From Pearl's (2009) backdoor criterion, however, we also know that if the right causal model is $X \rightarrow Y \leftarrow M \rightarrow X$, then data on M would allow the effect of X on Y to be identified. We could estimate the effect of X on Y for $M = 0$ and for $M = 1$ and take the average. Let's imagine that we think that this structural model *is* plausible. Substantively, we think we can gather data on how units are selected into treatment.

Suppose now that we aim to collect additional data, but that data on M for a single unit is far more costly than data on X and Y for a single unit. We thus face a choice between gathering *a lot* more data on X and Y (say, for 2,000 more cases) or gathering a *little* data on M for a subset of cases – just 20 in this illustration. Which should we do? Are 20 cases sufficient to learn enough

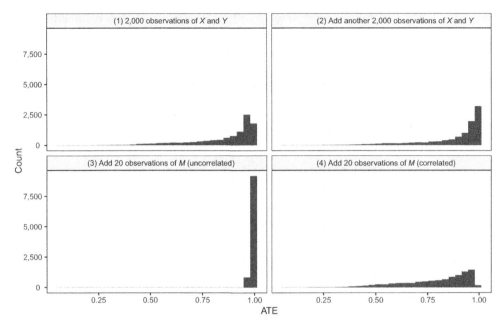

Figure 14.1   Posteriors on the ATE given different strategies and data patterns

about the causal model to find out whether the correlation between X and Y is spurious or not?

We get an intuition for the answer by imagining the inferences we might draw in three extreme cases and comparing these to the base case. Figure 14.1 illustrates. The figures are generated by forming a model with $X \rightarrow Y \leftarrow M \rightarrow X$, strong priors that $\Pr(M = 1) = 0.5$, and flat priors on all other nodal types. In other words, in our priors, we think that M is equally likely to be a 0 or 1 but do not make assumptions about how it is related to X and Y. We first update the model with a set of X, Y data – and then choose between going wider and going deeper.

Panel 1 in Figure 14.1 shows our posterior distribution over the average causal effect from observation of the base data: 2,000 cases with X and Y perfectly correlated. The distribution is quite wide, despite the strong correlation, because the posterior includes our uncertainty over the nature of confounding. Our estimate for the ATE is 0.86 but with a posterior standard deviation of 0.1519. There is positive weight on all positive values of the ATE.

How can we improve on this estimate?

One possibility would be to go wide and collect X, Y data on an additional 2,000 cases. Panel 2 displays our posterior on the average causal effect with the addition of these 2,000 cases. We assume that the new data also displays a perfect X, Y correlation, like the first set of data. Again, we could not imagine correlational data that more strongly confirms a positive relation, and now we have twice as much of it. What we see, however, is that investing in gathering data on 2,000 additional cases does not help us very much. The mean of our posterior on the ATE is now 0.88, with a standard deviation of 0.1497. So the updating is very slight.

Suppose that, for the cost of gathering X, Y data on an additional 2,000 cases, we could drill down on a random subset of 20 of the original 2,000 cases and observe M in those cases. What might we learn?

Because we start out with a flat prior on how M will relate to X and Y, we display inferences for two possible realizations of that pattern. In Panel 3, we show the updating if M turns out to be uncorrelated with both X and Y. The mean of our posterior on the ATE now rises to 0.98, and the posterior standard deviation shrinks dramatically, to 0.004. Greater depth in a relatively small number of cases is enough to convince us that the X, Y relationship is not spurious.

Panel 4 shows inferences from the same "going deep" strategy but where M turns out to be perfectly correlated with X and Y. Now our estimate for the ATE shifts downward to 0.79, with a posterior standard deviation of 0.1632. In this case, we have no leverage to estimate covariation between X and Y within each M condition. However, we do not give up on the possibility of strong treatment effects. Indeed, while the data are consistent with perfect confounding and no true causal effect, they are also consistent with perfect confounding and a strong causal effect. We just can't tell these apart.

In other words, in this setup, what we observe from our "going deep" strategy can have a big impact on our inferences. One reason we stand to learn so much from process tracing so few cases is that the process tracing speaks to relationships about which we start out knowing so little: M's effect on X and M's effect on Y, effects on which the X, Y data themselves shed no light.

It is also interesting to note that we cannot learn as much by updating *only* using information from the 20 cases for which we have full X, M, Y data. Were we to use only the subset with this complete data – ignoring the other 1,880 cases – and observe M to be uncorrelated with X and Y, the mean of our posterior on the ATE would be 0.26 with a posterior standard deviation of 0.1218 (not graphed). The breadth provided by those 1,880 X, Y-only cases thus adds a great deal. While observing an uncorrelated M in 20 cases allows us to largely rule out M as a cause of any X, Y correlation, observing a strong X, Y correlation over a large number of cases provides evidence that X in fact affects Y.

We use this example to highlight a simple but stark point: There will be situations in which the expected gains from collecting more data on the same cases and from collecting the same data on more cases will be different, sometimes very different. The model and the prior data shape the tradeoff. In this particular setup, it is the confounding together with the large number of prior X, Y observations that makes depth the better strategy. Once we have learned from 2,000 X, Y observations, data of the same form from more cases will not change beliefs. Yet going deep – even if only in a few cases – provides information on parameters we know nothing about, helping us draw causal inferences from the X, Y correlation.

14.2 Simulation Analysis

While the results in the last section are striking, they depend upon particular realizations of the data under each strategy. When selecting strategies we, of course, do not know how the data will turn out. Our problem becomes, as in the clue- and case-selection analyses, one of figuring out the *expected posterior variance* from different strategies.

14.2.1 Approach

The more general, simulation-based approach that we introduce here is parallel to the approaches for clue- and case selection. The steps of this procedure are as follows:

1. **Model**. We posit a causal model, along with any priors or restrictions.
2. **Prior data**. We specify the data that we already have in hand. For the simulations below, we assume no prior data.
3. **Strategies**. We then specify a set of mixing strategies to assess. A strategy, in this context, is defined as a combination of collecting data on the same nodes for a given number of cases (randomly drawn from the population) and collecting data on additional nodes for some number of cases randomly sampled from the first set of cases.
4. **Data possibilities**. For each strategy, we define the set of possible data realizations. Whereas for case selection, the structure of the possible data

realizations will be the same for all strategies with a given N, possible data patterns in wide-versus-deep analyses involve much greater complexity and will vary in structure across strategies. This is because the number of cases itself varies across strategies. Also, whereas we fix the X, Y pattern for the purposes of case selection, here we allow the X, Y patterns we discover to vary across each simulation draw.

5. **Data probabilities**. As for case selection, we use the model and prior data to calculate the probability of each data possibility under each strategy.
6. **Inference**. Again, as for case selection, we update the model using each possible data pattern to derive a posterior distribution.
7. **Expected posterior variance**. We then average the posterior variances across the possible data patterns under a given strategy, weighted by the probability of each data pattern.

14.2.2 Simulation Results

We now explore alternative mixes of going wide and going deep for a range of models and queries, the same set that we examined for case selection in Chapter 13. We present the results in a compact form in Figure 14.2. The macro-structure of the figure is the same as that of Figure 13.2 in Chapter 13, with models being crossed with queries. Again, we focus on the reduction in expected posterior variance. To help with scaling, we plot the reduction in expected posterior variance *relative* to the expected posterior variance for the least deep and least wide strategy under consideration.

Within each panel, each line represents going wide to a differing degree: collecting X, Y data for $N = 100$, for $N = 400$, and for $N = 1,600$. As we move rightward along each line, we are adding depth: We show results for a strategy with no process tracing, for process tracing 50 of the X, Y cases, and for process tracing 100 of the X, Y cases. On the y-axis of each graph, we plot the reduction in expected posterior variance from each wide-deep combination, relative to a strategy with $N = 100$ and no process tracing.[1]

Looking at the figure as a whole, one pattern that leaps out is that there are gains from going wider for almost all model-query combinations. For some

---

[1] Note that the expected posterior variance is always 0 for queries that are already answered with certainty by the model itself, such as the probability of a negative effect in a model with negative effects excluded, and so the reduction in expected posterior variance is not defined. Note also that in this figure we exclude the 0.5% of observations with the highest variance in each set because of extreme skew in the distribution of variance estimates. This smooths the figures somewhat but does not affect substantive conclusions.

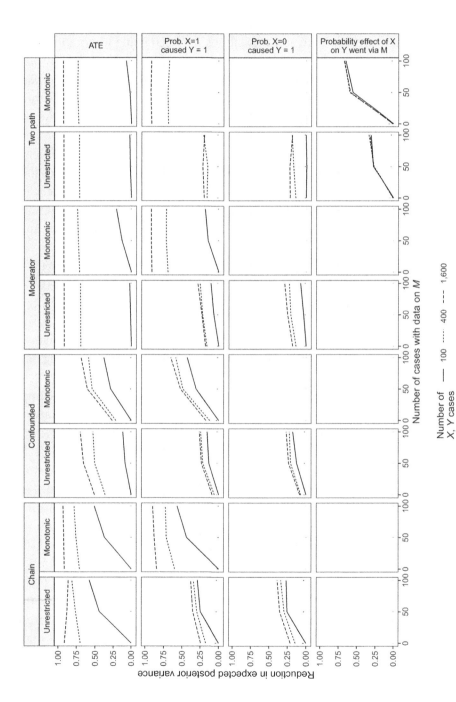

Figure 14.2 Reduction in expected posterior variance for different wide versus deep strategies, given different model-query combinations. Reductions are relative to the expected posterior variance for an $N = 100$, no process-tracing strategy

designs (the confounded model being a notable exception), we achieve close to a full reduction in posterior variance for the ATE as we go to 1,600 X, Y cases. We can also see, unsurprisingly, that the marginal gains to going wide are diminishing.

There are, however, some situations in which going wider appears to add little or nothing. One of these is where we want to estimate the probability that a positive effect runs through the indirect path in a two path model. For this query and model, we learn significantly from gathering more within-case information, but little from observing X and Y in a wider set of cases (see the two rightmost boxes in the bottom row).

Focusing just on the gains to depth, we see that these are more concentrated in specific model-query combinations. Going deep to learn about the ATE appears at best marginally advantageous – at least up to process tracing 100 cases – for the unrestricted moderator models and for the two-path models. Gains are also modest for the probability of positive or negative causation under these models.

On the other hand, we learn more from going deep, in both the unrestricted and monotonic chain models, and the confounded models (of course, except when the query is the probability that $X = 0$ caused $Y = 1$ in a monotonic model, where the model itself answers the query). And we learn from going deep for the query that the effect of X runs through M in the two-path model. As we saw with going wide, the marginal gains from going deep are diminishing.

In general, learning from going deep is stronger in the restricted models, but it is not limited to these. Thus, we don't need a built in probative value; rather, we *learn* about M's probative value (as discussed in Chapters 9 and 10) from the data.

Perhaps the most striking feature is the limited learning in the two-path model. Here, as with the moderator model, but unlike the confounded model, the ATE is identified without process data. But we do not see the gains from learning about M that we see in the chain model. In a two-path model, observing M correlated with X and with Y across a set of cases should allow us to learn about M's informativeness about the operation of an *indirect* effect, just as we can learn about M's probative value in a chain model. The problem is that knowing about the indirect effect in a two-path model contributes only marginally to the first three queries in the figure since these are about total effects. Thus, even adding monotonicity restrictions, which makes M *a priori* informative, does not significantly improve learning from M about total effects.

The important exception, when it comes to learning about the two-path model, is when it is the *pathway itself* that we seek to learn about. As we can see in the figure, we can learn a great deal about whether effects operate via M by observing M, even in an unrestricted two-path model. Interestingly, the gains from depth for causal-effect queries in an unrestricted chain model closely resemble the gains from depth for the indirect-effect query in the unrestricted two-path model. This similarity suggests that both kinds of model-query combinations allow for learning *about* M that, in turn, permits learning *from* M.

We also see that the context in which depth delivers the steepest gains of all is when we seek to learn about the probability of an indirect effect in a monotonic two-path model. Part of the reason is likely that M is *a priori* informative about the operation of the mediated pathway (as it is about the operation of effects in the monotonic chain model). Additionally, however, it appears that we start out with relatively high uncertainty about the pathway query because the model itself is quite uninformative about it. Thus, for instance, we learn much more from depth here than we do for a total effect query in a monotonic chain model: The monotonicity assumptions themselves already tell us a great deal about total effects, whereas they imply nothing about the path through which effects unfold. There is simply more to be learned from M about pathways than about total effects.

Most interesting, perhaps, is using the graphs to examine different wide versus deep tradeoffs we might face. Suppose, for instance, that we wish to learn about the probability that X caused Y in an unrestricted confounded model. We start out with X, Y data for 100 cases and have additional resources with which to collect more data. Let us further assume that the cost of collecting X, Y data for an additional 300 cases is equal to the cost of collecting M on 50 of the original 100 cases. Where should we invest?

We can read a fairly clear answer off the graph. As we can see in the relevant graph, we can expect to do better by adding depth than by adding breadth. In fact, even expanding our X, Y sample to 1,600 cases only gets us about as much leverage as we get from process tracing 50 cases.

We can also see how the optimal choice depends on what data collection we have already done or committed to. For the same example, imagine we do indeed commit to gathering data on M for 50 cases and then get additional resources. We would then expect to be much better by investing in an expansion to 300 X, Y cases than by process tracing the other 50 X, Y cases.

The chain models, both unrestricted and monotonic, also show clearly how expected learning from one strategy depends on how much of the other strategy we have already exploited. We can see for both the ATE and the probability of positive causation that the gains to depth are much greater if we have done less process tracing. Similarly, the gains from depth are much greater at lower numbers of X, Y cases.

A further question we can ask is: Where are *mixing* methods advantageous? And when are maximally wide or maximally deep strategies best? We can examine this question by comparing a strategy with maximal breadth and no process tracing; a strategy with maximal process tracing and minimal breadth; and a strategy in which we invest in a mixture of new data, by examining X, Y in 400 cases while process tracing 50 cases.

We see some places where we are best off going as wide as possible, at least for the ranges we explore in these simulations. For instance, if we wish to estimate the ATE in a chain model (unrestricted or monotonic), a pure "going wide" strategy is optimal. At the other extreme, when we seek to learn about the probability of an indirect effect from an unrestricted two-path model, we are best off process tracing our original 100 cases and gain nothing by expanding our sample.

In many contexts, however, the mixing strategy performs best. The advantage of mixing appears starkest for the confounded monotonic model. Suppose we start with only X and Y data for 100 cases under this model. If we can collect more data, how should we do so? A mixed strategy of expanding to 400 X, Y cases and process tracing 50 of them does much better than either a purely extensive strategy of analyzing X, Y in 1,600 cases or a purely intensive strategy of process tracing all 100 cases, for estimating both the ATE and the probability of positive causation.

14.3 Factoring in the Cost of Data

We can also use these results to think through optimal allocations of resources with varying prices for breadth and depth. To illustrate, consider the unrestricted chain model, where we see similar expected posterior variance for the probability of positive causation query from the following three combinations of wide and deep (first column, third row in Figure 14.2):

1. Maximally wide: 1,600 wide + 0 deep
2. Maximally deep: 100 wide + 100 deep
3. Mixed: 400 wide + 50 deep

Which strategy is optimal will depend on the relative cost of collecting X, Y data for a new case (which we normalize to a cost of 1) and collecting M for an existing case (at cost d per observation).

For this model-query combination, the widest strategy is better than the deepest strategy if and only if $1,600 < 100 + 100d$, that is, when $d > 15$. The mixed strategy is better than the maximally deep strategy if and only if $400 + 50d < 100 + 100d$, that is when $d > 6$. And the maximally wide strategy is better than the mixed strategy if and only if $1,600 < 400 + 50d$, or $d > 24$. Thus, roughly speaking, if $d < 6$, then our ordering is deepest > mixed > widest; if $6 < d < 15$, our ordering is mixed > deepest > widest; if $15 < d < 24$, our ordering is mixed > widest > deepest; and if $d > 24$, our preference-ordering is widest > mixed > deepest. We can, thus, see that the mixed strategy is optimal across a broad range of d, though for sufficiently cheap or expensive within-case data gathering, it may be optimal to go purely wide or purely deep.

14.4 Conclusion

As we found in our analysis of case selection in Chapter 13, the merits of different combinations of breadth and depth depend on the query we are trying to answer and the model we are working with. And as for case selection, the approach that we propose to make the wide-versus-deep tradeoff is one that can take account of both the expected learning and the costs of different options.

While the scope for general rules of thumb is limited, one striking pattern that we tend to see, across simulations, is diminishing marginal returns to both going wider and going deeper. This suggests that optimal strategies will likely involve some level of mixing of the two approaches. There are, however, certain extreme situations in which optimal strategies involve either maximizing going wide or maximizing going deep. A striking example is the two-path model (with possibly direct effects of X on Y and effects passing through M). For the simple ATE, the gains under this model all arise from going wide; whereas, for determining whether effects passed through M, all the gains arise from going deep. Again, the main lesson remains the same: The benefits of any given research design will depend on what kind of question we are posing to what kind of model.

Part IV

Models in Question

15 Justifying Models

We outline strategies for justifying models on the basis of prior data and thus empirically grounding beliefs about the probative value of clues.

The approaches to inference that we have described always involve updating beliefs given data and a model. So to get going, you need to start with a model of some form.

We see two broad responses to this problem.

One is to emphasize the model-contingent nature of claims. Some causal models might reasonably reflect actual beliefs about the world – for example, one might be convinced that treatment was randomly assigned, that there is no interference, and that units are independently sampled. All of these beliefs may be unwise, of course. But if held, then a simple model such as that represented by an $X \rightarrow Y$ DAG is more a representation of beliefs about a simple process in the world than a model *of* the world, in the sense of a simplified representation.[1] Recognizing that we are generally dealing with models that we do not really believe results in a reposing of the question: The question becomes not whether the assumptions are correct but whether the model is useful for some purpose (Clarke and Primo, 2012). The next chapter expands upon this idea.

A second approach is to seek to justify a model empirically. We describe such approaches to empirical model justification in this chapter. We take up the problem in two steps. First, we focus on process tracing and ask whether and when, given a causal structure, we can empirically derive the probative value of clues. Second, we briefly summarize an approach to discovering causal structures, the key input for both process tracing, and mixed-method inference.

---

[1] Even in this simple case there are ways in which the representation is a model, not least the coding of events as a variable involves a form of modeling.

15.1 Justifying Probative Value

The problem of justifying assumptions is acute for case-level process-tracing inferences, for two reasons. First, the beliefs that come into play in generating probative value for our clues are beliefs over the distribution of *individual-level* effects, not just beliefs over average effects. We need beliefs, for instance, about the probability of seeing some clue, K, in a given case if $X = 1$ causes $Y = 1$ in the case. This puts us up against the fundamental problem of causal inference (Holland, 1986). Second, in single-case inference, we have limited opportunity to learn about our model from the case at hand; so the beliefs we go in with are critical. Indeed, for case-level queries, inferences might be little more than conditional applications of a model.[2]

The question we pursue in this chapter is whether and under what conditions we can empirically justify those beliefs that yield probative value for our clues.[3]

15.1.1 Nothing from Nothing

We start with a discouraging result. Many of the models we have looked at – especially for process tracing – include a good deal of structure. Assumptions might include:

- conditional-independence assumptions
- assumptions of no confounding
- monotonicity assumptions or other restrictions such as no interactions

What happens if we make none of these assumptions? One way to think about this question is: Can we start with a DAG that makes none of these assumptions and then use observational data – that is, learn from those data – to render clues informative about causal effects?

Suppose that we would like to be able to learn from a candidate clue, a node M that is possibly a mediator or perhaps a moderator in the sense that it is realized after some explanatory variable X and before some outcome variable Y. We work through this problem under favorable conditions, a world in which in fact (though unknown *ex ante* to the researcher):

---

[2] Though it is certainly possible to learn from a single case that the model itself is wrong – for example, if events are observed that are assigned 0 probability under a model.

[3] The question was already addressed in Chapters 9 and 10; here, we gather together some particularly sharp positive and negative results.

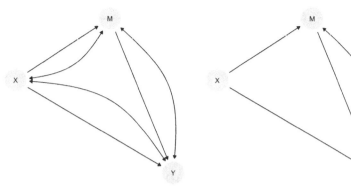

Figure 15.1 Two models. The model on the right might be justified if X is known to be randomized

- X causes Y through M
- X is a necessary condition for M, and M is a sufficient condition for Y – and so Y is monotonic in X and
- there is no confounding

We also assume that we have access to large amounts of observational data on X, M, and Y.

We work through inferences for two types of models in which X can have both indirect and direct effects on Y (Figure 15.1). We impose no restrictions on nodal types in either model. Even though there are only three nodes, Model 1 has 128 causal types ($2 \times 4 \times 16$). In addition:

- In Model 1 we allow confounding between all pairs of nodes. This results in 127 free parameters.
- In Model 2 we assume that X is known to be ("as if") randomized, but we still allow for confounding between M and Y. There are now only 64 free parameters.

We generate data from the true model and then update Model 1 and Model 2. Then we query the models to see how case-level inferences depend on M. The results are shown in Figure 15.2. The query of interest is whether X caused Y in an $X = 1$, $Y = 1$ case. We can inspect the figure to determine whether M is now informative about this query under trained versions of Model 1 and Model 2.

We find that even with an auspicious monotonic data-generating process in which M is a total mediator, M gives no traction on causal inference under

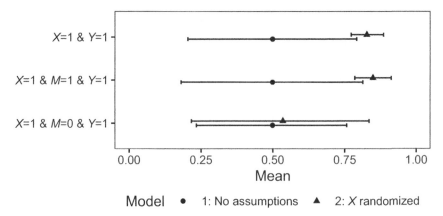

Figure 15.2 Can updating our models on large-*N* data render *M* informative? Model 1: No knowledge of structure; Model 2: *X* known to be randomized. Error bars show 95% credibility intervals

Model 1 – our beliefs have wide variance and are essentially unresponsive to *M*. In contrast, when *X* is known to be randomized, as in Model 2, we have tight posteriors, and *M* gives considerable leverage. If we observe $M = 0$, we would downgrade confidence that *X* caused *Y*.

This example nicely illustrates the Cartwright's (1989) idea of "no causes in, no causes out." We also think it poses a challenge to any process-tracing exercise that aspires to model-independence: observational data alone are not sufficient to generate a justification for process-tracing inferences for three-node problems even when in reality causal structures are simple.

15.1.2 Justifying the Classic Process-Tracing Tests

Now, on a more encouraging note, we show the possibility of justification of each of the four classical "qualitative tests" described by Collier (2011) and drawing on Van Evera (1997), at least when treatment assignment is as-if randomized.

Recall that the four tests are "smoking gun" tests, "hoop" tests, "doubly-decisive" tests, and "straw-in-the-wind" tests. A hoop test is one which, if failed, bodes especially badly for a claim; a smoking gun test is one that bodes especially well for a hypothesis if passed; a doubly-decisive test is strongly conclusive no matter what is found; and a straw-in-the-wind test is suggestive, though not conclusive, either way. Of course, Bayesian inference involves continuous probabilities, not discrete test categories, but we speak to these categories for heuristic purposes.

The key point is that probative value for case-level inference can be derived from data in which randomization of a causal variable can be assumed. Deriving probative value from data contrasts with approaches in which researchers are meant to have more or less direct knowledge of the priors and likelihoods.

In Humphreys and Jacobs (2015), for instance, formalization involves specifying (a) a prior that a hypothesis is true and, *independently* of that (b) a set of beliefs about the probability of seeing a given data pattern if the hypothesis is true and if it is false. Updating then proceeds using Bayes' rule. However, this simple approach suffers from two related weaknesses. First, there is no good reason to expect these probabilities to be independent. Our prior beliefs about the hypotheses constitute beliefs about *how the world works*, and beliefs about how the world works should have implications for the conditions under which clues are likely to be observed. Second, there is nothing in the setup to indicate how beliefs about the probative value of clues should be established or justified.

Both of these problems are resolvable in the context of inference from fully specified causal models. We illustrate first by using an idealized example to show that a case-level "doubly-decisive" test can be justified by population-level data from factorial experimental designs (see also our discussion in Chapter 5); we then generalize to all four tests.

Suppose that we have observed experimental data on just X and Y across a large set of cases, allowing us to infer that $\Pr(Y = 1|X = 1) = \Pr(Y = 1|X = 0) = .5$. Here, we have an average treatment effect of 0. But suppose, further, that our query is whether $X = 1$ caused $Y = 1$ in a particular case with $X = 1, Y = 1$. The marginal distributions we have observed so far are consistent with a world in which X never affects Y. But less obviously, they are also consistent with a world in which X always affects Y (sometimes negatively, sometimes positively). And they are also consistent with many possibilities in between these extremes.

Now let's say that we have lots of data on a third variable, K, and find (a) that $K = 1$ arises with 50% probability and (b) that the marginal distributions of Y given X and K are as follows:

- $\Pr(Y = 1|X = 0, K = 0) = 1$
- $\Pr(Y = 1|X = 1, K = 0) = .5$
- $\Pr(Y = 1|X = 0, K = 1) = 0$
- $\Pr(Y = 1|X = 1, K = 1) = .5$

Table 15.1 Known probabilities from a model with $X \to Y \leftarrow K$ justifying classic test types for clue K given $X = Y = 1$

	Doubly decisive	Hoop	Smoking gun	Straw-in-the-wind
$\Pr(K = 1)$	$\frac{1}{2}$	$\frac{9}{10}$	$\frac{1}{10}$	$\frac{1}{2}$
$\Pr(Y = 1 \mid X = 0, K = 0)$	1	1	$\frac{1}{3}$	$\frac{1}{2}$
$\Pr(Y = 1 \mid X = 1, K = 0)$	$\frac{1}{2}$	$\frac{1}{2}$	$\frac{2}{3}$	$\frac{3}{4}$
$\Pr(Y = 1 \mid X = 0, K = 1)$	0	$\frac{1}{3}$	0	$\frac{1}{4}$
$\Pr(Y = 1 \mid X = 1, K = 1)$	$\frac{1}{2}$	$\frac{2}{3}$	$\frac{1}{2}$	$\frac{3}{4}$
$\Pr(X \text{ causes } Y \mid K = 0)$	0	0	$\left[\frac{1}{2}, 1\right]$	$\left[\frac{1}{3}, \frac{2}{3}\right]$
$\Pr(X \text{ causes } Y \mid K = 1)$	1	$\left[\frac{1}{2}, 1\right]$	1	$\left[\frac{2}{3}, 1\right]$

We thus see that, in cases in which $K = 1$, $X = 1$ is a necessary condition for $Y = 1$. So if $K = 1$, then $X = 1$ certainly caused $Y = 1$ (since, in that case, were X zero, then Y would certainly be 0). On the other hand, were $K = 0$, then $X = 0$ would be a sufficient condition for $Y = 1$, which means that in this case, $X = 1$ most certainly did *not* cause $Y = 1$. We have then that, if $K = 1$, then certainly $X = 1$ caused $Y = 1$, whereas if $K = 0$, then certainly $X = 1$ did not cause $Y = 1$.

This example demonstrates it is, in principle, possible to justify a doubly-decisive test on the basis of infinite experimental data – provided that the case about which we seek to make inferences can be considered exchangeable with (that is, we have no reason to think it works differently from) the cases in the experimental data.

Table 15.1 shows how this logic generalizes to different types of tests. For each test, we first show the inferences from the data available to us (first five rows); we then show the inferences on whether $X = 1$ causes $Y = 1$ in cases where $X = 1$ and $Y = 1$ as a function of K.

Note that some entries in Table 15.1 appear as ranges. This reflects the fact that, unless we are at edge cases, the estimand here is not identified even with infinite experimental data. In practice, we expect never to be at these edges. However, despite not being identified, bounds can be placed on causal quantities. For instance, for the hoop test, when $K = 1$, the bounds are $[.5, 1]$. The reason that the probability of causation here cannot be *less* than 0.5 is that:

1. We can see from the distribution of Y given X when $K = 1$ that X has a positive effect on Y at least one third of the time (the average effect is one third, and so there is a positive effect for at least one third of units; indeed,

Table 15.2 Classic tests with probative value inferred from (simulated) data, for query: Does X have a positive effect on Y in this case (given K)?

Given	Straw-in-the-wind	Hoop	Smoking gun	Doubly decisive
–	0.483	0.474	0.536	0.490
$K=0$	0.312	0.042	0.488	0.009
$K=1$	0.638	0.523	0.907	0.976

it is possible that there is a positive effect for 2/3 of units and a negative effect for the remaining 1/3).

2. We can see that in two thirds of cases $Y = 1$ when $X = 1, K = 1$.
3. So at *least* half of these cases in which $Y = 1$ when $X = 1, K = 1$ are cases for which $Y = 1$ *because* $X = 1$.

In these examples, the fact that queries are not point-identified with infinite data does not detract from the fact that K is informative in the ways associated with the different types of tests.

So much for infinite data. Is it possible to justify classic tests with inferences on finite data starting with flat priors? Using the procedures given in Chapter 9, the results in Table 15.2 show that it is. For these results, we imagine four different data-generating $X \rightarrow Y \leftarrow K$ models. The models vary in the amount of weight they accord to three different nodal types for Y – as well as in λ^K. We then simulate 1,000 observations from each model and update an agnostic $X \rightarrow Y \leftarrow K$ model.

In particular, for the doubly-decisive test, we generate the data from a model in which all units have nodal type $\theta^Y = \theta^Y_{0001}$, and so the presence of K is necessary and sufficient to render X causal for Y. For hoop tests, we generate data from a model in which there are also θ^Y_{0101} nodal types: that is, cases in which K matters but X does not. Given these cases, observation of $K = 0$ guarantees that X does not matter, but observation of $K = 1$ does not guarantee that X does matter. To generate smoking gun tests, our data-generating model has a distribution over θ^Y_{0001} and θ^Y_{0011} types – in which X always matters when $K = 1$ but *might* not matter when $X = 0$. For straw-in-the-wind tests, we imagine a distribution over all three types.

In Table 15.2, we show the inferences we would now draw from observing $K = 1$ versus $K = 0$ in a single case, based on updating a model that has no restrictions and flat priors over all nodal types. The query is whether X has a positive effect on Y in a given case. Each column-labeled with the classic test names – represents our beliefs about K's probative value as derived from data generated by the four models we described above. These indeed conform to expectations. In the "hoop test" column, we see that (having updated based on data from one of the four data-generating models), we have formed beliefs such that observing $K = 1$ in a case slightly boosts our confidence that X has a positive effect on Y, while observing $K = 0$ dramatically undermines our confidence in such an effect. In the smoking gun column, we see that (having updated based on data from another one of the four data-generating models) we have formed beliefs such that observing $K = 1$ in a case greatly boosts our confidence that X has a positive effect on Y, while observing $K = 0$ slightly undermines our confidence in such an effect.

We underline that we have here *derived* the probative value of the clue from observed data and a model that was entirely agnostic about the clue's probative value (but which did assume *some* priors on causal types). In particular, the model that we start with has no restrictions on Y's nodal types, has flat beliefs over the distribution of K, and imposes no assumption that K is informative for how Y responds to X. It does, however, assume that X and K are unconfounded root nodes, as might be the case if these were experimentally manipulated.

For both of these examples, we have focused on moderators as clues. For results on mediators as clues, see Dawid et al. (2022), which establishes that mediators in chain models can produce hoop tests but are generally unable to generate smoking gun tests.

This approach to thinking about process-tracing tests is quite different from that described in existing (including Bayesian) treatments such as Collier (2011), Bennett (2015), Fairfield and Charman (2017), or Humphreys and Jacobs (2015). Rather than having a belief about the probative value of a clue, and a prior over a hypothesis, inferences are drawn directly from a causal model that embeds a clue in a network of possible causal effects. Critically, with this approach, the inferences made from observing clues can be justified by referencing a more fundamental, relatively agnostic model, that has been updated in light of data. The updated model yields a prior over the proposition, beliefs about probative values, and guidance for what conclusions to draw given knowledge of K.

15.2 Empirical Discovery of Causal Structure

In the preceding discussion of learning about probative value for process tracing, we have taken causal structure – the DAG itself – as given. Moreover, even when we are engaged in mixed-data inference on multiple cases – where we can start with *only* the DAG – we still need to start with some causal structure. Where does knowledge of causal structure come from?

One approach is to treat causal structure as just one more level in our multi-tiered hierarchy of models. We can entertain multiple models and specify priors over the causal structure. One could, for instance, have beliefs over two causal models that are mutually incompatible because arrows between two nodes point in opposite directions. In this case, uncertainty reflects uncertainty over models but learning involves not just updating model parameters but also updating over model structure.

This is a perfectly coherent approach but given the complexity of inferences *conditional on* a causal structure, we do not pursue this strategy further here. Instead, we briefly describe approaches to "causal discovery" – strategies to derive causal structures from data.

The empirical discovery of causal structure is a very large field of inquiry, and we cannot do it justice here. For a review, see Glymour et al. (2019). We seek, rather, to illustrate the possibility of causal discovery.

To do so, we demonstrate three situations in which there is a true – but unknown model – relating X, M, and Y to each other. Critically, we assume that there are no unobserved confounding relations (this is a requirement for the "PC" algorithm but not for the "Fast Causal Inference" algorithm). In each situation, we show the true relationship and the "skeleton" of the model as discovered by a prominent technique that uses a "constraint-based algorithm" – examining whether observed data correlations are consistent with one or another set of conditional-independence relations.

In Figure 15.3, we represent the true models from which simulated data are generated. The objective is then to see how much of this true causal structure the discovery algorithm can recover from the data. In the first true model, X affects Y directly and indirectly through M. In the second model, Y has two causes that do not influence each other. Finally, in the third model, X causes Y through M but not directly. When we simulate data from these models, we assume monotonicity but otherwise a flat distribution over nodal types. As noted, we also assume no confounding: There is nothing not represented on the graph that affects more than one node.

In Figure 15.4, we show the structures that we recover. In all situations, we correctly recover the skeleton: which nodes are connected to which nodes. Note that, for any link where we have an "o" on both ends of the link, we do not know in which direction causal effects flow.

In the first situation, the skeleton is unrestricted: We have correctly *not* excluded links between any two nodes, but we have not learned about the

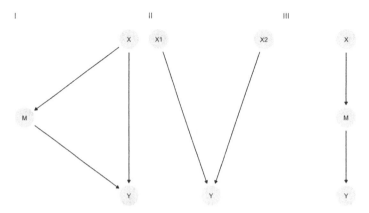

Figure 15.3   DAGs from three structural causal models

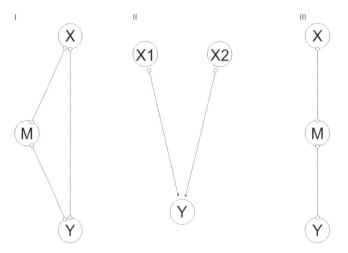

Figure 15.4   (Partially) recovered DAGs from data. Circles indicate uncertainty regarding whether an arrow starts or ends at a given point

directions of effects. In the second situation, however, we have fully recovered the causal structure. Thus, the algorithm has figured out that X_1 and X_2 are not children of Y. The algorithm sees, in essence, data patterns that are distinctively associated with colliders: X_1 and X_2 correlated conditional on Y but not otherwise. In the last setup, we have not figured out the direction of the causal arrows, but the inference is still rather impressive. Although X, M, and Y are all correlated with each other, the algorithm has figured out that there should be no direct link between X and Y – by observing that X and M are not correlated with each other *conditional* on M.

Note also that, in all three situations, if we have access to all relevant variables, the true graph can be recovered with additional knowledge of the temporal ordering of the variables.

The assumption that we have captured all nodes that might generate confounding is critical to these results. Yet these examples provide grounds for hope that causal models can be discovered and not simply assumed. If all relevant nodes are known and measured – a tall order for sure – causal structures can be identified from data.

We have shown that the models used for both process tracing and mixed-methods inference can be constructed from weaker models. This provides some defense against concerns that these approaches require assuming models that cannot be justified. In both cases, however, we also see that justification is not easy, sometimes not possible, and itself requires assumptions, albeit weaker ones.

16 Evaluating Models

We describe strategies for figuring out whether a model is likely doing more harm than good and for comparing the performance of different models to one another.

Throughout this book, we have maintained the conceit that you believe your model. But it is also obvious that even the most nonparametric-seeming models depend on substantive assumptions and that these are almost certainly wrong. The question then is not how much you believe your model (or whether you really believe what you say you believe) but whether your model is useful in some sense. How can we evaluate the usefulness of our models?

16.1 Four Strategies

In this chapter, we will describe four strategies and show them at work for a running example in which we know a model poorly captures an assumed causal process. We will then turn the four strategies loose on the two models that we examined in Chapters 8 and 10.

Here's our running example. Imagine a true causal process involving X, M, and Y. Say that X affects Y *directly*, M never has a negative effect on Y, and X has no effect on M (and so there is no indirect effect of X on Y) via M. But imagine that researchers wrongly suppose that the effect of X on Y runs entirely through M, positing a model of the form $X \rightarrow M \rightarrow Y$.

The problem with the posited model, then, is that it represents overly strong beliefs about independence relations: It does not allow for a direct effect that is in fact operating.

We are perfectly able to update using this too-strong $X \rightarrow M \rightarrow Y$ model and data – but the updated model can produce wildly misleading causal

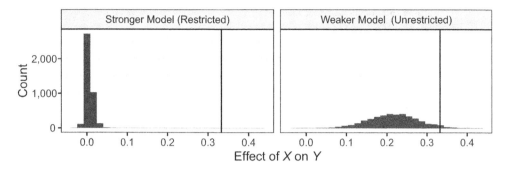

Figure 16.1 A restricted model yields a credibility interval that does not contain the actual average effect

inferences. We show this using a set of 200 observations simulated from a model that has direct effects only and an average effect of X on Y of $1/3$.

In the left panel of Figure 16.1, we show the estimated average treatment effect of X on Y when using these data to update the $X \to M \to Y$ model. In the right panel, we show the inferences we would make using the same data but using a model that makes weaker assumptions by allowing for direct effects: an $X \to M \to Y \leftarrow X$ model. With both models, we start with flat priors over nodal types.

We represent the (stipulated) true average effect with the vertical line in each graph.

As we can see, the weaker (i.e., more permissive) model performs alright: The true effect falls within the posterior distribution on the ATE. However, the stronger model, which excludes direct effects, generates a tight posterior distribution that essentially excludes the right answer. So, if we go into the analysis with the stronger model, we have a problem.

But can we *know* we have a problem?

In the remainder of this section, we explore a range of diagnostics that researchers can undertake to evaluate the usefulness of their models or to compare models with one another: checking assumptions of conditional independence built into a model; checking the model's fit; using "leave-one-out" cross-validation; and assessing model sensitivity.

16.1.1 Check Conditional Independence

First, even before engaging in updating, we can look to see whether the data we have are consistent with the causal model we postulate. In particular, we can check whether there are inconsistencies with the Markov condition that

Table 16.1 Regression coefficient on
X given $M = 0$ and $M = 1$

M	Estimate	Std error	p-value
0	0.359	0.088	0.000
1	0.163	0.108	0.134

we introduced in Chapter 2: that every node is *conditionally independent* of its nondescendants, given its parents.

In this case, if the stronger model is right, then given M, Y should be independent of X.

Is it?

One way to check is to assess the covariance of X and Y given M in the data. Specifically, we regress Y on X for each value of M, once for $M = 1$ and again for $M = 0$; a correlation between X and Y at either value of M would be problematic for the conditional independence assumption embedded in the stronger model.

Note that this form of diagnostic test is a classical one in the frequentist sense: We start by hypothesizing that our model is correct and then ask whether the data were unlikely given the model.

We report the regression coefficients on X in Table 16.1. It is immediately apparent that we have a problem. At both values of M, and especially when $M = 0$, there is a strong correlation between X and Y, evidence of a violation of the Markov condition implied by the stronger model.[1]

Identifying the full set of conditional independence assumptions in a causal model can be difficult. There are however well developed algorithms for identifying what sets, if any, we need to conditional on to ensure conditional independence between two nodes given a DAG.[2]

16.1.2 Bayesian p-Value: Are the Data Unexpected Given Your Model?

A second – though clearly related – approach asks whether features of the data we observe are in some sense unusual given our updated model.

---

[1] In applying the Markov condition, we also need to take into account any unobserved confounding. For instance, suppose that there was an unobserved confounder of the relationship between M and Y in the $X \to M \to Y$ model. Then, we would *not* expect Y to be independent of X conditional on M. In this case M acts as a collider between X and another unobserved cause of Y; so conditioning on M introduces a correlation between X and this unobserved cause, and thus between X and Y.

[2] R users can quickly access such results using the `impliedConditionalIndependencies` function in the `dagitty` package.

This approach is also quite classical: We are looking to see whether we should "reject" our model in light of inconsistencies between the data we have and the data we expect to see given our updated model. The idea is not to figure out whether the model is false – we know it is – but whether it is unacceptably inconsistent with data patterns in the world (Gelman, 2013).

An approach for doing this using simulated data from the posterior predictive distribution is described in Gabry et al. (2019).[3] The basic procedure we employ here is to:

1. Draw a parameter vector from the posterior,
2. Draw data using the parameter vector.
3. Calculate a test statistic using these data.
4. Repeat 1–3 to build up a distribution of test statistics.
5. Calculate the same test statistic using the real data (the observed statistic).
6. Assess how extreme the observed statistic is relative to the distribution of statistics generated from the posterior (e.g., the probability of getting a test statistic as large or larger than the observed statistic).

Note that in this straightforward calculation, we assess the probability of the data given the same model that generated the data; approaches could also be used that seek out-of-sample estimates of the probability of observing the observed data.

We note that the p-values generated in this way are not necessarily "calibrated" in the sense that given a true vector θ, the distribution of the p-value is not uniform (Bayarri and Berger, 2000).[4] It nevertheless gives an indication of whether the data are unusual given our model. As an illustration, imagine a simple $X \rightarrow Y$ model and imagine that in truth the effect of X on Y were 1. Say we observe N cases in which X and Y are indeed perfectly correlated; we update our model and then draw data from this updated model. What are the chances that the data we draw would also be perfectly correlated, like the data we put into the model? In fact, surprisingly, the answer is "low," and, moreover *how* low depends on N. See this result plotted in Figure 16.2. In other words, the extreme data we see can seem extreme to us – even after we have updated using the right model and extreme data.

Returning to our running example, we consider two test statistics and compare performance for the stronger and weaker model (Figure 16.3). First, we

---

[3] Tools in the bayesplot package can be used to show how typical the data we observe is for different models.

[4] A uniform distribution has the property that the probability of getting a value of p or less under the model is p.

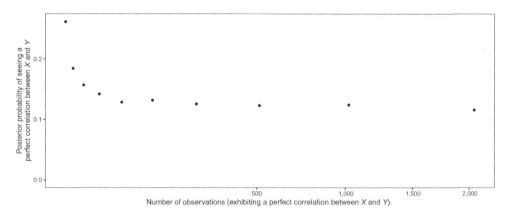

Figure 16.2 Bayesian p-values are not calibrated

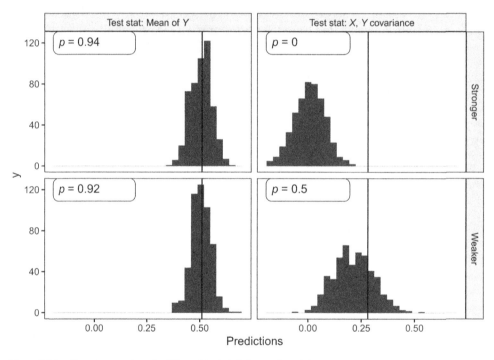

Figure 16.3 Bayesian p-values for different test statistics and models

look just at the distribution of the outcome Y to see how the actual distribution in the data compares to the predicted distribution from the updated model. Second, we look at the actual correlation between X and Y and see how this compares to the predicted distribution. In both cases we calculate a two-sided p-value by assessing the chances of such an extreme outcome as what we observe. If the observed data were at the mean of the predictive distribution, then we would have a p-value of 1. If they were at the 95th percentile (and the distribution of test statistics under the model were symmetric), we would have a p-value of 0.10.

For the first test, we see that the predicted distribution of the outcome Y is similar for both updated models; and the actual mean outcome is within the distribution of predicted mean outcomes. The p-values for the stronger (0.94) and weaker models (0.92) suggest that the observed mean Y value is not unusual for either model. No clues there. This is a fairly "easy" test in the sense that many models should have little difficulty producing a reasonable distribution for Y even if they are problematic in other ways.

When it comes to the correlation between X and Y, however, the two models perform very differently. The posterior predictive distribution from the stronger model is centered around a 0 correlation and does not even extend out as far as the observed correlation. The resulting p-value is 0, meaning that from the perspective of the stronger model the X, Y correlation in the data is entirely unexpected. A frequentist looking at the observed correlation between X and Y should feel comfortable rejecting the stronger model. The updated weaker model, in contrast, predicts a strong correlation, and the observed correlation is comfortably within the posterior predictive distribution, with a p-value of 0.5.

At first blush, the abysmal performance of the stronger model may seem surprising. Even after this model has *seen* the X, Y correlations in the data, the model still finds those correlations highly surprising. The $X \rightarrow M \rightarrow Y$ model fails to learn, however, because the strong assumptions on independence do not provide the flexibility it needs to capture the complex relations between X, M, and Y. The problem is that M is uncorrelated with X in the true data-generating process, so the stronger model learns that there is no indirect effect. But, at the same time, this model does not *allow* for a direct effect. Despite what would seem to be overwhelming evidence of a systematic X, Y correlation, a causal relationship connecting X to Y remains extremely unlikely given the X, M data pattern and the impossibility of direct effects. The stronger model just can't handle the truth. The weaker model, on the other hand, readily learns about the direct $X \rightarrow Y$ effect.

16.1.3 Leave-One-Out Likelihoods

A further class of model-validation methods involves cross-validation. Rather than asking how well the updated model predicts the data used to update it, cross-validation uses the data at hand to estimate how well the model is likely to predict new data that have not yet been seen.

One way to do this is to split the available data, using one subsample to update and then assessing predictions using the other subsample. We focus here, however, on a "leave-one-out" (LOO) approach that uses *all* of the available data to estimate out-of-sample predictive performance.

In the LOO approach, we update the model using all data points except for one and then ask how well the model performs in predicting the left-out observation. We repeat this for every data point in the dataset to assess how well we can predict the entire dataset.

Often, the LOO approach is used to predict a particular outcome variable. We, however, are interested in predictions over the joint realization of all nodes. Thus, we calculate the posterior probability of each data point, using the model updated with all of the other observations.

The LOO estimate of out-of-sample predictive fit, for a dataset with n observations, is then:

$$\prod_{1}^{n} p(y_i | y_{-i}, \text{model})$$

where y_{-i} is the data pattern with observation y_i left out, and y_i represents the values of all nodes of interest for observation i.

We implement LOO cross-validation of the stronger and weaker models using 200 observations generated from the same data-generating model employed above. We find that the LOO likelihood of the data under the stronger model is 4.12e-183 while the likelihood is 7.14e-179 under the weaker model. Thus, the weaker model represents an estimated improvement in out-of-sample prediction on the order of 1.73e+04.[5]

We can visualize the pattern in Figure 16.4, where we plot the likelihood of each possible data type under the stronger model against the likelihood of that data type under the weaker model. The distribution is much more compressed on the horizontal axis than on the vertical axis indicating how the stronger model is not able to differentiate as much across the data types as the weaker.

---

[5] These numbers (and later numbers) change from simulation to simulation based on the particular data we draw from the model.

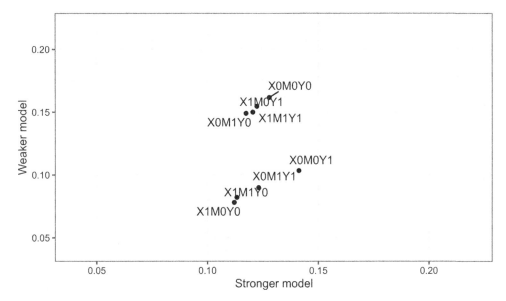

Figure 16.4   LOO likelihoods for different models

Notably, the stronger model is not able to "learn" from the data about the (*in fact*, operative) relationship between X and Y. The positive correlation arises because both models have "learned" from chance correlations in the data that different X, M combinations are differentially likely. The weaker model, however, also suceeds in dividing the data types into two groups: those with a positive X, Y correlation and those with a negative X, Y correlation and has correctly (given the true model) learned that the former is more likely than the latter. The stronger model is not sucessful in separating these sets out in this way.

In Figure 16.5, we then see how the likelihoods of each data type line up with the actual count of each data type. As we can see, the weaker model updates to likelihoods that fit the actual data pattern well while the stronger model does not; in particular the stronger model underpredicts cases that are on the diagonal and over-predicts cases that are off it.

We can also turn the tables and imagine that the *stronger* model represents the true data-generating process. We implement LOO cross-validation of the two models using 200 data points generated from the stronger model. In Figure 16.6, we see a comparison of the likelihoods of the data types under the two updated models and note that they are extremely similar. This represents an important asymmetry: the model that makes weaker

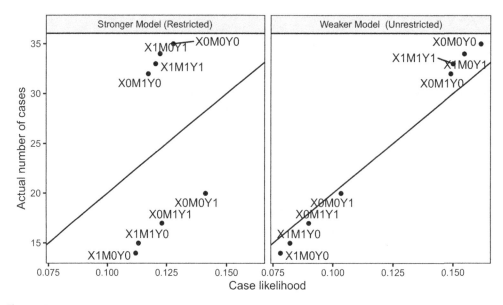

Figure 16.5 LOO likelihoods and data type counts for the stronger and weaker models

assumptions performs far better in handling data generated by a "stronger" true model than does the stronger model in learning about a process that violates one of its assumptions. Since the weaker model allows for both direct and indirect effects, the weaker *can* learn about the parameters of the true process in the first situation; but the strong model cannot do so in the second situation because it has by assumption ruled out a key feature of that process (the direct effect).

While it is difficult to see this in Figure 16.6, the stronger model performs better here than the weaker model. The likelihood of the data under the stronger model is now 1.25e–120, compared to the likelihood of 8.38e–126 under the weaker model. Thus, the weaker model represents an estimated loss to out-of-sample prediction on the order of 6.69e–06. This is not surprising insofar as the stronger model *precisely* models the data-generating process while the extra parameters in the weaker model allow for "learning" from chance features of the data.

These examples display features of out-of-sample prediction accuracy familiar from a regression context. In a regression framework, adding parameters to a model may improve fit to sample – generating gains to out-of-sample prediction accuracy when the new parameters pick up systematic features of the data-generating process – but run a risk of over-fitting to

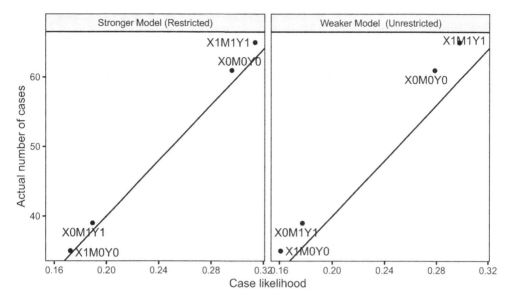

Figure 16.6   Data prediction of a restricted and unrestricted model when in fact the data are generated by the unrestricted (stronger) model

chance patterns in the data. Similarly in a causal models framework for a model with weaker assumptions and more parameters. We saw that the weaker model performed much better when the true process involved direct effects since the extra parameters, allowing for direct effects, captured something "real" going on. But the same model performed slightly worse than the stronger model when there were no direct effects to pick up, such that the extra parameter could only model noise.

16.1.4 Sensitivity

The last approach we consider brackets the question of which model is better and asks, instead: How much do your conclusions depend on the model? You can worry less about your assumptions if the conclusions are not strongly dependent on them.

For the running example, we already saw in Figure 16.1 that conclusions can depend dramatically on the model used. This alone is reason to be worried.

To illustrate how to think about sensitivity for a process-tracing example, consider a situation in which we are unsure about posited parameter values: that is, about the probability of particular effects at particular nodes.

Table 16.2 Inferences on the probability that X caused Y upon seeing $M = 0$ or $M = 1$ for a range of possible values of λ_{10}^Y

λ_{10}^Y	Prior	$M = 0$	$M = 1$
0.00	0.167	0.000	0.25
0.05	0.183	0.068	0.25
0.10	0.200	0.125	0.25
0.15	0.217	0.173	0.25
0.20	0.233	0.214	0.25
0.25	0.250	0.250	0.25

It is likely to be the case in many research situations that we are considerably uncertain about how to quantify intuitive or theoretically informed beliefs about the relative likelihood of different effects.

Suppose, for instance, that we begin with an $X \rightarrow M \rightarrow Y$ model. And suppose, further, that we believe that it is unlikely that M has an adverse effect on Y. But we are not sure *how* unlikely that adverse effect is. (We assume all other nodal types are equally likely.) Finally, say that we want to use the observation of M to draw an inference about whether $X = 1$ caused $Y = 1$ in an $X = Y = 1$ case.

How much does our inference regarding X's effect on Y – when we see $M = 0$ or $M = 1$ – depend on this second stage assumption about the probability of a negative $M \rightarrow Y$ effect?

We answer the question by looking at posterior beliefs for a range of possible values for the relevant parameter, λ_{10}^Y. In Table 16.2, we examine a range of values for λ_{10}^Y, from 0 to 0.25. For each parameter value, we first show the resulting prior belief about the probability that $X = 1$ caused $Y = 1$. We can see that, before we observe M, we think that a positive $X \rightarrow Y$ effect is more likely as a negative $M \rightarrow Y$ effect becomes more likely. This stands to reason since a negative second-stage effect is one possible process through which a positive $X \rightarrow Y$ effect might occur. And higher values for λ_{10}^Y come disproportionately at the expense of types under which X cannot affect Y.[6]

In the next two columns, we show the posterior belief we arrive at when we observe $M = 0$ and then $M = 1$, for each λ_{10}^Y assumption. Looking at the last column first, we see that our inference from $M = 1$ does *not* depend at

---

[6] Increasing weight on λ_{10}^Y is drawn equally from λ_{00}^Y, λ_{11}^Y, and λ_{10}^Y, with the first two of these three representing null effects.

all on our beliefs about adverse $M \rightarrow Y$ effects. The reason is that, if we see $M = 1$, we already know that M did not have a negative effect on Y, given that we also know $Y = 1$. Our beliefs are purely a function of the probability that there are positive effects at both stages as compared to the probability of other causal types that could yield $X = M = Y = 1$, a comparison unaffected by the probability of a negative $M \rightarrow Y$ effect.

Our inferences when $M = 0$, on the other hand, do depend on λ_{10}^Y: When we see $M = 0$, our belief about a positive $X \rightarrow Y$ effect depends on the likelihood of *negative* effects at both stages. We see, then, that the likelier we think negative effects are at the second stage, the higher our posterior confidence in a positive $X \rightarrow Y$ effect when we see $M = 0$.

Even though our inferences given $M = 1$ do not depend on λ_{10}^Y, the amount that we *update* if we see $M = 1$ *does* depend on λ_{10}^Y. This is because λ_{10}^Y affects our belief, prior to seeing M, that $X = 1$ caused $Y = 1$. Working with a low λ_{10}^Y value, we start out less confident that $X = 1$ caused $Y = 1$, and thus our beliefs make a bigger jump if we do see $M = 1$ than if we had worked with a λ_{10}^Y higher value.

However, to the extent that we want to know how our assumptions affect our conclusions, the interesting feature of this illustration is that sensitivity depends on what we find. The answer to our query is sensitive to the λ_{10}^Y assumption if we find $M = 0$, but not if we find $M = 1$. It is also worth noting that, even if we observe $M = 0$, the sensitivity is limited across the range of parameter values tested. In particular, for all λ_{10}^Y values below parity (0.25), seeing $M = 0$ moves our beliefs *in the same direction.*

We can use the same basic approach to examine how our conclusions change if we relax assumptions about nodal-type restrictions, about confounds, or about causal structure.

We also note that, in cases in which we cannot quantify uncertainty about parameters, we might still be able to engage in a form of "qualitative inference." There is a literature on probabilistic causal models that assesses the scope for inferences when researchers provide ranges of plausible values for parameters (perhaps intervals, perhaps only signs (positive, negative, zero)), rather than specifying a probability distribution. For a comprehensive treatment of qualitative algebras, see Parsons (2001). Under this kind of approach, a researcher might willing to say that they think some probability p is not plausibly greater than 0.5, but unwilling to make a statement about their beliefs about where in the 0 to 0.5 range it lies. Such incomplete statements can be enough to rule out classes of conclusion.

16.2 Evaluating the Democracy–Inequality Model

We now turn to consider how well our model of democracy and inequality from Chapters 8 and 10 fares when put to these four tests.

16.2.1 Checking Assumptions of Conditional Independence

Our model presupposes that P and I are independent and that P and M are independent. Note that the model is consistent with the possibility that, conditional on D, there is a correlation between M and P or between I and P, as D acts as a collider for these pairs of nodes.

To test these assumptions, we in fact need to depart from the dataset drawn from Haggard et al. (2012) because these authors only examined cases in which $D = 1$, those that democratized. Thus, we cannot use these data to assess the relationships not conditional on D or conditional on $D = 0$. We generate observations on all four nodes for a broader set of cases by pulling together measures from multiple sources, with the aim of modeling democratization that occurred between 1990 and 2000.[7] We describe this data in more detail in Appendix.

We check some of the model's assumptions in relation to conditional independencies through a set of simple regression models, with results displayed in Table 16.3. In the first two rows, we examine the simple correlation between P and I and between P and M, respectively. We can see from the estimates in the first row that the data pattern is consistent with our assumption of unconditional independence of I and P. However, we also see that there *is* evidence of an unconditional correlation between P and M, something that is excluded by our model.

We can dig a little deeper, however. The model *also* implies that P should be independent of I given M. We test this assumption in rows 3 and 4 of the table, where we examine the conditional independence of P and I given $M = 0$ and given $M = 1$. Here, the evidence is also troubling for our model, as we see a relatively strong negative correlation between P and I when $M = 0$, and positive correlation when $M = 1$.

While we cannot identify the correct model from this data pattern, one possible explanation could be that pressure has a direct effect on mobilization, making mobilization the product of inequality and pressure jointly.[8] A

---

[7] The data that we use to measure mobilization, from Clark and Regan (2016), cover only the 1990s.

[8] There is, in fact, also a strong positive interaction between I and P in a linear model of M.

Table 16.3 Regression coefficients to assess conditional independence

Correlation	Given	Estimate	Std error	p-value
P, I	—	0.000	0.114	1.000
P, M	—	0.291	0.131	0.029
P, I	M == 0	−0.220	0.111	0.053
P, I	M == 1	0.467	0.260	0.098

model with an arrow running from P to M would make the model consistent with the unconditional correlation between these two variables, the conditional correlation between P and I given M (since M would now be a collider for I and P), as well as the unconditional independence of I and P. A possible way forward – which we do not pursue here – would be to now amend the model and evaluate the revised model against an independent set of data.

16.2.2 Bayesian p-Value

We turn next to evaluating the democratization model using the Bayesian p-value approach, and for this purpose can return to the data that we coded from Haggard et al. (2012)'s qualitative vignettes. In the two panels of Figure 16.7, we plot the posterior predictive distributions from our updated model for three quantities of interest: the outcome D, the correlation between I and M, and the correlation between I and D. In each graph, we indicate with a vertical line the mean value for these quantities for the data at hand and report the p-value: the probability of the observed data conditional on our model.

As we can see, both visually and from the p-values, the model performs well (or at least, does not signal issues) in the sense that the data that we observe are not unexpected under the model.

16.2.3 Leave-One-Out Likelihoods

Turning to "leave-one-out" model assessment, we now consider comparing our base model (the "restricted model") to two models that make weaker assumptions. In one (the "partially restricted" model), we drop the assumption of monotonicity of M in I. In a second alternative ("unrestricted model"), we make no monotonicity assumptions for any of the causal relations.

Figure 16.8 shows the relationship, for each model, of the likelihood of each data type against the number of cases of that data type in the data.

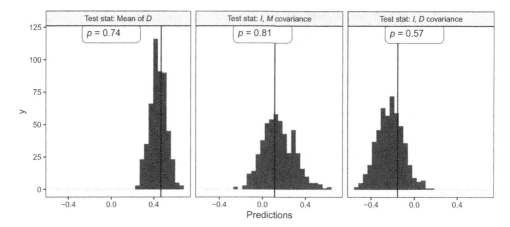

Figure 16.7   Three tests for the Inequality and Democracy model

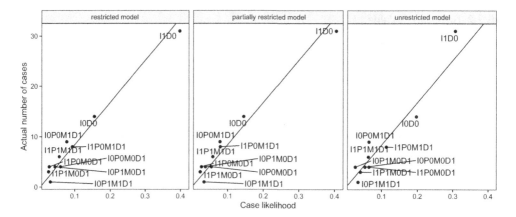

Figure 16.8   LOO data predictions for three versions of the Inequality and Democracy model

A data type here is defined as a possible combination of realized values on all nodes (I, P, M, and D). In each plot, the diagonal line represents equality between the proportion of expected cases under the model and the proportion of actual cases. Just eyeballing the relationships, you can see that the plots are very similar. The unrestricted model has, however, somewhat more compressed (and so, less sensitive) predictions. If we were to fit a line on the graphs we would have an adjusted R^2 of 0.92 for the unrestricted model and 0.97 and 0.98 for the partially restricted and unrestricted models, respectively.

More formally, we calculate the LOO likelihood for each model as 2.09e-73 for the restricted model, 2.69e-74 for the partially restricted model, and 9.16e-74 for the unrestricted model. In other words, we see that the most restricted model performs best on this criterion, though the differences between the models are not large.

16.2.4 Sensitivity to Priors

In our base model, we assume a set of monotonicity relations among nodes. How much do conclusions depend on these restrictions? We answer the question by comparing our conclusion with these restrictions to what we would conclude without this assumption. As above, we compare the fully restricted model to a partially restricted model and a fully unrestricted model.

We first show results for population inference from a mixed-methods analysis. As seen in Figure 16.9, our inferences regarding the overall effect of I on D are not very sensitive to the monotonicity assumption at M. However, they are extremely sensitive to the other monotonicity assumptions made in the model: As we can see, the effect goes from around -0.25 to 0 when we remove all restrictions.

Our unconditional inferences about the share of $I = 0, D = 1$ cases in which inequality mattered are not sensitive to the monotonicity assumptions. In particular, in cases with $I = 0, D = 1$ we are about equally likely to think that democratization was due to low inequality given any of the models. However, inferences conditional on M are highly sensitive to the restrictions. When we see that in fact there was no mobilization, our attribution increases in the restricted model but decreases in the unrestricted model. In the fully unrestricted model, our inferences are not affected at all by observation of $M = 0$.

Why is this? In the partially restricted model, we entertain the possibility that low inequality mattered not just directly but also, perhaps, by inducing protests. However, when we observe no protests, we rule out this possible pathway. In the restricted model, we do not think that democratization could have been produced by low inequality via demonstrations – but nevertheless entertain the possibility of mobilization that is *not* due to inequality, which could nevertheless be the cause of democratization. In this case, observing no mobilization removes a rival cause of democratization, not a second channel.

In all, we judge the conditional inferences as very sensitive to the monotonicity assumptions we put in place. Defending a particular set of claims requires a stronger defense of the model employed than would be needed if this were not the case.

We now consider a process tracing analysis in which we stipulate the probabilities of nodal types rather than learning about them from the data. For

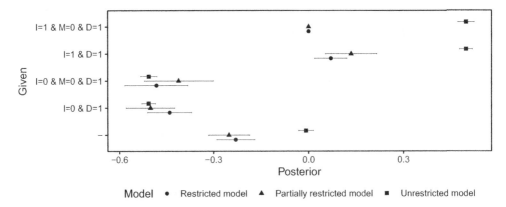

Figure 16.9   ATE of *I* on *D* for three models under different conditions

this setup, we compare our restricted model (M_1) to an alternative model (M_2) in which we allow for negative effects of *I* on *M*, but consider them to be *unlikely* rather than impossible (with null and positive effects somewhat likely). We refer to these priors as "quantitative priors" in the sense that they place a numerical value on beliefs rather than a logical restriction. Specifically, we define model M_2 with prior probabilities on the elements of θ^M as: $p(\theta^M = \theta^M_{10}) = 0.1$, $p(\theta^M = \theta^M_{00}) = 0.3$, $p(\theta^M = \theta^M_{11}) = 0.3$, and $p(\theta^M = \theta^M_{01}) = 0.3$. This is in comparison to the $(0, 0.33, 0.33, 0.33)$ distribution implied by the fully restricted model, M_1.

In Figure 16.10, we compare findings for a set of cases with different data realizations.

The results differ in various modest ways. For cases with $I = 0, D = 1$ we ask whether the low inequality caused democratization. There are some differences here when we are looking for negative effects of inequality, though the ordering of inferences does not change. The differences appear in the cases of Albania and Nicaragua, where $M = 1$. Under priors fully constrained to monotonic causal effects, we see that observing $M = 1$ makes us think low inequality was less likely to have caused democracy because $M = 1$ represents an alternative cause and because low inequality cannot cause democratization via *M* if $I \rightarrow M$ effects cannot be negative. However, if we allow for a negative effect of *I* on *M*, even while believing it to be unlikely, we now believe a negative effect of inequality on democratization, conditional on mobilization, to be more likely since now that effect *can* run from $I = 0$ to $M = 1$ to $D = 1$.

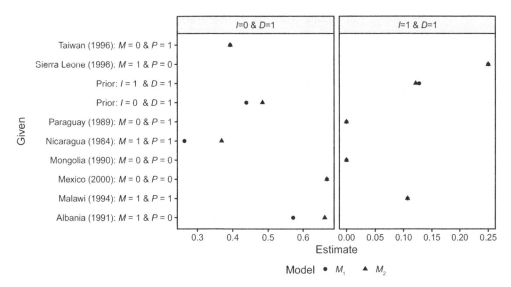

Figure 16.10 Inferences under alternative quantitative priors

Thus, our estimate for Albania and Nicaragua goes up under M_2 relative to M_1. We see, likewise, that mobilization, M, becomes less *informative* about the effect, as the estimates for Albania ($M = 1, P = 0$) are more similar to those for Mexico ($M = 0, P = 0$), and those for Nicaragua ($M = 1, P = 1$) to those for Taiwan ($M = 0, P = 1$).

Turning to cases with high inequality and democratization, inferences about the probability of positive causation are unaffected by the assumption about the effect of I on M. The reason is that, since we still maintain a monotonicity assumption for the direct effect of I on D (no positive effects), the only question is whether there was an indirect effect. Since we maintain the assumption of a monotonic effect of M on D, it remains the case in both models that observing $M = 0$ rules out a positive indirect effect. If however $M = 1$, then I did not have a negative effect on M and the only question is whether $M = 1$ because of I or independent of it – which depends only on the relative sizes of θ_{11}^M and θ_{01}^M. These remain the same (and equal to one another) in both models.

Overall the evaluation of the democracy and inequality model paints a mixed picture. Although the model is able to recreate data patterns consistent with observations, the inferences from within-case observations discussed in Chapter 8 depended on assumptions about processes that, while theoretically compelling, can *not* be justified from observation of broader data patterns even under relatively heroic assumptions on causal identification.

16.3 Evaluating the Institutions—Growth Model

Now we use these four techniques on our second application studying institutional quality and economic growth. Recall that we used data from Rodrik et al. (2004) to assess the causes of economic growth, focusing specifically on the effects of institutions and of geography.

16.3.1 Check Assumptions of Conditional Independence

Our model presupposes unconditional independence between M and D and between R and D. We can see from the simple unconditional regressions reported in Table 16.4 that a dependence exists that is not allowed for in our model. Mortality and distance are related, as are distance from the equator and institutions.

We might consider then a model that allows for an arrow from D to M. In this case, we have a violation of the exclusion restriction. Even still, one might expect that taking account of possible dependencies might not greatly alter analysis since we in effect block on each variable when assessing the effect of another. We will revisit this question when we assess model sensitivity.

16.3.2 Bayesian p-Value

We turn next to evaluating the institutions and growth model using the Bayesian p-value approach, and for this purpose can return to the data that we coded from Rodrik, Subramanian and Trebbi. In the two panels of Figure 16.11, we plot the posterior predictive distributions from our updated model for two quantities of interest: the outcome Y, the size of a country's economy, and the correlation between M, the settler mortality rate and R, the quality of institutions. In each graph, we indicate with a vertical line the mean value for these quantities for the data at hand and report the p-value: the probability of the observed data conditional on our model. This shows the odds of observing the data we see if we assume our model is true.

Table 16.4 Regression coefficients for M and R on D (estimated separately)

Relation	Estimate	Std error	p-value
$D \rightarrow M$	-0.373	0.105	0.001
$D \rightarrow R$	0.241	0.111	0.033

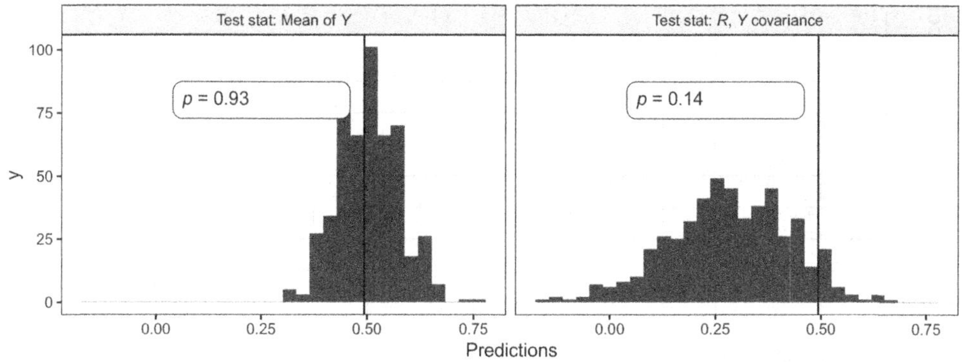

Figure 16.11 Bayesian p-values for the Institutions and Growth model

The distribution for the R, Y covariance has a somewhat low p-value, suggesting that the model does not update on the correlation between R and Y sufficiently; even after observing the data we remain surprised how strong this relation is. The figure looks essentially identical if we instead use the weaker model in which we allow a D to M link.

16.3.3 Leave-One-Out Cross-validation

Figure 16.12 shows the LOO likelihoods for the models with and without a D to M path.

We can see here that the LOO likelihoods are relatively similar for the different models. This suggests our monotonicity restrictions are not having an enormous impact on the plausibility of the model through this test. The LOO likelihood is 2.67e-92 for the base model and 1.65e-88 for the model that allows a $D \rightarrow M$ path.

The points off the 45 degree line in Figure 16.12 confirm, and provide greater detail about, the weakness in the model that we uncovered in our analysis of Bayesian p-values. We can see that we are systematically underpredicting cases in which $Y = R = 1 - M = 1 - D$, which is why the model finds the true Y, R correlation "surprising."

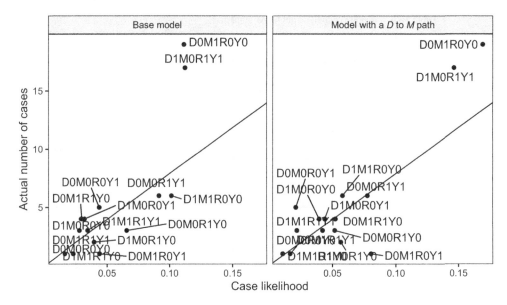

Figure 16.12 LOO data predictions for alternative models

16.3.4 Sensitivity to Priors

We test for sensitivity to three features of the base model: the assumption of a monotonic effect of mortality on institutions, the exclusion restriction (no direct M to Y path), and the exclusion of a D to M path. How much do conclusions depend on these assumptions? We answer this question by comparing our conclusions with these assumptions to what we would conclude by relaxing them. As above, we compare the baseline model in which all three assumptions are embedded to a one-by-one relaxation of each assumption.

We first show results for population inference from a mixed-methods analysis, in Figure 16.13. As we can see, our inferences are reasonably stable across models, whether we are estimating the average effect of R on Y, the share of $R = 1, Y = 1$ cases in which institutions mattered, or the share of $R = 0, Y = 0$ cases in which institutions mattered. The most consequential model assumption appears to be that of monotonicity for the effect of R on Y.

We now consider the consequences of the same model assumptions for case-level queries. Whereas for the democratization model we explored case-level queries under different assumed nodal-type probabilities, here we draw case-level inquiries from the updated model and use the "uninformative-

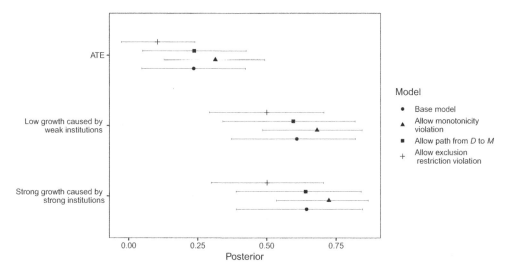

Figure 16.13 Sensitivity of population-level inferences to different model assumptions

case" query ($\hat{\pi}$) procedure (see section 9.3.2.1). Figure 16.14 shows the inferences we make given the same four different models for four types of cases. We focus the analysis here on cases with weak institutions and poor growth, but with differing values for M and D. We can see, in terms of the substantive conclusions we would draw, that patterns of inference for all cases are similar across the first three models. For instance, learning that there was high mortality makes you more likely to think that Nigeria did poorly because of poor institutions, regardless of whether we require monotonicity in the R to Y relationship or exclude a D to M path. The inferences are strongest in the case in which monotonicity is not imposed, but qualitatively similar across the first three rows. Case-level inference looks very different – indeed, becomes impossible – if we allow an arbitrary violation of the exclusion restriction: We gain nothing at all from observation of M and D.

Overall, the evaluation of the institutions and growth model in Figure 16.14 suggests reasonably robust data-based case-level inferences. However, these case-level queries do depend critically on the plausibility of the exclusion restriction to identify the relation between institutions and growth.

In summary, neither model emerges with a spotless bill of health. In both setups, our probing points to areas where the models' assumptions appear to be weighing on conclusions. Ultimately, however, the sensitivity of conclusions to model assumptions seems greater for the inequality model where monotonicity assumptions appear quite consequential.

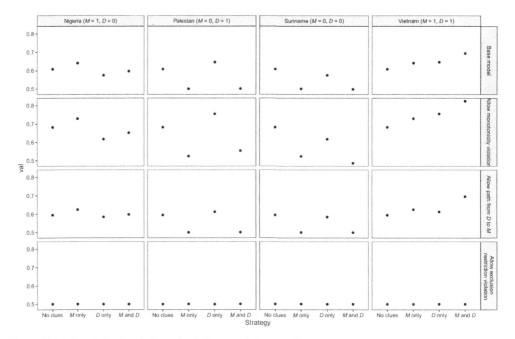

Figure 16.14 Sensitivity of probative value to three model assumptions

16.4 Appendix

Data sources for the expanded inequality and democratization data set:

- **Inequality**: We measure inequality, I, using the Gini estimates from the University of Texas Inequality Project (Galbraith, 2016). As we want to measure inequality at the beginning of the period, we take the Gini measure for each country that is closest in time to the year 1989. We then dichotomize the variable using the median value for the period as a cutoff.
- **Mobilization**: We measure M using the Mass Mobilization Protest Data from Clark and Regan (2016). To capture the kinds of mobilization on which redistributive theories of democratization focus, we restrict our focus to protests in the demand categories "land farm issue," "labor wage dispute," "price increases, tax policy," and "political behavior, process." We also include only those gatherings with a size of at least 1,000 protesters. We code a country case as $M = 1$ if and only if, during the 1990s, it experienced at least one protest that meets both the demand-type and size criteria.

- **Pressure**: We draw on the GIGA Sanctions Dataset to measure international pressure, P. Specifically, we code a country case as $P = 1$ if and only if the country was the target of democratization-focused sanctions during the 1990–2000 period.
- **Democratization**: We use dichotomous democracy measures from Cheibub et al. (2010) in two ways. First, we filter countries such that our sample includes only those that were not democracies in 1990 ($N = 77$). We then use the democracy measure for the year 2000 to determine which countries democratized, coding as $D = 1$ those and only those cases that Cheibub et al. code as democracies in that year.

17 Final Words

This book builds off the simple idea that we can usefully learn about the world by combining new evidence with prior causal models to produce updated models of how the world works. We can update a given model with data about different parts of a causal process, with, possibly, different types of data from different cases. When asking specific questions – such as whether this caused that or whether one or another channel is important – we look up answers in our updated model of causal processes rather than seeking to answer the question directly from data.

This way of thinking about learning, though certainly not new, is very different from many standard approaches in the social sciences. It promises benefits, but it also comes with risks. We try to describe both in this closing chapter.

The approach stands in particularly stark contrast to the design-based approach to causal inference, which has gained prominence in recent years. Advances in design-based inferences show that it is possible to greatly diminish the role of background assumptions for some research questions and contexts. This is a remarkable achievement that has put the testing of some hypotheses and the estimation of some causal quantities on firm footing. It allows researchers to maintain agnostic positions and base their inferences more solidly on what they know to be true – such as how units were sampled and how treatments were assigned – and less on speculations about background data-generating processes. Nothing here argues against these strengths.

At the same time, there are limits to model-free social science that affect the kinds of questions we can ask and the conditions that need to be in place to be able to generate an answer. Most simply, we often don't understand the "design" very well, and random assignment to different conditions, if possible at all, could be prohibitively expensive or unethical. More subtly, perhaps, our goal as social scientists is often to generate a model of the world that we bring with us to make sense of new contexts. Eschewing models, however, can make it difficult to learn about them.

Drawing on pioneering work by computer science, statistics, and philosophy scholars, we have outlined a principled approach to mobilizing prior knowledge to learn from new data in situations where randomization is unavailable and to answer questions for which randomization is unhelpful. In this approach, causal models are *guides* to research design, *machines* for inference, and *objects* of inquiry. As guides, the models yield expectations about the learning that can be derived from a given case or set of cases and from a given type of evidence, conditional on the question being asked. As inferential machines, models allow updating on that query once the data are in hand. Finally, when we confront a model with data, we learn about the parameters of the model itself, which can be used to answer a range of other causal questions and allow the cumulation of knowledge across studies. To complement the conceptual infrastructure, we have provided software tools that let researchers build, update, and query binary causal models.

17.1 The Benefits

Strategies centered on building, updating, and querying causal models come with striking advantages.

Many questions. When we update a causal model, we do not estimate a single causal quantity of interest: We learn about *the model*. Most concretely, when we encounter new data, we update our beliefs about *all* parameters in the model at the same time. We can then use the updated parameters to answer very broad classes of causal questions, beyond the population-level average effect. These include case-level questions (*Does X explain Y in this case?*), process questions (*Through which channel does X affect Y?*), and transportability questions (*What are the implications of results derived in one context for processes and effects in other contexts?*).

Common answer strategy. Strikingly, these diverse types of questions are all asked and answered in this approach using the same procedure: forming, updating, and querying a causal model. Likewise, once we update a model given a set of data, we can then pose the full range of causal queries to the updated model. In this respect, the causal models approach differs markedly from common statistical frameworks in which distinct estimators are constructed to estimate particular estimands.

Answers without identification. The approach can generate answers even when queries are not *identified*. The ability to "identify" causal effects has been a central pursuit of much social science research in recent years. But identification is, in some ways, a curious goal. A causal quantity is identified if, with infinite data, the correct value can be ascertained with certainty – informally, the distribution that will emerge is consistent with only one parameter value. Oddly, however, knowing that a model, or quantity, is identified in this way does not tell you that estimation with finite data is any good (Maclaren and Nicholson, 2019). What's more, the estimation of a non-identified model with finite data is not necessarily bad. While there is a tendency to discount models for which quantities of interest are not identified, in fact, as we have demonstrated, considerable learning is possible even without identification, using the same procedure of updating and querying models.[1] Updating non-identified models can lead to a tightening of posteriors, even if some quantities can never be distinguished from each other.

Integration. Embedding inference within an explicit causal model brings about an integration across forms of data and beliefs that may otherwise develop in isolation from one another. For one thing, the approach allows us to combine arbitrary mixes of forms of evidence, including data on causes and outcomes and evidence on causal processes (whether from the same or different sets of cases). Further, the causal-model approach ensures that our findings about *cases* (given evidence about those cases) are informed by what we know about the *population* to which those cases belong, and vice versa. And, as we discuss further below, the approach generates integration between inputs and outputs: It ensures that the way in which we update from the data is logically consistent with our prior beliefs about the world.

A framework for knowledge cumulation. Closely related to integration is cumulation: A causal-model framework provides a ready-made apparatus for combining information across studies. Thinking in meta-analytic terms, the framework provides a tool for combining the evidence from multiple independent studies. Thinking sequentially, the model updated from one set of data can become the starting point for the next study of the same causal domain.

Yet organizing inquiry around a causal model allows for cumulation in a deeper sense as well. Compared with most prevailing approaches to

---

[1] There is a large literature on partial identification. See Tamer (2010) for a review.

observational inference – where the background model is typically left implicit or conveyed informally or incompletely – the approach ensures *transparency* about the beliefs on which inferences rest. Explicitness about assumptions allows us to assess the degree of sensitivity of conclusions to our prior beliefs. Sensitivity analyses cannot, of course, tell us which beliefs are right. But they can tell us which assumptions are most in need of defense, pinpointing *where more learning would be of greatest value.* Those features of our model about which we are most uncertain and that matter most to our conclusions – be it the absence of an arrow, a restriction, a prior over nodal types, or the absence of confounding – represent the questions most in need of answers down the road.

A framework for learning about strategies. As we showed in Chapters 12 and 13, access to a model provides an explicit formulation of how and what inferences will be drawn from future data patterns and provides a formal framework for justifying design decisions. Of course, this feature is not unique to model-based inference – one can certainly have a model that describes expectations over future data patterns and imagine what inferences you will make using design-based inference or any other procedure.

Conceptual clarifications. Finally, we have found that this framework has been useful for providing conceptual clarification on how to think about qualitative, quantitative, and mixed-method inference. Consider two common distinctions that dissolve under our approach.

The first is with respect to the difference between "within-case" and "between-case" inference. In Humphreys and Jacobs (2015), for instance, we drew on a common operationalization of "quantitative" and "qualitative" data as akin to "dataset" and "causal process" observations, respectively, as defined by Collier et al. (2010; see also Mahoney, 2000). In a typical mixed-method setup, we might think of combining a "quantitative" dataset containing X and Y (and covariate) observations for many cases with "qualitative" observations on causal processes, such as a mediator M, for a subset of these cases. But this apparent distinction has no meaning in the formal setup and analysis of models. There is no need to think of X and Y observations as being tied to a large-N analysis or of observations of mediating or other processes as being tied to small-N analysis. One could, for instance, have data on M for a large set of cases but data on Y or X for only a small number. Updating the model to learn about the causal query of interest will proceed in the same basic manner. The cross-case/within-case dichotomy plays no role in the way inferences are drawn: Given any pattern of data we observe in the cases at hand, we are always assessing the likelihood of that data pattern under different values of the model's parameters. In this framework, what we have conventionally thought of as qualitative and quantitative inference strategies are not just integrated; the distinction between them breaks down completely.

A second is with regard to the relationship between beliefs about queries and beliefs about the informativeness of evidence. In many accounts of process tracing, researchers posit a set of prior beliefs about the values of estimands and other – independent – beliefs about the informativeness of within-case information. We do this for instance, in Humphreys and Jacobs (2015). It is also implicit in approaches that assign uniform distributions to hypotheses (e.g., Fairfield and Charman, 2017). Viewed through a causal models lens, however *both* sets of beliefs – about the hypothesis being examined and about the probative value of the data – represent substantive probabilistic claims about the world, particularly about *causal relationships* in the domain under investigation. They, thus, cannot be treated as generally independent of one another: Our beliefs about causal relations *imply* our beliefs about the probative value of the evidence. These implications flow naturally in a causal-model framework. When both sets of beliefs are derived from an underlying model representing prior knowledge about the domain of interest, then the same conjectures that inform our beliefs about the hypotheses also inform our beliefs about the informativeness of additional data. Seen in this way, the researcher is under pressure to provide reasons to support beliefs about probative value, but more constructively, they have available to them a strategy to do so.[2]

17.2 The Worries

While we have found the syntax of Directed Acyclic Graphs (DAGs) to provide a flexible framework for setting up causal models, we have also become more keenly aware of some of the limitations of DAGs in representing causal processes (see also Dawid 2010 and Cartwright 2007). We discuss a few of these here.

---

[2] As an illustration, one might imagine a background model of the form $X \rightarrow Y \leftarrow K$. Data that are consistent with X causing Y independent of K would suggest a high prior (for a new case) that X causes Y, but weak beliefs that K is informative for X causing Y. Data that are consistent with X causing Y if and only if $K = 1$ would suggest a lower prior (for a new case) that X causes Y, but stronger beliefs that K is informative for X causing Y.

Well-defined nodes? A DAG presupposes a set of well-defined nodes that come with location and time stamps. Wealth in time t affects democracy in time $t + 1$ which affects wealth in time t. Yet it is not always easy to figure out how to partition the world into such neat event bundles. Wealth in 1985 is not an "event" exactly but a state, and the temporal ordering relative to "Democracy 1985" is not at all clear. Moreover, even if events are coded into well-ordered nodes, values on these nodes may poorly capture actual processes, even in simple systems. Consider the simplest setup with a line of dominos. You are interested in whether the fall of the first domino causes the fall of the last one. But the observations of the states of the dominos at predefined points in time do not fully capture the causal process as seen by observers. The data might report that (a) domino 1 fell and (b) domino 2 fell. But the observer will notice that domino 2 fell *just as* domino 1 hit it.

Acyclic, really? DAGs are by definition acyclic. And it is not hard to argue that, since cause precedes effect, causal relations *should* be acyclic for any well-defined nodes. In practice, however, our variables often come with coarse periodizations: There was or was not mobilization in the 1990s; there was or was not democratization in the 1990s. We cannot extract the direction of arrows from the definition of nodes this coarse.

Coherent underlying causal accounts. The approach we describe is one in which researchers are asked to provide a coherent model – albeit with uncertainty – regarding the ways in which nodes are causally related to each other. For instance, a researcher interested in using information on K to ascertain whether X caused Y is expected to have a theory of whether K acts as a moderator or a mediator for X, and whether it is realized before or after Y. Yet it is possible that a researcher has well-formed beliefs about the informativeness of K *without* an underlying model of how K is causally related to X or Y. Granted, one might wonder where these beliefs come from or how they can be defended. We nonetheless note that one limitation of the approach we have described is that one cannot easily make use of an observation without a coherent account of that observation's causal position relative to other variables and relationships of interest.

Complexity. To maintain simplicity, we have largely focused in this book on models with binary nodes. At first blush, this class of causal models indeed appears very simple. Yet even with binary nodes, complexity rises rapidly as the number of nodes and connections among them increases. As a node goes from having 1 parent to 2 parents to 3 parents to 4 parents, for instance, the number of nodal types – at that node alone – goes from 4 to 16 to 256 to 65,536, with knock-on effects for the number of possible causal types (combinations of nodal types across the model). A move in the direction of continuous variables – say, from binary nodes to nodes with three ordinal values – would also involve a dramatic increase in the complexity of the type-space.[3] There are practical and substantive implications of this. A practical implication is that one can hit computational constraints very quickly for even moderately sized models. Substantively, models can quickly involve more complexity than humans can comfortably understand.

One solution is to move away from a fully nonparametric setting and impose structure on permissible function forms – for example, by imposing monotonicity or assuming no high-level interactions. Inferences then are *conditional* on these simplifying assumptions.

A second approach might be to give up on the commitment to a complete specification of causal relations between nodes and seek lower dimensional representations of models that are sufficient for specific questions we care about. For instance, we could imagine representing an $X \rightarrow Y$ model with just two parameters rather than four (for Y): Define $\tau := \theta_{10}^Y - \theta_{01}^Y$ and $\rho := \theta_{11}^Y - \theta_{00}^Y$, both of which are identified with experimental data. These give us enough to learn about how common different types of outcomes are as well as average effects, though not enough to infer the probability that X caused Y in an $X = Y = 1$ case.

Unintended structure. The complexity of causal models means that it is easy to generate a fully specified causal model with features that we do not fully understand. In the same way, it is possible to make choices between models, unaware of differences in assumptions that they have built in.

Consider two examples:

- We specify a model $X \rightarrow Y$ and assume flat priors over nodal types. The implied prior that X has a positive effect on Y is then 0.25. We then add detail by specifying $X \rightarrow M \rightarrow Y$ but continue to hold flat priors. In our more detailed model, however, the probability of a positive effect of X on Y is now just 0.125. Adding the detail requires either moving away from flat priors on nodal types or changing priors on aggregate causal relations.

---

[3] If, for instance, we moved to nodes with three ordered categories, then each of Y's nodal types in an $X \rightarrow Y$ model would have to register three potential outcomes, corresponding to the three values that X takes on. And Y would have $3 \times 3 \times 3 = 27$ nodal types (as Y can take on three possible values for each possible value of X).

- We specify a model $X \rightarrow Y \leftarrow W$ and build in that W is a smoking gun for the effect of X on Y. We add detail by specifying $X \rightarrow M \rightarrow Y \leftarrow W$. This means, however, that W cannot be a smoking gun for Y unless the $X \rightarrow M$ relation is certain. Why? To be a smoking gun, it must be the case that, if $W = 1$, we are sure that X causes M and that M causes Y, which requires an arrow from W to M and not just from W to X.

In such cases it is of course possible to query different models to make sure that new features have not been introduced unintentionally.

Model dependence of conclusions. One striking aspect of some of the analyses presented here is how sensitive conclusions can be to what would seem to be quite modest changes to models. We see two ways of thinking about the implications of this fact for a causal-models framework.

One lesson to draw would be that there are tight limits to building inference upon causal models. If results in this approach depend heavily on prior beliefs, which could be wrong, then we might doubt the utility of the framework. On this reasoning, the safer option is to rely on design-based inference to the extent possible.

An alternative lesson also offers itself, however. To the extent that our inferences depend on our background causal beliefs, a transparent and systematic engagement with models becomes all the more important. If inferences depend on models that are not explicitly articulated, we have no way of knowing how fragile they are, how they would change under an alternative set of premises, or what kind of learning we need to undertake if we want to generate more secure conclusions.

We do not see causal models as the only way forward or as a panacea, and we are conscious of the limitations and complexities of the approach we have outlined, as well as the need for extension and elaboration along numerous fronts. Yet we think there is value in further development of forms of empirical social science that can operate with analytic transparency outside the safe inferential confines of random assignment.

17.3 The Future

The future, as we see it, lies in improvements in cumulation, coordination, and model grounding.

Cumulation. The cumulation of knowledge requires integration.

As we acquire new evidence – perhaps from observation of additional cases or new events – we want to be able to update our general beliefs about how the world works by integrating new information with the existing store of knowledge. At the same time, we want our inferences about individual cases to be informed by our beliefs about how the world works in general. Causal models provide a natural framework for cumulating knowledge in this way. We have spelled out in this book how an individual researcher can use models to join up new data with prior beliefs and ground case-level inferences in beliefs about population-level parameters. In a scientific discipline, however, cumulation must also operate *across* researchers. For a field to make progress, I need to update *my* beliefs in light of *your* new evidence and vice versa.

There are more collaborative and adversarial ways to think about this kind of learning across researchers. One more collaborative approach is for researchers to agree on an underlying causal structure. Then, new data will lead not just to individual updating but also, hopefully, to convergence in beliefs – a feature that should hold for identified causal queries, but not universally. This is a nontrivial ask. Not only do I need access to your evidence, but we have to be operating to some degree with a common causal model of the domain of interest; otherwise, the data that you generate might fail to map onto my model. One approach is for researchers to agree on an overarching causal model that nests submodels that different researchers have focused on.

However, in practice, there may be little reason to be optimistic that individual researchers will naturally tend to generate models that align with one another. Not only might our substantive causal beliefs diverge, but we might also make differing choices about matters of model construction – from which nodes to include and the appropriate level of detail to the manner of operationalizing variables. Indeed, it might also be that generating comprehensive models undermines the goal of generating simple representations of causal processes.

Even in an adversarial context, however, we believe the approach described in this book would add value: It would require researchers to be clear and precise about their distinct models. Then these rival models, rather than being aggregated into a single model, could be pitted against each other using tools like those we describe in Chapter 16.

Coordination. Turning causal models into vehicles for knowledge cumulation in a field will thus require coordination around models. We are under no illusion that such coordination would be easy. But productive coordination would not require prior agreement about how the world works.

One possibility would be to fix (provisionally, at least) the set of nodes relevant in a given domain – including outcomes of interest, potential causes, and mediators and moderators implicated in prevailing theories – and how those nodes are defined. Individual researchers would then be free to develop their own models by drawing arrows and setting priors and restrictions in line with their beliefs. Coordination around model nodes would then guide data collection, as teams running new studies would seek to collect data on at least some subset of the common nodes – allowing, in turn, for all models to be updated as the new data come in.

Another possibility would be to exploit modularity, with different researchers or projects modeling different *parts* of a causal system. For instance, in the field of democratization, one set of researchers might model and collect data on links between inequality and democratization; others might focus on the role of external pressures; while still others might focus on inter-elite bargaining. Coordination would operate at the level of inter-operability. Modules would have to have at least some overlapping nodes for updating from new data to operate across them. Ideally, each module would also take into account any confounding among its nodes that is implied by other modules.

Another more minimalist mode of coordination would be for researchers to develop models that agree only on the inclusion of one or more outcome nodes. As new data comes in, models would then be set in competition over predictive performance.

Coordination would also require agreement on some minimal qualities that models must have. For instance, we would surely want all models to be well defined, following the basic rules of DAG construction and with clear rules for operationalizing all nodes.

Grounding. Most of our models are on stilts. We want them grounded. One kind of grounding is theoretical. As we show in Chapter 6, for instance, game-theoretic models can be readily translated into causal models. The same, we believe, can be done for other types of behavioral theories. Clear informal theoretical logics could underwrite causal models also. A second approach would be subjective-Bayesian: Models could be founded on aggregated expert beliefs. A third – our preferred – form of grounding is empirical. As we discuss in Chapters 9 and 15, experimental data can be used to anchor model assumptions, which can, in turn, provide grounds for drawing case-level inferences. Ultimately, we hope the benefits from mixing methods will flow in both directions.

We have taken a deep dive into the world of causal models to scope out whether and how they can support social scientists engaging in qualitative and mixed-methods research. We emerge convinced of the promise of the framework. Embedding our beliefs in a causal model enables rich forms of integration, allowing us to cumulate knowledge across cases, types of evidence, settings, study designs, and levels of analysis to address a vast array of causal questions. The framework also provides a coherent machinery to connect theoretical structures to empirical analyses. We have shown how this integration can strengthen the underpinnings of case-oriented research, providing microfoundations not just for the classic process tracing tests but for case-level probative value in general. We have, however, also emerged with a sharpened appreciation of how difficult it can be to justify our starting assumptions, of the extraordinary computational and conceptual complexity arising from all but the simplest causal models, and of the sometimes strong sensitivity of conclusions to our representations of causal processes. We conclude with cautious optimism: convinced of the need both to re-center social science research on causal models and to keep these models permanently under scrutiny.

Part V

Appendices

Term	(Typical) Symbol	Meaning
Ambiguities matrix	A	A matrix of 0s and 1s that maps from causal types (rows) to data types (columns). We call it an ambiguities matrix because the mapping from causal types to data types is many to one: Each causal type produces a unique data type, but a data type can be produced by many causal types.
Causal function	$f_Y(X, \theta_Y)$	A function that maps from the possible values of the parents of a node to the possible values of the node. A change in the value of an argument is interpreted as a controlled change. Thus, $f_Y(X = 1, \theta_Y) - f_Y(X = 0, \theta_Y)$ can be interpreted as the change in Y as X's value is manipulated from 0 to 1. See Note 2.1.
Causal model	M, M'	A triple containing: (1) a partially ordered set of (endogenous and exogenous) nodes, (2) a set of functions, one for each endogenous variable, specifying how it responds to the values of earlier variables in the ordering, (3) a probability distribution over exogenous variables. Note that (1) and (2) together define a "structural causal model" whereas (1), (2), and (3) describe a "probabilistic causal model" which we refer to simply as a causal model. See Definition 2.1.
Causal type	θ	A causal type is a concatenation of nodal types, one for each node. The causal type of a unit fully describes what values that unit takes on at all nodes and also how that unit would respond to all interventions. Example: $(\theta_0^X, \theta_{01}^Y)$ is a causal type that has $X = 0$ and $Y - 0$ but would have $Y = 1$ if X were set to 1. Types like this are written in code in `CausalQueries` as X0.Y01.

Term	(Typical) Symbol	Meaning
Clue	K	A variable or collection of variables whose values are potentially informative for some query.
Conditional independence	$(A \perp\!\!\!\perp B \mid C)$.	Two (sets of) variables (A and B) are conditionally independent given some third (set of) variables (C) if, for all a, $\Pr(A = a \mid B, C) = \Pr(A = a \mid C)$. See Definition 2.2.
Credibility interval		A set of possible values within which we believe a parameter lies with some specified probability. In tables we often use "cred low" and "cred high" to indicate the lower and upper bounds of a 95% credibility interval.
DAG		Directed acyclic graph. A graphical representation of a structural causal model, indicating nodes, parent – child relations, and relations of conditional independence.
Data strategy	S	A plan indicating for how many nodes data of different types will be gathered. A data strategy might indicate what new data will be gathered at one point as a function of what has already been seen at earlier points.
Dirichlet priors	α	Nonnegative numbers used to characterize a prior distribution over a simplex. The implied mean is the normalized vector $\mu = \alpha / \sum_{(j} \alpha_j)$ and the variance is $\mu(1-\mu)/(1+\sum_j \alpha_j)$. See Section 5.1.4.
Data type or event type		A possible set of values on all nodes (including, possibly, NAs). Example: X0Y1 $= (X = 0, Y = 1)$.
Endogenous node	X, Y	A node that is a function of other nodes (whether these are just exogenous nodes, or a mix of endogenous and exogenous nodes). All substantive nodes in a model are typically endogenous in that they, minimally, have an exogenous (θ^j) node pointing into them.
Event probability	w	The probability of a data type or event type arising. Example: $w_{01} = \Pr(X = 0, Y = 1)$.
Exogenous node	θ^X, θ^Y	A node that is not a function of other nodes in a model. Exogenous nodes are often not represented on causal graphs, but in general there is implicitly one exogenous node for each endogenous node. In this book's use of causal models, exogenous nodes typically represent nodal types.

Term	(Typical) Symbol	Meaning
Flat priors		We say priors are flat when they place equal weight on all possibilities. For instance, we refer to a Dirichlet as describing flat priors when α is a vector of 1s.
Mediator	M	A mediator is a variable (node) that lies along the causal pathway of one variable to another and through which a causal effect may pass. For instance, in an $X \rightarrow M \rightarrow Y$ model, M is a potential mediator for the effect of X on Y.
Moderator	K, M, W	A moderator is a variable that affects the effect of one variable on another. For instance, in an $X \rightarrow Y \leftarrow K$ model, K is a potential moderator, potentially altering the effect of X on Y.
Multinomial distribution		A probability distribution reporting the probability of a given distribution of outcomes across categories.
Nodal type	θ^X	The way that a node responds to the values of its parents. Example: θ^Y_{10}, sometimes written Y10 is a nodal type for which Y takes the value 1 if $X = 0$ and 0 if $X = 1$.
Parent (child)	$pa()$	X is a *parent* of Y if a change in X possibly induces a change in Y even when all other nodes in the graphs are fixed. Y is a *child* of X if a change in X possibly induces a change in Y even when all other nodes are fixed. On the graph, an arrow from X to Y indicates that X is a parent of Y and that Y is a child of X.
Parameter	λ	An unknown quantity of interest. In many applications in the book, λ^V_x denotes the share of units that have nodal type x on node V. In models with unobserved confounding, parameters are often thought of as the conditional probabilities of nodal types. Example: $\lambda^Y_{01\mid\theta^M=\theta^M_{01}} = \Pr(\theta^Y = \theta^Y_{01}\mid\theta^M = \theta^M_{01})$.
Parameter matrix	P	A matrix of 0s and 1s that maps from parameters (rows) to causal types (columns).
Posterior	$p(\lambda\mid d)$	A probability distribution over a set of parameter values after observing data.
Potential outcomes	$Y_i(0), Y_i(1)$	The values that a unit *would take* on under a specified set of conditions – for instance, if X were set to 0 or X were set to 1. See Note 2.1.

Term	(Typical) Symbol	Meaning
Prior	$p(\lambda)$	A probability distribution over a set of parameter values before observing data.
Query	Q, q	A question asked of a model, either about the values of nodes or the values that nodes would take under specified operations. We use lower case q to represent the answer to the query (the estimand), which is the realization of Q. *Simple* queries, such as the probability that X has a positive effect on Y, ask about the probability of some set of causal types. *Complex queries* such as the average treatment effect, ask for summaries of simple queries: in a binary setup, the share of units with a positive effect less the share of units with a negative effect.

Bibliography

Acemoglu, D., Johnson, S., and Robinson, J. A. (2001). The colonial origins of comparative development: An empirical investigation. *American Economic Review*, 91(5):1369–1401.

Acemoglu, D. and Robinson, J. A. (2005). *Economic Origins of Dictatorship and Democracy*. Cambridge University Press, New York.

Angrist, J. D. and Imbens, G. W. (1995). *Identification and estimation of local average treatment effects*. Technical working paper, National Bureau of Economic Research.

Ansell, B. W. and Samuels, D. J. (2014). *Inequality and Democratization*. Cambridge University Press, New York.

Aronow, P. M. and Miller, B. T. (2019). *Foundations of Agnostic Statistics*. Cambridge University Press, Cambridge.

Bareinboim, E. and Pearl, J. (2016). Causal inference and the data-fusion problem. *Proceedings of the National Academy of Sciences*, 113(27):7345–7352.

Bayarri, M. and Berger, J. O. (2000). P values for composite null models. *Journal of the American Statistical Association*, 95(452):1127–1142.

Beach, D. and Pedersen, R. B. (2013). *Process-Tracing Methods: Foundations and Guidelines*. University of Michigan Press, Ann Arbor, MI.

Bennett, A. (2008). Process tracing: A Bayesian perspective. In Box-Steffensmeier, J. M., Brady, H. E., and Collier, D., editors, *The Oxford Handbook of Political Methodology*, pages 702–721. Oxford University Press, Oxford, UK.

Bennett, A. (2015). Appendix. In Bennett, A. and Checkel, J., editors, *Process Tracing: From Metaphor to Analytic Tool*, pages 276–298. Cambridge University Press, New York.

Bennett, A. and Checkel, J. (2015a). Process tracing: From philosophical roots to best practices. In Bennett, A. and Checkel, J., editors, *Process Tracing: From Metaphor to Analytic Tool*, pages 3–37. Cambridge University Press, New York.

Bennett, A. and Checkel, J. T. (2015b). *Process Tracing: From Metaphor to Analytic Tool*. Cambridge University Press, New York.

Blair, G., Coppock, A., and Humphreys, M. (2023). *Research Design: Declaration, Diagnosis, Redesign*. Princeton University Press, Princeton, NJ.

Boix, C. (2003). *Democracy and Redistribution*. Cambridge University Press, New York.

Bollen, K. A. and Jackman, R. W. (1985). Political democracy and the size distribution of income. *American Sociological Review*, 50(4):438–457.

Brady, H. and Collier, D. (2010). *Rethinking Social Inquiry: Diverse Tools, Shared Standards*. Rowman & Littlefield, Lanham, MD.

Cartwright, N. (2007). *Hunting Causes and Using Them: Approaches in Philosophy and Economics*. Cambridge University Press, Cambridge.

Cartwright, N. (1989). *Nature's Capacities and their Measurement*. Clarendon Press.

Cheibub, J. A., Gandhi, J., and Vreeland, J. R. (2010). Democracy and dictatorship revisited. *Public Choice*, 143(1–2):67–101.

Chickering, D. M. and Pearl, J. (1996). A clinician's tool for analyzing non-compliance. In *Proceedings of the National Conference on Artificial Intelligence*, pages 1269–1276.

Clark, D. and Regan, P. (2016). Mass mobilization protest data. *Harvard Dataverse*.

Clarke, K. A. and Primo, D. M. (2012). *A Model Discipline: Political Science and the Logic of Representations*. Oxford University Press, New York.

Collier, D. (2011). Understanding process tracing. *PS: Political Science & Politics*, 44(4):823–830.

Collier, D., Brady, H. E., and Seawright, J. (2010). Sources of leverage in causal inference: Toward an alternative view of methodology. In Collier, D. and Brady, H. E., editors, *Rethinking Social Inquiry: Diverse Tools, Shared Standards*, pages 161–199. Rowman and Littlefield, Lanham, MD.

Cook, T. D. (2018). Twenty-six assumptions that have to be met if single random assignment experiments are to warrant "gold standard" status: A commentary on Deaton and Cartwright. *Social Science & Medicine*, 210:37–40.

Copas, J. (1973). Randomization models for the matched and unmatched 2×2 tables. *Biometrika*, 60(3):467–476.

Coppock, A. and Kaur, D. (2022). Qualitative imputation of missing potential outcomes. *American Journal of Political Science*, 66(3):681–695.

Cowell, R. G., Dawid, P., Lauritzen, S. L., and Spiegelhalter, D. J. (1999). *Probabilistic Networks and Expert Systems*. Springer, New York.

Creswell, J. and Garrett, A. L. (2008). The "movement" of mixed methods research and the role of educators. *South African Journal of Education*, 28:321–333.

Dahl, R. A. (1973). *Polyarchy: Participation and Opposition*. Yale University Press, New Haven, CT.

Dawid, P. (2010). Beware of the DAG! *Proceedings of Workshop on Causality: Objectives and Assessment*. PMLR: 6:59–86.

Dawid, P., Humphreys, M., and Musio, M. (2022). Bounding causes of effects with mediators. *Sociological Methods and Research*, OnlineFirst, https://doi.org/10.1177/0049124 1211036161.

Druckman, J. N., Green, D. P., Kuklinski, J. H., and Lupia, A. (2011). Experimentation in political science. In Druckman, J. N., Green, D. P., Kuklinski, J. H., and Lupia, A., editors, *Handbook of Experimental Political Science*, pages 3–14. Cambridge University Press, New York.

Dunning, T. (2012). *Natural Experiments in the Social Sciences: A Design-Based Approach*. Strategies for Social Inquiry Series. Cambridge University Press, Cambridge.

Earman, J. (1992). *Bayes or Bust? A Critical Examination of Bayesian Confirmation Theory*. MIT Press, Cambridge, MA.

Fairfield, T. and Charman, A. (2017). Explicit Bayesian analysis for process tracing: Guidelines, opportunities, and caveats. *Political Analysis*, 25(3):363–380.

Fairfield, T. and Charman, A. E. (2022). *Social Inquiry and Bayesian Inference: Rethinking Qualitative Research*. Cambridge University Press, New York.

Fearon, J. and Laitin, D. (2008). Integrating qualitative and quantitative methods. In Box-Steffenmeier, J. M., Collier, D., and Brady, H. E., editors, *Oxford Handbook of Political Methodology*, pages 756–776. Oxford University Press, Oxford, UK.

Fisher, R. A. (2017). *Design of experiments*. Hafner, New York.

Frangakis, C. E. and Rubin, D. B. (2002). Principal stratification in causal inference. *Biometrics*, 58(1):21–29.

Gabry, J., Simpson, D., Vehtari, A., Betancourt, M., and Gelman, A. (2019). Visualization in Bayesian workflow. *Journal of the Royal Statistical Society: Series A (Statistics in Society)*, 182(2):389–402.

Galbraith, J. K., et al. (2016). The University of Texas inequality project global inequality data sets, 1963–2008: Updates, revisions and quality checks. In Basu, K. and Stiglitz, J.E., editors, *Inequality and Growth: Patterns and Policy: Volume II: Regions and Regularities*, pages 98–135. Palgrave Macmillan, New York.

Galles, D. and Pearl, J. (1998). An axiomatic characterization of causal counterfactuals. *Foundations of Science*, 3(1):151–182.

García, F. M. and Wantchekon, L. (2015). A graphical approximation to generalization: Definitions and diagrams. *Journal of Globalization and Development*, 6(1):71–86.

Gardner, M. (1961). *The Second Scientific American Book of Mathematical Puzzles and Diversions*. Simon and Schuster, New York.

Gelman, A. (2013). Two simple examples for understanding posterior p-values whose distributions are far from uniform. *Electronic Journal of Statistics*, 7:2595–2602.

Gelman, A., Carlin, J. B., Stern, H. S., Dunson, D. B., Vehtari, A., and Rubin, D. B. (2013). *Bayesian Data Analysis*. CRC Press, Boca Raton, FL.

George, A. L. and Bennett, A. A. (2005). *Case Studies and Theory Development in the Social Sciences*. The MIT Press, Cambridge, MA.

George, A. L. and McKeown, T. J. (1985). Case studies and theories of organizational decision making. *Advances in Information Processing in Organizations*, 2(1):21–58.

Gerber, A. S., Green, D. P., and Kaplan, E. H. (2004). The illusion of learning from observational research. In Shapiro, I., Smith, R. M., and Masoud, T. E., editors, *Problems and Methods in the Study of Politics*, pages 251–273. Cambridge University Press, Cambridge, UK.

Gerring, J. (2006). *Case Study Research: Principles and Practices*. Cambridge University Press, New York.

Geweke, J. and Amisano, G. (2014). Analysis of variance for Bayesian inference. *Econometric Reviews*, 33(1–4):270–288.

Glymour, C., Zhang, K., and Spirtes, P. (2019). Review of causal discovery methods based on graphical models. *Frontiers in Genetics*, 10:524.

Glynn, A. and Quinn, K. (2007). *Non-parametric mechanisms and causal modeling*. Technical report, working paper.

Glynn, A. and Quinn, K. (2011). Why process matters for causal inference. *Political Analysis*, 19:273–286.

Goertz, G. and Mahoney, J. (2012). *A Tale of Two Cultures: Qualitative and Quantitative Research in the Social Sciences*. Princeton University Press, Princeton.

Good, I. J. (1950). *Probability and the Weighing of Evidence*. Griffin, London.

Good, I. J. (1984). The best explicatum for weight of evidence (C197). *Journal of Statistical Computation and Simulation*, 19(4):294–299.

Gordon, S. C. and Smith, A. (2004). Quantitative leverage through qualitative knowledge: Augmenting the statistical analysis of complex causes. *Political Analysis*, 12(3):233–255.

Haggard, S. and Kaufman, R. R. (2012). Inequality and regime change: Democratic transitions and the stability of democratic rule. *American Political Science Review*, 106(3):495–516.

Haggard, S., Kaufman, R. R., and Teo, T. (2012). Distributive conflict and regime change: A qualitative dataset. *Political Science Publications*, 5.

Hall, N. (2004). Two concepts of causation. In Collins, J., Hall, N., Paul, L. A., editors, *Causation and Counterfactuals*, pages 225–276. MIT Press, Cambridge, MA.

Hall, P. A. (2003). Aligning ontology and methodology in comparative research. In Mahoney, J. and Rueschemeyer, D., editors, *Comparative Historical Analysis in the Social Sciences*, pages 373–404. Cambridge University Press, New York.

Halpern, J. Y. (2015). A modification of the Halpern-Pearl definition of causality. *arXiv preprint arXiv:1505.00162*.

Halpern, J. Y. (2016). *Actual Causality*. MIT Press, Cambridge, MA.

Halpern, J. Y. and Pearl, J. (2005). Causes and explanations: A structural-model approach. Part I: Causes. *Journal for the Philosophy of Science*, 56(4):843–887.

Heckerman, D. E., Horvitz, E. J., and Nathwani, B. N. (1991). Toward normative expert systems: The pathfinder project. *Methods of Information in Medicine*, 31:90–105.

Hernán, M. A. and Robins, J. M. (2006). Instruments for causal inference: An epidemiologist's dream? *Epidemiology*, 17(4):360–372.

Herron, M. C. and Quinn, K. M. (2016). A careful look at modern case selection methods. *Sociological Methods & Research*, 45(3):458–492.

Hoffrage, U. and Gigerenzer, G. (1998). Using natural frequencies to improve diagnostic inferences. *Academic Medicine*, 73(5):538–540.

Holland, P. W. (1986). Statistics and causal inference. *Journal of the American Statistical Association*, 81(396):945–960.

Hume, D. and Beauchamp, T. L. (2000). *An Enquiry Concerning Human Understanding: A Critical Edition*, volume 3. Oxford University Press, New York.

Humphreys, M. and Jacobs, A. M. (2015). Mixing methods: A Bayesian approach. *American Political Science Review*, 109(4):653–673.

Humphreys, M. and Weinstein, J. M. (2009). Field experiments and the political economy of development. *Annual Review of Political Science*, 12:367–378.

Huntington, S. P. (1993). *The Third Wave: Democratization in the Late Twentieth Century*. University of Oklahoma Press, Norman, OK.

Imai, K., Keele, L., and Tingley, D. (2010). A general approach to causal mediation analysis. *Psychological Methods*, 15(4):309.

Jeffreys, H. (1998). *The Theory of Probability*. Oxford University Press, Oxford.

Kaye, D. H. (1986). Quantifying probative value. *BUL Review*, 66:761.

Kaye, D. H. and Koehler, J. J. (2003). The misquantification of probative value. *Law and Human Behavior*, 27(6):645–659.

King, G. (1998). *Unifying Political Methodology: The Likelihood Theory of Statistical Inference*. University of Michigan Press, Ann Arbor, MI.

King, G., Keohane, R., and Verba, S. (1994). *Designing Social Inquiry: Scientific Inference in Qualitative Research*. Princeton University Press, Princeton.

Knox, D., Lowe, W., and Mummolo, J. (2020). Administrative records mask racially biased policing. *American Political Science Review*, 114(3):619–637.

Knox, D., Yamamoto, T., Baum, M. A., and Berinsky, A. J. (2019). Design, identification, and sensitivity analysis for patient preference trials. *Journal of the American Statistical Association*, 114(528): 1–27.

Laplace, P.-S. (1901). *A Philosophical Essay on Probabilities*, volume 166. Cosimo, New York, translated by F. W. Truscott and F. I. Emory edition.

Lewis, D. (1973). Counterfactuals and comparative possibility. In Harper, W.L., Stalnaker, R., and Pearce, G., editors, *Ifs: Conditionals, Beliefs, Decision, Chance, and Time*, pages 57–85. Springer, Dordrecht, Holland.

Lewis, D. (1986). Causation. *Philosophical Papers*, 2:159–213.

Lieberman, E. S. (2003). *Race and Regionalism in the Politics of Taxation in Brazil and South Africa*. Cambridge Studies in Comparative Politics. Cambridge University Press, Cambridge.

Lieberman, E. S. (2005). Nested analysis as a mixed-method strategy for comparative research. *American Political Science Review*, 99(3):435–452.

Lieberman, E. S. (2010). Bridging the qualitative-quantitative divide: Best practices in the development of historically oriented replication databases. *Annual Review of Political Science*, 13:37–59.

Lindley, D. V. (1956). On a measure of the information provided by an experiment. *The Annals of Mathematical Statistics*, 27(4):986–1005.

Linz, J. J. and Stepan, A. (1996). *Problems of Democratic Transition and Consolidation: Southern Europe, South America, and Post-communist Europe*. Johns Hopkins University Press, Baltimore.

Maclaren, O. J. and Nicholson, R. (2019). What can be estimated? Identifiability, estimability, causal inference and ill-posed inverse problems. *arXiv preprint arXiv:1904.02826*.

Mahoney, J. (2000). Strategies of causal inference in small-n analysis. *Sociological Methods & Research*, 28(4):387–424.

Mahoney, J. (2008). Toward a unified theory of causality. *Comparative Political Studies*, 41(4–5):412–436.

Mahoney, J. (2010). After KKV: The new methodology of qualitative research. *World Politics*, 62(1):120–147.

Mahoney, J. (2012). The logic of process tracing tests in the social sciences. *Sociological Methods & Research*, 41(4):570–597.

Manski, C. F. (1995). *Identification Problems in the Social Sciences*. Harvard University Press Cambridge, MA.

Meltzer, A. H. and Richard, S. F. (1981). A rational theory of the size of government. *Journal of Political Economy*, 89(5):914–927.

Menzies, P. (1989). Probabilistic causation and causal processes: A critique of Lewis. *Philosophy of Science*, 56(4):642–663.

Méon, P.-G. and Sekkat, K. (2005). Does corruption grease or sand the wheels of growth? *Public Choice*, 122(1):69–97.

Mosley, L. (2013). *Interview Research in Political Science*. Cornell University Press, Ithaca, NY.

Palfrey, T. R. (2009). Laboratory experiments in political economy. *Annual Review of Political Science*, 12:379–388.

Parsons, S. (2001). *Qualitative Methods for Reasoning under Uncertainty*, volume 13. MIT Press, Cambridge, MA.

Pearl, J. (2009). *Causality: Models, Reasoning and Inference*. Cambridge University Press, Cambridge, UK.

Pearl, J. (2010). An introduction to causal inference. *The International Journal of Biostatistics*, 6(2):1–62.

Pearl, J. (2012). The causal foundations of structural equation modeling. In Holye, R.H., editor, *Handbook of Structural Equation Modeling*, pages 68–91. The Guildord Press, New York.

Pearl, J. and Bareinboim, E. (2014). External validity: From do-calculus to transportability across populations. *Statistical Science*, 29(4):579–595.

Peressini, A. (1999). Applying pure mathematics. *Philosophy of Science*, 66(S3):S1–S13.

Pierson, P. (1994). *Dismantling the Welfare State?: Reagan, Thatcher and the Politics of Retrenchment*. Cambridge University Press, Cambridge, UK.

Przeworski, A. and Limongi, F. (1997). Modernization: Theories and facts. *World Politics*, 49(2):155–183.

Raiffa, H. and Schlaifer, R. (1961). *Applied Statistical Decision Theory*. Division of Research, Harvard Business School, Boston.

Rodrik, D., Subramanian, A., and Trebbi, F. (2004). Institutions rule: The primacy of institutions over geography and integration in economic development. *Journal of Economic Growth*, 9(2):131–165.

Rohlfing, I. (2012). *Case Studies and Causal Inference: An Integrative Framework*. Research Methods Series. Palgrave Macmillan, New York.

Rohlfing, I. (2013). Comparative hypothesis testing via process tracing. *Sociological Methods & Research*, 43(4):606–642.

Rohrer, J. M. (2018). Thinking clearly about correlations and causation: Graphical causal models for observational data. *Advances in Methods and Practices in Psychological Science*, 1(1):27–42.

Rubin, D. B. (1974). Estimating causal effects of treatments in randomized and nonrandomized studies. *Journal of Educational Psychology*, 66(5):688–701.

Sachs, J. D. (2001). *Tropical Underdevelopment*. National Bureau of Economic Research, Working Paper 8119.

Saunders, E. N. (2011). *Leaders at War: How Presidents Shape Military Interventions*. Cornell University Press, Ithaca, NY.

Scharf, L. L. (1991). *Statistical Signal Processing: Detection, Estimation, and Time Series Analysis*. Addison-Wesley, Reading, MA.

Seawright, J. (2016). *Multi-method Social Science: Combining Qualitative and Quantitative Tools*. Cambridge University Press, New York.

Seawright, J. and Gerring, J. (2008). Case selection techniques in case study research: A menu of qualitative and quantitative options. *Political Research Quarterly*, 61(2):294–308.

Small, M. L. (2011). How to conduct a mixed methods study: Recent trends in a rapidly growing literature. *Annual Review of Sociology*, 37:57–86.

Spirtes, P., Glymour, C. N., Scheines, R., and Heckerman, D. (2000). *Causation, Prediction, and Search*. MIT Press, Cambridge, MA.

Splawa-Neyman, J., Dabrowska, D., Speed, T., et al. (1990). On the application of probability theory to agricultural experiments. Essay on principles. *Statistical Science*, 5(4):465–472.

Stan Development Team. (2020). *Stan modeling language users guide and reference manual*. Technical report.

Stokes, S. (2001). *Mandates and Democracy: Neoliberalism by Surprise in Latin America.* Cambridge Studies in Comparative Politics. Cambridge University Press, Cambridge, UK.

Swank, D. (2002). *Global Capital, Political Institutions, and Policy Change in Developed Welfare States.* Cambridge Studies in Comparative Politics. Cambridge University Press, Cambridge, UK.

Tamer, E. (2010). Partial identification in econometrics. *Annual Review of Economics,* 2(1):167–195.

Thelen, K. and Mahoney, J. (2015). Comparative-historical analysis in contemporary political science. In Mahoney, J. and Thelen, K., editors, *Advances in Comparative-Historical Analysis,* pages 1–36. Cambridge University Press, New York.

Van Evera, S. (1997). *Guide to Methods for Students of Political Science.* Cornell University Press, Ithaca, NY.

Waldner, D. (2015). What makes process tracing good? Causal mechanisms, causal inference, and the completeness standard in comparative politics. In Bennett, A. and Checkel, J., editors, *Process Tracing: From Metaphor to Analytic Tool,* pages 126–152. Cambridge University Press, New York.

Weller, N. and Barnes, J. (2014). *Finding Pathways: Mixed-method Research for Studying Causal Mechanisms.* Cambridge University Press, New York.

Western, B. and Jackman, S. (1994). Bayesian inference for comparative research. *American Political Science Review,* 88(2):412–423.

Woodward, J. (1979). Scientific explanation. *The British Journal for the Philosophy of Science,* 30(1):41–67.

Index

Acemoglu, Daron, 190
Ambiguities matrix, 163, 168, 227, 237, 409
Ansell, Ben, 190

Bareinboim, Elias, 291
Bayes Rule
  Continuous parameters, 105
  Definition, 103
  procedure, 117
Bayesian *p*-value, 374, 385, 390
  procedure, 375
Bayesian Updating
  Implementation with MCMC methods,
    116
  Simple illustrations, 101
Bennett, Andrew, 8, 155
Beta distribution, 107
Binary data, 56
  Non-binary data, 246
Boix, Carles, 21, 190

Cartwright, Nancy, 19
Case selection, 12, 234
  Common strategies, 320
  Findings from simulations, 335
  General strategy, 331
Causal ancestor, 27
Causal descendent, 27
Causal discovery, 369
Causal explanation, 24
Causal functions, 36, 60, 63, 67, 68, 70, 71, 83,
    148–151, 409
  Definition, 31
  Relationship with structural equations, 31
Causal models, 192, 208, 409
  Definition, 29
  Development and democratization, 69
  Government survival, 302
  Inequality and democratization, 23, 190, 192,
    213, 215, 260, 317, 384
  Institutions and growth, 207, 216, 267
  Meltzer-Richard, 190

Military interventions, 65
Probabilistic causal model, 38, 409
Sensitivity, 381, 399
Simplifying, 53
Steps, 55
Structural causal model, 10, 19, 32, 37–39, 133,
    138, 409
Welfare state reform, 60
Causal types, 25, 34, 157, 160, 224, 409
CausalQueries, 13, 56, 95, 185, 199, 215, 227,
    229, 237, 247, 253, 255, 289, 378
Charman, Andrew E., 111, 122, 322
Checkel, Jeffrey, 155
Cheibub, José A., 200, 395
Chickering, David M., 224, 254–256
Clark, David, 394
Clarke, Kevin A., 8, 147
Clues, 115, 116, 119, 123, 143, 169, 170, 172, 175,
    177–179, 186, 205, 214, 218, 270, 301, 308,
    365, 368, 410
Collider, 51, 52, 57, 174, 179, 211, 374,
    384, 385
Conditional independence, 50, 57, 373, 390,
    410
  Definition, 41
Confounding, 40, 47, 62, 139, 179, 209, 211–213,
    260, 272, 273, 280, 286–288, 290, 322, 343,
    349–351, 363, 405
  Unobserved confounding, 47, 54, 139, 160, 207,
    222, 233, 275, 369
Context, 35, 38, 291
Counterfactual model, 19
Cumulation, 11, 283, 398, 403

DAGs, 27, 44, 159, 221, 410
  Case level DAG, 256
  Confounding, 47
  reading conditional independence, 49
  Rules, 45
Data strategies, 15, 112, 113, 410
  Case selection procedure, 320, 328

Clue selection procedure, 301, 302, 309, 310, 317
   Dynamic strategies, 314
   Wide or deep procedure, 351
Data type, 410
Dawid, Philip, 368
d-connection, 53
Design based inference, 3
Designing Social Inquiry, 5
Dirichlet distribution, 106, 225, 234, 295
d-separation, 53, 172, 211, 256
Dunning, Thad, 7

Estimation, 229
Event probability, 146, 227, 237, 410
Exclusion restriction, 140, 392, 393
Expected learning, 334
Expected squared error
   Definition, 143
   Relation to expected posterior variance, 146

Fairfield, Tasha, 111, 122, 123, 322
Fisher, Ronald, 3
Fork, 50, 51, 223

Gabry, John, 375
Gelman, Andrew, 294, 375
George, Alexander, 8, 155
Gerring, John, 8, 322
Good, Irving John, 111

Haggard, Stephan, 190
Hall, Ned, 8
Halpern, Joseph, 89
Herron, Michael C., 322
Hume, David, 20

Identification, 75, 140, 255, 282, 390, 398
   Partial identification, 244
Instrument, 179, 208, 212, 246

Jeffreys, Harold, 112

Kaufman, Robert, 190
Kaye, David, 111
Keohane, Robert, 5, 344
King, Gary, 5, 344
Knox, Dean, 236, 286

Learning, 110
   Expected learning, 114, 115, 145, 305, 338
      Definition, 113
   Principles, 181
Likelihood, 103, 105, 118, 228, 238

Likelihood principle, 234
Limongi, Fernando, 69
LOO cross validation, 378, 391
   procedure, 378
LOO likelihood, 385
Loss, 113
   Expected loss, 113, 114

Mahoney, James, 8
MCMC sampling, 116
Measurement error, 248
Mediator, 175, 186, 195, 308, 314, 368, 411
Meta-analysis, 293
Mill, John Stewart, 329
Mixed methods, 5, 11, 237, 347
Models
   Analytic, 147
   As quantities of interest, 4
   Game theoretic, 147
   Higher level, 138
   Lower level, 135, 138, 140
Moderator, 186, 308, 314, 411
Multinomial distribution, 228, 411

Nash equilibrium, 147
Nodal types, 34, 68, 79, 84, 160, 170, 224, 411
Nodes
   Child, 27, 411
   Clue nodes, 172
   Endogenous, 29, 37, 40, 410
   Exogenous, 29, 37, 38, 135, 410
   Parent, 27, 34, 411
   Root nodes, 30

Overdetermination, 88

Parameter, 225, 411
Parameter matrix, 227, 411
Pearl, Judea, 6, 9, 20, 29, 53, 74, 133, 224, 254–256, 291, 348
Pierson, Paul, 60
Posterior distribution, 411
Posterior mean, 109
Posterior variance, 109, 141, 145, 302
   Expected posterior variance, 141, 145, 334, 338
      Relation to expected squared error, 146
Potential outcomes, 6, 21, 26, 36, 83, 411
Primo, David M., 8, 147
Principal stratification, 21, 33
Prior distribution, 38, 103, 106, 118, 412
Priors, 56, 160, 225
   Flat, 181, 182, 213, 232, 268, 322, 411
   Jeffreys, 56, 108, 109

Probative value, 5, 114, 170, 256, 362
    Definition, 111
    Derived from data, 239
Process tracing, 5, 12, 116, 119, 155, 157
    Applications, 189
    Procedure, 159
    Tests, 122
Przeworski, Adam, 69

Qualitative methods, 4, 10, 13, 344
Qualitative tests, 5, 169
    Doubly decisive, 122, 364, 366, 368
    Hoop, 122, 125–127, 364, 366, 368
    Smoking gun, 122, 125, 127, 364, 366, 368
    Straw in the wind, 122, 364, 366, 368
Queries, 79, 82, 84–87, 93, 94, 124, 166, 170, 336,
        412
    Sample average treatment effect (SATE), 219,
        220
    Actual causation, 88
    Average causal effects, 80
    Case level, 278
    Case level effects, 75
    Causal attribution, 78
    Causal paths, 82
    Complier average causal effect (CACE), 246
    Conditional, 231
    Conditional average treatment effect (CATE),
        82, 242, 292, 293
    Conditional queries, 230, 239
    Direct effects, 269, 276
    Indirect effects, 83, 269
    Informative case query, 240
    Population level, 276
    Uninformative case query, 240
Quinn, Kevin M., 322

Randomization
    as-if randomization, 4
Regan, Patrick, 394
Replication study, 254
Research design, 11, 12, 15, 28, 53, 307
Robinson, James A., 190
Rodrik, Dani, 208, 268

Sampling, 234, 235
Samuels, David, 190
Saunders, Elizabeth, 65
Seawright, Jason, 7, 322
Selection effects, 212, 286
Sensitivity analysis, 373
Spillovers, 251
stan, 116, 229
Structural causal model
    Definition, 29
Structural equations, 9, 10
    Examples, 32
    Relationship with causal functions, 31
Surrogates, 178, 179

Theory, 131
    and empirical research, 8
    as explanation, 131
    Gains from, 138
Transportation, 291

Unobserved confounding, 162

Van Evera, Stephen, 119, 122, 126, 170
Verba, Sidney, 5, 344

Wisdom, 141, 144
    Expected, 146

Made in United States
North Haven, CT
28 December 2023

46748683R00239